Wings of Their Dreams

To the Purdue people of yesterday and today who have dedicated their lives to flight and to the next generation of visionaries who will fashion tomorrow on the wings of their dreams.

Wings of Their Dreams

PURDUE IN FLIGHT

John Norberg

Purdue University
West Lafayette, Indiana

Printed in the United States of America

Library of Congress Cataloging-in-Publication Data

Norberg, John.
Wings of their dreams : Purdue in flight / John Norberg.
p. cm.
ISBN 1-55753-362-8 (hardcover)
1. Aeronautics--Research--Indiana--Lafayette. 2. Purdue University--Research. I. Title.
TL568.P87N67 2003
629.13'007'2077295--dc22

2003017634

"There shall be wings! If the accomplishment be not for me, 'tis for some other. The spirit cannot die; and man . . . shall have wings. . . ."

—Leonardo da Vinci

Table of Contents

Acknowledgments

This book was authorized by former Purdue University President Steven Beering. His vision for the story of Purdue in flight is the genesis of this work. It has also received the support of President Martin Jischke. Joe Bennett, vice president of Purdue University Relations, has been the guiding force of this project.

Because of time constraints and a desire to complete this book during the 2003 Centennial of Flight, a great deal of help was needed. The chapter on Amelia Earhart was researched and written by Jo Ellen Meyers Sharp. Katherine Markee, Purdue Special Collections Librarian, provided great help in this project.

This work is also thanks to the outstanding contributions of designer Tim Thompson; Tom Bacher, director of Purdue University Press; Jeanne Norberg, director of the Purdue News Service; Dave Brannan, director of Purdue Marketing Communications; and editors Jessica Burdge, Abby Jones, and Jennifer Tyrrell. Sue Honey spent long hours transcribing taped interviews and played an important role in this work.

Thanks to Craig Ryan, author of *The Pre-Astronauts: Manned Ballooning on the Threshold of Space;* C. V. Glines, of the James H. Doolittle Library, University of Texas, Dallas; Al Blackburn, author of *Aces Wild: The Race for Mach 1;* Charles Moore, professor emeritus, New Mexico Institute of Mining and Technology; and Purdue Professor Mike Nolan for their reviews of this history. Charles Holleman, professor emeritus, Purdue Aviation Technology, contributed a great deal of information with Jim Maris, former head of Purdue Aviation Technology, and Jerry Goldman of the Purdue Aeronautics Corporation. Thanks to Tom Farris, head of Purdue University Aeronautical and Astronautical Engineering, and Tom Carney, head of Purdue Aviation Technology, for their assistance and guidance. Also thanks to A. F. Grandt Jr., W. A. Gustafson, and L. T. Cargnino, authors of *One Small Step: The History of Aerospace Engineering at Purdue University,* for their great help. And thanks to Purdue Professor Emeritus George Palmer for his help and advice.

Finally, thanks to my wife, Jeanne, and family for their patience and support.

—John Norberg, June 2003

Foreword

Wings of Their Dreams

One of the questions people often ask me is why I think so many astronauts have come out of Purdue University. As I write this, the number of Boilermakers who have gone on to fly in space is twenty-one with one more astronaut waiting for his first flight. I'm certain that number will increase in the future. No other public university is in Purdue's league.

There really isn't a simple answer to the question, but if you read this book, I think you'll recognize that Purdue's astronaut phenomenon is not a fluke. It's really just one of the results of Purdue having a unique combination of historic strengths. It begins with engineering. Purdue graduates engineers who understand both the theoretical and practical sides of their profession. They are problem solvers who know how to think fast when the chips are down, and that's something NASA values highly. Neil Armstrong demonstrated this quality in 1969 when he took control of the Apollo 11 lunar lander to avoid large rocks littering the intended landing site and manually landed on the lunar surface with only seconds of fuel remaining.

Another characteristic of Purdue that has led so many people into space is what I would call a questing spirit. This is dramatized most vividly in the stories of the early days of aviation that John Norberg recounts in *Wings of Their Dreams.* The men and women who took to the skies in the early twentieth century understood very well the risks they were taking. They had none of the technical support, pre-mission modeling, or redundant systems that NASA provides for those of us who fly into space.

When Purdue graduate James Clifford Turpin was flying for the Wright brothers, he was literally inventing maneuvers as he sat at the controls. There was no one to teach him because these things had never been done before.

When Amelia Earhart set out to circle the globe in a Purdue-sponsored Lockheed Electra, she wasn't only flying into unknown territory. She was also testing the limits of human endurance and the physical limits of the marvelous new machines that made flight the most exciting development of the twentieth century. Like Amelia, many other early aviators gave their lives in the course of learning how far, how fast, and how high they could go. Danger is built into the story of flight. Even though we have made air travel the safest form of transportation ever devised, there will always be men and women pushing back the frontiers of flight because they yearn to do something that no one else has done.

No matter how many times I fly, I still feel the thrill of leaving the earth and the freedom of moving in three dimensions with ease. And I always remember that, even in the most routine flight, we are doing something not natural and that we are subject to the laws of nature and the possible consequences of not being careful. We were not born to fly, but that does not mean we were not meant to fly. We could not overcome the obstacles of weight and gravity solely with the strength of our bodies, but we did it with our intellect and through the courage and determination of the pioneers whose stories are told so well in this book.

These qualities have manifested themselves in many ways at Purdue University. Every student there learns of the exploits of Neil Armstrong and Amelia Earhart and of the tragedy of Virgil "Gus" Grissom and Roger Chaffee, who died while preparing for a historic step in our country's space program.

Purdue's history is full of equally important or exciting events that are not as well known. President Edward Elliott recognized the vast economic and social impacts aviation would have and decided that it had a place in academia. Grove Webster took Purdue's flight training program daringly into the arena of commercial aviation. Boilermaker alumnus Iven Kincheloe became known as "The First Spaceman" and died doing what he loved, just as America reached the threshold of space. Forgotten by most people, he lives on as a legend among pilots.

These are the kinds of stories that emerge from *Wings of Their Dreams.* Purdue and its people were there at the dawn of the age of human flight. They helped steer the course through the transition from barnstorming to revolutions in military strategy and transportation. They led the leap to space travel that will take humankind beyond the bounds of our solar system.

We don't know where we will go from here, but we do know that we will continue to push back the frontiers of air and space travel. The journey that began at Kitty Hawk has just begun. The first century of flight is a prelude to progress that we can't yet imagine. I was fortunate to attend a university that had the vision, the courage, and the innate curiosity to place itself in the center of the story of the first one hundred years of flight. Purdue has not just gone along for the ride. It has been at the controls and helped keep the machine aloft. When the history of flight's second century is written, I think the story will be even more exciting, and I'm certain Purdue University and its graduates will have played major roles.

—Jerry L. Ross

Introduction

When they talk about flight, the words you hear most often are "living a dream."

Whether they are jet pilots or astronauts or people who trail-blazed aviation in wood and muslin biplanes nearly one hundred years ago, flight means something more to these people than occupation, transportation, or even speed and power. They have a passion for being in the air, a love for the freedom that is theirs when they escape the confines of the earth and reach for the heights above. Rather than fighting nature, when they put their wings to the sky, they feel a part of it, at one with the wind.

At the dawn of the twentieth century, many people thought men and women were not meant to fly. They were wrong. Human flight occurs within and as part of the indisputable laws that govern our natural world.

One hundred years ago, Wilbur and Orville Wright accomplished controlled, powered flight in a heavier-than-air machine at Kitty Hawk, North Carolina. The two men stopped to shake hands in the moment before their great success. They looked one another squarely in the eyes before Orville took his turn and stepped onto their flying machine that windy morning of December 17, 1903. Biographers have quoted witnesses to the day as saying they looked like two men saying goodbye for the last time.

Confident in what they could do, perhaps they were saying goodbye to an age. Perhaps they were wondering about the possibilities they were about to release into the twentieth century. Perhaps they realized their world and all the world would never be the same.

It took less than sixty-six years to go from Kitty Hawk to the Moon. The history of aviation passed through the twentieth century like a rocket, going faster and higher every second. It is an incredible history. And like all history, it is shaped by the incredible stories of men and women whose passion for flight dominated their lives.

Purdue University and its people are a part of this story, from its first days, to its pioneering era through war and peace, to the emergence of commercial transportation, to the Moon, to the space shuttles and space stations, to Mars. Someday, they will be a part of everything that is yet to come.

This book tells the stories of some of these people. This is the story of Purdue's involvement in flight and the development of flight at the university as it was emerging throughout the nation and world. It is certainly not the complete history of flight at Purdue. That work would be many volumes. There are many more Purdue people whose lives were filled with the evolution of flight than this book could possibly include. And while the focus of this work is on the people who fly, there is also a great and extensive research history involving Purdue and its people that stretches from the first days of flight to the space age. Purdue graduates by the thousands work in the aviation and space industries, for NASA and its many private contractors, for the companies that are developing air transportation of the future. Theirs is another great story.

The story of flight and the story of Purdue are forever entwined. Both emerged from the revolution in thought and technology that leaped out of the late nineteenth century and shaped the one hundred years that were to follow. Flight and Purdue evolved together, and as the university and its people advanced aeronautics and astronautics, those sciences advanced the university's great international reputation.

Purdue graduate Richard Covey, who flew as a space shuttle pilot and commander, says the people of Purdue have an enormous and unique pride in the university's accomplishments with flight. Through support of Purdue, its alumni and friends feel a part of the story. Purdue celebrates the twenty-two astronauts who emerged from the campus. Purdue along with Massachusetts Institute of Technology (MIT) have graduated more astronauts than any nonmilitary academy. The first and last men on the Moon are Purdue graduates—Neil Armstrong and Eugene Cernan. They are all frequent visitors on campus, and on occasion, many of the twenty-two come as a group. They enjoy meeting one another as much as everyone else enjoys meeting them.

Why did Purdue graduate so many people who would fly into space? There are five general reasons: Purdue offers outstanding educational opportunities, with special strengths in engineering and technology, attracting top students; Purdue has one of the top ROTC programs in the nation, attracting people who want to take advantage of the military opportunities in flight; Purdue has its own airport, the first university-owned airport in the nation; Purdue had a master's degree program in cooperation with the U.S. Air Force Academy that brought seven young men to West Lafayette who would go on to fly in space; and finally, Purdue's reputation as a university that produces astronauts has attracted people for the past forty years and continues to attract new students today.

Purdue also has a leadership history of university presidents who have supported flight, from James Smart, who helped position the institution, to Edward Elliott, who believed land-grant universities should do for flight what they had done for agriculture, to Frederick Hovde, Arthur Hansen, Steven Beering, and Martin Jischke, who is an aeronautical and astronautical engineer.

The story of Purdue in flight begins with the Wright brothers and Cliff Turpin, who worked with the Wrights and thrilled hundreds of thousands of people across the nation with his flying demonstrations. It is the story of pioneers such as Jimmie Johnson and Charles McAllister, who would be among the world's first test pilots and part of the country's first flight aerobatic teams. It is the story of Ralph Johnson, who was part of the birth of commercial aviation. It is the story of George Haskins and Grove Webster, who helped bring flight to Purdue. It is the story of Amelia Earhart, who flew out of Purdue and into history. It is the story of test pilots George Welch and Iven Kincheloe, who went where no one had been before. It is the story of Malcolm Ross, who flew balloons up to the stratosphere. It is the story of twenty-two astronauts who lived their dreams, including Neil Armstrong and Eugene Cernan, along with Virgil "Gus" Grissom and Roger Chaffee, who both died in the tragic Apollo 1 fire. It is also the stories of eighteen astronauts who graduated from Purdue and are profiled at the end of each chapter.

The history of flight is a step-by-step process with each person building on the accomplishments of others. When Neil Armstrong stepped on the Moon, it was not only his success, and it was not only the result of the thousands of people who worked on the Apollo program. It was a success shared by the research, experiments, expertise, and daring of everyone throughout time who advanced our knowledge of flight. In a larger sense, perhaps Armstrong's landing and first step on the Moon were the most shared accomplishments in human history. That was the day the world stood still to experience and marvel at a single event that inspired and uplifted the human spirit.

Visionary people in the late nineteenth century positioned Purdue to become not just a good university, but a great one, whose influence and reputation would reach around the world. These people did not know what technologies would emerge to dominate the world to come. They only knew Purdue should be a part of it.

So, too, Purdue is being positioned today to be a leader in the sciences, technologies, engineerings, and arts that will dominate the next one hundred years. We cannot know what is to come, but we know that, because of the investments being made today, more generations of Purdue students will leave the university and help to shape the world of flight.

They will succeed as others have before them—on the wings of their dreams.

Wings of Their Dreams

Buzz Aldrin: Contact light! Okay, engine stop . . . descent engine command override off.
Charlie Duke: We copy you down, *Eagle.*
Neil Armstrong: Houston, Tranquility Base here. The *Eagle* has landed!
Duke: Roger, Tranquility. We copy you on the ground. You've got a bunch of guys about to turn blue. We're breathing again. Thanks a lot.
Aldrin: Thank you.
Duke: You're looking good here.
Armstrong: Okay, we're going to be busy for a minute.
Duke: There are lots of smiling faces in this room, and all over the world.
Aldrin: There are two of them up here.
Mike Collins: And don't forget the one in the command module.

—July 20, 1969

If I have seen further . . .
it is by standing upon the shoulders of giants.

—Sir Isaac Newton
Letter to Robert Hooke, February 5, 1675

Chapter One

Let us hope that the advent of a successful flying machine, now only dimly foreseen and nevertheless thought to be possible, will bring nothing but good into the world; that it shall abridge distance, make all parts of the globe accessible, bring men into closer relation with each other, advance civilization, and hasten the promised era in which there shall be nothing but peace and goodwill among all men.

—Octave Chanute,
Progress in Flying Machines, 1894

It was a fine, fresh day, the kind that arrives in Indiana near the end of spring—before summer's humidity slinks in, after winter's chill has been beaten back once and for all.

On June 10, 1908, 262 seniors at Purdue University, nearly all of them men, filed into a building named for a woman—Eliza Fowler Hall. It was commencement day.

The hall was practically new, having only been finished in the past five years, and it was a showcase of the campus. It featured a pipe organ with strong, full sounds that filled every inch of the 500-seat auditorium and spilled outdoors onto the sparse, green landscape of the young university.

On this commencement day, Eliza Fowler Hall was filled beyond capacity with graduates, administrators, faculty, and families all excited at the prospects of a promising age, an exciting century that was only eight years old. All present wondered what possibilities the twentieth century would hold for these young men and the handful of women who made up the graduating class. What promise and potential was waiting to meet them? The future had never looked more exciting than that spring day in 1908. In fact, it was a time when barriers between the impossible and possible were being broken. Improbable dreams were coming true.

It was the age of inventions, of flourishing technology that seemed to know few limits, maybe none. Ideas were springing forth from the minds of research scientists and spare-timers tinkering in their workshops, people who explored possibilities with enthusiasm and wonder. Their discoveries and ideas were beginning to change the world.

The telephone, the light bulb, the wireless telegraph, the skyscraper, and the automobile had all recently come into being, capturing the public eye and fancy. The travel time to distant shores had shortened, and it seemed to a public that was only forty-three years past the Civil War that the world was rapidly shrinking. It was an exciting time to be alive.

It was a time when some men and women were beginning to believe ingenuity and technology could accomplish any task, if people simply put their minds to it. It was an attitude that wouldn't diminish until after the sinking of the *Titanic* four years later, until the carnage of the Great War, whose shadow was not yet visible to the class of 1908.

The year 1908 marked the thirty-fourth commencement in the history of Purdue — "a notable event" the *Lafayette Daily Courier* reported in its evening edition. "The class that went forth from the halls of old Purdue was one of the most loyal and progressive in the history of the university," the newspaper reported.[1]

What the writer didn't understand that day—what no one who crowded into Eliza Fowler Hall could have comprehended—was that two members of this small class would soon play major roles in one of the most exciting stories of all time. From this class of 262 people, at this young Midwestern university in the heart of Indiana, emerged two men who would make their mark as engineers and adventurers and push the limits of a fledgling technology that would very soon change the world—flight!

These two men, along with a third from the class of 1907, mark the beginning of Purdue's involvement in the history of aviation—the story of incredible human accomplishment that took less than sixty-six years to go from Kitty Hawk to the Moon.

Nothing before in history had ever developed as rapidly as flight. Orville Wright would know Charles Lindbergh. Lindbergh would know Neil Armstrong. Armstrong would go on to personally inspire the men and women planning human exploration of Mars. Each step of the way people built on previous accomplishments, standing on the shoulders of those who came before them, building on dreams as old as time.

Purdue, its alumni, and its faculty would play a major role every step of the way in this remarkable record of flight. Purdue would have the first university airport and among the first programs in aeronautics and astronautics. Purdue would finance the final flight by Amelia Earhart, who was a counselor for women at the university when the mission was conceived. Purdue alumni would help the Wright brothers. They would become among the nation's first test pilots and among the first members of flight demonstration teams. They would take balloons into the stratosphere, pilot the X-planes, and hold speed and altitude records from 1910 until the modern era. A Purdue alumnus would be one of the first two people to fly faster than the speed of sound.

Purdue astronauts would include Virgil "Gus" Grissom, one of the original astronauts of Mercury 7. They would include Neil Armstrong and Eugene Cernan, the first and last men on the Moon.

As the twenty-first century began, Purdue would have one of the top-ranked aeronautical and astronautical engineering programs in the world with a record in research that had helped to shape aviation and space. It would have one of the largest and best aviation technology programs and twenty-two alumni who had been selected as astronauts. By the twenty-first century, about 37 percent of all U.S. manned space flights had launched with a Purdue alumnus on board. Robert Foerster, a Purdue graduate, was among the ten finalists to be "Teacher in Space."

The story of Purdue and flight go hand in hand. Both were new at the start of the twentieth century, and by the start of the twenty-first, they had both impacted the world. Much of Purdue's great record of accomplishment that places it on this international stage would emerge from its achievements in flight. But the people attending the 1908 Purdue commencement had no idea about any of this. In their wildest dreams, they never imagined what was about to take place.

At the dawn of the twentieth century, many people in the United States and Europe were still struggling to accomplish a new form of flight that would launch the new age. Some of the best and brightest scientists of the day had tried and failed. Their dismal results were reported in newspapers. Eight years into the century, the public was just becoming aware that this new form of flight had actually been accomplished.

Oh, people had been flying in baskets strapped beneath balloons since the late eighteenth century. That was common knowledge to everyone. Dirigibles were well known. Brilliant engineers had been flying gliders with enormous success. The science of gliding was greatly advanced in the 1890s by work at Miller Beach in the Indiana Dunes where pilots hung on for dear life as odd-looking contraptions with multiple wings soared over sandy shores.

But this was different. What had been accomplished in the United States by Wilbur and Orville Wright in 1903, to little fanfare and public notice—and some misunderstanding—was powered, controlled, and sustained flight in a heavier-than-air machine. And if that terminology is cumbersome for people today, imagine the problem people had with it in the first decade of the twentieth century.

The fact that flight had been accomplished was not overnight, international news. It evolved slowly. In 1903, the *New York Times* story index carried nineteen entries for "aeronauts," most of them referencing balloonists and mentioning nothing about the Wright brothers. In 1904, there were twenty-five stories. In 1905, under the heading "aeronautics," which included ballooning and dirigibles, there were thirty-six stories. In 1906, the list grew to ninety-seven, including one story on January 7, page three, about "a machine invented by Orville and Wilbur Wright that flies without air balloon or gas bag." On March 18, 1906, the *Times* reported on page five that the "Aero Club of America had honored the Wright brothers for practical invention of a flying machine." There were 111 stories about aeronautics in 1907, 270 in 1908. By 1909 the list of stories, in small type, fills more than five large pages in the *Times* index.

Major events connected to flight swirled around the Purdue graduation in June 1908. That summer Orville Wright would write for the first time an article detailing the brothers' work and accomplishments in the respected magazine *Century*.

If not everyone in Purdue's Fowler Hall that June 1908 fully understood what was happening in this new science and technology, graduate James Clifford Turpin understood. And so did his classmate, Frederick L. Martin. They would become among the first Purdue graduates to tie the university's name and reputation permanently to flight.

Graduation day was a moment that actually linked eras, although no one yet knew it. Civil War veterans sat through that ceremony, fanning themselves in the growing heat of the crowded room. And somewhere in Eliza Fowler Hall that June day in 1908 sat people who, sixty-one years later, would watch on television as Neil Armstrong placed his boot on the surface of the Moon. Who could possibly have imagined that graduation day where the world was going—and so quickly?

The thoughts of Turpin and Martin were certainly in the sky that June day as Harvey Wiley, one of Purdue's first professors and a man who had gone on to become one of the nation's most distinguished researchers, rose to give his commencement speech from a flower-and-fern-filled stage.

Wiley had become chief of the U.S. Bureau of Chemistry and head of the Department of Pure Food in the U.S. Department of Agriculture. He had forever placed his seal on American history by being the driving force behind federal legislation that removed deadly preservatives from food. The same law took substances such as cocaine, morphine, and heroin off the shelves of corner drug stores. It was Wiley's determined and persistent research that resulted in the first U.S. Pure Food and Drug Act. It was a great honor for Purdue to have such an important and famous man speaking at its commencement.

Taking the podium at Purdue, Wiley gave a talk that was well received for its gentle humor and insightful advice. Work hard, Wiley told the assembled graduates. It is the only path to success.

"Every year the chances for great fortune, which formerly were abundant in this country, diminish," he said. "There is no more virgin soil, few undiscovered mines, almost no unexploited projects."[2] Almost no unexploited projects?

James Clifford Turpin and Frederick Martin must have smiled at such a shortsighted statement from a far-sighted man. Flight—the powered, controlled, sustained, heavier-than-air machine variety—was still a most unexploited project five years after it had first been accomplished.

On the morning of December 17, 1903, Orville and Wilbur Wright wheeled their latest flyer out of its shed on the sandy shore of Kill Devil Hills, Kitty Hawk, North Carolina. The day was cold, clear, and windy. At 10:35 A.M. Orville started the engine, which was connected to eight-foot propellers by bicycle chains manufactured by the Diamond Chain Company in Indianapolis. The Wright brothers and an assistant had built the engine themselves in their Dayton, Ohio, workshop. Orville positioned himself centered on the lower wing of the biplane, lying on his stomach. From that position he powered the fragile looking flyer with his left hand and hips. Approaching takeoff, the flying machine ran on a wooden rail into winds gusting up to twenty-seven miles per hour. The speed was slow enough that Wilbur ran along side, keeping pace with the flyer until it rose into the air after a forty-foot run.[3]

Orville was in the air for only twelve seconds and traveled only 120 feet, but that was all it took for the Wright brothers to accomplish what no one had done before: powered, controlled, sustained flight in a heavier-than-air machine.

Both brothers took the controls that day, each dressed in their standard work gear: ties, coats, and starched white shirts. Wilbur followed Orville and flew for 195 feet. Orville tried again and flew 200 feet, staying in the air fifteen seconds. On the last flight of the day, they accomplished what they really considered success when Wilbur flew 852 feet and remained in the air for fifty-nine seconds. Some people would have rounded off those fifty-nine seconds and called it a perfect minute, but Wilbur and Orville Wright were all about exactness and precision. Science had brought them to this moment and led to their success. Fifty-nine seconds it would be.

A small group of people assembled to witness the great event. Orville had arranged for one of them to snap a photograph just as the Wright Flyer lifted off from the sandy dunes. The photo captured Wilbur standing to the side, his legs spread apart, and his arms at the ready as if he would try to catch the plane and throw it back up into the sky if it dared come back too soon. The photo captured Orville lying on the lower wing of the biplane, working the controls, desperately trying to stay aloft—no easy task for a man who was discovering the principles of flight every second he stayed in the air.

The photo is one of the most amazing ever taken. No one was standing on the beach to photograph Christopher Columbus as he waded to shore in the New World, but someone did snap a photo as the Wright brothers entered the new world in the sky. It was, perhaps, the first world-changing moment captured on film. From that moment on, every breakthrough in aviation and space would be captured on film.

The birth of aviation had been thousands of years in the making. 1700 B.C. Greek mythology told the story of Icarus flying on wings made of feathers and wax. He fell to his death when he flew too high, too close to the sun. The message for the ages to come was clear: Keep your feet on the ground. Don't reach too high.

But people who wanted the freedom of birds didn't listen. In A.D. 1010, an English monk named Eilmer of Malmesbury broke his legs when he tried to fly with wings attached to his body. Crippled, he remained convinced that flight was possible.[4] In 1300, Marco Polo told incredible stories of people tied to kites sailing in the air over China. Not all of those people went up voluntarily. Not all landings were smooth—or even successful.[5] In about 1500, Leonardo da Vinci used his study of science and knowledge of the laws of nature in plans to conquer the air.

Experiments in flight went on and on—and down and down. Suddenly, something incredible happened, the first breakthrough. In Paris, France, November 1783, Pilatre de Rozier and the Marquis d'Arlandes made the first successful manned balloon ascent, traveling five miles and reaching a height of three thousand feet in a balloon that was the brainchild of Joseph and Etienne Montgolfier, brothers who had earlier noted that bits of paper rise in the heat of open fires. Through careful experiments they discovered that bags filled with hot air from a fire would float upward. The brothers used this discovery to first launch an unmanned balloon, and then a basket of animals, before sending de Rozier and d'Arlandes into the sky above Paris,[6] and they thereby established a test flight protocol that would be repeated by NASA in the earliest days of the U.S. space program almost two centuries later.

Present to witness that first manned balloon flight was a scientist and diplomat from the New World—Benjamin Franklin. Franklin was appalled that people wondered out loud about the purpose of flight beneath a balloon. "What good is it?" he asked, and then he gave his own answer. "What good is a newborn baby."[7]

Balloon progress developed and advanced rapidly. Ten days after the first hot air balloon flight, Jacques Charles and Nobel Roberts lifted off from Paris and covered twenty-seven miles beneath a balloon filled with hydrogen.[8] In 1785, de Rozier used a hot air balloon and a gasbag in an attempt to cross the English Channel. The balloon exploded, killing de Rozier.[9] Later in 1785, Jean-Pierre Blanchard completed a crossing of the English Channel, thereby continuing French domination of ballooning.

In 1793, Blanchard took his balloon to America and made the first successful flight in the New World before a group of dignitaries including George Washington, John Adams, Thomas Jefferson, James Madison, and James Monroe—the current and the next four presidents of the United States.[10] Flight had reached the New World in a big way.

Ballooning continued to be popular throughout the nineteenth century. It became a major spectator event, and by 1859, there were estimates that three thousand ascents had been accomplished, many of them at U.S. county fairs and urban celebrations.[11]

The year 1859 was an important one in the history of flight for Lafayette, Indiana, in Tippecanoe County, the home of Purdue. On August 17, 1859, Lafayette was the origination site of the nation's first airmail delivery. John Wise from Lancaster, Pennsylvania, piloted the balloon named *Jupiter* carrying 123 letters and 23 circulars. Wise was a noted balloonist who added to his prestige by using the title "professor."[12]

In July 1859, Wise had attempted the first airmail delivery launching from St. Louis heading toward New York City. He made it as far as Henderson, New York, before his balloon crashed in a storm and the mail was lost. The flight was officially classified unsuccessful because the mail did not reach its destination, but he had flown about eight hundred miles in a journey that took more than twenty hours. That was a balloon record for the day.

The attempt in Lafayette was scheduled for August 16. Some people estimated the crowd that gathered to watch that day at fifteen thousand. Others went as high as thirty thousand. The huge difference makes it impossible to even guess how many people might have actually been on hand. The important point is that it was probably the largest group of people that had ever gathered in Lafayette, leaving news reporters and authorities unable to come up with an accurate estimate.

Schools were let out so children could witness the historic event. The railroads, whose location in Lafayette had assured prosperity for the growing town, ran special excursions to bring in crowds from surrounding areas. It was a big day for hotels, so much so that "before 11 o'clock it seemed the rural areas had been depopulated," the *Lafayette Daily Courier* reported.[13]

The *Jupiter* balloon was filled at the gas works on the corner of Vine and what is now Fourth Street, and then it was moved, fully inflated with Wise in a basket beneath it, along what is now Fifth Street. At the head of the procession was a band followed by the Lafayette Guards, who wore plumes in their hats. Band, guards, and balloon—it was quite an impressive procession, and one that had never been seen before or has been seen since.

Near Fifth and Main, telegraph wires crossed the street. They had not been removed as planned, so Wise had to hop his balloon over them. The balloon was secured with ropes while it was raised above the wires. But one rope slipped from its securing and the balloon came dangerously close to crashing into the side of the tall Lahr Hotel. To save the balloon—and himself—Wise "determined to let her go," according to the *Courier.*

"She mounted the heavens . . . and in a few seconds had attained an altitude of several thousand feet, when Mr. Wise opened the valve and the balloon settled gracefully to earth, making a beautiful landing . . . opposite the home of Mr. Robert Jones, Esq." the newspaper reported.[14]

Once back to earth, the balloon was moved along South Street toward the Courthouse Square for a launch. Wise had lost some gas in the incident with the wire, so he tossed out more than two-thirds of the sand bags he had on board for ballast. He then gave a speech to the gathered crowd and told them if the currents in the upper atmosphere were favorable, this would be an even more notable trip east to the seaboard than his earlier attempt from St. Louis. Wise seemed concerned about his potential to make it: "I will only say that this shall be as long a voyage eastward as a proper energy will enable me to make it," he said. "With that, I bid you all farewell."[15]

For a moment, everyone stood still while a photographer snapped his shot. The crowd roared. Wise waved. The balloon was released from its moorings.

Nothing happened.

The balloon, Wise, and the mail stayed right there on the ground. There was frantic activity as more ballast was removed.

Nothing.

Wise went nowhere as the impatient crowd waited. The *Courier* said, "It at once became evident that the balloon had been too much exhausted [getting over the telegraph wire] to overcome the stubborn gravity of the aeronaut's avoirdupois."[16] It was a nice, nineteenth-century newspaperman's way of saying that Wise was too big for what the balloon had left. So Wise's 120-pound son was recruited to make the ascent while his father cheered from the sidelines. It became a staged event to satisfy the large crowd, and the boy brought the balloon down after a short flight just to the outskirts of the city.[17]

There were other problems at the launch according to the *Courier.* It was a mid-August afternoon, which can be intensely hot in Indiana. The reporter from the *Courier* complained that with no public drinking fountains, many in the crowd were left to cool off in the town's saloons.

"The crowd—a colossal drunk," a newspaper subhead stated. "That the crowd . . . was the largest ever assembled at Lafayette on any occasion is generally conceded," the paper said. "In such a crowd and considering the extreme heat of the day, it is not astonishing that there was a vast amount of drunkenness. There were poor facilities for obtaining water and those who were compelled to enter the saloons to quench their thirst generally took something stronger than Adam's ale. The result, to sum up, was a drunken attachment to almost every gas post and a lien upon half the buildings in the city. . . . Men who are compelled to enter saloons and other public places where liquor is sold for the purpose of obtaining a glass of water feel under obligations to patronize the bar as acknowledgement of the courtesy. They take a drink, which only serves to make room for another—another—and another."[18]

To prove its point, the newspaper also reported, "The Mayor's Office was crowded [the following morning] with whiskey-soaked and lager-inflated jail-birds . . . who fell into the hands of Marshal Evans."[19] All pleaded guilty and were fined five to ten dollars, depending on the circumstances.

The next day, with another large crowd on hand, Wise successfully launched his balloon at 2:00 P.M. According to the *Courier*, "the beautiful air vessel moved off gracefully to the southeast, but after reaching an elevation of about two thousand feet, the local current changed to the west and, after remaining in full view for 50 minutes, suspended as it were almost over the city, the balloon was lost in the dim distance on the Southwest."[20]

Southwest, of course, was not the direction in which Wise wanted to travel to reach "the seaboard," as they called his eastern destination.

The *Courier* was less than confident about the potential for success. "The ascension from this city was grand and beautiful in the extreme, but in view of the fact that the local currents are adverse, we have little to hope from the experiment as a trans-continental voyage. It does not seem possible that Mr. Wise will be able to make any considerable progress toward the seaboard, and we shall not be surprised to hear of his descent this evening somewhere in Southern Illinois or Western Kentucky. The fact is that the aerial ship *Jupiter* is about as well adapted to the navigation of the upper current as Mr. Wise is adapted to preach the gospel."[21]

The grand trip to the seaboard was, in fact, terminated on a county road south of Crawfordsville at 7:08 P.M. that same evening. Total flight time was five hours and seven minutes. Wise had tried to reach the upper atmosphere currents he believed would take him east, but he failed. Understanding the value of publicity, he decided to come down on the public square at Crawfordsville, but the current carried him further south.

The *Courier* exposed the prejudices of the time in describing the attempts Wise made to land safely back on earth. "He threw out his rope to an Irishman, but the son of Erin had never before seen a balloon and, half-frightened out of his wits, refused to touch it," the newspaper reported. "Mr. Wise insisted, but Paddy refused to touch it, crossing himself . . . dodged behind a tree just in time to avoid a loaf of bread which the aeronaut had thrown at him. At half a mile further on, Mr. Wise observed some women in the road near a farmhouse. After a great deal of persuasion, [he] induced them to take hold of the rope and pull the balloon to the ground. . . . So endeth the transcontinental voyage. That this was only 'trans-county-nental' is no fault of the great aeronaut. His balloon was not suitable for a long voyage, nor was it possible to make one except under a combination of the most favorable circumstances."[22]

Wise was met and taken into Crawfordsville for the evening. The mail's trip to New York City was completed by the railroad, but Wise had successfully flown the initial leg, accomplishing the first airmail voyage.[23]

There was more to the flight than airmail. Wise was true to his title "professor." He had joined with Lafayette's Dr. Charles Wetherill to conduct ozone experiments during the flight. Wetherill, an accomplished chemist who, in just a few short years, would be named by President Abraham Lincoln as the first chemist in the U. S. Department of Agriculture, worked with Wise to create equipment that could monitor the ozone during the high airmail flight.

Wetherill had theories about the relationship between changes in ozone and health. In 1854, he noted there had been a great deficiency of ozone and that year had been marked by a cholera epidemic.

On his *Jupiter* trip, Wise carried Wetherill's experiment. It consisted of paper covered with a paste of starch. Added to this was a small amount of iodide of potassium. The ozone, Wetherill said, would "liberate" the iodine that would combine with the starch creating a blue color on the paper.[24]

The Wetherill family would eventually have an important impact on Purdue's standing as a science research center. Wetherill's son, Richard, was born in Lafayette in 1859—the year of the great airmail flight. Richard Wetherill attended Purdue and went on to become a physician who studied in Berlin and Vienna in addition to the United States. He established a practice in Lafayette in 1886 and taught some courses at Purdue. His will provided funds for student scholarships at Purdue as well as for the Wetherill Building on the university campus, which helped perpetuate the momentum of scientific discovery in Lafayette and Purdue.

With the launch of *Jupiter* that August day in 1859, Lafayette was officially in the history books, connected to flight for the first time. And perhaps, even more importantly, the community was connected to the research possibilities of flight.

Wise also became the first person to see the Lafayette area from above. Here is his description as told by the *Courier*: "The view is among the most beautiful ever beheld. The Grand Prairie stretching away to the westward seemed like a mammoth pleasure garden, dotted here and there with pleasant summerhouses and with the woodland enclosing it like a hedge fence. Lafayette, Crawfordsville, Attica, and eight villages in full view, the river, the [Erie] canal, and railroads altogether presented a panoramic picture of singular and impressive beauty."[25]

During the Civil War, both federal and confederate armies used balloons for military reconnaissance. Wise became a Union Army balloonist. In September 1879, at the age of seventy-one and considered the nation's top balloonist, he died in an accident over Lake Michigan.

In the postwar period, the age of ballooning began to wane. Balloons were much too subject to the "mercy of the winds."[26] Meanwhile, a new technology was developing that would change the world and have a particular impact on flight: the internal combustion engine.

In 1876, German Nicholas A. Otto demonstrated the first successful gas- (not gasoline) powered internal-combustion, four-cycle engine. It was the first practical alternative to the steam engine. In 1885, another German, Gottlieb Daimler, invented a gasoline-powered internal-combustion engine, and in less than a year, Karl Benz received the first patent for a gasoline-fueled car. The first motorcycle also appeared in 1885.

Turpin and Martin, along with most of the other graduates in the Purdue class of 1908, were born in 1886 just as this new age of engines, cars, and motorcycles was emerging. Turpin and Martin came to Purdue to study mechanical engineering. They came to study engines.

Purdue, as a land-grant university launched in the tradition of educating the masses of people, held a philosophy that changed education in the United States forever, expanding it beyond the rich and elite and opening it to common people. In 1862, President Abraham Lincoln signed the Land-Grant College Act. It provided public land in the west that states could sell, using the proceeds to start colleges where people would be taught agriculture and the mechanical arts.

Purdue opened its doors to thirty-nine students in 1874, but the young institution would need a great deal of work to become a top university; developments took place rapidly. In 1879, a School of Mechanics was founded, and in 1882, a School of Mechanical Engineering appeared with a full curriculum in this up and coming discipline.

At that time, according to *One Hundred Years of Progress,* a brochure about the story of Purdue Mechanical Engineering, "Purdue was still engaged in a life and death struggle to justify its existence. Engineering education was only a generation removed from the blacksmith's shop and had yet to define its position in academia."[27] In fact, when Indiana Governor James "Blue Jeans" Williams spoke at the Purdue commencement in the spring of 1877, he started by saying, "Eddicate a boy and he won't work." It was an opinion that was widely shared.[28]

The fact that Purdue took on this struggle to offer degrees in engineering is partially credited to early Purdue President Emerson White, a man who saw the need for training young men in engineering. He was also stern and had "little tolerance for campus frivolities such as fraternities, smoking, fashionable young ladies, or the new-fangled contraption known as the bicycle."[29]

In fact, it was Harvey Wiley, the nationally acclaimed, distinguished speaker at Purdue's 1908 commencement, who first ran afoul of the stern policies of White and the entire Purdue University Board of Trustees.

Wiley had started at Purdue in 1874 as one of six original faculty members. In 1880, Wiley peddled the first bicycle in Tippecanoe County. It was not a great occasion in the eyes of White and the board. To them, the bicycle was bad enough, but to make matters worse, Wiley wore knickers while he peddled across the campus.

At a board meeting, one member of the board stated, "Imagine my feelings . . . on seeing one of our professors dressed up like a monkey and astride a cartwheel riding along our streets!"[30]

Upon hearing that, Wiley resigned. While his resignation was refused, he eventually left Purdue in 1883, moving to Washington, D.C., where people were more tolerant of bicycles and knee breeches. His return to Purdue for the 1908 commencement was his first visit since leaving.

In his absence, engineering at Purdue had progressed, and mechanical engineering had come into its own. According to Purdue's mechanical engineering history, "By the late 1880s the public had begun to accept the concept of formal engineering education. Indiana high schools restructured their programs to produce better-qualified applicants, and large numbers of them began seeking admission. In 1887 and 1888, the Schools of Civil and Electrical Engineering were created."[31]

Purdue's School of Mechanical Engineering quickly established itself as a worldwide center for research and learning in steam engines and transportation. So when the twentieth century arrived, the eventual evolution to a new manner of transportation—air travel—was a logical progression.

In 1891, the School of Mechanical Engineering acquired the Schenectady, an 85,000-pound steam engine locomotive. According to *One Hundred Years of Progress,* "The Schenectady brought the School of Mechanical Engineering and Purdue an instant international reputation for innovation and bravado. It . . . identified Purdue as an early leader in transportation research. . . . As early as 1893, Russian visitors to the World's Fair in Chicago made a point of stopping in Lafayette to see the Schenectady locomotive roaring away in place at eighty miles per hour, surrounded by students and faculty performing tests."[32]

At the turn of the century, Purdue was the place in the nation and the world for railroad locomotive testing. Railroad companies brought their best new equipment to West Lafayette for evaluation.

While railroads were dominating transportation and shaping history, more innovations were being studied at Purdue's School of Mechanical Engineering. In 1892, Purdue acquired an Otto-Cycle gas engine—"the first in any engineering education laboratory in the United States." That engine launched the study of gas engineering at Purdue. "The installation of the Otto in Mechanics Hall preceded by at least a year the known manufacture of any American automobile. The Otto burned gas, not gasoline, and was used primarily by students making comparative studies of gas and steam engine efficiencies. During the first decade of the new century, many mechanical engineers believed gas and gas engines might prove to be the primary source of industrial power. Research of gasified coal aroused considerable interest as an alternative to steam-generated power. In 1906, a complete gas plant was functioning in Heavilon Hall"—the new state-of-the-art building where Mechanical Engineering was located. Even before that plant was put into operation, gasoline engines were beginning to redirect the thrust of research and teaching at Purdue.[33]

In 1905, an automotive testing plant was constructed in Heavilon Hall. Students and professors worked on a Lambert Runabout, a White Steamer, an Overland, a Ford, and a Cole.[34] By 1900, there were 599 students enrolled at Purdue. Eighty-four percent of them majored in engineering. The largest enrollment was in mechanical engineering with 202 students—almost 34 percent of the entire student body.[35]

Purdue, which was gaining an international reputation in the study of engines, power, and transportation, had a great deal to offer students such as Turpin and Martin. The developments in engines came along at the same time as rapid progress in flight and the two separate technologies were destined to merge. As engines became smaller, lighter, and more powerful, they became practical for powering flying machines.

After a decade of development, in 1900 German Ferdinand von Zeppelin combined a gas engine with balloon technology and came up with a powered airship called a dirigible, or Zeppelin. Flight took a huge step forward. Meanwhile, other people were experimenting with gliders.

German Otto Lilienthal died in a glider accident in 1896, but his carefully researched scientific work advanced the technology, and he was widely studied by others. One of those who studied him was Octave Chanute. Born in Paris, Chanute came to the United States as a child. He became a very successful engineer, designing the first railroad bridge over the Missouri River. He also designed the Kansas City and Chicago stockyards.

In the mid-1890s, Chanute turned his attentions to gliders and began experiments at Miller Beach in the Indiana Dunes, not far from his Chicago home. In a very short time, steel mills would be built near Miller in a new town named Gary. Because of Chanute, northern Indiana was on the map as a center of progress in the quest for flight. As a widely respected engineer, Chanute wrote books and articles about his research in flight and became a popular lecturer.

In 1899 in Dayton, Ohio, the idea of powered flight struck the interest of Orville and Wilbur Wright. Their workshop was near the family home of James Clifford Turpin.

Within four years, the Wright brothers took what they could learn from Lilienthal and Chanute, added their own ideas including new controls and propeller design, combined it all with a gasoline engine, and accomplished flight.

The Wright family had close ties to Indiana. Orville and Wilbur Wright's father, Milton, was born in Rush County, Indiana, in 1829. At twelve years of age, Milton moved with his family to Fayette County, Indiana, where he grew up and became an ordained minister in the United Church of the Brethren.

Milton Wright married Susan Koerner in 1859—the year of Lafayette's airmail flight. And after several moves around this young state, they settled in a three-room house near Millville, Indiana, eight miles east of New Castle. It was here that Wilbur Wright was born a Hoosier in 1867. In 1871, the family settled in a new home in Dayton, Ohio, at 7 Hawthorn Street, where Orville was born that August. The family continued to relocate until the two young men finally settled again in Dayton.[36]

After their mother died in 1889, Orville and Wilbur set out together searching for a calling in life, as well as a steady income. By 1892, they had found what they planned to make their life work: bicycles. The brothers began repairing, selling, and eventually building their own bicycles in a Dayton shop at 1127 West Third Street, not far from the Hawthorn Street home.

By the 1890s, bicycling had become a national passion, and the Wright brothers were doing quite well with their business. They began to work on flight during their spare time toward the end of the decade. The leap from bicycles to flight was not as great as it might seem.

Contrary to many others of the day, Wilbur Wright believed a major aspect of flight involved balancing a machine in the air. And that was not unlike the skill of balancing a bicycle on land. In fact, on several occasions—and at least once in court testimony—Wilbur Wright would use bicycling analogies to explain how the brothers developed their techniques of flight.

At one point in *The Bishop's Boys*, author Tom Crouch writes, "The development of a system to control an airplane in flight rested on . . . Wilbur's understanding of how a bicycle is turned to the left."[37]

Crouch, and many others who have studied the Wright brothers, says it was Wilbur who first became interested in flight. Later in his life, Wilbur noted that in 1896 he had read items in Dayton newspapers about glider experimentations. The idea was planted in his head, and like a seed, it took root and grew.

Crouch writes, "millions of people around the globe were sufficiently fascinated by flight in nature to read an occasional book on the subject. [However] very few ever attempted to build their own wings. Wilbur's peculiarly receptive frame of mind had set the Wrights apart."[38]

In 1899, Wilbur Wright wrote a letter to the Smithsonian Institution asking for information about the study of flight. The letter still exists, and along with the Kitty Hawk photo, it is among the most historical documents associated with flight.

Wright Cycle Company
1127 West Third Street
Dayton, Ohio
May 30, 1899

The Smithsonian Institution, Washington:

Dear Sirs: I have been interested in the problem of mechanical and human flight. . . . My observations . . . have . . . convinced me . . . that human flight is possible and practicable. It is only a question of knowledge and skill just as in all acrobatic feats. Birds are the most perfectly trained gymnasts in the world and are specially well fitted for their work, and it may be that man will never equal them, but no one who has watched a bird chasing an insect or another bird can doubt that feats are performed which require three or four times the effort required in ordinary flight. I believe that simple flight at least is possible to man and that the experiments and investigations of a large number of independent workers will result in the accumulation of information and knowledge and skill which will finally lead to accomplished flight.

. . . I am about to begin a systematic study of the subject in preparation for practical work to which I expect to devote what time I can spare from my regular business. I wish to obtain such papers as the Smithsonian Institution has published on this subject, and if possible a list of other works in print in the English language. I am an enthusiast, but not a crank in the sense that I have some pet theories as to the proper construction of a flying machine. I wish to avail myself of all that is already known and then if possible add my mite to help on the future workers who will attain final success. I do not know the terms on which you send out your publications, but if you will inform me of the cost I will remit the price.

Yours truly,
Wilbur Wright[39]

The reply from the Smithsonian included some pamphlets and articles and recommended books by, among others, Chanute and Samuel Pierpont Langley. Langley served as secretary of the Smithsonian Institution and was the man many thought would be the first to accomplish powered, controlled, sustained flight in a heavier-than-air machine—if anyone ever could.

Years later Wilbur explained his letter to the Smithsonian. "My brother and I became seriously interested in the problem of human flight in 1899. . . . We knew that men had . . . adopted human flight as the standard of impossibility. When a man said, 'It can't be done; a man might as well try to fly,' he was understood as expressing the final limit of impossibility. Our own growing belief that man might nevertheless learn to fly was based on the idea that while thousands of the most dissimilar body structures, such as insects, fish, reptiles, birds, and mammals, were flying every day at pleasure, it was reasonable to suppose that man might also fly. . . . We accordingly decided to write to the Smithsonian Institution and inquire for the best books relating to the subject."[40]

The brothers began working in their West Third Street shop in Dayton, carrying out test flights at Kitty Hawk, North Carolina, where winds were ideal for their research. While their first flights were accomplished in 1903, it would be 1909 before the Wrights were widely recognized.

The year 1908 would be a break-through year in flight. Just twenty-five days before the Purdue graduation, correspondents from the *New York Herald*, the *New York American*, the *London Daily Mail*, and *Collier's Weekly* had hidden themselves in pinewoods at Kitty Hawk, North Carolina, to see for themselves if rumors about the Wright brothers were true. Their dispatches made headlines in major cities, but the general public remained skeptical, unconvinced, or simply unaware. In June 1908, when one of those "hidden" correspondents tried to sell his story to a major U.S. magazine, his work was returned with this comment from the editor: "While your manuscript has been read with much interest, it does not seem to qualify as either fact or fiction."[41]

In a book approved by Orville Wright, *The Wright Brothers: A Biography*, author Fred C. Kelly, who would later write a biography of Purdue benefactor David Ross, told of the public attitude in May of 1908. "After publication of many dispatches from these eyewitnesses at Kitty Hawk and front page headlines, it might have been expected that the fact of human flight would now be generally accepted. As [Byron] Newton had written to his paper, there was 'no longer any ground for questioning the performance of these men and their wonderful machine.' [Arthur] Ruhl in *Collier's* had told how the correspondents had informed the world that 'it was all right, the rumors true—that man could fly.' Yet even such reports by leading journalists still did not convince the general public. People began to concede that perhaps there might be something in it, but many newspapers still did not publish the news."[42]

In June 1908, people remained unsure what to think of controlled, powered flight. But by July—appropriately on Independence Day—the influential magazine *Scientific American* offered a prize to anyone in the world who could fly one kilometer in a straight line. A dashing young man named Glenn Curtiss, whose spirit for technology and adventure would help define his age, would capture the prize. The recognition of flight was developing quickly.

In August 1908, Wilbur Wright literally wowed the skeptical people of France with spectacular flying demonstrations that made worldwide news. One month later, on September 17, 1908, accomplished flight recorded its first fatality. Army Lieutenant Thomas Selfridge died in the crash of a plane piloted by Orville Wright. Wright escaped with serious, but not fatal, injuries.

In the summer of 1908, right after the Purdue graduation, people in the United States and throughout the world began to understand that after thousands of years of inventing and experimenting and gazing into the endless, clear, blue sky, humankind had finally "slipped the surly bonds of Earth" to "touch the face of God."[43]

In his commencement speech on June 10, 1908, Harvey Wiley was brilliant and inspirational in his message to the young graduates—even if he did incorrectly believe that there were almost no unexploited projects left.

He said, "Three weeks ago I attended a conference to consider the best means of preserving our natural resources. We heard much spoken of preservation of forests, waterways, mines, and soil. But what are all these resources without that crowning resource of all—our people? And of our people, what part is more important than youth?

"No matter how successful you may be in your career, what wealth and honor you may acquire, you [graduates] are richer today than you will ever be in the future. Rockefeller and Carnegie would gladly exchange all their millions for the youth you possess.

"How are you going to use this great wealth for the benefit of the world. . . ?

"The young man who succeeds is . . . the one who never gives up. No matter how hard his fortunes may be, he still hopes, because he feels within himself that he is capable of doing something—and that he will do something."[44]

Frederick L. Martin would meet his destiny sixteen years after graduation.

The first person from the Purdue University class of 1908 to "do something" was James Clifford Turpin. He practically walked from that commencement into the sky, into the enthusiastic hearts of an American public who turned Turpin and other birdmen of the day into overnight, international heroes.

Charles Walker

Flight emerged with the birdmen of the early twentieth century, and within two generations, a new term was being used for people who pushed the limits of the sky: *astronauts.*

Charles Walker was born into the space age, the era of rockets and astronauts, and he grew up to live his greatest dreams.

Among Walker's earliest memories are three television programs that brought the dream of space travel into the reality of American living rooms in the mid-1950s. The programs brought together two giants of the twentieth century—two men from two very different fields. Both were visionaries. And in the 1950s, when they joined for a series of television programs about space, they influenced a nation. Wernher von Braun was a German physicist responsible for many of the achievements of the U.S. space program in the 1950s–1970s, including the Explorer satellites, Jupiter rockets, and the Project Mercury. Walt Disney was a businessman and the owner of a movie and television studio who was just breaking into theme parks. Both were charming and charismatic, and they believed in the future and potential of a U.S. manned space program.

Their first space program aired on March 9, 1955. It was titled "Man in Space." Next, later in 1955, came "Man and the Moon," and finally "Mars and Beyond," which aired on December 4, 1957.

This is how Walker became interested in space as a boy growing up in Bedford, Indiana: "I remember seeing those programs and saying to myself, 'This space exploration has to be fun. I want to be a part of that,'" Walker says. "Our nation was beginning to seriously develop rockets. They were principally intercontinental ballistic missiles, but there was always the talk that these would also be used to send manned missions into space. You know, for a kid of seven years old, that was pretty exciting stuff. It caught my attention. Jet aviation records were being set at places like Edwards Air Force Base. This whole cultural focus on aviation and space in the 1950s really got me excited."

Bedford, in southern Indiana, is the largest town in Lawrence County. The second largest town is Mitchell, twelve miles to the south. And Mitchell, Indiana, by the late 1950s, had its own hometown space hero in native son Virgil "Gus" Grissom, a Purdue University graduate. Grissom had been selected as one of the original Mercury 7 astronauts. In July 1961, he became the second American to launch into space.

"Every fall Mitchell has its premier social event—the Persimmon Festival," Walker says. "And in 1960, Gus Grissom participated in that festival. In addition, NASA had shipped into town a full-size mock-up of the Mercury capsule. When I saw that, my eyes were just wide open, and I was saying, 'You know, this is cool.' The space program had come not quite to my hometown, but twelve miles away was close enough. And here was a guy who was going into space, and he came from just down the road!"

Walker watched on a black-and-white television set in a study hall at Bedford Junior High when Alan Shepard launched into space in May 1961. In high school he focused on science, math, and technology, where he had interests and strengths. The whole time he kept a close watch on NASA as it moved through the Mercury and then Gemini programs. When it came time to pick a university, Walker wanted to follow in Grissom's footsteps. He enrolled at Purdue University.

His parents, his friends, everyone who knew him through those days, uses the same word to describe Walker's attitude: *focused.*

"When I arrived at Purdue, I knew what I wanted to do," Walker says. "I remember one of the early interviews, and they said, 'Okay, freshman year you're going into general engineering.' I said, 'I don't want to go into general engineering. I want aero-astro engineering.'"

He got the opportunity to study aeronautical and astronautical engineering in his sophomore year after he completed the general introductory program all freshmen engineers take. During his years at Purdue, encounters with pioneering astronauts like the first and last Americans on the Moon, Neil Armstrong and Eugene Cernan, Purdue graduates themselves, only reinforced Walker's determination to be a part of the space program.

In the spring of 1971, Walker accomplished his dream. He graduated from Purdue with a degree in aeronautical and astronautical engineering and went right to work—as a civil engineering technician, land acquisition specialist, and forest firefighter for the U.S. Forest Service.

"Well, I graduated right in the middle of the last big slump in aerospace employment," he says.

He had job offers to work as an engineer, but for Walker, it was going to be NASA or the aerospace industry. Nothing else would do.

He had worked summers with the U.S. Forest Service, and since he couldn't find a job in aerospace, he fell back on his old connections while he continued his job search. His dreams would have to wait—but not long.

He soon found employment as a design engineer with the Bendix Aerospace Company where he worked on aerodynamic analysis, missile subsystem design, and flight testing. He was also employed at the Crane Division, Naval Surface Warfare Center, in southern Indiana as project engineer with the Naval Sea Systems Command. He worked in computer-controlled manufacturing systems.

"All this time I was still looking for that space job," Walker says. "I paid my own way to travel to professional society meetings and built contacts. I wrote letters to industry contacts, and I was interviewed several times by several companies. I finally found the position I was looking for."

In 1977, he went to work with the McDonnell Douglas Astronautics Company as a test engineer on the aft propulsion subsystem for the space shuttle orbiters. This was four years before the first space shuttle flight in 1981. At McDonnell Douglas, Walker was interested in developing space-flight hardware with commercial application.

"I really was focused on the commercial possibilities of exploiting the unique environments of space, particularly microgravity," he says. "McDonnell Douglas had just started a research and development program in that very vein. They said, 'Okay, we'll bring you on. Get going on it.' Walker was involved in equipment design and development. Meanwhile, McDonnell Douglas was negotiating with NASA to test its equipment on space shuttle flights.

"I went to my management," Walker says. "I said, 'You know, if this stuff flies in space, I want to go with it.'"

He became the first industrial payload specialist to fly on a space shuttle in August 1984. He flew on two other shuttle missions in April and November 1985.

As a payload specialist he was not a NASA astronaut, but rather he flew on the missions as a McDonnell Douglas employee. With the company paying NASA for the marginal costs of his flights, he became the first paying—and working—passenger into space.

Walker now works for The Boeing Company in Washington, D.C. Would he like to fly in a space shuttle again?

"I'd love to," he says. "The experience is more than you can ever imagine. The psychological, physical, and emotional experience is just awesome." Like the love for aeronautical and astronautical engineering he learned as a boy, the love and lure of space travel stays with a person for life.

Chapter Two

To invent a plane is nothing.
To build one is something.
To fly is everything.
—Otto Lilienthal

James Clifford Turpin cut a dashing figure in his senior class photo that appeared in the 1908 Purdue University yearbook, *Debris.* He was stylishly dressed in a mid-calf-length coat and a cardigan sweater. His starched, white collar held a dark tie, and his pants were well tailored, breaking right at the shoe. He wore a cap that was tilted to the side of his head giving him a determined, confident, almost cocky look as the camera caught for posterity his knowing smile.

He was a handsome fellow—dashing, nearly six feet tall, black hair, blue-gray eyes. He looked like a young man who could have been modeling the latest styles for a fashion magazine of the day.

According to the yearbook, Turpin—they called him "Turp"—was in the Mechanical Engineering Club, which would be expected since that was his major. He was well-rounded and belonged to the Harlequin Club, which in 1907 performed the first theater production at Purdue called "The President of Oolong." Turpin was a member of Phi Delta Theta Fraternity and ran track at the university.

Under each student's list of activities, the *Debris* staff added some brief remarks—comments that were half in jest and half serious. They were designed so that the students would be able understand all the inside jokes, but no one would be afraid to show the yearbook to their parents.

The remarks about Turpin open with this quotation: "J. C. Turpin, Dayton, Ohio," as if he commonly introduced himself that way and then abruptly stopped talking, thinking you had all the information you needed for the moment.

Members of Turpin's family say he was a man of few words who let his accomplishments do the speaking.[1] So the yearbook staff was joking when they called him "the man with a vocabulary and a record of 1,500 words per minute." He had a reputation on campus as a young man who understood engines.

"He is a gasoline expert," the *Debris* staff said, "and has proved his worth in college, showing some of the profs a few new turns. He works hard when he has to, does not carry anything to excess except smoking, and is a good fellow in every sense."

In a very short time after graduation Cliff Turpin—as he was known everywhere outside Purdue—would show a few new turns in gasoline engine technology to a lot of people, including Orville and Wilbur Wright who lived in his home town of Dayton, Ohio.

In fact, the Wright brothers' workshop was located not far from the home where Turpin grew up and lived with his parents before and after graduating from Purdue. The Wright workshop once had been a place where they sold, repaired, and manufactured bicycles. By 1908, the Wrights were busy designing and testing the flying machines that were still quite new to the entire world.

What was taking place in the Wright workshop from about 1900 through 1908 could not have slipped past Turpin, a young man who had the mind of an engineer, a passion for engines, and the heart of an adventurer.

With scientific and engineering work that was about to shake the entire world taking place within blocks of his home, Turpin made certain his daily evening walks took him past the Wright workshop. There he would stop, watch, and often talk with the talented Wright brothers.

Turpin's father, James, was anxious for his son to receive the best education. And there was a reason: he wanted Cliff to return home after graduation from Purdue and work in the family business. James Turpin wanted to manufacture motorcycles. The Turpin's New Era Motorcycles went into production in Dayton in 1909 with Cliff, a Purdue graduate, helping run the company.

An official biography, approved by Turpin late in his life when he was inducted into an elite group of pre-1915 flyers known as the Early Birds, talked about his long evening walks that included stops at the Wright workshop.

"Clifford became interested in the activities of the Wright brothers as he would walk out West Third Street and pass their shop, occasionally stopping in to watch them at their work," the biography states. "He soon became acquainted with both brothers who observed his increasing interest in what they were doing."[2]

After accomplishing powered, controlled, sustained flight in their flying machine in 1903, the Wrights had returned to Dayton with much work to do. They knew they still had a long way to go. They needed better controls for their machine. They needed to learn how to pilot it better. There was no one to give them flight instructions. They were writing flight manuals as they invented and experimented. And they needed to develop a better engine that was lighter, but at the same time more powerful and efficient. Twice in May 1904 they had displayed their flying machine for reporters. Twice it accomplished only short hops with engine power being a central problem.[3]

They built equipment in their workshop on Third Street and, when the weather was right, ran flight tests in an area outside of Dayton known as Huffman Prairie. By 1905, the Wright brothers had developed what they considered to be a reliable machine. They spent most of the next two years working on patents and marketing.

In 1908, the Wrights split up, temporarily. They divided their work and traveled separately away from Dayton. Orville went to Fort Myers, Virginia, where he was injured demonstrating the flying machine to Army officials. Wilbur traveled to France to show the world what they had accomplished.

By June 1909, when the brothers returned to Dayton, they were international celebrities. In that year, the knowledge of what they had accomplished finally took hold. President Taft even held a ceremony for the Wright brothers at the White House.

On June 10, 1909—exactly one year after Turpin's graduation from Purdue—the East Room of the White House was filled with dignitaries as Taft addressed the brothers, noting that he was a bit too large to fly. Taft did understand one of the key elements that led the Wrights to succeed where so many others had failed: hard work.

"You made this discovery by a course that we of America feel is distinctly American—by keeping your nose right at the job until you had accomplished what you had determined to do," Taft said.[4]

Back home in Dayton, June 17–18 was named "Wright Brothers' Home Days Celebration." There were huge ceremonies. Hundreds of local grade-school children sat together on bleachers wearing red, white, and blue clothing that formed a human flag. These children formed the backdrop for a speaker's podium where the high and mighty of Dayton praised the two men who brought so much honor to their hometown. There were parades and bands. It was a time of great pride for a community that saw itself claiming international esteem.

Early in the morning on June 19, 1909, the day after it all ended, the Wrights, "ever keeping their nose right at the job at hand," caught a train and traveled to Fort Myers, Virginia, continuing their efforts to interest the U.S. Army in their flying machine.

Since Turpin returned to Dayton with his Purdue degree in June 1908—and we know the Wright brothers spent most of the next twelve months out of town—it's likely that he first became involved with Orville and Wilbur even before he left for college in the fall of 1904. As a high-school student, or at the latest during summer breaks from Purdue, Turpin probably began his visits to the Wright workshop observing the fascinating activity that was taking place there: the birth of aviation. He continued those contacts with the Wrights after graduation whenever they were in town.

In the Early Birds' biography, Turpin confirmed, "when the Wrights learned that [he] was a graduate engineer, they invited him to join their group."[5]

In several interviews with newspaper reporters many years later, Turpin added more details. In 1954, he told the *Purdue Alumnus* that Orville Wright had approached his father asking for help. According to the *Alumnus*, "Cliff was working for his father who manufactured gasoline engines. Orville Wright came to [the Turpins] with motor trouble. . . . After two or three months, they solved the problem."[6]

It was the fall of 1909 when the Wright's offered Turpin full-time employment. Before he took the job, Turpin had to "wrangle" consent from his parents.

By 1911, New Era Motorcycles was out of business, and Cliff Turpin was enshrined as one of the heroes of the age, a daring birdman who enthralled hundreds of thousands of people across America with his flights in the air—spectacular, daring flights that defied every law of nature people had been taught to believe since childhood: birds fly, not people.

Turpin's first efforts focused on improvements to the Wright engine. He also "assisted in developing several major improvements to the aeroplane [itself] and its controls."[7]

That puts him on the ground floor of the birth of aviation, working with the Wright brothers on their flying machine at a time when progress in aviation was being advanced every day. In 1910, the Wright brothers introduced a new flying machine with a redesigned forty-horsepower, four-cycle engine that Turpin probably had a hand in designing and building.

By 1910, other people were building flying machines. The Wrights believed that some of them were infringing on their patents, and they initiated legal actions that would go on for many years.

Even before 1910, competitors to the Wrights, people such as Glenn Curtiss, were putting on air shows and drawing thousands of people who paid to gather at fair grounds or in fields outside of town to watch men fly.

Flight was quickly capturing the imagination of a nation. The Wright brothers did not approve of the daredevil stunts people were using to entertain these crowds. At the same time, they realized that they, too, would have to enter this arena to maintain their dominance in the young world of flight. They understood if they did not enter the exhibitions, they would be left behind. By January 1910, the Wrights had decided it was time to enter the flight exhibition business.[8]

The Wright brothers trained their first handful of pilots in Montgomery, Alabama, choosing the southern location because the weather in Dayton during the winter of early 1910 was too cold and severe for reliable flying day in, day out. In Montgomery, Orville trained three young pilots: Walter Brookins, Arch Hoxsey, and Spencer Crane. When the weather improved up north, Orville left Brookins in charge at Montgomery and returned to Dayton.

At Huffman Prairie in Dayton, the Wright brothers gave flight training to A. L. Welsh, Duval LaChapelle, Phil O. Parmalee and Cliff Turpin. In May, Brookins arrived from Montgomery. He trained Ralph Johnstone and Frank Coffyn.[9]

Many of these new pilots, including Turpin, lead by Roy Knabenshue, formed the Wright exhibition flying team.

By June 1910, Turpin was no longer content confining his work to the ground and building better engines. He wanted to fly. He was twenty-four years old. What young man with his background wouldn't want to take one of the new flying machines up into the air to see and feel what only a handful of very select people in the whole world had been privileged to experience?

A Dayton newspaper dated August 1910 carried the headline "Society Man to Turn Aviator." The article not only established a historical record of when Turpin started flying. It also said a lot about the Turpin family. "Mr. Clifford Turpin, a member of the exclusive younger society set of Dayton and associated with his father, James Turpin, in the New Era [Motorcycle] Company, will study aviation under the Wrights and train to become an operator."[10]

As Parmalee and Turpin learned to fly together, they became quick friends forming a Big Ten bond. Parmalee was an alumnus of the University of Michigan, and the two college graduates found they had much in common.

Not everyone who wanted to fly with the Wrights was successful. Getting a flying machine off the ground and keeping it there was a difficult process. Some washed out during flight instructions. Some of those who were trained did not make it on the exhibition circuit.

One man who successfully learned to fly from Turpin and others on the Wright team was Cal Rodgers. In 1911, with the sponsorship of a grape soft drink named Vin Fizz, Rodgers attempted to become the first person to fly across the United States. He did it in eighty-four days having survived five terrible crashes that seriously damaged the flying machine he appropriately named the *Vin Fizz*. Rodgers ended the flight on crutches. He failed to receive a cash prize for his accomplishment because it had taken him too long, but he did gain national publicity for his accomplishment.

The U.S Army sent two men, Second Lieutenant Thomas Milling and Second Lieutenant Henry H. Arnold, to Dayton to learn how to fly from the Wright group. Turpin was one of the primary instructors, and both the Army officers were successful in their training and became among the first military pilots.

During World War I, Milling was placed in charge of Air Service training in Europe. Later he was named as chief of staff of the Air Service, First Army, American Expeditionary Force. He eventually helped create U.S. laws, rules, and regulations for air travel, advocated a strong air service, served during World War II, and retired as a brigadier general.

Henry "Hap" Arnold would become commanding general of the U.S. Army Air Corps during World War II. He has been called the father of the modern U.S. Air Force. Arnold's memories of those days paint a wonderful picture of what it was like to take to the air in a flying machine. His recollections come from his book, *Global Mission*:

"Back in the early 1900s when the area surrounding Dayton was not so thickly populated, there were many small farms—one in particular located about nine miles out of town at a place called Simms Station. Later, it was sometimes called Huffman Field. . . . It was a cow pasture. . . . It had a large thorn tree at one end and at the other end was a fairly large wooden shed. . . . Every morning a man would arrive in a wagon. . . . He'd hitch his horses alongside the fence around the cow pasture and sit there and wait in the wagon until noon and then he'd get out, untie his horses, turn them around, and slowly shaking his head, solemnly drive back to Dayton. The man was the local undertaker."[11]

There were two seats, side by side, in these Wright aeroplanes. The instructor and trainee were positioned on these hard seats that were attached to the lower wing. The previous practice of lying on the wing had been abandoned because Orville Wright got a stiff neck trying to hold his head up during flights that lasted half an hour or more.[12] The pilots held their hands on levers, their feet on a bar.

Arnold said would-be pilots at the Wright trainings first learned about flying machine controls using a ground simulator. They learned sitting in an old plane that was balanced on two sawhorses.

Getting the real flying machines off the ground, keeping them in the air, and landing them without killing yourself were difficult tasks, and different designers were building their aeroplanes with different controls. Experienced pilots needed to learn all the different control techniques for all the different flying machines, how their engines worked, and how to care for them. Arnold experienced this need for varied working knowledge of different aircrafts, including wing warping, the important Wright technique of altering the surface of the wings—a process that would eventually be taken over by ailerons:

> . . . In the Wright plane, the airman's feet rested on a slender bar before the wing. For the elevator, the Wright pilot moved a vertical stick. There were two of these sticks, one outside of each seat for whichever pilot happened to be flying the plane. But there were not two complete sets of controls. The third stick, between the two aviators, though it moved fore and aft, was for lateral balance and rudder. The top portion of this middle lever was hinged to rock laterally and was connected by a rod to a quadrant on the same shaft as the warp control. The rudder could be moved either in combination with the warping or independently. Operation of the warp-rudder lever as a whole warped the light wings and simultaneously moved the rudder the correct amount for maintaining straight flight during adjustment of lateral equilibrium. A right turn, for example, was achieved by pulling the lever back to lift the left wing and simul-

> taneously rotating the hand trip an appropriate number of degrees to the right for right rudder. After the turn was started, the pilot eased back to normal attitude for level flying. This scarcely instinctive procedure had to be mastered before one could go into the air as a Wright pilot. The old plane mounted on a sawhorse was how you began.
>
> The lateral controls were connected with small clutches at the wing tips and grabbed a moving belt running over a pulley. A forward motion, the clutch would snatch the belt, and down would go the left wing. A backward pull and the reverse would happen. The jolts and teetering were so violent that the student was kept busy just moving the lever back and forth to keep on an even keel.[13]

The message from this passage is clear: flying in those early days was very difficult and only the best were able to master it.

Arnold's total flight instruction time was typical and consisted of three hours and forty-eight minutes in the air over the course of eleven days, which excluded the Sunday Christian Sabbath. The Wrights did not permit flying on Sunday, but the flight students were sometimes welcomed at their home for Sunday dinner where their sister, Katherine, worked very hard overseeing the preparation.

According to Arnold, after three hours and forty-eight minutes, he had been taught all the facts and insights that the instructors knew. From that point on, a person had to go up in the air and learn for himself or herself, hopefully coming down at a time and place of his/her own choosing. Instructors, in fact, were still learning about the art and science of flight themselves every time they went up.

When something went wrong and a pilot crashed, Arnold said everyone assumed it was pilot error. They never considered the possibility that there was something drastically wrong with the flying machine. To think that would have been too frightening for the men who had to go back up in those machines day after day.[14]

There were few instruments on the planes to help the early flyers. "The only instrument used on airplanes when I began to fly was a piece of string tied to the front crossbar on the skids," Arnold wrote. "When it stood out directly to the rear, everything was okay—the pilot was flying correctly. When it drifted to one side or the other, the plane was in a skid."[15]

These planes were flying faster than fifty miles per hour, reaching heights hundreds and even thousands of feet in the air. The pilots' own strength holding on to the controls was the only thing that held them in the chair. There were no seat belts in those early flying machines.

Arnold told of one accident some years later when a military student was in the air over water with his flight instructor. They were suddenly bounced out of their seats. Arnold said, "Jack Towers was thrown from his seat. The pilot was tossed clear. Since [the pilot] had no parachute, he didn't have a chance and dropped like a rock into the ocean. Towers, rattling around between the wings, strut, and wires, managed finally to grab a wire and hang on until the plane hit the water."[16]

Miraculously, Towers survived by staying with the plane until it hit the water and then swimming free as the wreckage slipped beneath the waves.

"After that," Arnold said, "we all used seat belts."

Arnold discovered other problems he was not prepared to encounter. The custom was to sit on the wing and turn your hat backwards so the wind wouldn't carry it away. The pilots were concerned about losing their hat in the wind. In the earliest days, less thought was given to wind in their eyes.

Arnold said on one occasion when he was coming back for a landing "a bug hit me in the eye and left one of its transparent wings sticking to my eyeball. The pain was terrific; blinded by tears I could scarcely see to make my landing. As a matter of fact, it was some days before the doctors were able to find that transparent wing and remove it. The possibility of being rammed dead by a bug had not occurred to us before. After that, we wore goggles."[17]

Training others to fly was part of the job of the Wright exhibition team flyers, but the main occupation of Turpin and the others was to take aviation to the American people who wanted to witness this miracle with their own two eyes.

In 1910, the Wright team and other flyers of the day became fast national celebrities. They demonstrated flight and competed in speed, elevation, duration, and other contests against international assemblies of birdmen. Flying became an enormously popular *sport,* and that's the word newspapers of the day often used to describe aviation, much to the chagrin of the Wrights, who wanted it to be an industry, a money-making industry.

The birdmen were among the first national sports stars of the United States. For example, the *New York Times* didn't limit front-page coverage to air shows on the east coast. They carried dispatches about air shows from Chicago, St. Louis, and even San Diego and Seattle. The birdmen were front-page news everywhere as they pushed the limits of what was possible, performing daring stunts designed to outdo one another.

The pay for the birdmen was good—if they didn't get killed. It was even better for the Wright brothers who did not fly at all in these exhibitions but received the profits. The Wrights brothers ran a tight ship.

In *The Bishop's Boys,* Crouch writes, "Pilots in the Wright camp were subject to strict supervision. All the standard family rules were in effect. There was no drinking, gambling, or flying on Sundays. The pay was a set fee of twenty dollars per week and fifty dollars for every day a man flew. For the Wright Company, it was an ideal arrangement. The brothers demanded $1,000 for each day that [the exhibition team members] flew at a meet. The company received $6,000 per man for a standard one-week meet, plus any prize money earned; the pilot received $320. Small wonder that the year 1910 was a good one for the Wright Company; profits approached $100,000."[18]

The first air show the Wright team took part in was at the Indianapolis Motor Speedway during the week of June 13, 1910. It was a major event and it brought aviation back to Indiana where Octave Chanute had performed many of the early experiments on gliders at the Dunes. However, Turpin did not fly at Indianapolis.

As exhibitions continued from one coast of the country to the other, men and aeroplanes couldn't fly from one event to the next. The distance between exhibitions was too far. Instead, they rode the rails. Flying machines were disassembled, packed in crates, placed on trains, and shipped to an exhibition site. When the exhibition was over, everything was crated up again and sent by train to the next location.

Every plane had a crew consisting of the pilot, a motorman in charge of the engine, assemblymen who were in charge of crating and uncrating the flying machines, and tent men who set up tents at each location. These tents served as hangars and also places where people would be allowed a close look at the flying machines—a close look for an extra price.

Crowds numbered into the thousands and tens of thousands depending on where the exhibitions took place. People came from everywhere to see these birdmen. They sat in grandstands and stood in fields. Local newspaper photographers were taken up for a ride and the next day in their home town papers citizens saw—for the first time—what their communities looked like from a bird's-eye view. It was overwhelming. People stood awestruck as they watched these machines leave the ground and fly overhead. They were frightened. They were terrified that they would witness a tragedy—and often they did—but they were spellbound. There were many accidents among the flyers at the air shows. There were many deaths.

Within the Wright exhibition team, Hoxsey and Johnstone were immediately called the "Stardust Twins" for their daredevil stunts. They did a "Dive of Death," plunging nose first from 1,000 feet "with a pull-out at the last possible minute."[19]

Wilbur Wright was not happy with these stunts. He read about them in newspaper accounts, and he wrote his exhibition flyers to protest. The brothers had no intent of sponsoring death-defying carnival shows. They took flight as a serious business, a growing industry—not a sideshow. They wanted their flyers to introduce aviation to the public, not to scare people half to death.

A stern Wilbur Wright wrote this to his flyers: "I am very much in earnest when I say that I want no stunts and spectacular frills put on the flights. . . . If each of you make a plain flight of ten to fifteen minutes . . . keeping always within the inner fence wall away from the grandstand and never more than 300 feet high, it will be just what we want."[20]

That letter slowed the Wright team members down temporarily, but it didn't stop them for long. The birdmen knew what the public was paying to see at the air shows, and they were paying to see something more than flight. They wanted excitement.

Johnstone was first. He died in an accident at an exhibition on November 17, 1910. Hoxsey was killed a month later.

Throughout 1910, air shows became the most thrilling events ever witnessed. And while Turpin did not fly in Indianapolis, he was quickly a part of the show. He made his first performance in Missouri, October 1–7, 1910.

A Sedalia, Missouri, newspaper dated October 1, 1910 gave this account: "The airplane exhibitions are indisputably the greatest attraction ever secured by the fair directors to entertain people. . . . When Turpin approached the grandstand on his first trip around the track, he met with a spontaneous outbreak of applause—the spectators, fairly going wild in their demonstration of approval and praise. Again and again he was greeted with deafening cheers, which drowned the whirring of the big motor that propelled the aeroplane."[21]

Another newspaper account from Sedalia reported on a race that people from Missouri would have to see to believe: a contest between an aeroplane flying dangerously low and an automobile speeding around an oval track:

> The most sensational, thrilling, and novel speed contest ever witnessed in Missouri was held yesterday afternoon at the fair grounds. It was a five-mile race between a rambler—a forty-five-horse power racing automobile—and a Wright aeroplane, driven by aviator Clifford Turpin, who was making flights daily at the fair. The contest was the concluding number on the day's amusement program, and it was nearly 6:00 P.M. when the race was commenced. Yet thousands of people waited to witness the marvelous exhibition by the man-bird and the daredevil in the auto. Spectators were well repaid for waiting, and not one of them would have missed the spectacle for a small fortune.
>
> The start was made at the three-quarter pole, and the biplane quickly took the lead. The auto [raced] down the stretch with the speed of the New York Central's Empire Express. The second mile was made by the biplane, at the rate of a mile a minute, with the rambler a close second. Round and round the track the two machines flew at a dizzying pace, the airplane hugging the top of the fence along the backstretch, and it looked as if Turpin was trying to hold [the automobile] in a pocket, and keep him from getting the lead.
>
> At the commencement of the fourth mile, it was even-money that either the auto would win or there would be a dead heat. Turpin, however, had a surprise up his sleeve, and he sprung it at the finish of the last half-mile of the race. The aviator, during the race, had been laying his course in the infield, paralleling a track on the homestretch, in order to avoid the poles and guy wires used in the athletic performances. But

> he was not asleep at the opportunity to perform the unexpected. Coming down the home stretch to the finish, the last mile, the aviator drove his machine over the racetrack, between the grandstand and judge's stand. The spectators in the grandstand held their breath in amazement, and then a roar of applause, loud enough to be heard a mile, burst forth spontaneously. Thousands of men were on their tiptoes, yelling like mad, and ladies turned the air white with their waving handkerchiefs.
>
> Turpin crossed the wire just as the rambler was turning into the homestretch, nearly a quarter of a mile to the rear. The distance of five miles had been made in five minutes and thirty-one seconds, almost a mile a minute. It was a pretty wild race and a contest that will always be remembered by all who saw it.[22]

From Sedalia the team moved directly to St. Louis for one of the most famous air shows of all time. It took place from October 8–18, and it was here that Theodore Roosevelt became the first former or current U.S. president to fly. He was in the air for four minutes with Hoxsey as his pilot.

It was at St. Louis that Turpin received his pilot's license from the Aero Club of America. France was already issuing pilot's licenses when the Aero Club of America decided to follow suit. Regulations stated, "All candidates shall satisfy the officials of the Aero Club of America of their ability to fly at least five hundred yards, and of their capability of making a gliding descent with the engine stopped, before their applications will be entertained."[23]

The first five licenses had been issued in June 1910. They were given alphabetically to people already known to qualify. License number one went to Glenn Curtiss. Next came Frank Lahm, Louis Paulhan, and finally Orville Wright and Wilbur Wright.[24]

On October 18, 1910, Turpin was issued license number twenty-two, the twenty-second issued in the United States. He kept it all his life.

From St. Louis, Turpin and the Wright team traveled to Belmont Park on Long Island, for a meet that lasted from October 20–30.

Turpin had been flying for less than six months when his fraternity, Phi Delta Theta, started covering his exploits. An article in the fraternity magazine dated November 1910 was headlined, "The Young Mechanical Engineer James Clifford Turpin:"

> The young mechanical engineer who is the subject of discussion has been out of school only two years and has been connected actively with the development of aeroplanes only about four months[sic]. But being associated with the foremost exponents of the science of building aeroplanes and the navigation of the air, he has attained a prominence excelled by few in this most distinguished field of human endeavors.
>
> The Wright aviators including Brookens, Hoxsey, Turpin, Welch, and Johnstone with Knabenshue, are at the present time perfecting the Wright biplane, by exhaustive tests and public exhibitions—and, incidentally, reaping a harvest of gold without precedent.
>
> They are all young men, boys almost, in the experimental stage of development, at least. Older men are not so well adapted to the work, apparently, as [young] men are—with their boy's enthusiasm of mind, combined with a determined heart and reckless irresponsibility of young men not yet married. Whether it is accidental or all these men are of this kind is not known.[25]

The fame and the daring of these young men attracted welcome attention from female fans. A newspaper article from November 1910 reported that young women were flirting with the Wright flying men wherever they went. It reported that Welch, Coffyn, and Johnstone were married. Brookins, Hoxey, Turpin, and Parmalee were the eligible bachelors. "Cut out the list girls and paste it on the inside of your bonnet. The information ought to prove valuable to many and keep a good many lovesick girls from innocently trying to lure Wright aviators in the path of married blessedness. The feminine world seems to think there is something unusual about an aviator, yet they are only human. Women, young and old, all over the land, have worshiped the Wright's septet. Offers of marriage received by the plucky man-birds would make mighty interesting reading. It comes as good dope that 500 women from

Columbus [Ohio] and other places have written, asking permission to ride in the aeroplane that will carry a bolt of silk from Dayton to Columbus Monday, and making inquiries about who and what kind of fellow will drive the biplane."[26]

This was an era when people gathered around pianos in family parlors and sang popular songs of the day. One of these songs was "Come, Josephine, in My Flying Machine," which was also known as "Up She Goes!" On the cover of the sheet music was a young man seated on a Wright Flyer, his hands on the controls. Seated beside him, admiring his skill was a young woman flying in a full, long dress, a large hat, and a flowing scarf. This song shows the romance attached to flyers from 1910 to the twenty-first century.

> *Oh, say! Let us fly, dear. Where kid? To the sky dear. Oh you flying machine! Jump in Miss Josephine. Ship ahoy! Oh, what a joy! What a feeling. Where boy? In the ceiling so high, hoopla! We fly to the sky so high.*
>
> *Come Josephine, in my flying machine, going up she goes, up she goes! Balance yourself like a bird on a beam, in the air she goes, there she goes.*
>
> *Up, up a little bit higher, Oh my! The moon is on fire. Come Josephine in my flying machine, going up all on— Good-bye.*
>
> *One, two, now we're off dear. Say you, pretty soft dear. Whoa! dear, don't hit the moon. No dear, not yet, but soon. You for me, oh gee! You're a fly kid. No me, I'm a sky kid. Gee, I'm up in the air about you.*[27]

In 1910, romance was truly in the air. What did it feel like to fly, sitting on the wing of a Wright Flyer? People of 1910 were as excited about seeing Earth for the first time from an aeroplane as another generation would be in the late 1960s to see photographs of Earth for the first time from the Moon.

Frank R. Robertson was a travelogue writer and speaker in 1910 who had an opportunity to fly with Turpin:

> No more Pullman cars. No more ocean liners for me. Now I know what it must seem like to the birds spreading their wings for the first time. What did it feel like? I don't know. I was too busy lamenting the fact that I didn't have a camera to look upon the motion picture of Mother Earth as it opened up in all its vastness beneath me.
>
> I expected that the roar of the motor would be deafening, but really I forgot there was a motor. I braced myself for a series of rough bumpings after we started out from the hangar, but a motorcar could not have started off with a more luxurious sense of restful ease. The gentle run of thirty yards on the field . . . and the earth fell away beautifully, as the treetops disappeared and tangled up in the distance. A sense of absolute super-human mastery, the mental disassociation with all things earthly, and the potential feeling that one holds ever-lasting space at the command of a turn of a lever. My, it was superb. I might almost say sublime. A gentle turn to right or a gentle turn to left by my skilled pilot who had impressed me from the first contact on the earth below as a clever, straightforward, cheerful, practical, know-his-business sort of a companion, whose very master touch inspired further confidence the higher we mounted. Just a gentle touch I say, and the air seemed to do his bidding.
>
> One hundred and fifty feet up, Turpin said we were going forty-five miles an hour. Oh, but say that is the way to get pictures of the world over, and the six minutes we were in the air seemed like as many seconds. I didn't want to come down. If I could just have gone on and on and on and on [and] dropped down long enough for each travelogue per day, and returned between times.[28]

At the end of the 1910 flying season, Turpin and the other flyers returned home, but Turpin did not stay long in Dayton. The Wright brothers placed him in charge of their exhibit at the New York Aero Show held at Grand Central Palace.

The Wrights sent select people a very formal invitation to the show. One went to Turpin's parents. In beautiful script it stated, "The Wright Company announces to Mr. and Mrs. James Turpin the first exhibitions of its 1911 aeroplanes to be held at the Grand Central Palace from December 31 to January 7. The company will be represented by Mr. J. Clifford Turpin, who will take pleasure in extending every courtesy."[29]

Turpin was a good choice for the assignment. Along with Parmalee he was among the best educated of the Wright flyers. He had a tremendous amount of knowledge about key features of the plane, especially the engine. And he had all the social skills from his years at Purdue and his younger days in Dayton society.

When the 1911 air show season started, Turpin and the other birdmen alternated between giving flight lessons in Dayton and traveling the country demonstrating flight to an eager public. In May, Turpin flew in Hartford, Connecticut. In June, he was at an air show in New Hampshire.

As Turpin traveled the country bringing aviation to America, flight came to West Lafayette and his alma mater, Purdue University. It happened on Tuesday, June 13, 1911, and by all accounts, it was one of the most spectacular days in the history of Tippecanoe County.

An Aero Club had been organized at Purdue in 1910. Professor Cicero B. Veal in the School of Mechanical Engineering was the force behind the group.[30] But members of this group did not fly. The first demonstration of flight and aircraft occurred during Purdue Gala Week, a Purdue tradition in which alumni return to campus for an official weekend of reunion events [in the early part of the century, it occurred close to graduation, which took place in June], in June 1911, three years after Turpin's graduation.

In June 1911, the Purdue Alumni Association joined with the *Lafayette Morning Journal*, a forerunner of today's *Journal and Courier*, to sponsor a spectacular event called Aviation Day on campus at Stuart Field, the area where Elliott Hall is located today.

Purdue's birdman, Turpin, did not take part in the event. It featured Lincoln Beachy and George Witmer, both exhibition flyers for Glenn Curtiss, the main rival of the Wright brothers. All the exhibition flyers were national celebrities in 1911, but Beachy was one of those who stood above the rest in public adulation. He was known for daredevil stunts, going into deep dives, and only pulling out at the last second. In 1911, he made international headlines flying over Niagara Falls and then underneath a steel bridge.

Adding to the excitement of Aviation Day in West Lafayette, Purdue President Winthrop Stone and George Ade, a writer and one of the university's most distinguished graduates, had each vowed to fly with the visiting aviators.

Ade had a great interest in flight. In 1908, he had penned a musical comedy, "The Fair Coed." In it he referred to an aeronautical engineering department at the fictitious "Indiana Institute of Technology," which to Ade could only have meant Purdue. If the first mention of aeronautical engineering at Purdue was fictitious, it was visionary. Turpin might have performed in this play. The Purdue Harlequin Group that he belonged to staged it in West Lafayette before it went to Broadway.

The Lafayette newspapers were filled with stories about Aviation Day as the big event drew near. Crowds began arriving in Lafayette early on June 13, 1911, according to the *Lafayette Morning Journal.* People poured into town "by train, interurban, automobile, buggy, and foot," the paper reported.[31] A Monon train arrived at 10:30 A.M. bringing more than 1,000 people from Michigan City. Hotels, restaurants, and businesses all through Lafayette were packed with people getting ready for the big event—an event that was put off until afternoon because of morning winds.[32]

It all sounds very much like the celebration that took place when *Jupiter* launched in 1859. Grandchildren of the men and women who had gathered to watch the first airmail were now gathered in Lafayette to watch the community's first heavier-than-air machines fly.

"Before twelve o'clock the visitors began going to West Lafayette and the university," the *Morning Journal* reported. "From then on until after four o'clock the street cars, the levee, and the sidewalks were crowded.

"When the gates to Stuart Field were opened at two o'clock, the people were packed and jammed about them for hundreds of feet. At the automobile gate, the great number of panting automobiles waiting seemed to be in a hopelessly chaotic state, stretched in all directions. When the gates were opened it was all the policemen could do to keep the cars from trying to enter two and three at a time. But with the exception of a few bent fenders and broken lights there were no accidents. From the time the first car entered the field until after the meet had started there was a steady stream of machines [automobiles] entering and lining up in their places. Nearly 250 automobiles were parked on the field and every available space was taken. At the main gate there was a steady stream of people entering from two to four o'clock. Every seat in all but the covered bleachers was taken, and hundreds of people were forced to stand throughout the entire meet, their interest so great that they were unmindful of the fact."[33]

The newspaper estimated more than 7,500 people were gathered at Stuart Field. Additionally, another 10,000 people were watching from other locations and the *Morning Journal* proclaimed it "the largest crowd that has ever gathered in Lafayette." But those reporters hadn't been to the *Jupiter* launched fifty-two years earlier.

Winds throughout the morning and early afternoon left people worried that the flying machines might not attempt to leave the ground. As the crowds lined Stuart Field, two Curtiss biplanes sat idle at the southwest corner of the area attracting the attention of everyone. Each person impatiently waited for the machines to be moved in preparation for flight, but nothing happened.

Finally, at 3:30 P.M. Beachy himself became impatient. Worried about disappointing the gathered thousands, he had his aeroplane wheeled to the center of the field. A huge roar of applause burst from all parts as Beachy paced proudly to his flying machine and mechanics began final tune-ups in preparation for flight. When all was ready, the aeroplane was wheeled to the southeast corner for takeoff. With Beachy seated at the controls and his hands on the steering wheel, a mechanic spun the propeller and the eight-cylinder engine huffed and puffed and started with such a heavy burst of exhaust it blew a huge cloud of dust right into the faces of the well-dressed people seated in the south bleachers. There was an absolute stillness in the crowd. People froze in position, holding their breath in anticipation. The only sound in West Lafayette was the rumble of Beachy's engine "as the first aeroplane ever moved under its own power in this part of the country."[34]

It moved slowly at first, and people wondered how it would ever gain enough speed and power to lift off from the earth. They worried the winds would push it back down, but as it rolled along Stuart Field on three wheels, the aeroplane gradually gained speed. It rushed past the center of the field, heading north, and all at once to the glee of the crowd the wheels lifted off from the ground, and Beachy rose up and up and up to the gasps of people in the bleachers. The instant the aeroplane left the ground the silence of the day was broken. The crowd spontaneously rose "as one" and cheered wildly for Beachy who was climbing higher and higher and could not have heard them above the rumble of his engine.[35]

The *Morning Journal* estimated Beachy was only forty feet above the ground when a gust of wind grabbed hold of his aeroplane and tilted it dangerously. People held their breath. Their hearts jumped. "But with never slackening speed the plane rose higher and higher until it seemed but a huge bird far above," the paper reported. "At intervals the roar of the motor would reach the spectators, who gazed above, spellbound."[36]

Twice Beachy circled the field, and people twisted their necks to watch a sight they had never seen before in their lives. He then began a long descent, skimming over the heads of the crowds in the south bleachers before bringing his aeroplane to the ground like a falling feather. The machine traveled about a hundred yards on the ground before Beachy brought it to a stop, turned off the engine, got out, and began walking across the field as the crowd of thousands erupted into a deafening roar of adulation.[37]

Flight had arrived at Purdue University.

Witmer was next, and he flew a plane that had given him many problems just days earlier in Evansville. There was a long delay in getting his machine prepared, but the crowd waited patiently. Finally, it was ready to fly, and Witmer repeated the steps Beachy had taken to get his machine into the air. Witmer circled the field twice, landed, and was greeted by another thundering applause.[38] The day was far from over.

Beachy went up again, this time to show people the heights these machines were capable of achieving. He flew up and up, circling the field, and then heading out over the Wabash River toward Lafayette until he appeared as just a speck in the sky. He returned with a rapid descent and a landing that thrilled the crowd. The *Morning Journal* said Beachy had reached a height of three thousand feet.[39]

It was again Witmer's turn, and his mechanics worked furiously on his troubled engine that refused to hit on all cylinders, a sound even the uninformed in the crowd could spot as serious trouble. Finally, Witmer decided he could not keep the crowd waiting any longer. With his engine sputtering he took off. Beachy also lifted off, following close behind. With both aeroplanes in the air, Beachy nearly stopped the hearts of everyone. He dipped, he dropped, he swooped, and people were stunned as he pulled himself out of what seemed sure death time and again. Twice he allowed his aeroplane to fall within what seemed to observers as just a few feet off the ground before yanking it back up into the sky. It was then that Beachy spotted an automobile pulling away from the field. He would have none of that. He steered his plane toward the auto, swooped down, and flew right overhead as the occupants cowered into their seats. At the last second, Beachy pulled out to the cheer and laughter of the crowd.[40]

With all the attention on Beachy, the crowd did not notice that Witmer was also still flying and his engine was misfiring badly. It sputtered and gradually drew the attention of everyone, including Beachy, who stopped his death-defying stunts. Witmer was flying far away from the field when his engine stopped dead, and he began a descent that had the crowd holding its breath once again. He dropped into a Purdue farm pasture about a half-mile south of State Street. "The crowds on Stuart field were in an uproar and hundreds ran to the scene," the *Morning Journal* reported. "There was a sigh of relief when it was announced Witmer was not injured." It was, Witmer later said, the fourth time this particular engine had failed him. He vowed to replace it.[41]

There was only one disappointment. Stone and Ade did not fly. The *Morning Journal* reported that the birdmen, Beachy and Witmer, determined the winds were too severe to carry passengers aloft. There were also later reports that the Purdue University Board of Trustees had decided the stunt was too dangerous to allow their president to fly.[42]

The 3,000 feet that Beachy reached in Lafayette was nothing compared to what Turpin was doing. In 1911, at Asbury Park, New Jersey, Turpin flew to a height of 9,400 feet. It took him two hours and forty-five minutes to reach that height.[43]

It was an elevation record when he accomplished it and, although new elevation records were being set almost every week in 1911, Turpin's became the first of many that would be set by Purdue alumni.

The year 1911 was spectacular for Turpin who was touring with his best friend and fellow Wright exhibition flyer, Parmalee. From August 12–20, hundreds of thousands of people in Chicago witnessed Turpin, Parmalee, and many other birdmen in one of the greatest aviation exhibitions ever held in the United States. The location—Grant Park, right on the lakefront in downtown Chicago—could not have been better.

Bleachers seating seventy-five thousand people helped to form a huge oval all around Grant Park. But people also watched from various locations around the downtown as the aeroplanes flew over Lake Michigan, up and down the lakefront, and over the city itself.

Prominent Chicagoans who hoped to earn back their investments through gate proceeds sponsored the exhibition. But they also provided thirty thousand good, free seats, showing their main intention was to promote Chicago and aviation.

"Chicagoans of prominence undertook to bring this about because of their Chicago spirit," said an article in the *Chicago Tribune.* "The meet is not for profit. If anything is left it will go to charity. If nothing is left but debts, the supporters of the plan will pay them and say nothing."[44]

In all, prizes worth $80,000 were offered.

"The international aviation meet is a genuine competition, not merely an exhibition of flying," the *Tribune* reported. "It will embrace races and contests every day—actual races between the best of flying machines—contests in accuracy in flying over prescribed courses, in quick stopping and starting, in alighting, maneuvering, in passenger carrying, and in such warlike developments as sending wireless messages and dropping bombs."[45]

Nearly every well-known American flyer was in Chicago for the event, along with a number of birdmen from Europe. Thirty-eight birdmen entered the exhibition. Three withdrew before it even began because of accidents before arriving in Chicago.

The *Tribune* was filled with stories leading up to the event. Special sections provided daily coverage of activities. A headline on August 13 read, "Whether we suffer from aeromania or rave with aviation, it's all the same—the air bug's got us and we're proud."[46]

Purdue graduate John McCutcheon, an editorial cartoonist for the *Tribune*, went up as a passenger during the exhibition. It marked his second flight, his first coming a year earlier in Dayton, Ohio.

In his book *Drawn from Memory*, McCutcheon recalls his first flight in Dayton with Parmalee as the pilot. "I remember rattling through the weeds at a terrific speed—no concrete runways then!—and circling over the adjoining fields at about 700 feet. I sat on the lower wing of the biplane with my feet on a small bar below and clung to the struts. I think the pressure of my grip must show to this day. The pilot sat beside me with two control levers in his hands. The engine was suspended above us and two big propellers, connected by chains, were behind us, between the two wings. It was extremely primitive, crude and awkward, but it did go up and after ten or fifteen minutes came safely down . . . as they turned the plane to run it into the hangar the crankshaft broke squarely in two."[47]

That was not the sort of incident that instilled confidence. But McCutcheon was hooked. McCutcheon's drawings caught the spirit of Chicagoans. He drew a window washer strapped to a high-rise building, watching aeroplanes as he worked high above the city streets saying,

"None of that for me! Too dangerous." Another drawing featured two aviators reading newspaper headlines about a fatal train wreck. "Wonder if they'll ever make railroad travel absolutely safe," one asks the other.[48]

A second *Tribune* cartoonist had a different slant on the event. He drew a birdman piloting his aeroplane over a baseball field, so he could watch the game. The headline was this: "Yes, someday flying machines will be of practical use."[49]

Daredevil tricks started on the first day of the Chicago air show. "The crowd held its breath as a man thousands of feet in the air slanted his plane and slid down an invisible mountain as if to crash his machine to splinters," the *Tribune* reported. "The spectators gasped as he started his motor, tipped up his elevating planes and flew along parallel to the earth and rose again to experience the sensation anew. The thousands gave forth a mumble of incredulity as they saw a machine start circling in the upper air and follow huge spiral curves to the ground. It whistled and cheered as a man would 'throw' his machine toward the ground, 'bounce' it upward, and go rollicking over the course, suggesting nothing so much as the possibility that he was on an invisible roller coaster, the speed and dimensions hitherto unrealized by amusement park builders."[50]

The *Tribune* said hundreds of thousands of people jammed along Michigan Avenue, watching eleven aeroplanes in the air at one time. Birdman Lee Hammond was spared from death when his aeroplane suddenly dropped sixty feet, landing in Lake Michigan. The machine sank instantly, but the aviator was not badly injured, and he began swimming to safety before a boat picked him up "almost exhausted" if not almost scared to death.[51]

Turpin did not fly the first day of the meet. But he was in the air more than two and half hours the second day and a quick nine minutes the third. A number of pilots intentionally held back from flying on the opening day saving their best stunts for later. But no reason is given for Turpin's brief showing the third day.

The euphoric mood in Chicago changed on the fourth day of the exhibition.

The *Tribune* reported, "While 50,000 spectators were looking on—and under as fair a sky as ever blessed the city—two aviators flew to death in the aeroplanes at Grant Park yesterday afternoon. One young man, a wealthy Pittsburgh amateur in a biplane, was dashed to the ground and crushed to death. He fell fifty feet. The other, a Chicago youth, was drowned two hours later when his monoplane dived 600 feet into Lake Michigan.[52]

The aviators who died were William Badger of Pittsburgh, who was trying to descend swiftly toward the ground before pulling back up in the last second, and St. Croix Johnstone, whose aeroplane fell into the lake for unexplained reasons. Turpin said, "Badger was one of the finest fellows entered in the meet. Johnstone was a sober, serious fellow, and we respected him."[53]

The next day McCutcheon drew a cartoon that featured the Grim Reaper, wearing a summer straw hat, entering the exhibition along with unnoticing, happy, men, women, and children. "Late in coming," McCutcheon wrote. "But he came."[54]

In four days there had been thirteen other accidents involving fourteen birdmen who miraculously suffered no injuries. The *Tribune* provided a list of aviation fatalities for the year 1911 up to the mid-August event. The total number killed in less than eight months was forty. And before the week was completed, another pilot had been killed in England.

Turpin was not a big winner at Chicago. The big winner was a British flyer, Thomas Sopwith, who won $13,120—a major sum in 1911. Turpin won $450.

McCutcheon wrote that he received permission to go up during the exhibition from Orville Wright himself. According to McCutcheon the two sat down at a lunch, McCutcheon looked silently at Wright, and the world's first pilot knew exactly what the cartoonist was thinking.

"Yes," Wright said. "You can go in the biplane race." McCutcheon later wrote, "The race was to be around four pylons over a course scarcely a mile long. There were several entries. I learned with some uneasiness that the pilot of [my] Wright plane was named Coffyn [pronounced coffin], Frank Coffyn. After lunch I was asked to go to the Wright hangar to have my heart examined. It was pounding so hard with excitement that I feared I might not pass the test, but all was well and I walked back to my seat. On my way, I passed, still lying on the field, the wreck of the plane in which William Badger had just been killed.

"I tried to talk casually to my friends in the box and, when the time arrived, to appear unconcerned as I saw Coffyn's plane trundle out before the crowd. Then I had the fun of suddenly arising and handing my hat to one of the ladies in the party. 'Will you hold this for me please? I am going to fly in this race.'

"The resulting sensation was entirely satisfactory, and I strode down the ramp and out onto the field and took my place in the plane. It was the same open type without fuselage in which I had flown before. The signal was given, we started. Soon we were up and began rounding the pylons, one after another, at what appeared to me a horrifying angle. On the ground [a friend] was standing with Orville Wright and he has often told me how scandalized Wright was at the way Coffyn was banking those turns. At no time were we over fifty feet from the ground.

"On one of the laps I caught sight of an ambulance racing across the field below us. Turning gingerly in my seat, I followed its direction and saw, projecting out of the lake, part of the plane in which St. Croix Johnstone had just been killed. . . .

"Lincoln Beachy, who had flown at Purdue's Stuart Field, did some remarkable stunting. From about a thousand feet he would dive down and then skim just over the cars in Michigan Avenue or, costumed in old-fashioned women's garb, he would go hedgehopping down the field from end to end. . . ."[55]

"It may be wondered why with all this enthusiasm I never tried to learn to fly myself," McCutcheon wrote. "For a fellow who couldn't back a car out of a garage—let alone tune in correctly on a radio football game even when Purdue was playing—there was never any temptation."[56]

The next meet for Turpin after Chicago was August 26, flying with Parmalee in Des Moines, Iowa. Turpin was soon setting people buzzing in Colorado when he vowed to attempt a flight over Pike's Peak.

A newspaper article was headlined "World Famous Aviator in Colorado Springs; Clifford Turpin, Wright Airman, Ready for Carnival Flights; says 'Pike's Peak or Bust.'"[57]

"Eager to soar through the dizzy heights above Pike's Peak, Clifford Turpin, one of the world's most daring birdmen, who, with P. O. Parmalee, will be at the cynosure of all eyes in the big carnival aviation meet here this week, arrived in Colorado Springs yesterday afternoon. The aviator is not an assuming young fellow, in spite of the fact that he holds, or has held, several world records. There is nothing boastful in his demeanor."[58]

The newspaper reporter asked Turpin if he could fly over Pike's Peak. "We'll, you can never be sure of that," Turpin answered. "But we're going to try. It's this way: I prefer to save any possible boasts until the thing has been done."[59]

According to the *Colorado Springs Gazette*, "Turpin was the second aviator [in history] to ascend over a mile, and in his fourteenth month career in the thrilling profession, [he] has dazzled more crowds than any other man, with the possible exception of his partner, Parmalee, and one or two others. 'Aren't you afraid?' he was asked. 'Afraid?' he repeated. 'I'm afraid I don't know, yet, what the word fear means.' The speaker was not boastful in his reply, merely truthful."[60]

Turpin then launched into a talk about the future of aviation. As an engineer and gasoline engine expert, he understood what was at the heart of flight: engines.

"The entire future of the aeroplane rests upon the dependability of the engines," he said. "When we get an engine that will be absolutely dependable, then there will be no limit to achievements of the airmen. We are gradually approaching that desirable era in engine building. So far, we are by no means at a loss if our engines stop when we are a few thousand feet in the air. "[61]

According to the *Colorado Springs Gazette* account, Turpin held "the American endurance record for staying in the air for three hours and forty-five minutes. And, he has the undisputed record for carrying the greatest number of passengers of any aviator in the world. [Turpin and Parmalee] can be depended on to make the flight around Pike's Peak as sensational as ever has been pulled off in the United States."[62]

The *Daily News* in Denver reported twenty thousand people in Colorado Springs shouted and cheered as they watched Turpin and Parmalee fly at an exhibition. People became so excited, the newspaper reported, young women were trying to leave the bleachers to run out in the field and "embrace their heroes" and would have succeeded "had not their fathers stepped between." "Death rather than disdain, was courted by one Parmalee, who in a fierce fight with the wind . . . triumphed. [Meanwhile] his pal, Cliff Turpin, his nerves all tingling with emotion, sat alone in his tent and prepared himself . . . to win the plaudits of the crowd."[63]

At one point in the Colorado Springs event, Turpin watched from the ground in horror as Parmalee's aeroplane dropped toward the horizon and out of sight a great distance away. Turpin hopped on a horse and raced to the accident scene. Parmalee survived and was cheered by all on his return to the exhibition area.[64]

Bad weather—and wise judgment—prevented Turpin and Parmalee from attempting a flight over Pike's Peak.

The birdmen hopped all around the country, entering exhibitions wherever they took place. On September 12, 1911, Turpin was in Grand Rapids, Michigan.

According to newspaper accounts, during one flight demonstration there his engine stopped dead at one thousand feet. He had a passenger on board, and he gave that man and the crowd watching the thrill of their lives when he glided his machine safely down into a marshy field near a river.

As the Grand Rapids newspaper reported, "Descending from an altitude of nearly 1,000 feet, traveling at the speed of seventy miles an hour, his plane inclined at an angle of nearly fifty degrees to a marshy field below, without injury to himself, passenger, or machine. The accident came as a thrilling end to a spectacular flight of the daring young aviator, carrying J. E. Worthing, a newspaperman as a passenger."[65]

In Springfield, Illinois, that autumn, Turpin narrowly escaped injury again:

> The Wright aviator thrilled the fair crowds with a pretty flight this morning. . . . He also came within a few inches of adding another chapter in the already large volume of air tragedies. Turpin had been in the air eight minutes and had circled above the cattle in the stock barns near the coliseum. He was returning to the racecourse when he encountered unexpected downward air currents. The aviator was taken by surprise. Before he could gain absolute control of the machine, he was within ten feet of the tops of the trees to the southwest of the barns. For a few seconds, he was unable to turn the path of the machine upward. Turpin and the machine, at high rate of speed, were descending straight into the clump of trees when—but ten feet above the trees, with the certain wreck of his machine should the big craft continue its descent—Turpin mastered the situation and turned the nose of his machine upward. He shot up like a rocket and continued his trip to the racecourse where he descended. 'That is about as close as I want to come to the top of the trees,' Turpin said, after he had motored his airplane to the ground. 'The air currents above the forest of trees took me by surprise. The air currents were very strong and batted the machine downward with terrible force.'[66]

Weather continued to be a problem in Illinois. The people of Peoria had convinced Turpin to fly to their city after the exhibition in Springfield. He tried in spite of conditions.

Turpin's account in a Peoria, Illinois, newspaper of what it was like to fly sitting on the wing of an open aeroplane when the cold wind howled reveals the affects of winds and weather on these early birdmen:

> When I headed the plane for Peoria, the watch stood exactly at 3:26. I sailed over north Springfield at an altitude of about 200 feet. Beginning slowly, I gradually arose in the air to find less windy lanes and warmer levels in the air. I kept the machine going up all the way from Springfield to Lincoln. Instead of finding less wind, however, the breeze kept growing stronger. . . . I judge I was up around 2,000 feet. I was being thrown from side to side. My hands were so numb that I hardly knew I had hold of the levers. They were so cold that I felt my fingertips burning up with that needle-like sensation that comes from extreme cold. There was hardly a minute when the possibility of going to earth was not imminent. The longer I rode, the more I thought it had been a foolish thing to leave my hangar at all on such a day.
>
> Coming on toward Lincoln, I became confused. You know, there are three sets of tracks running into town. For a few minutes I almost lost my bearings, the wind getting under the goggles into my eyes so that I could hardly see my map because of the moisture on the lens of the glasses and the water in my eyes and the wind across my face. Sometimes I could hardly get my breath because of the sudden gusts. One thing was a cinch. There was a possibility that I might fly off at a tangent unless I found out where I was. With Lincoln in sight, I steered towards the northeast section of the city, and landed in a big vacant lot at a place about a mile northeast of the courthouse. There were several hundred people around when I came down. Despite the numbed condition I was in, I made a good landing and brought the machine to a stand still without straining a wire. I got five gallons of gasoline, inspected my engine, and found everything working lovely.

> It was just 4:30 when I landed in Lincoln. I started again for Peoria after a twenty-five minute wait, during which I tried to get warm. I hoped that with the coming of evening, there might be a lessoning of the wind. There was nothing like that. When I got up again, instead of going down, the wind seemed to have increased. The buffetings were worse than before. I just couldn't find a level from which to escape the gale. . . . The breeze was racing against me at a thirty-mile gait. It was a struggle all the way the wind growing stronger every minute. I was blown out of my course repeatedly. The cold was becoming more intense. You have no idea how cold it is at 1,000 feet above the ground.[67]

At one point the wind was blowing at him so hard that Turpin felt like he was standing still. That's when he knew he had to give it up. He landed in a farm field and sought refuge with the farm family that night.

Many years later, Turpin would say his most frightening experience occurred in Louisville, Kentucky, November 2–5, 1911, when a mechanic failed to set into place cotter pins that were needed to hold the wing struts. "Luckily, the wings didn't collapse until after the plane landed," Turpin said.[68]

Newspaper accounts of that Louisville air show said Turpin and Parmalee "gave an exhibition of flying that has never been equalized in Kentucky. Despite the heavy wind that was blowing, they each made several flights and thrilled the spectators at one time by playing cross-tag with each other while in the air. The first event of the afternoon was a military drama entitled 'On The Mexican Border.'" The infield of the racetrack served as a battlefield. The fighting forces were made up of members of the first Kentucky regiment, and for twenty minutes they furnished spectators with a thrilling battle scene with Turpin and Parmalee flying overhead in "dips of death and other hazardous feats. . . . Without any doubt, they are two of the greatest aviators in the world."[69]

Through the summer and fall of 1911, Turpin and other pilots often carried mail and sometimes even transported commercial goods. This was done for publicity purposes and the distances were short, but they became among the first examples of airmail and air cargo service by flying machines.

By the end of November 1911, the exhibition season east of the Rocky Mountains came to an end with the cold, windy weather of winter approaching. The Wrights by this time were growing disenchanted with the exhibition flights because of the daredevil stunts that continued to take place and the number of accidents and pilot deaths. They decided to stop participation in the exhibitions.[70]

A 1911 St. Louis newspaper article: "Death List Causes Wrights to Retire." The article details their decision:

> Appalled by the fatalities among their aviators, the Wright brothers, motors and aeroplane specialists in America, have decided to retire from the exhibition field. They will seek to develop a taste among American sportsmen for the art of flying and will try to create a demand for their aeroplanes by establishing training schools to teach sportsmen to fly. The facts became known yesterday from the visit of J. Clifford Turpin, one of the Wright aviators, who was sent from Dayton, Ohio to address the Aero Club of St. Louis at its annual meeting last night. In his address, Turpin was guarded in his statements concerning the intentions of the Wrights. During the day in confidential talks with the members of the Aero Club of St. Louis, Turpin was more explicit regarding the plans for his employers. They are tired of having their men dashed to death for the purpose of the Roman holidays, and are taking the position that American sportsmen, if they want to, can fly their own holidays of this sort. Prior to their decision to retire from the exhibition field, special field dates were made which will keep their aviators busy the remainder of the year, or until about November. But they will not add to their list of fliers. Only four men, Turpin, Brookins, Parmalee, and Cousins, will show for them this year. Welch, one of the men who exhibited for them, will have charge of one of their training stations, but will not give exhibition flights as he did last year.[71]

If the Wrights were through with exhibitions, their flyers were not yet ready to quit. There were air shows and contests planned on the west coast during winter and spring of 1912. And the flyers wanted to participate.

Aware of the decision to pull out of air shows, on November 29, 1911, Turpin and Parmalee entered a contract with the Wright Company for the lease of two aeroplanes and equipment. It was an expensive proposition for the two young men. For a six-month lease on two machines, a Wright model EX and a Wright Model B—both used—along with extra parts and accessories, Turpin and Parmalee agreed to pay $4,736.90.[72]

On top of that, they agreed to post a $3,000 surety bond to guarantee the planes. They also agreed to pay the Wright Company $100 for every day a plane was used in an exhibition, fifty dollars for each day each machine was flown for other purposes such as taking passengers aloft, and five dollars per day for each day a tent was used, not to exceed $120.

This was serious money in 1911, but there was serious money to be won and made by giving people air rides. A January 1912 meet in Los Angeles was approaching with $80,000 in prize money. And some wealthy people were willing to pay as much as $500 for Turpin and Parmalee to take them up for a twenty-minute ride.[73]

In January 1912, Turpin and Parmalee were in Los Angeles for that huge exhibition at Dominguez Field. The fact that they were flying on their own, independent of the Wright Company, hit the *New York Times*, which on January 16 reported "friction over prizes" lead to the breach.[74]

If there was friction, the Wrights and Turpin remained on friendly terms and corresponded by letter through the winter of 1912. Freed, from the rules and regulations of being part of the Wright brothers' team, Turpin made headlines in Los Angeles with several stunts.

At one point he was deputized by California police and probably became the first pilot ever to use an aeroplane and field glasses to search from the air for bandits who had shot a sheriff's deputy. Turpin didn't find the man, but he did make the front page of newspapers.[75] He also used his flying skills for what was called "the first wedding trip in a flying machine."[76]

In California, Neal Cochran, a former employee of the Wright brothers in the days when they made bicycles in Dayton, Ohio, married his bride, Leona Cowan, seated in Turpin's plane. When the vows were completed, Turpin took them up for a ride. A steamship followed the aeroplane as it flew over water—just in case.

According to a Dayton newspaper article about the event, "'Don't you think your wedding trip was a little dangerous?' was a question suggested to the pretty bride. 'Not a bit,' she responded showing a row of pearly teeth. 'I just love excitement, anyhow, and I knew that there was no danger. Mr. Turpin is a fine pilot and landed us safely. It was a swell trip and one that no other bride has taken.'"[77]

The bride was reported to be an amateur actress who perhaps believed publicity about the stunt would advance her career in California. "She may go on the stage as 'The Aviator Girl,'" the newspaper reported.[78]

During an exhibition in Venice, California, Turpin decided he needed something special to attract a crowd. He settled on a parachute jump. He hired a man named "Mr. Rose" whose previous experience in flight involved being shot from a cannon in a circus. Rose's parachute was stuffed into a bucket-like container which was attached to the side of the aeroplane. When Rose jumped, the parachute unfurled from the bucket.

Turpin had to take his aeroplane up to two thousand feet for the jump, and during the half-hour ascent a strong wind came up. When Rose jumped, the wind carried him out to sea. Fortunately, boats saw Rose falling and picked him up soon after he hit the water, narrowly averting disaster.[79]

The Los Angeles exhibition at Dominguez Field was a huge success, drawing thousands of spectators. Turpin and Parmalee were not big money winners and there were problems with the organizers. In a letter to Orville Wright dated February 13, 1912, Turpin said they found themselves forced into a position where they threatened not to fly unless the organizers agreed to pay their contracted fees.[80]

In Los Angeles, there were daily dangerous stunts staged to excite the crowds.

Beachy, who had thrilled people in Lafayette and Chicago and throughout the nation, drew people to the Los Angeles meet by promising a woman would fly his aeroplane; and it happened. Sometimes, later, it was reported that Beachy himself had made the flight dressed as a woman—the same stunt he had used in Chicago. It set the tone for much that was happening in the Los Angeles meet.

Beachy would be dead in three years. He crashed at the Panama-Pacific International Exposition in San Francisco on March 14, 1915, eleven days after his twenty-eighth birthday. The death of the popular flyer would hasten an end to exhibition flying throughout the United States.

In the middle of the Los Angeles event in 1912, the *New York Times* commented the dangers of the sport, "As a show the 'aviation meet' in Los Angeles promises to be as successful—that is to say profitable—as its promoters hoped. The performers are repeating all the feats that startled the world when they were done as something new . . . and if no fatal accidents occur to disturb the equanimity of the spectators, no harm will have been done. When reading the daily dispatches from Los Angeles, however, one gets the impression that flying of this particular sort is a rather futile business, interesting and amusing rather than important, not at all the thing that is really going to advance aerial navigation. The contestants are constantly tempted to win unthinking applause by recklessly taking desperate chances, and the more people are astonished by the performance of dangerous stunts, the less appreciation will they have for the sane and comparatively safe sort of flying that means something for the future of aviation. The Wrights are fully justified in avoiding exhibitions of this kind. The aeroplane is an invention with possibilities of too much [potential] to be thus used without a certain impropriety or without a certain loss of dignity for all participating in or promoting the exhibitions."[81]

Turpin talked about the excitement of flying with a Los Angeles newspaper reporter. He said, "I have been in motorcyclist contests and took part in fast automobile races, but aviation is the hardest, most nerve-racking of them all. The reason I say it is the most intense and difficult is that it requires the most nervous strain of all time. When a man is up in the air, his mind is on his work and he is on constant strain to properly guide the aircraft—to listen intently every moment for a slight defect in his engine, to watch his surroundings at all times. Then, when an airman is not in the air, he is all the time thinking about flying. I always carry five mechanics around. They keep my motor in good running order. But I'm compelled to do the greater part of the work myself, when they do not understand the finer points. Flying also requires the maximum amount of physical power at all times, while in the air. After I've been up in a flight, I return to the earth simply exhausted by the exertion necessary for the flight. There is no real fear about flying, except what the newspapers create."[82]

The newspaper reporter said people were "naturally afraid to take a trip in the airship. But when they come to an aviation meet, they see how smoothly the airplane goes sailing through the air, and ninety percent of them are not only willing, but eager for a ride."[83]

In fact, when a man said he would give $5,000 to any birdman who could talk his wife into flying, Turpin took up the challenge. The newspaper did not report whether or not Turpin was successful.

"The fact that the aviation is a young man's sport, is well exemplified in the case of Turpin, who . . . is only twenty-four years old," the newspaper reported. "When one learns the ages of the birdmen, now before the public, those who have retired from the sport, and those who have given their lives in furtherance of [its] scientific advancement, it is seen that practically everyone is under the age of thirty. We older fellows are more cautious and do not care to risk our lives as the younger fellows do. . . . Turpin's home is Dayton, Ohio, but he says he expects to go to Palm Beach, Florida, after this week to enjoy beach life. However, he may decide to remain in Los Angeles and enjoy the breezes of the old Pacific Ocean and our beaches."[84] Turpin stayed in California—but not to enjoy the ocean and beaches.

In a February 13, 1912, letter to Orville Wright, Turpin says, "For the past two Sundays we have been giving exhibition flights at Venice [California] which is practically the same as Atlantic City on the Eastern Coast. Besides receiving a good guarantee, we have the privilege of carrying passengers and this contract has proven to be a very nice source of income. In fact, it has been such a good drawing card for the resort that they have asked us to sign a ten-week Sunday contact with them. But this contact has not been closed as yet, as we are still holding out for a higher price."[85]

Orville and Wilbur Wright might have raised an eyebrow at the Sunday flying and wondered where their invention was leading.

Turpin also had other thoughts on his mind during his time in California. In the letter he tells Orville Wright that he has read about a new machine the Wright brothers had been testing. Turpin says he has heard, the Wrights might enter this machine in exhibitions the coming summer. "[I] feel confident that I can handle [it] as well as anyone, with the exception of course of yourself and would like to have the opportunity of piloting this machine—for I feel that it will be a winner, if we do not have motor trouble. Hoping to hear from you in regards to this."[86]

Turpin wrote a second letter to Orville Wright from Los Angeles on March 2, 1912. "Dear Sir: I am taking the liberty of writing to you again concerning the aero-related events of this coming summer. . . . Several large meets are going to take place, and I would like very much to know whether you contemplate building a machine [to compete] in these classes and also whether we could make arrangements with you to [acquire one of the aeroplanes] on a rental basis."[87]

Turpin said he had propositions from other aeroplane manufacturers, including the archrival of the Wright brothers, Glenn Curtiss. "But [I] do not wish to reply to same, for several reasons, until I hear from you," Turpin wrote. "You are in a position and have had more experience in building these racing machines than they and therefore I believe that if you do turn out a plane of this nature that it will go faster than any other plane manufactured by any other company in the country."[88]

Orville Wright responded on March 12. "My dear Cliff: I was pleased to get your letters telling of what you have been doing in the West, and I am glad that prospects are looking brighter now than when you first arrived on the Coast. We have not yet decided as to whether we will have an exhibition team this coming summer or not, but in case we do, it will consist of only one or two men. Of course, we would prefer taking some of the men we have already had than starting again with a novice. We have been getting a good many inquiries for exhibition flights." Wright goes on to say they have been doing very well with the new machines, and he is willing to provide one to Turpin on a rental basis.[89]

That April, the original contract between Turpin, Parmalee, and the Wright brothers was extended to June so the flyers could participate in meets in the Northwest.[90] The first was in Vancouver, Canada, on May 24, 1912.

In a book titled *Canada's Flying Heritage*, Frank H. Ellis wrote that Turpin and Parmalee gave "a most credible performance on the outskirts of Vancouver. . . . Their flight headquarters was Hastings Park, later described by the young airmen as the most dangerous field they had ever known. The area was small in extent, surrounded by high and heavy forest, and was crossed at one end by an electrical power line. Yet the flyers met the hazards with courage and skill, making in all seven takeoffs and landings. The machine they used [a second one was left at the border since customs duties were too high to admit both] was a well-made, two-seater biplane with the engine and propeller in front . . . known as a tractor airplane. The contract for two days flying included a feature unique in Canadian air history: a parachute jump from a plane in flight. Only four such jumps had been made anywhere in the world and none in Canada, so this exploit would constitute a record worth witnessing."[91]

According to Ellis, people parachuting at that time did not use harnesses to strap themselves to the chutes. He said, "The courageous parachutist simply grasped the trapeze bar which was attached to the parachute by suitable cords, and the straining muscles of his own strong hands and arms were all he could rely upon to forestall a sudden trip to eternity when the jolt of the opening chute all but wrenched him from his hold."[92]

There were several successful parachute jumps, and the entire exhibition was a huge success. "Later, Parmalee and Turpin ran into difficulties when trying to return to the United States," Ellis wrote. "The Canadian railway refused to ship their plane as baggage, while to send it by freight would have meant a late arrival for their next contract. . . . Finally, they secured the services of a taxicab owner-driver. They loaded the [aeroplane] engine onto the back seat of his big Winton touring car, and on top they packed the fuselage, with blankets and pillows for padding, and the wings protruding fore and aft. The three men and the machine, after making a slow, tedious, but safe journey, reached their destination with time to spare."[93]

Turpin and Parmalee went on to Seattle for an exhibition there. In Seattle, Turpin made a flight on May 30 before a crowd of people packed into the grandstands. He was bringing his plane in for a landing at 2:45 P.M. that day—right in front of the crowded grandstand—when an amateur photographer crossed in front of his landing path. Turpin swerved the machine to avoid hitting the photographer. As he swerved away from the landing, "his left rudder wing struck an iron pipe . . . at the edge of the race track," the *Los Angeles Times* reported.[94]

The aeroplane spun on the iron pipe and broke free, sending the machine careening into the grandstands filled with people, the propellers still turning. One man, George Quinby, a civil engineer, was killed instantly when the propeller hit him. "Quinby's face was cut off," the *Los Angeles Times* reported. More than ten other people were injured, several seriously.

The *L.A. Times* reported, "Many saved their lives the moment the machine struck by throwing themselves flat on the ground. With the sound of shivering timbers and snapping steel, the machine [hit] with a crash against the front row of boxes in the grandstand, falling directly into the screaming mass of humanity beneath it. Women shrieked and fainted, and, as with one voice, a great cry went up from the thronged grandstand, all rising to their feet. Then for a moment there was silence. All held their breath. This was broken by the moaning of the injured and the excited trampling of the crowd pouring down the grandstand to get a closer view."[95]

Somehow, Turpin survived. According to the *L.A. Times*, "When Turpin's machine struck the grandstand and tumbled into the crowd, knocking people left and right, Turpin was hurled sideways out of his seat. Although not badly injured, the right side of his face struck the piano wire bracings and steel tubular frame. When the unconscious man was picked up, he presented a terrible sight. This was true in the case of most of the victims, the injuries being of a peculiarly ghastly nature due to the sharp projections of the plane and the razor-like edges of the big, laminated, wooden propeller. Features and limbs were sliced off as with a knife, and several minutes after the accident took place a severed nose and finger were picked up in front of the grandstand."[96]

Automobiles rushed the injured to nearby hospitals. They included a ten-year-old boy with a fractured skull.

In spite of the disaster, forty-five minutes after the accident Parmalee took to the air to fulfill the terms of their contact. He circled the field once and offered to perform a parachute jump, using the same jumper he and Turpin had worked with in Canada. But exhibition officials decided to call off the rest of the performance.

Police held Turpin in Seattle pending an inquest. He was quickly and fully cleared as soon as the accident was reviewed.

With Turpin recovering from his injuries, Parmalee took their remaining machine to Yakima, Washington, for another contracted exhibition. On June 1, he attempted a flight in Yakima into heavy winds. It was against his better judgment. His mechanic tried to persuade him not to fly.[97] A crowd of people was waiting to see him, and he probably felt that he and Turpin needed the money because of the financial loss from the wrecked aeroplane in Seattle.

Parmalee took off. He quickly lost control on a turn and crashed into an apple orchard. He died instantly from a crushed skull.[98] Parmalee was twenty-five years old. (Coincidentally, the accident occurred the day after Wilbur Wright died in Dayton, Ohio, after a short illness.) At this point, five of the nine men who had served on the Wright exhibition team formed in 1910 had died in crashes. A sixth would die in a 1928 crash.[99]

Devastated, a still recovering Turpin traveled to Yakima to claim Parmalee's body. Traveling by train, he accompanied it to St. John's, Michigan—Parmalee's home—for burial. Parmalee had been scheduled to fly in his hometown at the county fair that coming August.[100]

In 1916, Turpin wrote his personal impressions on aviation for the *Purdue Engineering Review.* He called flying "one of the most alluring of sports:"

> The landing . . . is by far the most difficult . . . for it is only at this time in coming close to the ground that the operator realizes the extreme speed of the machine. When one considers that a machine of extremely light construction and weighing around 1,200 pounds with the operator is compelled to land at the rate of fifty to sixty miles per hour on sometimes very rough ground, one can easily understand the skill it requires to avoid demolishing the planes.
>
> My first lesson, and also my first ride in an aeroplane, was to me an extremely disagreeable experience. The nearest approach to a comparison is that of riding in an automobile at the rate of fifty or sixty miles per hour over very rough roads. The statements of my passengers whom I took up in later days that they had enjoyed the experience immensely, I always took with a grain of salt, as I knew very well that while they were glad to have had the experience, they were more glad to again be able to place their feet on solid ground. . . .
>
> In the early days of flying the greatest source of trouble was the motor. Under the most favorable circumstances, the motors only developed thirty-five horsepower and their life in the air was about twenty hours. I have many times had the experience while in the air of having an exhaust valve drop through the head of a piston and come out through the bottom of the crankcase. . . . By flying at a fairly good height of say approximately 2,000 feet, this would mean that in case your motor stopped, if landing conditions were not available directly underneath, you could glide a distance of over a mile and in this radius, you could easily pick out favorable landing conditions.

> One experience above all others will always remain vividly impressed upon my mind. This occurred in California in a flight from Venice to Long Beach, a distance across country of about twenty miles. . . . The day was exceedingly foggy and the clouds hung at a distance of not over 1,000 feet above the earth. As I knew the course well between these two points, I decided to mount above the clouds in order to strike better atmospheric conditions. . . . After flying for what I considered to be the proper time to cover the distance between these two places, I began to make my descent. Upon coming through the cloud banks I found that instead of being near Long Beach, the wind had carried me over ten miles out to sea. Under these conditions I was absolutely at the mercy of my motor for if it had stopped at that time, there would have been nothing for me to do but make a landing in the water. . . . However, in this case as in many others, my motor power remained faithful to the last and I was able to reach shore without further qualms.
>
> The aeroplane of today has been refined in many details over the machines of five years past as to workmanship, construction, far superior motors. But as to the handling of the plane and as to the safety of the operator exclusive of the above features, no advancements have been made.
>
> This step, however, is bound to see the light of day within the near future, and it is my opinion that in the next twenty-five years, aviation will have advanced to the point where there will be comparative safety in the operation of aeroplanes.[101]

That is what Turpin believed. Comparative safety was some twenty-five years away. When Turpin wrote that report, he was thirty years of age. He was living in Boston. He had married an actress, and they had adopted a little girl. He was a very happy man with a full life.

Turpin would live to be seventy-nine years old. For many years he shunned eligible membership in exclusive flight organizations. He avoided publicity.

In December of 1949, when "Hap" Arnold, a general in the U.S. Air Force, discovered where Turpin was living, there was a quick exchange of letters. "It would be grand to see you again to get together for a little 'hangar flying,'" Arnold wrote in a letter dictated in mid-January 1950. It was mailed posthumously. Arnold died January 15, 1950, before he even signed it. The letter to Turpin had been among his last acts.[102]

Turpin lived into 1965. He watched space launches on television—launches including fellow Purdue graduate Virgil "Gus" Grissom. He was thrilled with how far flight had come, but he said little about his role in it all.

He did give rare interviews. In 1964, a reporter for the *Cape Cod Standard Times* interviewed him. "The imagination knows no bounds," Turpin said. "I believe they'll . . . put a man on the moon by 1968. These astronauts are the same breed of cat as we were. They are adventurers dedicated to aviation. . . ."[103]

He reread a statement he had made in 1911. "You have no idea what that feeling of being beyond the reach of man is like. . . . When a man has only one thing between him and eternity, he gets to love that thing and the idea that the aeroplane is inspired with a soul has often come to me at these lonely heights."[104]

In the end, Turpin enjoyed playing with his two young grandsons on Cape Cod where he lived in retirement. Only rarely did he mention to them that one day, long ago, he had been a birdman and one of the most daring and famous people of his time, setting records, thrilling crowds, creating aviation as he flew. Cliff Turpin lived a long full life without regrets. But from the day he crashed into the grandstands in Seattle on May 30, 1912, he never set foot in any airplane of any kind ever again.

Loren Shriver

The history of flight advanced rapidly in the days of the Wright brothers, Cliff Turpin, and Jimmie Johnson. It has moved even more rapidly in the lifetime of Loren Shriver, who was born during World War II when jet airplanes were just emerging. Forty years later he would fly a space shuttle.

When Shriver started high school in the farming community of Paton, Iowa, in 1958, the first Mercury 7 astronauts had just been named. By the time he graduated from high school in 1962, the Mercury program was completed and Gemini was underway. By the time he graduated from the U.S. Air Force Academy in 1967, Gemini was over, the Apollo program was being finalized, and Neil Armstrong was only two years from the first landing on the Moon. Eighteen years after graduation, Shriver took his first space shuttle flight.

Shriver was helped along the way by a special Air Force cooperative master's degree program at Purdue University.

"I don't know what first attracted me to flying," Shriver says. "I just know from an early age, probably intermediate school, I always had been interested in flight. I wanted to learn to fly. I don't know of any one event that sparked that interest. It just always seemed to be there."

The Air Force Academy was a logical choice. And it had an exciting opportunity to offer. In the fall of 1962, Academy officials had contacted Purdue University about starting a special program for its graduates. The Academy was an undergraduate school, but the Air Force wanted to offer its top students the opportunity to earn a master's degree quickly after graduation The plan was, during their undergraduate years, top students would take advanced courses at the Academy and would then compete to take part in a master's degree program at Purdue beginning in June after graduation and ending the following January. The degree would be in a field that sounds exciting today and must have seemed incredible to students in the early 1960s—astronautics.

The first fifteen students arrived in June 1963. Between 1963 and 1976, nearly 150 Academy graduates took part in the Purdue program—fifteen at a time in the early years with the number later dwindling to six. The program produced an incredible number of astronauts—seven: Loren Shriver, John Blaha, Roy Bridges Jr., John Casper, Richard Covey, Guy Gardner, and Gary Payton.

Even as he studied for an advanced degree in astronautics, Shriver remained focused on becoming an Air Force pilot.

"The space program while I was in high school, through college, and afterwards, you realize—gosh, what those guys are doing looks like a lot of fun," Shriver says. "But it seemed like a remote possibility that I'd be able to participate."

He served in Thailand during 1974, came home, and was accepted at the Air Force Test Pilot School at Edwards Air Force Base. He was working as a test pilot at Edwards in 1977 when NASA announced it was taking applications for astronauts.

"I looked over my credentials, and I had the right education, the right flight experience, and test pilot experience," Shriver says. "I thought, why not put in an application? So I did."

He was accepted along with thirty-four others who were being prepared for the Space Shuttle Program. The astronaut class also included Purdue graduates Don Williams and Richard Covey. Almost 9 percent of the class had "Purdue" written on a diploma.

Shriver was the pilot on a mission in January 1985, and commander on missions in April 1990, and July 1992. During the 1990 mission, crew members deployed the Hubble Space Telescope. In 1993, Shriver became Space Shuttle Program manager, launch integration, with responsibilities including final shuttle preparation, mission execution, and return of the orbiter to Kennedy Space Center if landing occurred at Edwards Air Force Base.

In 1997, he became deputy director of the Kennedy Space Center for Launch and Payload Processing. In 2000, he became deputy program manager for Houston operations for the United Space Alliance, Space Shuttle Program. The United Space Alliance (USA) is one of the prime NASA contractors for operating the space shuttle system. In Houston, it does mission operations work, astronaut training, flight-controller training, and mission analysis. USA employs ten thousand people who work on space suits, orbiter projects, shuttle software, and much more.

Shriver has taken his career one step at a time. "Going from the farm to this was an evolution of thoughts and ideas and goals," he says. His shuttle flights were "pretty fantastic experiences." So is the work that has followed.

Chapter Three

Flying wasn't complicated in those days.
You just got in and flew.

—Jimmie Johnson

Summer, 1935—
Jimmie Johnson stood in front of the bathroom mirror, bending and stretching his lathered face. His steady right hand held a light grip on the straight-edge razor he slipped across his sharp features. His face was weathered from years of wind blowing across the open cockpit of his airplanes, from the drips of hot oil that shot out of leaky engines landing on his cheeks and chin.

Shaving was a morning ritual as familiar to Johnson as the feel of wind beneath his wings, the instinctive balance between a pilot, his hands, and his airplane floating in the quiet morning air.

This morning, Johnson's eyes and concentration were less on what he was doing and more on the boy who sat nearby, legs crossed on the floor. Johnson's eyes darted from the mirror, down to his side where his son sat staring. The boy watched his father closely, studying and memorizing every stroke of the blade.

Jim Johnson idolized his father. If he wanted anything from his life, he wanted to be just like his dad. He already had his name. He wanted to look like him, act like him, be like him, and know what to do—no matter what the problem—like him. Most of all, he wanted to fly an airplane, just like his dad.

His father was a storyteller who could recite "Hiawatha" and other legendary, lengthy poems line for line from memory, adding emotion that made them real. No one had more fun than his three children when they were all gathered together and he went into one of his long poems—nobody, except maybe Jimmie Johnson.

More than poems, Johnson enjoyed telling his children stories about all kinds of people and places—some of them true, some of them fairy tales, some of them science fiction straight from the imagination of writers like Jules Verne.

"Now you listen to me, Jim," Johnson said to his son as he finished running the straight-edge razor across the side of his face. "Airplanes are the future. I know that they are. We haven't seen anything yet. There are planes that are going to fly higher and faster than anything we could ever imagine. Do you know what? One day, people are going to fly to the Moon. This isn't science fiction I'm talking about. This is a fact. I don't know if I'm going to live to see it. I hope I do. I might not. But I'll tell you what, you'll see it. You will. One day man will reach the Moon. And I want you remember that I told you so."

The boy's eyes opened wider with each sentence his father spoke. It stirred his imagination and he accepted it as fact. If it weren't so, his father would not have said it.

Like a snapshot in his memory, the boy never forgot that morning. The father never forgot it either, never forgot the dreams for the future he had promised his son. And he never stopped believing in them.

In 1941, Jimmie Johnson, who by then was the owner of a five-cent-to-a-dollar store in Germantown, Ohio, received a letter from the Illinois Aeronautics Commission. It informed him that the Illinois Writers Project was putting together a new publication that would come out in 1942 called *Who's Who in Aviation.* Johnson was being asked to send his biography for inclusion.

"Other books of this kind have been published, but none has given full coverage to the field," the letter said. "*Who's Who In Aviation* will include all branches of aeronautics, both civil and military, in the United States and its possessions."

Some people in Germantown were surprised that the quiet storekeeper was being included among the most important flyers of all time. "Well, I guess there was no way they could avoid it," Johnson would explain. "Every time they went back to the early days and looked at an important airplane, they would find out I was one of the first to fly it."

When the book appeared, Johnson's occupation was listed as merchant. "B.S. Purdue University, 1907; . . . learned to fly Curtiss School, North Island, San Diego, California, 1914; . . . civilian test pilot for U.S. government at Langley Field, Virginia, and McCook Field, Dayton, Ohio, 1917–1921. . . . "

The lengthy entry went on to mention Johnson's affiliation with a list of aviation companies. It was an impressive entry, but it didn't tell the story.

It didn't tell the story of a young man who wanted to fly so badly that he left his job and security for a chance in the sky; the story of a man who was among the first pilots of aeroplanes that landed on water; a man who was among the first American pilots of the autogyro, a predecessor of the helicopter; a flight instructor who taught one of the legends in aviation how to fly. It didn't tell the stories of the early days: aeroplanes landing on cows, cross-country air races, loop-the-loops, and doctors trying to decide what to do about a woman who wanted to fly.

Jimmie Johnson lived the early history of flight.

He was born in the old south in Helena, Arkansas, right across the river from Memphis, Tennessee. He started life in a railroad family and became one of the world's first real test pilots.

"Jimmie came to us on a slow train from Arkansas," the 1907 *Debris* said. Johnson's graduation photo shows his hair neatly parted and trimmed above the ears. He wore a dark suit, a starched white shirt, and a light tie. He had earned a bachelor's degree in mechanical engineering and belonged to the Mechanical Engineering Society, the athletic association, and the Ohio Club because his family had moved from Arkansas to Fremont, Ohio.

To the staff of the *Debris*, Johnson was still a southern boy from rural Arkansas. "He is a good fellow, gentle disposition, seldom flustered, well bred, very neat, and really a gentleman," the editors wrote. "The successor for the position he has held in a Purdue cozy corner for four years has already appeared."

Exactly what that last sentence means is lost to time. But it would indicate Johnson was a quiet young man who probably found a nice little spot to study where he could watch the world passing by and chart the role he would play in the possibilities unfolding before him.

He was born July 19, 1885; his middle name was Mussey, a family name. His father died when he was young, but there must have been money in the family to take care of the widow and her children. In addition to Johnson having a university degree, all three of his sisters also went to college. It was very rare for young women of that time to receive the benefits of an expensive education.

Johnson was probably lured to Purdue by its fame as a railroad engine center. His study of mechanical engineering at the young university put him in direct contact with some of the best engine technology of the day. His senior thesis, "An Efficiency Test of an Allis-Corliss Engine," was filled with technical data.

As involved as he was with engines, Johnson had an early eye for the sky. Throughout his life he told people he first took an interest in flight while at Purdue and wrote a paper about airplanes during his junior year in 1906. That is a very early date in the history of aviation.

His first job after graduation was with a power company in Cheboygan, Michigan. It was a good job and put him on a career path, but Johnson's dreams were much higher: they were in the sky. He never fully explained what prompted him to leave that solid job with steady income. Maybe it was just so obvious to him he always thought everyone would understand. If we don't have it from his own words, we can draw a pretty clear picture of what happened.

Beginning in 1910, air shows became hugely popular all across the nation. Daring pilots, birdmen, competed for big money in air races often jointly sponsored by newspapers and civic groups interested in promoting their community as a progressive place to do business.

Johnson, a young man with an adventurous spirit, could not have missed what was happening in the sky overhead. If he didn't see one of those air shows in person, he certainly read about them in the newspapers. Maybe he even went to a show that featured Cliff Turpin, one of the original Wright exhibition flyers. Turpin had gained national fame as a birdman. His exploits were written up in Purdue alumni publications. Since both Turpin and Johnson were mechanical engineers at the same university and graduated just one year apart, they certainly would have known one another. Turpin's success could not have missed Johnson's attention, and it might have captured his spirit.

Johnson's story picks up in 1914 when he shows up at Glen Curtiss's flying school—one of the original, great flying fields of the twentieth century—in San Diego, California. Curtiss was one of America's first great pilots and aviation business leaders—and the Wright brothers' competition.

The Wright brothers made the first flight, but Glenn Curtiss was not far behind. And perhaps no one in those early days had a greater genius for the potential of flight, for promoting it, and for training people how to fly.

Curtiss became a premiere designer for airplanes in the early twentieth century. In 1911, he opened the flying school in San Diego where Johnson trained. It became a place where many aviation firsts were accomplished. Among the planes tested in San Diego was the flying boat, which took off from and landed on the water. Johnson would become one of the flying boat's first pilots.

In 1914, when Johnson arrived in San Diego, he made a quick friendship with another young man interested in flight named Walter Lees. Completely taken by the lure of aviation, Lees left the University of Wisconsin after his sophomore year and headed for Curtiss's school in San Diego.

The two young men rented a room together in San Diego. They got up every morning at 5:00 A.M. and took a trolley to a pier and a motor launch to North Island where the flight school was located. According to Edith Dodd Culver's book *Tailspins: A Story of Early Aviation Days*, they spent whatever money they had on flight lessons and lived on milk and bananas.[1]

Curtiss must have liked what he saw in Johnson and Lees. He was probably impressed by Johnson's engineering degree and knowledge of gasoline engines. Airplane engines of that time were constantly breaking down and engine failures often had fatal results. A pilot in those days needed more than training in flight. He needed to understand engines. A man with great talents in flying and in building and repairing engines became a very important man indeed.

Johnson himself always downplayed what he did. In a newspaper interview in the mid-1950s, he said, "Flying wasn't that complicated in those days. You just got in and flew."[2]

But it was far more difficult than that. In San Diego, Johnson became one of the best flyers in the Curtiss school, eventually earning full-time employment as an instructor.

By 1916, both Johnson and Lees left San Diego and went to Newport News, Virginia, where Curtiss had an east coast flying school. Almost as soon as they arrived, a young military officer based in nearby Washington, D.C., showed up and said he wanted to learn how to fly. It wasn't part of his military training so he paid for the lessons out of his own pocket. His name was Major William Mitchell. People who knew him well called him Billy.

In 1913, Billy Mitchell became the youngest man assigned to the general staff of the Department of War in Washington, D.C. Perhaps because of his youth he was open to new ideas, and he became an advocate of airpower at a time when most of the senior officers saw little use for flying machines in the military. "Men will some day wage war in the sky," Mitchell said.[3]

At the start of World War I, the U.S. government had fifty-four planes ready to fly and there were thirty-five military men trained to fly them.[4] Mitchell was one of them. He was a hero of the American Air Service during World War I. He returned home a brigadier general and became one of the first and most vocal advocates of a strong military air service. But other military and political figures of the day did not agree and let the Army Air Service dwindle in numbers and importance, much to Mitchell's protest. His fight with the Army ultimately led to court martial, he was found guilty, and left the service. Later, when World War II arrived and found the United States with a weak Air Service, he was vindicated.

Mitchell was not an instant success as a pilot. In his journal, Walter Lees wrote, "Billy [Mitchell] was a grand guy. And the first thing he told Jimmie when he started training was to forget that he was an Army major and to treat him as we did anyone learning to fly. One day Jimmie was sick and Mitchell [was assigned] to me and I soloed him. Mitchell was very erratic. One day he would be okay and the next day lousy. I just happened to catch him on one of his good days. He made two perfect flights this day."[5] Johnson called Mitchell stern and stubborn.[6]

Shortly after his first solo flight with Lees, Johnson worked with Mitchell again. Mitchell would fly by himself and then meet with Johnson on the ground to talk about how he was doing. Working on his landings, he did several just fine. He then took one too hard, too fast, with the tail too high and bounced back up into the air, flipped over, and landed upside down.

Johnson ran to the airplane to help Mitchell who was strapped in his seat, hanging upside down. He got the airman free and was relieved to find him unhurt. Brushing himself off, Mitchell had only one thing to say to his instructor. "Now what did I do wrong?"[7]

While Mitchell was fighting the Great War in France, Johnson did his service at home. He never joined the Army, but in 1917, as one of the best flyers in the country with an extensive background in engines, Johnson was assigned as a civilian government test pilot to Langley Airfield in Virginia. Langley was brand new, and Johnson's tenure there was a brief five months from June to October.

In October 1917, Johnson was sent to McCook Field in Dayton, Ohio, to train pilots for the Army and to test airplanes. Johnson's title was chief test pilot, thereby becoming one of the world's first people to have that honored title. He would stay at McCook until 1920. His friend Lees was also assigned to McCook.

McCook Field lies on what is now Wright-Patterson Air Force Base outside of Dayton. During World War I, it was a major location for airplane flight-testing and development of new aviation technology.

After witnessing the potential of airplanes, Congress established the National Advisory Committee for Aeronautics on March 3, 1915, which became more commonly known as NACA. Many years later, in 1958, the name would be changed to the National Air and Space Administration (NASA).

According to the official Wright-Patterson history, "Congress' foremost concern was the potential capability for America to provide an effective aerial force for its impending involvement in the war. Lacking American engineers with military aircraft design experience, the NACA, along with the Army and Navy, planned to build its own research and experimentation laboratory at Langley Field, Virginia. With Langley Field construction slowed by war pressures, the Aviation Section of the Signal Corps decided to pursue another location for its aviation research."[8]

That other location was north of downtown Dayton, a site approved by Army Colonel Edward A. Deeds on the counsel of Orville Wright and Dayton businessman Charles F. Kettering. The site was to be the location for "all Army aircraft engineering and procurement functions consolidated in one area."[9]

Construction of McCook Field began in October 1917, so Johnson arrived when it was brand new. The field was named for the "Fighting McCooks," a family that sent seventeen men to fight for the Union forces during the Civil War that had only ended fifty-two years before.

According to the official airfield history, "McCook Field was outfitted with the best that money could buy in 1917 for flight testing. This included a sod airfield and a 1,000-foot-long by 100-foot-wide macadam and cinder runway for use during inclement weather to prevent damage to the aircraft and its instrumentation. This early flight test instrumentation often amounted to little more than an altitude barograph with an ink pen tracing on a rotating paper drum balanced with a log book on the pilot's knees."[10]

It was the most exciting place in the world for a young man in love with flight and aviation engineering. Generations of pilots coming onto the scene after Johnson would consider work as a test pilot the best job on the planet—and the best road to another goal: space travel.

As the United States entered World War I in 1917, the Dayton-Wright Airplane Company was formed with Orville Wright on the board. The company produced the DH-4 airplane, an all-wood, two-seat biplane. By the end of World War I, 106 had been built. Each was called the Liberty plane, named for its Liberty engine. The Liberty did not see much action on the front but was widely used as a flight trainer. Johnson, no doubt, played a key role in flight tests for the Liberty.

Dayton-Wright also built the Curtiss JN-4. It was called a Jenny and was also used extensively in training. About four hundred were built, and after the war they were widely used by barnstorming and daredevil pilots.

According to the Wright-Patterson history, "For the decade after the war, the Airplane Engineering Department, renamed the Airplane Engineering Division, continued to serve as the center of all Army aviation research and development. McCook engineers kept the skies humming with flight testing from both McCook and Wilbur Wright Fields. In 1919 alone, there were 1,276 test flights recorded by McCook's Flight Test Section. McCook engineers tested numerous planes including American, Allied, and captured enemy planes.

"McCook pilots set numerous air records. In a supercharged open cockpit Packard-LePere LUSAC-11 two-seat biplane, Major Rudolph 'Shorty' Schroeder set a solo altitude record of 33,114 feet in 1920, freezing his eyelids open in the process. In 1925, Lieutenant James H. Doolittle, pushing a XCO-5 beyond 37,000 feet, temporarily lost consciousness in the thin oxygen and minus-seventy-degree temperature. These problems led the engineers at McCook to design protective clothing and other improvements such as closed cockpits, heated and pressurized cabins, and oxygen systems."[11]

In 1919, Billy Mitchell brought a British aircraft designer to McCook Field to build a long-range airplane capable of carrying a bomb load sufficient to sink a battleship.[12] Johnson was involved in all of this and remained at McCook until April 1921 when he and a friend, Al Johnson [of no relation], formed the Johnson Airplane and Supply Company in Dayton. A year later they started Johnson's Flying Service.

They did everything. They sold planes, they sold parts, and they flew people to destinations with their flight service. A catalog for the company boasts on the cover, "largest commercial aviation supply house in the country."[13]

They built successful airplanes. In 1924, a flight contest was held in Dayton, and since it was staged in the birthplace of flight, it attracted some of the best pilots and airplane designers in the nation. Jimmie Johnson was one of the winners and took home a prize of $3,000. He flew one of his company's own models, the Johnson-Driggs D-J-1. The official speed he reached to win his event was 64.1 miles per hour. There to shake his hand when he won was his former student, Billy Mitchell, with whom he posed for a newspaper photograph.

According to a Germantown, Ohio, newspaper reporter who interviewed Johnson in the 1950s, "The $3,000 didn't mean nearly as much as the honor and glory of winning. Johnson said the plane cost much more than that to build. Its top air speed was seventy-five to eighty miles per hour and the engine was a converted motorcycle motor."[14]

The Johnson partners had many adventures together. One of the most memorable adventures occurred when they advertised in Dayton that they were bringing a special airplane to town to show off its great speed. Al Johnson was flying to Dayton, but was held up by weather. When he finally landed at the Johnson Airfield, which was really a cow pasture, he landed on top of one of the residents: a cow. It destroyed the plane, but they had promised to show this exciting new airplane to the people of Dayton. So the two men got another plane, painted it to look like the one they had advertised, and flew it high over the airfield so that no one could see the difference.

In 1925, Johnson sold his interest in the companies to his partner and went off to seek his fortune. The "big boom" was on in Florida, and Johnson went down to gain a share of the prize. Years later he would say, "They lowered the boom on me. All I had when I came home from Florida was a dirty shirt."[15]

From 1927 to 1928, he worked for the Department of Commerce issuing pilot's licenses and inspecting airplanes. Next, he went to work for Buhl Airlines in Detroit where he was a salesman and test pilot. It was while working with Buhl that Johnson came across a unique new type of aircraft: the autogyro.

The autogyro looked like an airplane with short wings. It had conventional motors and propellers and rotary blades above the fuselage. It looked half helicopter, half airplane. A motor did not power the rotary blades on top. They were moved by the draft from the conventional engines and from the movement of the aircraft as it traveled forward. It was able to take off in a very short distance and could land straight down. It could even hover in a strong wind. They were not helicopters, which had not yet been perfected, but were an interesting cross between a fixed wing aircraft and what would become a helicopter.

Juan de la Cierva, a Spaniard, designed the first practical autogyro in the early 1920s, and Buhl designed the world's first pusher autogyro with the motor facing the rear of the plane, but by 1932, the Depression had taken Buhl out of business. Johnson was the first person to fly the autogyro in December 1931.

Johnson had worked in manufacturing in the Detroit area for a while, and in 1937, the family moved to Germantown, Ohio, and opened a five-and-dime store. He said, "At least we'll be able to eat the candy."[16] Later, during World War II, he worked for Fairchild Aircraft Company in Dayton.

In 1955, when MGM produced the movie *The Court Martial of Billy Mitchell,* starring Gary Cooper, Johnson was a special guest at the premier along with Mitchell's sister—Mitchell had died in 1936. Johnson's interest in and love for aviation never wavered, but after 1937, he never piloted a plane again.

Johnson wasn't the only pilot in the family. His wife was among the first women in the world to get a pilot's license. The Johnsons met in Dayton, Ohio, in 1920 and were married in 1925. The exact date of her first airplane flight is unclear; it was no earlier than the fall of 1921 and no later than the spring of 1922. Although she always remained unsure about the actual date, she was always certain about the man who literally swept her off her feet. His name was Jimmie Johnson.

She had completed two years of college—a rare accomplishment for a woman of her era. The Nineteenth Amendment to the Constitution guaranteeing women the right to vote had only been ratified in 1920, and women were slowly gaining the civil rights given to men. Gertrude Wilson was an educated woman who took advantage of these rights.

She went by the much less formal name of Trudy. She cut her hair short, which was not only stylish in the Roaring Twenties, but also practical for a young woman who spent considerable time wearing a leather helmet with the wind blowing in her face.

Trudy lived in Dayton, the epicenter for flight in the first days, and she could even recall watching an early Wright brothers' flight outside of town. Maybe this first exposure hooked her for life. Maybe that's the reason she was attracted to Johnson. He was the one who took her up on her first flight.

"I had to don a helmet and goggles," Trudy remembered years later, "and with much boosting, I managed to get a foothold on the 'step' of the wing, and get into the front seat of the cockpit. They strapped me in with a safety belt, and I was ready to go. I really do not remember any reactions from my flight. I do know I was not scared, but more thrilled than anything else."[17]

Johnson was competing in air races during those times. The prizes ran into thousands of dollars, which was big money in the 1920s.

Weight was a huge factor in those races. Regulations for the races required pilots to carry weight either in the form of sandbags or passengers squeezed into the front seat of the planes. Johnson liked the idea of passengers, and two young women were just the right weight that he needed.

Trudy Wilson became ballast for Jimmie Johnson. Joining them was one of Johnson's sisters. Photos from those days show two very excited women seated in the plane, with a very determined looking Johnson sitting in the rear pilot's seat. The first air race for Trudy was called "On to Detroit."

"In those days we did not have radios, no weather reports of any kind," Trudy said in a talk she gave in 1974 about the early days of flight. "You just got in and flew. We had a couple days of rain. Newspaper reporters came out each day and hung around to watch the takeoff and get pictures. One day, after a very stormy couple of hours, it cleared off—and this was it. I dashed out of my home, got my overnight bag, and was ready to go. As I was leaving, my mother made a last minute warning to me. It was, 'Now if you get sick, have him drop you off.'"[18]

The group of three—Johnson, his sister, and Trudy—took off from Dayton into the clear skies. They hit speeds of eighty miles an hour with the wind rushing past them as they sat in the open cockpits. They had to shout to be heard. To see where they were going they would lean out the side and look down upon the countryside below while oil flying out of the engine splattered their goggles until they couldn't see. A handkerchief was an important piece of equipment for a passenger flying in the 1920s.

The weather had cleared in Dayton, but they quickly caught up with the storm and had to land in a plowed farm field. They taxied up to the barn and asked the owner of the farm if they could use his telephone. It was a party-line telephone and everyone in the community was on the line talking about an airplane that had actually landed in the area. Johnson never got his call out.

A huge crowd gathered at the farm to watch the threesome take off when the weather cleared. They flew into the sky to the cheers of people below, but quickly caught up to the storm again.

Trudy Wilson had finally had enough. She and Johnson's sister caught a train in Toledo and headed back to Dayton. When the weather cleared, Johnson completed the flight to Detroit carrying sand bags for ballast. Trudy and Johnson's sister did get a lot of publicity for their efforts since they were the only women who took part in any aspect of the race.

At about the same time, an airport was being dedicated in Columbus, and pilots from all over the state and region were flying in to take part in the ceremonies and excitement. Trudy was becoming a regular passenger on Johnson's flights, and she joined him on the Columbus trip.

"Once again, I was the only female to fly into Columbus that day, and once again, newsmen and photographers were much in evidence," she recalled. "My outfit at that time consisted of knickers—and I felt much too conspicuous."[19]

The loose fitting, three-quarter-length pants were appropriate for women, but somewhat daring for those days. Trudy had few options. Women's dresses and skirts in the 1920s were hardly suitable for the harsh conditions found in flight. Just getting into an airplane seat in a skirt or dress would be an unpleasant experience, so Trudy opted for knickers when she flew. However, if she felt uncomfortable having her photo taken in them, she felt much more comfortable flying in them. She became more than ballast. She was a navigator.

"I flew quite a bit with Mr. Johnson," Trudy recalled. "I remember [he] contracted to put on an air show at the Harvest Home Picnic. No one knew where the place was, but I knew dimly, so I was asked to be the navigator. I told him if he would follow the Cincinnati Road, which later became State Road 25, I was sure I could spot the North Bend Road. I was not successful the first time, but on the second try we found the picnic grounds. We negotiated our stunts, which consisted of only one loop, some awe-inspiring dives, and sharp turns—and I think that was it, so we headed back to Dayton. I have forgotten the compensation we got. But at the time, it seemed like quite a sum for a few minutes of fun."[20]

Some Early Bird pilots claim Johnson was one of the first to perform loops in the air. Trudy was certainly one of the first women to ride in a plane that was doing loops.

Navigation in those days, when even good roadmaps were hard to come by, often consisted of following railroad or interurban tracks. The one thing pilots could count on from railroad tracks that ran through the farmland and countryside was that if you followed them long enough, they would eventually lead someplace, usually to a little town with a station. By the 1920s, many towns were painting their name on the roof of the stations so pilots overhead could identify where they were located. The best stations even had arrows pointing north painted on the roof. Water towers with town names were also welcome sights.

Eventually, Trudy decided if she was going to spend so much time in the air, she should learn how to fly. She was certainly allured by the thrill of flying a plane by herself, and it was an opportunity very few women experienced. It is estimated in those days there were fewer than three hundred women pilots in the United States.

But it was also probably a practical matter. If you're going to be in an airplane quite frequently, you might as well learn how to fly in case you ever have to take the controls in an emergency.

Johnson was a willing teacher, but there were other problems. "When I finally made up my mind to really learn to fly and get my license, the first thing was to get my physical examination," Trudy remembered. "Those days, you couldn't go to just any doctor. There would be a physician appointed in areas—I would say for a 100- or 200-mile radius.

"I was the first woman [pilot] this doctor had [seen], and he didn't seem to know exactly what to do. However, he did give me my physical. Then he asked me to sit down and talk it over with him. As there were few women flyers, they didn't know too much about us."[21]

Sitting alone with Trudy in his office, the doctor fumbled for words. He couldn't look directly into her young face. "Now you understand," he said, "and I know I don't have to tell you this. But you have to realize, of course, that once a month women . . . well, once a month women are, well—incapacitated."

"Incapacitated?" Trudy repeated.

"Yes, well you know this. But what you don't know is that if you fly during this time I am afraid you will be unable to control the airplane, you will crash, you will injury yourself, and you quite likely could be killed. Now I want you to think about this."

"How do you know?" Trudy asked.

"How do I know what?" the doctor said.

"How do you know I can't fly an airplane when I'm incapacitated?"

It was a good question, but one the doctor hadn't expected, and he again stumbled to explain. Since he had known she was coming for her flight physical, he said, he had spent a good part of the previous evening calling everyone he knew who had any experience with flight and pilots and especially female pilots. He found no one who had ever licensed a woman pilot or even knew a woman pilot. There was no record of this sort of thing. It was simply unheard of.

"Then how do you know I can't fly when I'm incapacitated?" Trudy asked.

"Well, I just know it," the doctor said. "I'm a physician."

"Did I pass my physical?" Trudy asked.

"Yes, certainly," the doctor said.

"Then I'm going to learn to fly," Trudy said.

Frustrated, the doctor relented with only one more bit of advice about her incapacities.

"Do not fly the day before," he told her. "Fly very little if at all during the time. And certainly never fly the last day."

She joined a flight class with six to eight young men. At first she flew separately, but decided it would be better if she could train at the same time as the others so she could learn by observation as well as experience.

There were only a couple instruments in the trainer plane: a tachometer, an oil pressure gauge, a compass, and an altimeter. There was also a gauge to indicate speed, but it was unreliable. "I presume there was a gas gauge, but where it was, I didn't have to worry about that," Trudy said. "The mechanics always saw to it that there was plenty of gas."[22] There was another instrument she compared to a carpenter's level with a bubble that floated from side to side "so you could determine whether you were flying level."[23]

Trudy probably had a good enough feel for flight from all her years as a passenger that she didn't need to rely much on her instruments. She had a remarkably relaxed attitude and gave a wonderful description of what flight was like in the 1920s.

"The plane I learned to fly was called a Dart," she said. "Why it was called that, I shall never know. It had an eighty- or ninety-horsepower motor. The cockpit had two seats—tandem. As a passenger, I always rode in the front cockpit, and now I had graduated to the rear. The first procedure was drilled into us. First, one must be sure there were blocks under the wheels. The mechanic would stand in front and yell 'switch off.' I'd lean over the cockpit and answer 'switch off.' He then would yell, 'switch on.' And I would answer. The last command would be 'contact' and when he heard the answer he would swing the prop and hope it would catch the first time.

"If it would start, that was just the beginning. We [had to] thoroughly warm up the motor, we would taxi out a short way to get away from the hangar, and there we would sit, pushing the throttle up a little at a time. This would take approximately ten minutes. I must tell you, I'm afraid I didn't know how it was supposed to sound when it was warmed up.

"Then we would taxi out on the field—and what a bumpy ride that would be. The fields were really farmlands [that were] mowed. Landing strips were farm fields just mowed more frequently than the surrounding land.

"There were no brakes of any kind [on the planes]. If one wanted to turn—and you surely had to turn—you blasted the motor and pushed your foot [pedal] in the direction you wanted to go—[keeping] the stick in a neutral position. After a very bumpy ride you would get to the end of the runway, head into the wind, and you'd be ready to go.

"I must say, if I was ever squeamish about flying at all, it had to be at takeoff. Having flown so much before, I knew the dangerous time was on the takeoff. Those days, motors weren't reliable and many times they would cut out. You must learn to keep going straight. There was no turning back to the field unless you had sufficient height. And every field had a water tank, and to me this was a mental hazard. Seems that is all I could see. After I was airborne and at a safe height, I am sure I always heaved a sigh of relief.

"I often wonder the feeling of the instructor in the front seat. He could, of course, take the stick and do the flying. But one would often hear of the student 'freezing' on the stick. What would happen, I do not know, unless the [instructor] would reach over to the back cockpit and hit the aspiring pilot and knock him out. If the instructor wanted to explain something, he would wiggle his control, throttle back the motor, put the nose down, and yell at the top of his voice what the instructions were."[24]

Finally, Trudy felt she was ready for her first solo. The plan was for Trudy to climb to about three thousand feet, get comfortable behind the controls alone in the sky, make some turns, complete a figure eight, fly around for fifteen minutes, and then land.

Trudy taxied to the runaway, revved up her motor, and started moving down the newly mowed field. She went faster and faster and, just when she was sure it felt right, she pulled back on the stick, and her Dart trainer plane lifted in the air to the cheer of those watching. She climbed higher and higher, focusing all her attention on her gauges and the sky in front of her. She leveled off at three thousand feet and quickly knew she was in complete control. She was flying this plane by herself. She could do it, and for the first time, she was absolutely sure of that.

Trudy leaned over the edge of the plane to get a glimpse of all those watching down below. But there was not a person in sight. The crowd that had watched her take off only moments before was gone. Completely. There were fewer people to be seen than on a normal day. In fact, she could see no one back at the airfield. She was convinced something had happened. Something terrible had diverted the attention of the all those people. She considered landing to see what was wrong and wondered if Jimmie was all right. But she decided to stay aloft the fifteen minutes and complete her solo. Everything was fine on the ground, she told herself, but where had everyone gone?

Trudy did her turns and then her figure eight. The wind was rushing past her leather helmet and around her goggles and hitting her exposed face. And that's when it hit her. She remembered. In all the excitement of the day, it had escaped her attention; now it finally came back to her. She was, in fact, "incapacitated," but nothing was going to stop her now.

She completed her flight, landed the plane on the grassy field with still no one in sight, and taxied toward the hangars. That's when she saw people coming out of the buildings, some walking, some running toward her. They all congratulated her as she jumped down from the plane after her first solo.

"Where were you while I was flying?" Trudy asked.

"We watched," Johnson said, "but we were afraid if you could see us it would make you nervous. So we all cleared out of sight."

For the next several days, Trudy circled the field while Johnson stayed on the ground, standing at the edge of the airfield, watching every move she made. One morning she landed, and Johnson came running to her airplane.

"You're doing this wrong," he said and jumped into the plane. As soon as he fasted the buckle in the front passenger seat, Trudy gunned the engine and they were off. It wasn't until they were airborne that Johnson signaled for her to power back the motor, so she could hear what he wanted to say. It wasn't important. Trudy had her first passenger following her solo.

"I first wore knickers for all my flying," Trudy said. "It was the most practical and simple thing to wear. But I felt everyone knew I was that 'woman flyer.' I finally found a knitted suit with a pleated skirt, which allowed me the freedom of climbing in and out of the plane. One day I had just landed when two car loads of people arrived—poured from the cars—came up to me and said, 'Where is she?' They had heard there was a woman flyer at the field and they wanted to see her. This was one time I didn't have knickers on." She was wearing pants, a heavy coat, a leather helmet, and goggles. She looked like a man.

"I simply said that as far as I knew there wasn't a woman flying right then," Trudy said, "and there really wasn't."[25]

After her flight training came to end, Johnson put Trudy in a small, single-seat, low-wing "pup" airplane. A motorcycle engine powered its single engine.

The first time she flew it, he told her to take it up to 2,500 feet and do some turns. She taxied out to the runway, but by the time she got there her knees had picked up the "putt-putt" shaking of the motor. Her knees and the motor eventually were knocking in the same rhythm.

She took it to six hundred feet, did her turns, and took it down immediately. It did not feel safe. She was ready to tell her husband she would never fly it again and would have said so, but she suddenly realized that was just what men would expect from a woman. She kept her feelings to herself, overcame her fears, and flew the "pup" quite often.

"One beautiful evening I just thought I would love a ride," she said. "There wasn't any wind, no clouds, a perfect summer evening. I was flying merrily along when something hit me on my knee! There wasn't any question in my mind—the plane was falling apart. I throttled back, headed down, began to look around, and found a small block of wood [that might have fallen off]. [Fortunately] it was only a piece of bracing and not a vital one at that. But I did decide to return to earth, that is for sure."[26]

"Now that I had my license, I found out there wasn't much I could do with it," Trudy said. "I could take up friends, but who wanted to fly with a woman? No one, I assure you. I did manage to take up a maid and one of my sisters-in-law. I could take up passengers, but not for hire."[27]

At one point the Johnsons lived on the St. Clair River, about sixty miles north of Detroit. On the other side of the river was Canada.

"When taking up my sister-in-law, I wanted to show her the country, so I flew across the river and over into Canada," Trudy said. "I never suspected I was breaking the law. I had no sooner landed [back home in the United States] when the Canadian and United States custom men appeared. I assured them I had not landed in Canada and would not do such a thing again. So they let the poor, ignorant woman go."[28]

Trudy liked to fly over the house and look at her children playing in the yard below. She would fly high above, circle around the house, and dip her wings to them. But they paid no attention.

"Their daddy [did the same, but] more spectacular," Trudy said. "He would zoom over the house, climb steeply, and dip his wings. They always got a thrill from him."[29]

As the years passed, Trudy became quite an experienced pilot and even accompanied her husband on the cross-country trips he made to California and New York. These were often made in cabin planes that were completely enclosed. This was quite a treat for someone used to flying in the open air. Johnson enjoyed having his wife with him on the long trips, and it was more than companionship. When he got tired, he could take a nap, and Trudy could fly the plane. He took his nap in the back section that was separated from the pilot's cabin by a door.

"I always rode up front with him," Trudy said. "How many, many times he instructed me if anything went wrong I should, without hesitating, get back to the door [and go to the back compartment]. It might mean a case of life or death. And each time he told me, I insisted I was going to stay right there by his side. If anything happened to him, it was going to happen to me. I sincerely meant it. But one day our motor blew a spark plug and made a horrible racket. Before Mr. J. could turn to tell me to get to the back, believe me, I was already there! I never will live that down."[30]

She loved joining her husband when he flew into air shows. There were no control towers, no radios, and people were flying in from all directions at once. It was all first come, first serve.

"At one time I flew to Philadelphia with Mr. J." Trudy said. "The first autogyros were in the making, and he wanted to fly one. It certainly was a queer looking contraption—but what fun it was to fly in it. After a couple trips alone, I went aloft with him. We would see something on the ground, maybe become curious, go down and hover over it, and then go on. While I never soloed in the gyro, I was allowed to handle it in the air."[31]

Sometimes she again flew as ballast with her husband when he was testing the limits of a new plane. On one occasion, he was planning to take the airplane to its limit in terms of height. As the pilot, he took along a canister of oxygen for himself. As the ballast Trudy just sat there and got dizzy.

While Trudy loved to fly, she always felt she was doing it without a purpose. It wasn't work. It was just for pleasure. Few people flew just for fun in those days. She had three children and a husband to take care of. Sometimes she wondered what she was doing up in the sky.

One day, while taking a flight over her home, Trudy looked down on her three children playing in the yard below. They didn't notice her floating through the air, doing things very few women of her time would attempt. They were children. They didn't know Trudy was a trailblazer not only for aviation, but also for women.

Flying there in the quiet sky, all alone, Trudy wondered who would take care of those children if something happened to her. It was a time when the death of a mother meant that children were often taken from the father and placed with a relative—or even in an orphanage. The thought sent a shudder up and down her spine.

She flew gracefully back to the airfield and landed her plane with the perfection and ease of the skilled pilot that she was. She taxied down the runaway and across the grassy field toward the hangars. At last, the plane rolled to a stop. She shut down the engine, took off her helmet and goggles, and climbed out of the cockpit onto the wing, stepping down to the hard ground. There was a distant smile on her face. She was the only person who knew why.

Trudy Johnson never piloted an airplane again in her life, but she never forgot the thrill. She never forgot how much she loved it. She never forgot what she had gone through to accomplish what she had done. In a speech in 1974, Trudy talked about all she had seen and accomplished.

"I still get a thrill each time I learn of records made in aviation," she said. "I wonder whether or not the advancement in the last fifty years can be duplicated in the next fifty years. It certainly seems impossible to me. But I am sure that there will be tremendous strides.

"Of course, I follow all aspects of flying as closely as I can. The astronauts and their program fascinate me. I have not missed a blastoff."[32]

She then wondered about the possibility of women becoming astronauts, and she was all for it. Trudy ended her talk that day with a smile on her face. There was just one thing she wondered as she thought about the first women being accepted by NASA as space astronauts: Would they be allowed to launch if they were incapacitated?[33]

In the 1950s, Jimmie and Trudy's son, Jim, was a pilot in the Navy. He was flying off an aircraft carrier in the Pacific Ocean. Jim Johnson had succeeded in following his father's footsteps; he was a pilot. In just a few years the son of one of flight's first pilots would take a Navy jet to the sound barrier.

While in the Navy, out on his ship, Jim received letters from his father. One day he got a surprise. Through the Red Cross, he received a telegram from his father back home. It was brief and to the point. It simply said, "That didn't count."

The son had no idea what the telegram was about, and he puzzled over it for several days. Finally, he came across a news story about a radar beam that had been sent from the earth and had bounced off the Moon.

He remembered the morning long, long ago when he and his father had talked while his father shaved. He remembered his father told him man would one day reach the Moon, but that radar signal didn't count. That's what Jimmie Johnson meant.

Jimmie Johnson died in the early morning hours of Wednesday, August 20, 1968. He believed to the very end.

Eleven months later a fellow Purdue alumnus, Neil Armstrong, stepped out of a lunar module and placed his foot on the surface of the Moon.

Gary Payton

Gary Payton was eight years old and living with his family in Rock Island, Illinois, when his Uncle John took him flying in a Piper Tri-Pacer airplane. He was hooked for life.

"I was half thrilled and half scared," Payton says. "But it was a lot of fun. Uncle John had been in the Navy in World War II. He was a mechanic on aircraft carriers. After the war he got his private license, and he was always talking about flying."

Payton made plans for a flight career, but he grew up in an age when people started looking even higher. The Soviet Union launched the *Sputnik* satellite in 1958. An American satellite soon followed. The space race was on.

"When *Sputnik* happened, that got my interest going on rockets," Payton says. "At that time our school system did a rapid turn around in teaching math and science. I was part of the targeted group in school. . . .

"I was just interested in aerospace in general, and of course, the mantra of aviation is higher, faster, farther. Rockets going into space as high and as fast and as far as you can go. So that's what was intriguing to me."

But even more than the flying in those days, he was interested in rockets and the engineering that made it all possible.

As he neared the end of high school, he applied for the Air Force Academy. He failed the eye exam. He enrolled at Bradley University in Peoria, Illinois, and the following year was able to gain admittance to the Academy. He eventually received a vision waiver to fly.

He applied for the cooperative master's degree program at Purdue and was accepted, requiring him to take upper-level courses as an undergraduate. "It was the toughest program at the Academy," Payton says.

Payton graduated from the Academy in 1971 and received his master's from Purdue in January 1972. He had pilot training at Craig Air Force Base, Alabama, and became an instructor pilot. In 1976, he was assigned to Cape Canaveral, Florida, as a spacecraft test controller, launching military satellites.

The Space Shuttle Program was developing at this time, and it was decided that all military satellites would be launched with the shuttle.

"The Air Force started a payload specialist program to better understand how the shuttle operated," Payton says. He became the first of those Air Force payload specialists.

Payton launched on space transportation system (STS) 51-C in January 1985. Purdue graduate Loren Shriver was the pilot. It was the first space shuttle flight dedicated to the Department of Defense.

Today Payton is the deputy for advanced systems in the Air Force Missile Defense Agency at the Pentagon in Washington, D.C.

He has traveled more than 1.2 million miles through space.

Chapter Four

Should the university decide to enter [aeronautical] research it would be one of the pioneers among colleges and universities of the country.

—George W. Haskins

It was an incredible day for George Haskins. It was an experience that in one sense must have seemed unreal to him. Yet, in another sense, as a visionary engineer, there were aspects that were probably exactly what he expected.

On July 20, 1969, Haskins watched on television as the *Eagle* lunar lander touched down, and astronauts Neil Armstrong and Edwin "Buzz" Aldrin prepared to walk on the surface of the Moon.

Haskins was seventy-seven years old that summer. He was eleven years older than powered flight that the Wright brothers had accomplished in 1903. His life had spanned the history of aviation from Kitty Hawk to the Moon. And as an engineer, a researcher, a college professor, a military commander, and a pilot, he had been involved in a great deal of the progress that ultimately built up to the moon landing success.

Haskins must have felt enormous pride as he watched the fuzzy, black-and-white image of Armstrong stepping down the ladder of the lunar module. Whatever personal feelings were inside him that day, he never mentioned them. He wasn't a boastful man. But he must have understood.

It was Neil Armstrong who took the first step on the Moon. It was George Haskins who took the first major step to bring flight to Purdue University, the school where Neil Armstrong would one day study and earn his degree along with many other leaders in aviation and space.

Haskins's early advocacy of flight at Purdue would lead to giant leaps in the years to come: an aeronautics program, the nation's first university airport, the hiring of Amelia Earhart, and the creation of a School of Aeronautical Engineering and Astronautical Engineering, one of the best and largest aviation technology programs in the nation.

And Haskins had another tie to the Apollo 11 mission in addition to the Purdue-Armstrong connection.

As he witnessed that lunar landing in 1969, his thoughts must have gone back fifty years. His memories must have stirred.

In the spring of 1910, students had formed a Purdue Aero Club. The faculty advisor was Professor Cicero B. Veal, a mechanical engineer who would go on to serve as chief of inspectors at the Curtiss plant in Buffalo during World War I. The purpose of the club was to assemble books on aviation and to build an airplane.[1] Perhaps they found some books, but there is no record of the club successfully building an airplane.

The group got immediate editorial support from the student newspaper, the *Exponent.* A May 18, 1910, article states, "If we may be pardoned for suggesting it, we feel that what the Aero Club needs is plenty of action. They should flap their wings, so to speak, and give flight to their latent impulses. When the aviators have made themselves felt, some benefactor may happen along to hasten developments."[2]

The club did help the Purdue Alumni Association and the *Lafayette Morning Journal* in planning and staging Aviation Day.

After the June 13, 1911, Aviation Day at Purdue on Stuart Field—when birdmen Lincoln Beachy and George Witmer thrilled seventeen thousand people—very few airplanes touched the sky over the Lafayette area. Maybe none. Aviation Day had rocked the community and inspired everyone with the thrill of flight. But the excitement of that day was followed by an eight-year void in Purdue aviation. However, there was some quiet stirring.

In the period that followed, Veal gave support to the study of aviation. In 1911, he delivered a paper about flight to the American Society of Mechanical Engineers. In 1913, he called on technical schools to show a greater interest in flight.[3]

There were faculty members at Purdue who agreed with him. But in the days before World War I, when flight was widely considered a sport or a hobby, the possibility of aviation as an academic program did not progress.

One aeroplane was built in Lafayette just before the start of World War I, but it never flew. And as it turned out, it was most fortunate that Lafayette's first home-built plane stayed on the ground.

Harry Roth was the builder. He is identified only as a "young enthusiast" with a lot of adventure in his heart. He also had some mechanical skill and a little money. Roth built the airplane out of bamboo, canvas, and piano wire in a livery stable behind the Mars Theater (now the Long Center for the Performing Arts).

Roth had purchased the plans for a Santos Dumont airplane and no doubt had great dreams of thrilling his friends and neighbors as he flew over Lafayette. But his parents had other ideas and Roth's plane never flew. It was instead put on display at Purdue's Locomotive Museum.

At some later point in time it was finally taken outside and started. The propeller broke loose and put on an excellent air show all by itself, flying through the air—no doubt as people ran for cover. It was reported to have cleared Heavilon Hall before returning to the earth.[4] Since the Heavilon Hall bell tower was the highest point on campus, it was a pretty spectacular flight—if only by a part of an airplane.[5]

During the war, Purdue and Lafayette had some brushes with flight. In 1918, a military plane flying from Indianapolis, Indiana, to Rantoul, Illinois, ran out of fuel and landed in a farm field south of Purdue. The pilot, who had committed a major error in gas calculation, walked to town. Of course he and his airplane quickly drew attention, and when he offered to put on a flight exhibition at the same Stuart Field that had been used on Aviation Day in 1911, his proposal was quickly accepted. Unfortunately, the pilot lost control of the plane and crashed from a height of about fifteen feet.[6]

On the eleventh hour of the eleventh day of the eleventh month in 1918, the Great War ended. During the war, flight had captured the imagination of many people, including young engineers at Purdue and recent graduates. Some of them had flown in spectacular air battles over Europe. Once having tasted the thrill of flight, these young men would never be bound to the earth again. They wanted to fly. One of these young men was George Haskins.

Haskins was born in 1892 in Waterville, Ohio, south of Toledo. It was the same year that Amos Heavilon made a donation to Purdue that would lead to construction of Heavilon Hall, at its time one of the finest university engineering facilities in the nation. Haskins was eleven years old when Wilbur and Orville Wright, from down the road in Dayton, accomplished powered, controlled, sustained flight in a flying machine at Kitty Hawk, North Carolina.

Still, it is likely Haskins heard little about flying machines until 1908 when newspapers in the United States began wide coverage of aviation and flight exhibitions in cities and towns from New York to California.

From the beginning, Ohio took particular pride in the Wright brothers and that certainly spread to Haskins's hometown. At some point in his life Haskins came to know Orville Wright.[7]

Haskins was twenty years old when he started college. He spent his freshman and sophomore years at Valparaiso University before enrolling in mechanical engineering at Purdue as a junior in the fall of 1914. The circumstances that took him from an Ohio farm to West Lafayette are not known, but he loved engineering and was probably attracted by the school's reputation.

The 1916 *Debris* says Haskins was a member of Delta Upsilon Fraternity. He was active in the Y.M.C.A. and the Glee Club. "George hails from our neighbor the Buckeye state," the yearbook says. "Before coming to Purdue he spent two strenuous but very pleasant years at Valparaiso. Although small and unassuming, he is yet a man of many affairs. He is a good consistent student and yet finds some time to delight his friends with a clear, rich tenor voice."

Haskins and the rest of his class graduated into difficult times. Europe was already deeply involved in war. The United States would enter in 1917. The 1916 yearbook features cartoons of young men resolutely marching off to the military as young women try to hold them back.

Haskins took his Purdue mechanical engineering degree and went to work with a company that pumped water out of the ground using compressed air.

In April 1917, three days after the United States entered WWI he enlisted and followed the lure of aviation that had attracted him even before he enrolled at Purdue. He applied for the air service.[8] He was accepted, received his training, and was selected, along with about seventy other young men, for special intensive study at MIT. The course work included newly advanced theories of aerodynamics, propeller and airplane design, and airplane engines.[9]

From MIT, he went to McCook Field in Dayton where he was an assistant to the chief engineer. McCook was not an ordinary airfield at this time. It was the key training and testing facility. Civilian Jimmie Johnson, from the Purdue class of 1907, was a chief test pilot at McCook, and the two Purdue men must certainly have come to know one another.

At the end of the war in 1918, Haskins, a lieutenant, remained in the military and pursued a career with the Air Service. He was enthused about the military and civilian potential for flight. In 1919, only three years after graduation, he returned to Purdue. The way he chose to return made newspaper headlines.

On Sunday, June 8, 1919, in its final edition of the semester, the *Exponent* reported, "Lt. George W. Haskins of Dayton, Ohio, will . . . come [to Gala Week] in a plane. He will arrive Sunday or Monday morning with resolutions of the Dayton Alumni Association drawn up at a meeting of that association Friday at the English Club. Haskins will probably be here all week and demonstrate aerial maneuvers with his plane. . . .

"This proposed means of journeying to an alumni reunion and Gala Week events will mark an epoch in the history of the university—since it will be the first time that an alumnus has returned in an airplane."[10]

The newspaper article has the sound of several last-minute decisions. The article appeared Sunday in the last edition of the *Exponent* until fall. The alumni meeting in Dayton where "resolutions" were drafted had just occurred two days earlier. Haskins still didn't know exactly when he would arrive or how long he would stay. He only knew he wanted to do something that had never been done before: arrive as an alumnus by airplane. The information for this news story sounds like it was wired to West Lafayette from Dayton just before the paper's deadline.

Haskins did become the first flying alumnus to return—but just barely. He arrived Sunday, June 8, the same day the newspaper article appeared. Alumnus John T. McCutcheon was also flying in with a pilot from Chicago. McCutcheon arrived Monday afternoon, one day later.

Haskins carried to Purdue a single resolution from the Dayton Alumni Club calling for the creation of an aeronautics program at Purdue. It arrived too late to make the official agenda of the Purdue University Board of Trustees meeting that week. There is no mention of it in the minutes of the meeting. But it attracted the media.

The *Lafayette Morning Journal* reported on Monday, June 9, "Lt. Haskins has been stationed [in] Dayton and left there at 11:20 [Sunday] morning. Although flying against a strong wind and having to stop twenty miles east of Indianapolis because of lubrication troubles in the engine and again in Indianapolis for gas and oil, he reached here and alighted on Stuart Field at 5:20. Besides attending the commencement exercises and visiting his fraternity brothers at Delta Upsilon house, Lt. Haskins is also here on official business in the matter of securing the cooperation of the university in carrying on research work in aerial navigation and by so doing recognizing the air service as one of the more important branches of military service."[11]

The resolution from the Dayton Club has the sound of something Haskins had proposed. There were powerful people in the military that wanted to dismantle the air power built up during the war. Haskins sided with those who felt this would be a major mistake. Perhaps he was trying to bolster the concept of a strong Air Service as well as an aeronautical engineering program at Purdue through the proposal.

Whoever first initiated the resolution, the Dayton Alumni Club certainly felt it was the appropriate place for this idea to originate. Dayton was, after all, the "birthplace of flight" and the home of important military and civilian aviation programs.

The *Morning Journal* article continued. "Lieutenant. Haskins stated that should the university decide to enter upon the research work it would be one of the pioneers among the colleges and universities of the country in the work and would greatly enhance its reputation as a technical institution in doing so.

"Although his engine is not working well, he will probably make a number of exhibition flights while he is here and it is his intention to start for Dayton about 1 o'clock tomorrow [Tuesday] afternoon—just at the time when the alumni luncheon is being held on campus."[12]

This young alumnus, only three years past his own graduation, might have been pushing his luck by upstaging the luncheon with his own takeoff right on campus. But this was the first Purdue reunion since the end of World War I and young men who had served were held in high esteem. Plans were already getting underway for a Union Building as a memorial to Purdue men who died in the war.

In addition to Haskins's flight on campus, the *Morning Journal* reported that Lt. Henry G. Boonstra, who was stationed in Indianapolis, would also be in the community to give exhibition flights that week. The paper said, "Lt. Boonstra is one of the best aviators who has ever been seen here and his flights are always marked by what—to the uninitiated—seem daring feats, but which to Lt. Boonstra are little more than common place of the sport."[13]

After a long lull in aviation at Purdue, there was a lot of flight taking place in a single week.

W. H. Robertson wrote a page-one column in the *Lafayette Morning Journal* and he used his commentary on Monday, June 9, 1919, to say, "If John Purdue, founder of Purdue University, could push aside the sod from the eternal temple in which he reposes amid a ground of pines on the campus and see members of the association returning for the annual reunion via the air route—he would doubtless be hugely amazed.

"That is one of the things an institution like Purdue does for young people. They may be compelled to scrimp and save in order to complete their college courses; they maybe be compelled to walk from the precincts of their alma mater in order to find a field upon which to wage their fight and conquer the world. Many of them have done that very thing; countless others will doubtless repeat the performance in the years to come. But if they have profitably employed their time as students, there is no doubt about their ultimate ability to come back by whatever method of conveyance appeals to their fancy."[14]

Two days later Robinson wrote, "Flying is become popular. It is the logical means of transportation if time and comfort are matters to be taken into consideration. Airplanes are becoming a sight so common that they no longer attract a great deal of attention in this city. It is the same in other cities."[15]

At the same time Robertson says this, it should be noted that every flight into and out of Purdue that week was being reported in his newspaper.

He continued, "There is one thing Lafayette should do, however, and that is provide a landing field for planes that visit this city. The cost would amount to practically nothing. All that is necessary is to secure a lease on a plat of ground on which a circle approximately 600 feet in diameter should be outlined by brick even with the ground. The circle should be painted white or kept whitewashed in the summer time in order that it might easily be located by visiting flyers. In the winter, the brick should be kept free of snow so that the circle would be distinguishable from above. If possible, a supply of gasoline and oil should be kept at the field, but this would not be necessary until the requirements are greater than at present.

"On Monday, two planes were damaged here as a result of inability of the aviators to choose proper landing places. They alighted safely, but when they attempted to ascend they came to grief by reason of the unfitness of the fields.

"Flying is not nearly as dangerous as the general public imagines. There are numerous accidents, it is true, but in practically every instance they result from stunt flying or to poor landing places."[16]

It would be nine more years before anyone in the community acted on Robertson's suggestion.

From all reports, Haskins got into and out of Stuart Field without problems. So the difficulties Robertson mentioned were apparently to the airplanes that carried Boonstra and John McCutcheon.

McCutcheon, the *Chicago Tribune* cartoonist who had reported on his previous flights with Wright exhibition flyers, also wrote about his airplane trip to Purdue and accompanied the story with drawings.

"How smooth and even the plane flies," he said, "and how beautiful the checkerboard of the fields looks! From up here the fields look like watered silk, half of them plowed and half of them green with wheat and oats. How comfortable the pilot looks! He takes it as easy as if he were loafing along at a fifteen-mile gait in a car."[17]

McCutcheon and his pilot had lunch in Rantoul, Illinois, and then got lost heading into West Lafayette. They landed in a Carroll County cow pasture and were given directions by an excited boy who ran out to greet them.

As the plane neared Purdue, a crowd that had been waiting for the famous cartoonist all afternoon at Stuart Field became excited. But the pilot decided he didn't have a large enough area to land. He saluted the assembled people in what he considered more of a tailspin[18] and flew off to land in an alfalfa field, "the propeller mowing off the alfalfa."[19]

John McCutcheon thought air travel was the only way to go. But not everyone agreed. The *Lafayette Morning Journal* reported, "Mrs. McCutcheon is coming by train."[20]

McCutcheon agreed with newspaper columnist Robertson and declared that every city the size of Lafayette should have a landing field. He predicted one day it would. And during an alumni banquet that Gala Weekend he followed up on the resolution flown in by Haskins and said that in order for Purdue to remain at the top in higher education, an aeronautical program would have to be initiated.[21]

Haskins returned to McCook and continued to advance in his military career. He also continued to promote aviation in general and in particular at Purdue. There would be no aviation at Purdue in 1919. Not yet. But that same year in Lafayette, Colorado, Jim Maris was born. And in thirty-six years he would arrive at Purdue to begin an aviation technology program that would grow to be among the best in the world.

In the spring of 1920, Haskins wrote at length about some of the technical aspects of flight in the *Purdue Engineering Review*. He saw great potential in its future—even if it did present some new problems. All new technologies brought people some problems, in addition to the great benefits, Haskins wrote. With the birth of electrical engineering, he said, people were shocked and burned. Water travel had seasickness, and now air travel called for medical treatments for conditions that included "heart dilation, oxygen wants, special nerve strain, and air sickness."

"It was because of these exceptional or unusual demands upon the human body that a special examination was prepared with a view to picking men best able to stand up under the great variety and intensity of stress and strain, as great as that in the airplane," he wrote. "It is not that a flier must be a superman, nor can one man properly fill all the diversified classes of work such as pursuit, reconnaissance, photography, bomb-dropping, and night flying. . . . Man was not originally intended to be a flyer. . . . The air fighting force . . . has its potentialities of disaster . . . and is doing great work in correcting the ills as they have been revealed.

"In closing," Haskins said, "it is desired to emphasize the vigor and extent to which commercial aviation has already been pushed, but even yet, the public, to a great extent, treats the whole affair as a dream of the future. Commercial aviation is its own reward and is a direct asset in time of war emergency, as the planes can be quickly converted. It needs guidance and encouragement.

"Already a route has been completed from Cairo to the Cape. There is talk of an expedition to the South Pole; there are transcontinental routes over many parts of Europe and good air service between Paris and London has been a fact for some time. South American countries have already looked upon aviation as a solution in opening obscure mining and other rich lands. Where a certain party of prospectors spent two months trying to arrive at a new rich, mining district . . . an airplane would have made the trip in a little over two hours.

"America is by no means dead, but has organized several companies. It is hoped that the foregoing has given the young engineers something to think about. The field is large, fortunes will be made, and only the surface has been touched in this new and promising industry."[22]

It is safe to assume in addition to "young engineers," Haskins was hoping his message would reach the Purdue University Board of Trustees.

W. O. Erwin, Purdue class of 1920, wrote the second article on aviation in the 1920 *Purdue Engineering Review.* It focused on the Air Service of the United Sates Army and concluded that "it seems that with the perfection of airplanes, new possibilities of use will be discovered until it is difficult to retrain one's forecasts of what the future holds in store. The possibilities are limitless."[23]

In the fall of 1920, a new Aero Club was started. Its members were all veterans. In the fall of 1921, Purdue finally responded to Haskins and the Dayton Alumni Club. Four elective courses were offered in aeronautical engineering through the Purdue School of Mechanical Engineering. An aerodynamics laboratory was created in Heavilon Hall. The lab was equipped with an airplane and several operating engines. Professor Martin L. Thornburg, a Purdue mechanical engineering graduate from the class of 1915 and an Air Service veteran, was in charge.[24]

Still in the Army at this time, Haskins supported fellow officer Billy Mitchell, a man who faced court-martial in 1925 growing out of his vocal criticism of the military for its failure to develop a strong Air Service after WWI.

While not as vocal as Mitchell, Haskins's, opinions were known in the military. And seeing that developments were proceeding in a direction that he could not support, Haskins left the Army Air Service as a captain in 1922. From 1924 until 1929, he was a representative with Drying Systems in Chicago.

Meanwhile, the study of aeronautics was progressing at Purdue but with frequent leadership changes. By 1928, two graduate classes were added, and the number of planes had grown to three, along with a collection of nine engines.[25]

In 1929, Haskins was recruited to Purdue, joining the faculty of mechanical engineering to teach in the field where he believed "fortunes will be made." One year later Neil Armstrong was born in Wapakoneta, Ohio.

Haskins was placed in charge of Purdue's aeronautics program that was just getting off the ground, and he worked extremely hard.

"For eight years of turbulent development, [he] carried a tremendous load," Knoll writes in *The Story of Purdue Engineering*. "In his time the Air Corp made substantial donations of equipment, the airport was established, and the Supercharger Laboratory placed in the vanguard of all such laboratories in the country. A wind tunnel of a twelve-inch cross section was constructed for tests on models. . . . In one period, Haskins taught nine different courses, counseled students, prepared laboratory plans, and 'supposedly,' he said, did research."[26]

In addition to his work at Purdue, Haskins continued flying and was a popular sight in rural Indiana.

One afternoon he was forced down in a farmer's field because of mechanical problems. The farmer helped Haskins repair the engine in return for a ride and the opportunity to see his fields for the first time from the air. They flew so late that Haskins couldn't get home before dark, so he spent the night at the farm home. The next day when he went to take off there was a bushel of fruit waiting in his cockpit.

In 1937, Haskins left Purdue having taken aeronautical engineering at the university from a small program to being on the verge of becoming a school. He went to work for the Civil Aeronautics Administration as an engine and propeller specialist. One of his special areas of expertise was superchargers and pressuring cabins for high altitude flying.

When the United States entered World War II, he was recalled to active duty. He was given several commands, was sent to MIT to do further research on superchargers, and eventually went to the Indo-China theater during the war.

A newspaper article written about him during the war states, "A few years back the Glenn Martin Aviation Company was sponsoring teams of combat fliers for test purposes. The teams had good planes, some of the best in the air in those days, but they were having difficulty in attaining proper altitude for certain maneuvers.

"'Get hold of George Haskins,' a company executive said. 'If anyone can straighten us out, he can.'

"So George Haskins was ordered to work on the problem, and after only two weeks of intensive study and work, he set an altitude record which still stands for the particular [censored] type of plane: 37,000 feet. Since then, many of the combat planes in use in the U.S. evidence marks of his influence in cowling, arrangement, and method of cooling."[27]

When the war ended, Haskins retired as a full colonel and returned to the Civil Aeronautics Administration. His son, Bill, studied for two years at Purdue before entering the Air Force in 1950. He flew F-86 fighter-bomber jets during the Korean War and eventually became a pilot for United Airlines.

George W. Haskins retired in Santa Monica, California, having spent his life taking flight, from open cockpit biplanes made of wood and cloth to the jet age. In retirement, he had the opportunity to watch the space age advance, which built on everything that had been done before.

He was proud that Neil Armstrong went through the program he helped start and build. And when the *Eagle* landed on the Moon July 20, 1969, he had a double joy in that accomplishment.

In 1928, when he married his first wife, Dorothy, he picked one of his closest friends to serve as his best man. The best man was a pilot for Standard Oil, and Haskins had known him for many years, dating at least to the days when they both served in the Air Service at McCook Field. The best man flew the newlyweds on their honeymoon. That best man was named Edwin Aldrin. Edwin Aldrin had a son who was given his name. But everyone called him "Buzz."

When Haskins watched the accomplishments of Apollo 11 in July 1920, he was observing one man—Armstrong—who had been through the aeronautics program that he had played a major role in creating and building. The other man walking on the Moon that day was the son of one of his best friends.

It was a great day for space and aviation. It was a great day for George W. Haskins, and it was fitting that a man who lived to see so much in aviation should reach that moment. He died just two months later.

Donald Williams

Don Williams was born on a farm not too far from where George Haskins landed his airplane in 1919, at Purdue University.

Williams graduated in 1960 from Otterbein High School; there were twenty-five students in his graduating class.

"We had a pretty small farm for that time," Williams says. "We owned a couple of hundred acres, and we leased another couple of hundred. When I was in school, I spent a lot of time out in the fields on tractors and other types of equipment. I remember on summer days, which were typically hot and you're dirty and dusty, an airplane would fly by overhead. Sometimes I'd see the contrail of a jet airliner or maybe just a small plane coming out of Purdue Airport. I can remember looking up at the sky and the airplanes from that tractor and thinking, 'That looks like a lot more fun than this is.'

"As it turns out, it was."

Williams enrolled at Purdue University with a Navy Reserve Officers Training Corps (NROTC) scholarship.

"I think Purdue's ROTC program is part of the reason the university has attracted so many astronauts," he says. "It's a large and really strong program.

"I loved Purdue, but it was challenging," he says. "Coming from a small high school and not really having a strong academic background, it was quite a step up. It was a challenge, but it was worth the work. Purdue gave me the foundation to go forward in the direction I wanted to go, which eventually led to being picked for the space program. At Purdue, I learned how to ask questions, where to go to find information, how to do technical analyses."

Williams graduated from Purdue in 1964, completed Navy flight training, and did four tours of duty in Vietnam, where he flew 330 combat missions. He was flying in the Vietnam War when Neil Armstrong landed on the Moon July 20, 1969.

"I was in awe," he says. "I was thinking, 'Wow, that would be nice to be part of that.' But I thought I'd never have a chance, so I put it out of my mind."

After Vietnam, Williams went to test pilot school. While flying as an engineering test pilot in Maryland, he learned that NASA was getting ready to accept applications for something new—the Space Shuttle Program.

"NASA decided they were going to need a lot more astronauts," he says. "The shuttle had a lot more capability. They were going to fly crews of up to seven or eight at a time, instead of two or three."

Williams went into NASA with the class of 1978. After being selected for the program, there is close to a year of training before the individual becomes qualified to fly.

"The idea is to give the folks who come into this business a year's worth of indoctrination—basic training in the shuttle and systems, and what's going on," Williams says. "You also get some flight training in the NASA jets used for space flight readiness. At any time during that year, an individual can make their own decision about whether or not this is what they really wanted to do. And of course, NASA can also make a decision about whether they picked the right people. If an individual decides it isn't the right thing to do, then that person can leave anytime during that first year with no stigma attached. You can go back to wherever you were before.

"So far, to the best of my knowledge, no one's ever done that because it's a pretty nice flying club."

Williams's first flight came seven years after his selection, on April 12, 1985. He was the pilot on STS 51-D.

"The shuttle flight deck looks like an airplane, if you've been in a cockpit of a 737 or 727 or an airbus," Williams says. It's not a roomy place. Williams describes the size as similar to that inside a recreation vehicle. "And not the big ones. Maybe the kind you tow behind a full-size truck," he says. Though the space seems small, once you are less affected by Earth's gravitational pull, you can use vertical space as well. Once you get into orbit there is really no up or down. So it seems more spacious.

Williams slept on the flight deck.

"We have a little sleeping bag that is just a piece of cloth with a couple of armholes in it and a zipper. It has some cloth ties that you can tie off on either end. You can actually sleep quite well just floating around. The trouble is, because of the air recirculation system, eventually you're going to run into something or somebody, and it wakes you up—or it wakes them up, which doesn't make them too happy."

On October 18, 1989, Williams was commander of STS-34 that successfully deployed the *Galileo* spacecraft on a journey to explore Jupiter. At the start of the twenty-first century, *Galileo* was still productive, although its time is running short.

"It's been fun to watch," Williams says. "People ask what did you do on your first shuttle flight and nobody remembers the satellite deployments and other activities. But people remember *Galileo.* We were the last humans to see the spacecraft before it went on its little journey to Jupiter, which, by the way, took seven years. The data that has come back from that mission has rewritten the textbooks."

Space flight is an incredible, life-changing experience, he says.

"One of the things you see from space when you look at Earth is there are no boundaries, except between the land and the sea," he says. "The only other boundaries on Earth are the ones that people have created. It really is one planet. And we need to learn to conserve its resources and get along with each other. I hope that a lot of other people get the chance to make that discovery."

Williams left NASA at the end of 1989. "I had reached my goal and decided it was time to try something different," he says.

He is a vice president for Science Applications International Corporation, which does work with NASA, other federal agencies, and many commercial customers.

Chapter Five

I will bet twenty thousand pounds against anyone who wishes that I will make the tour of the world in eighty days or less.

—Phileas Fogg,
Around the World in 80 Days, by Jules Verne

Others will fly around the world. But there will never again be a first time.

—Admiral Ashley Robertson,
San Diego, California, 1924

It was Thursday, March 20, 1924, a heady time in the United States when everything looked exciting and possible.

Army Major Frederick L. Martin reflected the positive attitude of the age as he smiled and taxied his open cockpit airplane to a stop at Sand Point Field in Seattle, Washington.

It was a big biplane, almost box-like, and it looked as if it was constructed for the long haul and endurance rather than speed.

Martin had a confident smile. He had a large square jaw that he pushed forward and a weathered face that was marked by lines of experience. He stopped his loud motor, bringing a sudden quiet to the area around him.

According to the *Seattle Post-Intelligencer,* "Martin looked down out of his cockpit and smiled a wide smile of surprised recognition. His hand shot out and was grasped by another hand. 'Hello, Schrader, old boy,' grinned [Martin] as Major O. H. Schrader . . . balanced himself on the wing of the plane. The two were classmates at Purdue University in '08."

Martin climbed down out of the high cockpit and greeted people who surrounded him on the airfield, including news reporters. "What does it mean to you to be named commander of the around-the-world flight," a reporter for the *Seattle Post-Intelligencer* asked him.

"It means everything to me," Martin answered. "It's the greatest opportunity I've ever had or ever will have. It's a trust of single honor that I had hoped for but hardly expected prior to the moment of notice that I had been selected as one of the four—and to command! We are expected to go through with it. And we will."[1]

Martin was a determined dead-serious man. When he said he would succeed, people believed him. He was a tall, straight solider, and a veteran of World War I who wore his uniform stiff and perfectly pressed. He was proud and carried an air of leadership about him. He was a Purdue University graduate with a degree in mechanical engineering.

In the spring of 1924, he was about to set out on the most exciting adventure possible in aviation, which many already considered the most exciting occupation in the world. Along with three other Army pilots and their one-man crews, Martin's mission was to command the first flight around the world. It was a trip that would stretch more than twenty-six thousand miles and it would take months of flights that never lasted longer than one day. It was almost unimaginable to people of the day. Around the world. They might as well try to fly to the Moon.

In 1924, airplanes were built of wood and wire and cloth. They had wooden propellers, few instruments, and engines that were known for failure and oil leaks. Airports were open fields—wherever they might be. It had only been twenty-one years since the Wright brothers flew at Kitty Hawk. It had only been thirteen or fourteen years since Cliff Turpin and other pilots thrilled the nation with air shows that often ended in disaster.

What made these men think that in 1924 they could accomplish something as monumental and unheard of as flying around the world? Imagine. Imagine if they had only known that in fourty-five years men would fly to the Moon and that the first man to do it would be born in just six years.

One of the greatest natural resources of America has always been the "can do" attitude of its people—people who believe in their hearts that if they work hard, they will succeed in the face of all the obstacles. And so it was that in the spring of 1924 four Army pilots and their four mechanics were preparing to leave Seattle to attempt a mission that had captured the spirit of the world.

Other nations were trying the same thing. Pilots from at least five other countries had plans to fly around the globe. American pride was at stake. In a sense, this was a race around the world. In a larger sense, this was a mission to create excitement about aviation and to show everyone what air power could accomplish.

Airplanes had attracted considerable attention during World War I, but after the fighting ended, people wondered what use these flying machines could possibly serve.

The National Defense Act of 1920 established Air Service as part of the Army. It fell to people who manned this program to prove to the Army, Congress, and the general public that the development of aeronautical technology was in the interest of the nation.

"The Air Service pilots who remained in uniform [after the war] were encouraged to show that airplanes had a vital role in national defense," C. V. Glines wrote in an article in the *Air Force* magazine "They began setting altitude, endurance, and speed records and were the first to cross the nation in less than a day, refuel in midair, and fly nonstop across the country. Each flight was carefully planned and, although there were failures, the successes were newsworthy and expanded the range of possibilities for the airplane. The announcement by the Air Service that eight of its airmen would attempt an around-the-world flight captured the public's attention."[2] It was front-page news from coast to coast. It was dinner conversation and front porch debate.

And the command for this earth-shaking mission had gone to Martin. He never said so publicly, but given his background of self-confidence and determination, he might have considered himself destined to lead this mission from the start.

He was born in 1882, before airplanes and automobiles, in the little Indiana town of Liberty. It was a small community where everyone knew one another and a boy could not be mischievous without his parents finding out about it before he could even get home. In those days before telephones and radios, Liberty was a town where people saw one another almost every day. It was a strong community.

In 1904, Martin enrolled at Purdue University. There is no record of what brought him to Purdue. It is safe to assume he was a bright young man in school who showed a talent for engineering, and there was no better place for him to build a career than at the nearby university that was offering students amazing opportunities to work with engines of all types and sizes.

Martin's major interest at Purdue was the military. Along with many young men of his era, he joined the military club. He also was active in the Mechanical Engineering Society and won numerals for football his sophomore, junior, and senior years.

Beneath his picture in the *Debris* dressed in a coat, tie, and bowler hat: "This ungainly Hoosier, hailing from Liberty, became possessed with the idea that he must become a soldier in order to uphold the name of his native town. He has succeeded in becoming one of the shining lights of the Purdue Army, and this weighs mighty heavily upon his mind. He wears his uniform whenever the occasion offers so that everybody may know he has one. His intended occupation he says is 'to do others,' but from his appearance, it would seem that he would be rather easily done."[3]

Martin left Purdue and was commissioned in the Army Coast Artillery with the rank of second lieutenant. He was promoted to first lieutenant on March 11, 1911. In 1913, he graduated from the Coast Artillery School at Fort Monroe, Virginia. He was based in Washington, D.C., where he had the opportunity to meet important people.

Meanwhile, his classmate Cliff Turpin had attracted so much national attention between 1910 and 1912 that his fame could not have escaped Martin or any other member of the Purdue class of 1908. Perhaps Turpin's accomplishments sparked something in Martin. Whatever inspired him, he became caught up in the national aviation excitement that filled the nation before and during WWI.

On July 1, 1916, Martin became a major. In 1917, he transferred to the aviation section of the Signal Corps. During the war he spent time in Washington and in Europe with the Occupation Army dealing with supply matters.

In 1920, when the Army Air Service was created, Martin was assigned to it. He was trained as a bombardment pilot and received his wings at Kelly Field in San Antonio, Texas, in 1921. He became commanding officer of the Air Service Technical School at Chanute Field in Rantoul, Illinois, not far from his Liberty, Indiana, home and Purdue University. By 1924, Martin had seven hundred hours of flight experience.

It was from Chanute Field that he was named to command the around-the-world flight. Following the war, the idea of an around-the-world flight had been in the thoughts of many people interested in aviation and in testing its potential. Just as explorers had once dreamed of sailing around the world, now people were dreaming of conquering the world through the air.

The mission was openly discussed by U.S. military officers and in 1923, Major General Mason M. Patrick, who headed the Army Air Service, officially endorsed the idea. He also took his endorsement a step further and appointed a committee to study how it could be done.[4]

"General Patrick, a veteran ground officer who had learned to fly at age sixty, felt justified that such an unusual undertaking would give the Air Service valuable experience in long-distance flying as well as secure for the United States the honor of being the first country to encircle the world by air," Glines and Stan Cohen wrote in *The First Flight Around the World*.[5]

Obviously, among the most difficult parts of the project would be getting across the Pacific and Atlantic Oceans. They determined that this would be accomplished by flying north to Alaska and traveling along the Aleutians Islands to Japan. Coming back to the United States, the route across the Atlantic would be accomplished by flying to England; up to the Orkney Islands in northern Scotland; across to Iceland and Greenland; and finally traveling via Labrador, Canada, following the route of Vikings from another time.

The official starting point for the journey was Seattle. The trip would pass through Canada, Japan, China, India, the Middle East, and Europe in addition to Iceland and Greenland, with stops in some of the most exciting and exotic cities: Shanghai, Hong Kong, Saigon, Bangkok, Rangoon, Calcutta, Delhi, Karachi, Baghdad, Bucharest, Belgrade, Budapest, Vienna, Strasbourg, Paris, London, Boston, New York, and Washington, D.C.

But there were problems in addition to passing over lengthy corridors of ocean. Real challenges were posed by extremes in climate, the lack of proper landing fields, and the stresses that would be placed upon the airplanes and engines during the long effort. Since it was the biggest and the most comprehensive project ever attempted by the Air Service, it was also the most thoroughly planned. Many government agencies contributed in addition to the Army Air Service.

"The State Department had to exert extensive diplomatic effort to arrange for visas and over-flight permissions," Glines wrote. "The Navy, other Army branches, the U.S. Coast Guard, the Commerce Department, the Aeronautical Chamber of Commerce, and American companies located in other countries to be visited were asked to support the effort logistically and stand by for search-and-rescue assistance."[6]

Five airplanes would be built for the project. Four would make the trip to increase the odds that at least one would succeed.[7] The fifth airplane was a prototype used for testing and ultimately kept on standby as a back up in case it was needed.

The planes would be constructed according to Air Service specifications—biplanes with separate, open-air pilot and passenger compartments. The planes were to be equipped with interchangeable wheels and floats so they could land either on the ground or on water.

Donald Douglas, who built seaplanes in Santa Monica, California, was chosen to build the airships. Each plane would have an altimeter, a turn-and-bank indicator, a drift indicator, and a compass. But that was about it. They were not equipped with radios.[8] They were big planes for the day—50-foot wingspans, 35.5 feet long, more than 14 feet high.

The journey was divided into six segments with people put in charge of each individual section. The planes would make stops at sixty-eight different locations around the globe and advance teams were assigned to visit each one, making preparations that included finding spare parts that would certainly be needed along the way.

At forty-one years old, Martin was the oldest and highest-ranking pilot selected. He was also the tallest. The other pilots were Lt. Lowell Smith, thirty-one; Lt. Leigh Wade, twenty-seven; and Lt. Erik Nelson, who was born in Sweden; and Lt. Leslie Arnold, age twenty-nine.

The pilots picked their own mechanics from a field of candidates. Martin selected Sgt. Alva Harvey; Smith picked Sgt. Arthur Turner; Wade picked Sgt. Henry Ogden; and Nelson selected Lt. John Harding, Jr. It was later determined that Turner could not make the journey because of a lung condition, and he was replaced by Lt. Leslie Arnold.

In the winter of 1923–24, they trained in Santa Monica, California, and at Langley Field, Virginia. A U.S. War Department release issued March 9, 1924, explained the plans:

> The crossing of the Atlantic and Pacific Oceans will present the greatest difficulty to be encountered in the flight around the world. It is impractical to attempt either the flight across the Atlantic or the Pacific Oceans, except by way of Iceland and Greenland in the Atlantic and the Aleutian Islands in the Pacific. Long water flights are not considered practical with the present equipment and facilities available to carry out the intricate navigation problems that would attend such an undertaking. It is also felt that a successful flight over the present route would not only be a greater accomplishment, but would afford an opportunity to open up realms to aviation that heretofore remained closed.

> The preparation of the landing fields over the entire route for the flight round-the-world would be highly impractical, both from the standpoint of expense and from the standpoint of time available for this work. Therefore, it has been decided that the portion of the route from Seattle, Washington to Calcutta, India, will be flown in ships equipped for water landing, as will be that portion of the route from Brough, England to the United States. The rest of the flight will be covered in land planes.
>
> Since the successful accomplishment of this vast undertaking depends almost entirely upon weather conditions, the time of year chosen for the start and the schedule planned were based entirely upon the necessity of taking advantage of the most favorable flying conditions along the most hazardous and isolated sections of the route. Specifically, they needed to get through some before the start of the rainy season and wait to start until the snowstorms cleared in Alaska.[9]

The plan called for the four planes to leave Santa Monica on March 15 and proceed to the official starting point at Seattle. April 1 was the target day to start the around-the-world flight with a landing in Washington, D.C., expected on August 10.

The War Department release listed four purposes for the mission:

"1. To gain for the Air Service additional experience in long distance flying and particular in the supply problems connected therewith;

2. To demonstrate the feasibility of establishing an airway around the world;

3. To test existing flying equipment under the extremes of climate conditions;

4. To secure for the United States, the birthplace of aeronautics, the honor of being the first country to encircle the world entirely by air."[10]

They did not list a fifth reason, which was perhaps understood by everyone in 1924 without the need to spell it out. The mission would generate considerable excitement throughout the nation and world about the possibilities of flight that were still being explored in 1924. They also, of course, wanted to make sure that no one flew around the world before Americans.

The race was on.

Martin has been described as "devout, dignified, and diplomatic."[11] He was also the only pilot who was married, and he had a six-year-old son, Robert.

In a 1990 interview with the PBS documentary series American Experience, Robert Martin said he remembered the around-the-world flight very well. "I recall it as if it was yesterday," he said. "I opened the paper and there it was: 'Air Force to send men around the world.' It was a race against other countries and they named about four of them. It mentioned my father as being in command, and I got this feeling of terror, fright. I was frightened for him and for the whole idea of the race.

"They had no directional finding equipment, they had no radios, they had no way to contact anybody or anything—open cockpit planes. When you realize how primitive it was you think 'Good God, you mean they were going to go around the world in those conditions?' It was absurd."[12]

If the flight would be tremendously difficult, the preparations in California provided a great deal of fun. They were close to Hollywood, and the movie starlets of the day were eager to get their photos taken with the daring young pilots. There were dates out on the town. "Dad was trying to ride herd on those guys, and they were having the time of the lives," Robert Martin said.[13]

Three of the four planes left Santa Monica on March 17, only two days later than planned. Martin had immediate problems and had to make a forced landing short of the airport at Sacramento, the planned destination for overnight. Repairs were made to his plane and he completed the journey that same day. The fourth plane, flown by Nelson, took off from Santa Monica on March 18. By March 20, they were all in Seattle, the official starting point.

In Seattle at Sand Point, wheels were taken off the planes and replaced with pontoons. It was there that the planes were named for American cities—no doubt greatly increasing the interest in those communities. The planes became the *Chicago, Boston, New Orleans,* and Martin's lead plane was appropriately named the *Seattle.*

Weather was a problem right from the start. They hoped to take off on April 4, but weather to the north looked bad. On April 5, Martin tried to take off but had difficulty getting out of the water. When Martin was unable to get away, the other pilots decided against even trying.

Finally on April 6, the mission was underway with the *Seattle* flown by Martin taking the initial lead. Martin had decided, however, that he would not be the lead plane each day. That job would be alternated among the four pilots.

In their book, Glines and Cohen describe the immediate weather problems the flyers encountered. "The planes headed over Puget Sound and Georgia Strait where they ran into fog. They let down to water level and plunged ahead to Queen Charlotte Sound where it became increasingly difficult to estimate their altitude above the water because of the glassy surface. When they reached the open sea, the fog dissipated, but they ran into snow squalls and the seas beneath them turned rough. At Campania Islands, they avoided snowstorms as best they could as they followed the Napean Sound, then through the Ogden Channel to Prince Rupert, British Columbia. The wind increased as they neared the area, and rain and hail pelted them brutally in their open cockpits. They reached Prince Rupert in a blinding snowstorm and landed at 4:55 P.M. They had flown 650 miles in eight hours, ten minutes."[14]

It wasn't a whole lot of fun. Fog, snow, wind, rain. It was a terrible start. And it was going to get worse. "It wasn't hard to fly," Martin's mechanic Ala Harvey would later remember. "But sometimes you wondered what was right ahead of you."[15]

Martin had problems landing at Prince Rupert. His pontoons dug into the water and the wing struts were damaged.[16] The mayor of Prince Rupert greeted the world flyers by saying, "Gentlemen, you have arrived on the worst day we've had in ten years."[17]

Weather held them for several days in Prince Rupert. On April 10 they took off for their next destination, Sitka, Alaska, 282 miles away. They departed Sitka on April 13 and ran into more Alaskan April weather: snow squalls, as described by pilot Nelson. "We had to descend to the edge of the water and crawl along the beach to keep from getting lost. . . . The beach was covered with snow and the air around us filled with it. Everything was one color [white], and we might almost have been flying in total darkness. Sometimes we flew so low that our pontoons almost dragged the water. Most of the time I flew standing up in the cockpit, braced against the back of the seat with my feet on the rudder bar so that I could look out over the front of the plane as well as over the side."[18]

They landed at Seward, Alaska, and on April 15, departed for Chignik. Martin had trouble again. Several times he lagged behind. The other pilots thought he would catch up, but eventually he disappeared from their view. Martin later explained, "After being in the air four hours and thirty minutes, Sgt. Harvey called my attention to the fact that our oil pressure was at zero. This forced us to land with the least possible delay."[19]

When they landed in a sheltered inlet, Harvey discovered a hole in the engine crankcase. There was nothing to do but stay with the plane. It was a cold, long night, and Harvey eased his sleep with a few sips of whiskey. He offered the bottle to Martin who declined. "Dad said, 'that's a poor blanket for you Harvey,' but he didn't criticize him—none of that nonsense," Robert Martin said.[20]

The next morning the two men spotted two Navy destroyers and signaled for help. One of the ships took the plane, pilot, and mechanic to a nearby village. "Upon going ashore, we learned this was the first calm day in eight months," Martin said.[21] Had it not been calm, they wouldn't have survived.

They radioed for a new engine, which later arrived by Coast Guard cutter. Meanwhile, ahead of Martin, Harvey, and the *Seattle*, it was discovered the *Boston* also needed a new engine. There were more storms and winds of fifty to seventy miles per hour. The trip was not off to a good start. Harvey had to work all night in the snow using light from a lantern to change engines on the *Seattle*. He finished on April 25.

"But ice had formed around the plane's pontoons and had to be broken up into pieces and floated down the creek before the plane could be moved to the open water of the bay," according to Glines and Cohen.[22]

Martin was able to take off, despite the ice. Problems continued as they flew on. "Two hours and fifteen minutes passed, during which we were far too busy keeping out of trouble to watch the map," Martin said, "but instead of the storm being local, it seemed as though we were never going to get through into clear weather."[23]

Finally, they reached Chignik. By this time, the other three planes had gone ahead to the next stop at Dutch Harbor, some four hundred miles away. Martin and Harvey had to wait in Chignik until April 30 before the weather cleared enough for them to continue. The around-the-world flyers had been traveling for three weeks and three days. They hadn't gotten very far, and two engines had already been lost.

The weather report from Dutch Harbor was favorable on the early morning of April 30, so Martin and Harvey climbed into the *Seattle* and took off, encouraged they would soon be joining the rest of the crew.

They did not arrive. No one heard from them. Their whereabouts unknown, the first news reports of missing men went out on May 1. By the morning of May 2, the *New York Times* reported on page one, "Army World Flier Missing in Alaskan Hop; Boats Search Along Storm Swept Coast."

"The best hope held was that Major Martin and his mechanician, Sgt. Alva Harvey of Cleburne, Texas, had taken refuge in some cove on the desolate, rocky coast of the Alaskan Peninsula," the *Times* reported. "The North Pacific Ocean has been lashed by terrific gales, the wind frequently reaching a velocity of 100 miles per hour. The air . . . has been filled all day with snow blown from the mountainsides and neighboring peaks."[24] The reports continued to be grim.

On May 3, the *Times* reported, "The search for Major Frederick L. Martin, commander of the American world flight squadron, and his mechanician, Sgt. Alva Harvey, missing since [April 30] widened and intensified today as dispatches received here indicated their plane had not been seen since they left Chignik for Dutch Harbor. . . . Fears are expressed here that, although the men may have found a safe haven in one of the small coves in the islets along the coast of the peninsula, they may be suffering from hunger and exposure. . . . [The] likelihood that Major Martin turned the nose of his cruiser over the Aleutian range of mountains instead of taking the longer route of skirting the Alaskan peninsula caused searchers today to turn inland. . . ."[25]

Dog sled teams were sent out to search, but they came back each night reporting the only thing they had seen were other search parties. Meanwhile, the other three planes were prepared to continue the around-the-world flight. They had to keep on schedule to avoid additional severe weather problems, such as being trapped by more Alaskan spring snowstorms, as their mission continued.

A dispatch in the *Times* on May 3 addressed the future of the mission. "President Coolidge has no disposition to call off the world flight because of the apparent loss of Major Frederick Martin, commander of the expedition, it was stated today at the White House by a spokesman for the president.

"Much as the president would regret it if the intrepid aviator is not found, he feels that the attempt to circumnavigate the globe by air was not undertaken without considering the dangers encountered, and unless some insurmountable difficulty should be met, the president sees no reason why the flight should not be continued. In the president's opinion, the loss of one of the machines would not constitute such an insurmountable difficulty."[26]

Patrick, the Air Service officer who had authorized the mission, wired an order to pilot Lowell Smith, second-in-command to Martin. Patrick told Smith to proceed from Dutch Harbor as soon as the weather cleared. Patrick's cable was to the point with the telegram style that used the word "stop" to end a sentence. "Do not delay longer waiting for Major Martin to join you (stop) See everything done possible to find him (stop) Planes number two, three, and four to proceed to Japan at earliest possible moment."[27]

On May 3, the planes left Dutch Harbor and flew 365 miles to Atka Island, the next stop in the Aleutians.

The desperate search for Martin and Harvey continued. May 4. May 5. May 6. Dog sled teams raced across the snow-covered countryside. Ships sailed day and night, up and down the ragged coastline. Small launches each with several men on board were sent out to explore narrow inlets. At night, search lights shined on the coast as the ships slowly moved forward while crew members looked for signs of life.

They saw nothing. May 7 passed. May 8. On May 9, the three remaining world flyers left Atka Island and headed 530 miles for Attu Island. It was their last stop before a journey of nearly nine hundred miles that would take them to the other side of the world from early twentieth-century America.

When the flyers landed at Attu they immediately asked for information about Martin and Harvey. There was nothing new to say, and the grim search continued to grab headlines across the country. Martin's wife and their eight-year-old son, Robert, waited for news in San Diego. Mrs. Martin's sister in Los Angeles sent her a letter on May 9. She used the only address she knew. 'To Aviator Martin's wife, Mrs. Martin, San Diego, Calif." In the return address location on the envelope she wrote, "U.S. Mail Service, carry this letter as fast as possible through."[28]

It arrived.

On May 10, the three remaining flyers prepared to leave the North American continent as soon as their equipment was ready and as soon as the weather changed for the better. It was one of the most critical parts of the mission.

May 11 arrived with the weather in the Aleutian Islands finally clear. The three remaining pilots prepared to leave.

On that same day, a tiny coastal village named Port Moller, a boat with five people on board pulled away from the wharf. On a nearby snowy beach they saw two men standing near the waterfront. They motored through the ice floes to investigate.

"Martin and Aid [Harvey], World Flyers, Are Safe," screamed a headline on page one of the *New York Times*. "Miraculously escaping death after crashing against a mountain peak in a fog and completely wrecking the former flag plane the *Seattle*, one of four United States

Army globe-encircling air cruisers, Major Frederick L. Martin and his mechanic, Staff Sergeant Alva L. Harvey, were safe tonight at Port Moller, 100 miles west of Chignik.

"The two American aviators, who escaped unhurt from their splintered plane on the mountainside, were forced down one hour and a half after leaving Chignik for Dutch Harbor shortly before noon on April 30. Only nerve and concentrated food rations saved their lives."[29]

In San Diego, Martin's wife received the news with tremendous joy and relief. She said she would ask her husband for just one promise: never fly again.[30]

Martin sent a telegram to Patrick. "Crashed against mountain in fog. Thirtieth 12:30. Neither hurt. Ship total wreck. Existence due to concentrated food and nerve . . . Awaiting instructions here." Patrick immediately wired back. "We rejoice and thank God that you are both safe and well. Confidence in you unabated. You have proved yourself. Still want you to command flight. Cannot arrange for you to overtake others by going west. You and Sgt. Harvey will report here without delay. Plan to send you east to rejoin flight at the furthest convenient point from which you can complete the journey with the rest of your command."[31]

Now attention turned to reuniting the three flying teams with their lost commander and his mechanic. The May 13 *New York Times* said, "Major Frederick L. Martin, world flight commander, and Staff Sergeant Alva L. Harvey, his mechanic, who escaped unhurt after wrecking their plane in a collision with a mountain on the bleak Alaskan peninsula, have been ordered by Secretary Weeks of the War Department to report to Washington immediately.

"The War Department has decided to provide them with another airplane (the fifth Douglass World Cruiser), now at Langley Field, and will dispatch them eastward to rejoin the world flight at the furthest convenient point."[32]

It was a bold plan. The Army at first considered packing the plane and shipping it from New York to Constantinople, Turkey (Istanbul), but by using this plan, it would take more than 100 days before the plane and crew would be ready to fly again, and the schedule called for the other three pilots to be beyond Turkey within that period of time. They next considered shipping the plane to London and then to Brough, England, to meet the other flyers. Using this plan, the plane would be ready to fly in fifty-four days. This was the recommended course.[33]

The plan met with favorable public response. The *Times* said Martin would have "the honor of leading his comrades on the homeward journey."[34]

On May 16, the three other world flyers took off from their last base on the Aleutian Islands and successfully flew to Japan with a short stop along the way at a Russian-occupied island where they were welcomed with vodka and told to move on.

Meanwhile reports began to filter out about the incredible ten-day hike to safety by Martin and Harvey. Martin blamed the accident on mirages. The *Times* reported, "Mirages among the Aleutian Islands which he followed, not suspecting the dangers that lurked beyond the atmospheric illusions, were the chief factors contributing to the wreck of the flag plane *Seattle* on the rugged slopes of a bleak, unnamed elevation on April 30.

"Martin said his route from Chignik on the morning of April 30 was first altered when he encountered a mirage twenty minutes after departure. Subsequent mirages occurred at frequent intervals thereafter until, he said. About 12:30 in the afternoon, realizing that he had been misled by the phenomena, he swung his plane south in an effort to reach the Pacific Ocean and crashed against a mountain shrouded in fog at an elevation estimated at 1,500 feet."[35]

Martin later offered this explanation: "In trying to cross a portage, which was supposed to be low ground, we suddenly saw a mountain looming ahead. I knew this couldn't be right and, thinking that we might have veered a bit too sharply in leaving Chignik Lagoon, I turned, flew back, took my bearings again, and flew over a level stretch for a short distance. As we were now flying over land with pontoons instead of wheels, we were getting rather concerned. But blue water was visible to the westward, so we headed for it in an effort to reach the sea again with the least possible delay.

"Our ceiling now was about two hundred feet, but somehow that body of water never got any nearer. Instead, we were approaching fog. I was now strongly inclined to turn back to Chignik and start all over again by way of the original course. But, as we had come this far and the water seemed near, we kept on. The fog grew so dense that it drove us down within a few hundred feet of the ground. Still, we found no water. Feeling certain that we had left the mountains behind us, I thought it would be safest to climb over the fog, which I felt sure would only extend for a short distance."[36]

Martin had taken on two hundred gallons of gasoline and oil to make certain they had enough fuel for the flight. Now his precaution was causing problems. The plane was heavy and slow to rise as Martin tried to pull above the fog.

The mountain jumped into Martin's view as if it had emerged out of nowhere. He tried to swing the plane higher but with limited success. As he struggled to clear the mountain, he caught glimpses of bare patches where snow had blown away. The ground rose rapidly to meet them. It seemed to Martin only an instant passed before they crashed in a barren treeless stretch where the mountain formed a gentle slope. After skidding for two hundred feet, the plane lay in pieces.

"We struck with terrible force," Martin said. "The fact that the ship had started slightly upward at that moment is perhaps the one incident which saved us from death."[37]

Martin suffered slight injuries to his face. Harvey emerged without a scratch. Stunned, they surveyed the situation. It was desperate. In his book *Around the World in One Hundred and Seventy-Five Days,* Glines describes the wreckage. "The right pontoon was under the left side of the fuselage with the left pontoon nearby. The pontoon struts were completely crushed and torn loose from the fuselage. The lower right wing was completely demolished. The upper right wing was pulled back about halfway between its original position and the tail of the plane. . . . The propeller was broken."[38]

There would be no repairing this airplane for further flight. The *Seattle* was finished. Martin said, "Our despair was a terrible experience. Further participation in the around-the-world flight was at an end. We thoroughly appreciated our plight as we knew this part of the western peninsula to be uninhabited, excepting by a few people at considerable distance along the shoreline."[39]

It was as though "they were on the moon," Robert Martin said.[40] Martin and Harvey assessed the cold, realized the day was passing and that they had to find shelter—soon.

They made their best estimate about their location and started walking down. Martin would later write, "The fog was very dense and was so white as to blend completely with the snow. The snow was deep and smooth, leaving practically no objects visible. This experience was very peculiar as the vision was limited to a few feet. It was found to be impossible to walk in a straight line as our sense of balance seemed to be affected. It was necessary to stop frequently and check our course on the compass [which was very inaccurate]. Invariably, we found we were walking other than in the desired direction."[41]

Realizing they were about to become hopelessly lost and after three hours in the bitter cold and dense fog, they returned to their wrecked airplane. They built a fire out of the broken wings and pontoons. And they created an igloo windbreak from chunks of ice that they had removed from the side of the mountain. It was there that they spent the first night. There would be ten more nights.[42]

Martin was despondent over loss of his command and a chance at history. Harvey often had to encourage him to continue on. "Dad thought the world of Harvey," Robert Martin said. "He thought Harvey had the guts of a blind burglar."[43]

They stayed with the plane all of May 1. The only nourishment they had carried was four sandwiches, a dozen malted milk tablets, and two thermos bottles of liquid concentrated food. They ate the concentrated food a teaspoon full at a time.[44]

"On May 2, the fog was as bad as ever," Martin said. "We worked our way to a valley and followed a stream which we thought would take us to the Pacific Ocean. We followed the stream west after a futile attempt at scaling the mountain, and that night camped in an alder thicket. Sleep was impossible, the heat from the fire built of dead alder limbs being insufficient to keep out the cold.

"On the morning of May 3, we retraced our steps to the plane, following our tracks in the snow. It was still foggy. We reached the wreck after eight and a half hours of climbing. Harvey appeared to be suffering with his eyes, and I think I was becoming snow blind. Boric acid found in bags on the plane helped his eyes."[45]

Harvey said the fog was so thick, if they got ten feet apart, they couldn't see one another. They couldn't sleep. As they sat in the cold snow at night they could only doze occasionally. They became very weak, eventually only able to walk twenty or thirty steps without stopping to rest. "I think Major Martin was suffering remorse more than me," Harvey said. "He'd been given a most important command and he'd lost that. It was hard for him to fight on."[46]

At one point during the walk just several feet away from their path, the mountain dropped sharply and, had they slipped, they would have fallen 1,500 feet to their death.[47] Again, they camped by the wreckage.

On May 4, they decided to accomplish what they had tried to do in the airplane: get above the fog for a clear view of where they needed to go. The two men walked up the mountain for several hours and finally reached an elevation where the sky was clear. Using binoculars, they found a small lake and started walking down toward it. At a point they estimated to be three miles from the shore of the lake, they were overtaken by darkness and decided to spend the night, again, in an alder thicket. Fresh bear tracks made for light sleep.[48]

"The morning of May 5 we started for the lake again, reaching it about noon," Martin said. "By this time my own eyes were in bad shape and Harvey was leading, breaking trail. I followed him, guiding his course, occasionally with a compass. That night we camped in a canyon near the lake, where beds were made from wild grass and alder brush. We each slept for the first time, about four hours at intervals that night."[49]

On May 6, they tried to find a way down, but gave up and returned to the canyon campsite. The next morning, after experiencing a night of tremendous cold, they started out again. They were near the end of their strength, but May 7 would be a lucky day for them. In the wilderness of the Alaskan mountains they found a trapper's cabin and went inside, finding a note indicating the cabin belonged to a man named John S. Johnson. They also found flour, canned milk, and baking powder. They made flapjacks.

"This was our only real food," Martin said. "We stayed there for three days during which time a storm that had developed on May 7 raged outside in all the ferocity known to the north. Had that storm overtaken us before our arrival at Johnson's cabin, we would have perished."[50]

Rested with at least some nourishment, when the weather finally cleared on May 10, they left the security of the camp and hiked down the mountain, confident they would find something before long. They walked twenty miles before they saw the smoke stacks of the cannery at Moller Bay and realized they would live to tell their experience. "There is nothing I can say which would measure my appreciation of the men at Port Moller," Martin said.[51]

It was May 25 before Martin and Harvey finally returned by boat to Bellingham, Washington. That same day, the other three crews were being greeted in Tokyo. Martin and Harvey were far behind the flight schedule. For several days there was no public announcement about what would be done to reunite the rescued crew with the other flyers, but there must have been extensive debate behind the scenes within the Air Service.

Finally, on June 3, the announcement was made. Martin and Harvey would not rejoin the others. Lieutenant Lowell Smith had been placed in command of the world flight. In what was without question the hardest decision of his life, Martin had withdrawn from the mission in a letter to General Patrick that same day:

> *My Dear General Patrick,*
>
> *I am very grateful to you for your continued confidence in me and for your telling me of your willingness to have me resume my place as commander of the world flight. It was discussed with you, before we started, and it was agreed that if any of us had to fall out, the flight would nevertheless go on. The success of this great undertaking is the essential thing and not the wishes or desires of any of the fliers.*
>
> *It was my misfortune to meet with an accident and since then Lt. Smith has had to carry on. The responsibility for a perilous part of the journey has rested on him, and he has borne himself well.*
>
> *While there is nothing I should like better than to rejoin the flight and again take command, by that time a considerable part of it will have been accomplished without me.*
>
> *In fairness to Lt. Smith, who succeeded me in command, I think he should so continue and himself bring the flight back to the United States.*
>
> *I therefore request Lt. Smith be notified that from now on he will be in full charge. I wish him all success in his conduct of the remainder of the flight around the world and I hope to join in welcoming him and the other fliers when the flight is ended.*[52]

The other three flyers in the *Chicago*, the *New Orleans,* and the *Boston* airplanes continued their journey and were welcomed as heroes at every stop. There were many more difficulties and dangers, but all were overcome until August 3, when the *Boston* made an emergency landing in the Atlantic Ocean, just off the coast of Iceland. An oil pump had broken.

The pilot, Leigh Wade, made a skillful landing in the choppy waters and signaled to another of the planes overhead to continue on and report his location. There was no hope of taking off in the choppy Atlantic waters. Furthermore, the repairs to the plane could not be made at sea.

After a long wait during which waves further damaged the plane, ships pulled alongside. The pilot and mechanic were taken on board, and there were attempts to save the *Boston.* They failed. By August 4, waves had damaged the planed beyond repair, and it was cut loose to sink in the Atlantic. Now, only two planes were left.

General Patrick acted quickly. The fifth Douglas World Cruiser—the one that had originally been offered to Martin—was still at Langley Field, Virginia. Patrick ordered it to be flown to Pictou, Nova Scotia, where it would be picked up by the *Boston* crew and flown to the end of the mission in Seattle. The backup plane was named the *Boston II.*

The *Chicago* and the *New Orleans* arrived in Pictou Bay, returning to the North American continent on September 3. The rest of the journey to the finishing point in Seattle would be relatively easy and a celebration every step of the way.

Patrick himself got into an airplane and flew it to greet the three crews when they reached Boston on September 7. On September 9, President Coolidge greeted them in Washington, D.C. Fifty thousand people cheered them in Dayton, Ohio. Expensive gifts such as gold medallions and silver tea sets were presented to the flyers at each stop in the United States. In San Francisco, the mayor presented each with a check for $1,250.[53]

They finally landed, three abreast so the finish would be simultaneous, at Sand Point Field, Seattle at 1:28 P.M. on Sunday, September 28, 1924. Fifty thousand people were waiting and cheering. Among the first to greet them was Major Frederick Martin.

"All Seattle Sees World Flight End," read the blaring headline in the *Seattle Post Intelligencer* the next morning. "Major Martin in tears as he is cheered."[54]

The trip had taken 175 days. The planes actually flew for 371 hours, 11 minutes. The distance traveled was 26,345 miles. The flyers made seventy-two stops in twenty-eight countries. Martin and Harvey, along with the other pilots and crews, received the Distinguished Service Medal.

Celebrations continued through the year as the Army sent the three successful crews on a victory tour. When they returned to Dayton on their victory tour, they met with Orville Wright.

All the flyers went on to successful careers in the military or private industry.

The two planes that completed the mission are now in museums; the *New Orleans* is housed at the Museum of Flying in Santa Monica, and the *Chicago* resides at the Smithsonian Air and Space Museum in Washington, D.C. The *Boston II* was scrapped in 1932. The *Boston I* remains at the bottom of the Atlantic. The wreck of the *Seattle* was still at the crash site until the 1960s. Parts were then removed to the Aviation Heritage Museum on Lake Hood, Anchorage, Alaska.[55]

There can be no question about the impact the crash had on Martin. He was deeply disappointed in his inability to complete the mission he had first commanded.

"My hopes and opportunities of a lifetime wrecked among the crags in the Aleutian Islands," he said.[56] It certainly felt that way to him in 1924. But before he retired, he would be a general, and on one more occasion, his life would directly intersect with world events and the history of flight. Martin's next appointment with destiny would be on December 7, 1941, in Honolulu, Hawaii.

Richard Covey

Richard Covey was born twenty-two years after Frederick L. Martin took off from Seattle in command of the around-the-world flight. And though Martin was born before the Wright brothers flew, Covey was born with a love for flight that has stayed with him all his life.

"I'm the son of a fighter pilot," he says. "My father flew P-47s and P-51s in the Pacific during World War II and the F-86 in Korea. I grew up with military aviation. That went very well with my interests, which were science and math. And when Alan Shepherd first flew into space, I was fascinated with the idea of men flying on rockets. I learned everything I could, mostly through *Life* magazine."

It didn't take him long to determine what it took to become an astronaut: you needed to be a military test pilot. And it didn't take him long to determine the best route to achieve that: the U.S. Air Force Academy.

"I went to the Air Force Academy, with the intent of being a career military pilot and officer, but also with the idea that I could leverage that into being a test pilot and/or an astronaut," Covey says.

Before he even arrived at the Academy, a friend of his father's visited the Covey family at their home in Fort Walton Beach, Florida. The friend was a professor of mathematics at the Academy. He told Covey to point his objectives toward the Academy's astronautical engineering program that included a direct tie-in to a master's degree at Purdue University.

"He said, 'Dick, this is the program that you need to get into and work for because it's absolutely a fantastic program to achieve your objectives and to challenge you,'" Covey says. "Even as a seventeen-year-old, I saw the beauty of being able to get my degree at the Academy and also be able to take graduate-level courses that were accepted by Purdue toward a master's degree."

He took that route. He graduated from the Academy in 1968, was accepted into the highly competitive Purdue program, and earned his master's degree in aeronautics and astronautics in seven months. He then entered U.S. Air Force flight training.

"My objective was to get into test pilot school as a fighter test pilot, so I had to do everything I could to get into fighter aircraft," Covey says. "I was fortunate enough to be able to do that. That also meant that I was going to go to Vietnam, because anybody that went into fighter aircraft in the early 1970s was going to Vietnam."

He served a total of eighteen months in Vietnam and flew 339 combat missions. His career stayed on path. In 1974, he was accepted into test pilot school and graduated in 1975 at the young age of twenty-nine.

He was on a fast track. In 1978, when NASA took a new class of thirty-five astronauts selected specifically to fly the space shuttle, he was in the group. That class doubled the size of the astronaut office.

Covey was pilot on STS-51 in 1985. In 1988, he was pilot on STS-26, the first launch after the *Challenger* accident.

"Each of my missions really was unique for a different reason," Covey says. "Clearly the one that people most remember and recognize is the first flight after *Challenger*. That was important to bring the shuttle back to flight. You know, a lot of people don't even remember what our payload was. But they remember the crew, and they focused on the crew."

He was commander on STS-38 in 1990 and STS-61 in 1993.

"On the last one, we repaired the Hubble Space Telescope," Covey says. "That clearly had national importance and historical significance. Remarkable science has resulted from that. I just continue to be amazed at what we learn from that one telescope. The capabilities of the telescope have continued to be improved, and its life sustained because of the fact that it was designed to be serviced by astronauts on the space shuttle."

After the Hubble mission, he retired from NASA and the Air Force. He now works for Boeing.

In 2003, he was asked by NASA to cochair a Return to Flight Task Force, following the *Columbia* accident.

"We will provide an external, independent assessment of NASA's implementation of the recommendations that are expected to come from the 'Columbia Accident Investigation Report,'" Covey says.

After the shuttle is flying again, he'd like to see a stronger commitment to space exploration.

"I think the challenge for our nation, for NASA, and maybe internationally is to find a path back to what I call real exploration, which is returning to the Moon, trying to get to Mars," Covey says. "There are a lot of challenges in doing that—not only technically but also financially. We have to find a way to do that."

He loved his years in the space program.

"I like to tell people I'm a smoke and fire guy," Covey says. "You know, I got in this space business because I wanted to ride rockets, and I wanted to bring spacecraft back through fiery re-entries and land them. The shuttle was the right means for me to accomplish that."

Chapter Six

There was a deeper reason for wanting to jump, a desire I could not explain. It was that quality that led me into aviation in the first place—it was a love of the air and sky and flying, the lure of adventure, the appreciation of beauty.

—Charles Lindbergh

Falling from a height of five thousand feet over rural Texas, Charles McAllister felt a jolt when his parachute opened.

He looked above him and saw the white silk canopy billowing as he drifted toward earth. It was a good feeling as he gripped the taught parachute straps with both his hands. Somehow, holding on made him feel better.

In the distance he could see the other pilot—a tall, lanky man floating toward the ground, still a little higher in the air. The other pilot's parachute was also fully opened. Everything was going to be fine.

When the two planes had collided in midair moments earlier, McAllister had been the first to jump. He didn't jump out of fear. He jumped out of experience, out of an instinct that instantly told him his airplane was finished, that he was going down either fast or slow, and that slow was better.

It was March 6, 1925. McAllister would never forget that day. Neither would the other pilot. As they drifted over thick fields of mesquite, McAllister was relieved when he realized that the light wind was blowing them toward an open farm field where the landing would be relatively easy.

The parachutes they were using had only been invented six years earlier, and some newspaper accounts would claim this was the first time two pilots from two planes had both parachuted after a midair collision—and both survived. Maybe those reports were true, but records like that hardly mattered to McAllister as his feet hit the ground and his body fell into the soft dirt. He was just glad to be alive.

An officer in the Army Air Service, McAllister quickly found the other parachute jumper, a cadet by the name of Charles—Charles Lindbergh—whom he forever blamed for the accident.

Seventy years later, McAllister was asked what Lindbergh said when the two men first got together once they were safely on the ground. "He didn't say anything," McAllister said. "I did all the talking."[1]

Among Lindbergh's many nicknames, they called him "Lucky Lindy." While Lindbergh rightly believed that his success as a pilot was due more to careful planning and skillful flying than to luck, he was certainly very lucky to have survived that March day in 1925.

Twenty-six months after crashing in midair with Purdue graduate McAllister, Lindbergh would become an overnight international hero and part of the history of aviation after completing the first solo, nonstop flight across the Atlantic Ocean.

Charles McAllister was born in Logansport, Indiana, in 1895. His life changed at the age of fourteen when he saw his first airplane. Eighty-six years later, he could still vividly recall that experience. He lived to be 101, an age when some memories fade but not the important ones. He never forgot the details about the day he saw his first flying machine. And he never forgot how he felt seeing it floating low in the sky.

He said, "The sun was just going down behind a slow rise in the west—a big red sun sitting on the horizon."As he watched the Indiana sunset, he saw a pilot take his airplane just barely above the flat fields of corn.

"He went just over the horizon, right into that setting sun," McAllister said.[2]

McAllister pursed that vision all this life. Upon graduation from high school in 1914, McAllister headed north and enrolled at Purdue University where he studied electrical engineering. His education was cut short when the United States entered the World War I. He enlisted in the Army and soon found himself stationed in England.

By the outbreak of World War I, Purdue had already established a flight tradition through men such as Cliff Turpin and Jimmie Johnson, men who were trailblazing the new exciting possibilities of aviation. If McAllister was disappointed that he didn't get into pilot training during the war, he never expressed it. He only said that flying at that time was very dangerous, the planes not well constructed, and the men not well trained. Many World War I pilots did not survive the war.[3]

At the end of the war, McAllister returned to Purdue and graduated in 1920. He spent the next several years trying to find his place in the world. For a time he worked for General Electric in Detroit. He was laid off during an economic downturn, and in 1921, he moved to Winter Garden, Florida, to take a job supervising the production line at a citrus packing plant. It was not where he wanted to be, but events that would impact his life had been swirling all around him.

In 1918, an Army air base named Brooks Field was established as a satellite to Kelly Field in San Antonio, Texas. Brooks became a primary flying school with more advanced training taking place at Kelly. Then in 1919, one of the most significant events in the history of aviation took place.

At McCook Field in Dayton, Ohio, on April 28, 1919, Leslie L. Irvin tested a new parachute designed by Major E. C. Hoffman of the U.S. Air Force Engineering Division. It used a short freefall and a ripcord. Purdue graduates Jimmie Johnson and George W. Haskins were both working at McCook at this time. Irvin broke his ankle when he landed, but he didn't care. "I would have been all right if everyone around me had not acted as though they were going to be my pallbearers," he reportedly said.[4]

Irvin established a company to produce the parachutes, and during the 1920s and 1930s, virtually every pilot who jumped from an airplane used equipment that bore his name.

The first pilot whose life was saved by an Irvin parachute was Lt. Harold R. Harris of McCook Field. In 1922, he successfully jumped from his disabled airplane. Realizing that many more would join Harris, it was decided a club made up of people whose lives were saved by parachutes was needed. It was called the Caterpillar Club, "symbolic of the silk worm which lets itself descend gently to earth from heights by spinning a silk thread upon which to hang."[5] Parachutes in the early days were made from pure silk. In 1922, Irvin started giving gold pins to every person who gained entry into the Caterpillar Club. Lindbergh and McAllister joined the still very select membership that March day in 1925.

Dissatisfied with his work at the packing plant in Winter Garden and having never forgotten a love for flight, McAllister rejoined the military and applied for the Air Service. He was sent to San Antonio, first to Brooks Field and then to Kelly and received his wings at Kelly Field in 1924. His life was in the sky, and he never would come down again.

Meanwhile, Lindbergh was also searching for his place in life. He had entered the University of Wisconsin at Madison in the fall of 1920—the same year McAllister graduated from Purdue.

But Lindbergh, too, had seen an airplane fly, and his life was never the same. In February 1922, just short of his twentieth birthday, Lindbergh dropped out of school with a single goal: flight. He opted for lessons through the Nebraska Aircraft Corporation in Lincoln, Nebraska. On April 9, 1922, he had his first flight as a passenger and his lessons soon followed.

In June 1922 in Lincoln, Lindbergh met Lt. Charles Hardin, a parachute maker who gave demonstrations to sell his product. Lindbergh had to try it. Here is Lindbergh's description of his first jump:

"When I decided that I too must pass through the experience of a parachute jump, life rose to a higher level, to a sort of exhilarated calmness. The thought of crawling out onto the struts and wires hundreds of feet above the earth, and then giving up even that tenuous hold of safety and of substance, left me a feeling of anticipation mixed with dread, of confidence restrained by caution, of courage salted through with fear. How tightly should one hold onto life? How loosely give it rein? What gain was there for such a risk? I would have to pay in money for hurling my body into space. There would be no crowd to watch and applaud my landing. Nor was there any scientific objective to be gained. No, there was deeper reason for wanting to jump, a desire I could not explain. It was that quality that led me into aviation in the first place—it was a love of the air and sky and flying, the lure of adventure, the appreciation of beauty."[6]

In his book *Lindbergh*, author A. Scott Berg tells a more harrowing story. "He asked Hardin for instruction, but not in the basic parachute jump. For his first exit from a plane in flight, Lindbergh wanted to try what was known as a 'double jump' in which one chute opens and is discarded, making way for a second one to deliver the jumper to the ground. One June evening against a clear sky, Lindbergh made a leap from 1,800 feet and the first chute opened perfectly. After a few seconds he cut it lose and waited for the second to open. But several seconds passed and he did not feel the tug that should have followed. Because he had never made such a descent before, Lindbergh had no idea that everything was not right until he began to fall headfirst. Another long moment later, the parachute at last blossomed, carrying him safely to earth. For the rest of this life, Lindbergh remembered feeling no panic over what might have happened to him, only how soundly he slept that night."[7]

By 1924, Lindbergh enlisted in the Army to receive flight training. That March he was assigned to Brooks Field in San Antonio and in the fall reported for advanced training to Kelly where McAllister was stationed.

It was a dangerous business. In February 1925, two cadets crashed and burned at Brooks Field. Eight months earlier, a pilot had been killed when two planes collided over Kelly—a situation similar to what would happen to McAllister and Lindbergh.

On March 6, 1925, Lindbergh was eight days away from graduation from Advanced Flight School. On that day, he and McAllister were assigned to a mission at five thousand feet. Three groups had been formed, each made up of three planes flying in a V formation. Lindbergh was flying the left position. McAllister, an officer who already had his wings, was in the right position. They were flying SE-5 planes, and their mock enemy was a plane flying below, a DH-4B.

When the mock attack began, Lindbergh dropped down from the left and McAllister from the right. Their planes collided and locked together. In his official report, Lindbergh wrote, "I passed above the DH and a moment later felt a slight jolt, followed by a crash. . . .

"I closed the throttle and saw an SE-5 with Lieutenant McAllister in the cockpit a few feet away on my left. He was apparently unhurt and getting ready to jump.

"Our ships were locked together with the fuselages approximately parallel. I removed the belt, climbed out to the trailing edge of the damaged wing—the ship was then in a nearly vertical position—and jumped backward from the ship as far as possible.

"I had no difficulty in operating the pull ring and experienced no sensation of falling. The wreckage was falling nearly straight down and for some time I fell in line with its path. Fearing the wreckage might fall on me, I did not pull the ripcord until I had dropped several hundred feet and into the clouds.

"During this time I had turned one half revolution and was falling flat and face downward. The parachute functioned perfectly; almost as soon as I pulled the ripcord and the risers jerked on my shoulders, the leg straps tightened, my head went down, and the chute was fully opened. . . .

"Next I turned my attention to locating a landing place. I was over mesquite and drifting in the general direction of a plowed field, which I reached by slipping the chute. Shortly before striking the ground I was drifting backwards, but was able to swing around in the harness just as

I landed on the side of a ditch less than 100 feet from the edge of the mesquite. Although the impact of the landing was too great for me to remain standing, I was not injured. The parachute was still held open by the wind and did not collapse until I pulled on one group of the shroud lines."[8] There is a saying about parachutes that Lindbergh knew quite well. It says, "If you need a parachute and haven't got it, you'll never need it again."

On March 14, Lindbergh graduated and was commissioned a second lieutenant in the Air Service Reserve Corps. Only nineteen cadets out of the original group of 104 that had started at Brooks made it.[9]

The following November, Lindbergh enlisted in the Missouri National Guard and he began flying the U.S. mail under contract in April 1926.

McAllister married in 1926 and remained in the military, spending time at several bases including Wheeler Field in Honolulu. By 1930, he was back on the mainland, this time in Dayton, Ohio, where he used his electrical engineering background to help design landing lights. From Dayton he was transferred to Maxwell Field in Montgomery, Alabama—the very location Wilbur Wright had founded for his early flying school.

At Maxwell, McAllister was selected for one of the world's first military precision flying groups called the Skylarks. It was a predecessor of groups such as the Blue Angels and the Thunderbirds.

The nation's first military aerobatic flying team was the Three Musketeers, which represented the First Pursuit Group at the 1928 National Air Races. In 1932, Captain Claire Chennault, who would later command the Flying Tigers in World War I, formed a group at Maxwell called the Flying Trapezers or Men on the Flying Trapeze.[10]

According to the official Maxwell base history, "He used a simple method to choose the team. Anyone who could fly with him in his P-12 for thirty minutes of head-spinning acrobatics would be selected. Only three were successful. By the time the aerial team disbanded in 1936, it had appeared in about fifty air shows and performed to the delight of an estimated audience of 50,000 people."[11]

Two other pre–World War II Army aerobatic teams were the Three Mugs of Beer and the Skylarks. The Skylarks aerial demonstration team was formed at Maxwell in 1935 and is described by the Maxwell base history. "Instructed by Chennault, the Skylarks performed many of the same stunts made popular by their predecessors; tight formation flying, loops in formation, barrel rolls, spins . . . the double formation roll, the inverted flight formation, and the snap roll from the top of a loop were all Skylark originals."[12] Captain McAllister was the leader of the Skylarks and the other pilots were Lt. Carl D. Storrie, Lt. Clayton E. Hughes, and Lt. Wilbur W. Airing.

In 1942, after the start of World War II, McAllister was assigned to Albuquerque, New Mexico, where he ran the B-24 flight-training program.

Although Lindbergh had publicly campaigned to keep America out of the war, once Pearl Harbor was attacked he helped the Allied effort in every way he could. In 1942, Henry Ford was preparing to build a B-24 bomber factory in Detroit, and he recruited Lindbergh to help him.

Lindbergh traveled extensively doing research including a trip to Albuquerque where he met with McAllister to learn more about the B-24. In a 1995 interview with the *Orange County (Florida) Register,* McAllister said, "He [Lindbergh] had matured a lot." He said Lindberg had little time for pleasantries, and they did not discuss their accident. "He was a non-drinker, a very naïve sort of fellow," McAllister said. "There were a lot of things he wasn't interested in and didn't want to learn."[13]

In *The Wartime Journals of Charles A. Lindbergh,* published in 1970, Lindbergh noted the meeting. "Breakfast with Colonel McAllister at 7:30 A.M. I received a note of invitation from him when I arrived at the hotel last night. McAllister and I collided our SE-5's while we were attacking an observation plane during maneuvers at Kelly Field in 1925. We both had to jump but landed without injury. McAllister, who was a student officer at the time, was a bit stuffy about it and claimed I ran into him. I didn't think so and thought he was out of place in the three-ship formation we were flying. However, it hadn't occurred to me to question who was at fault. We had been doing a dangerous type of flying, and our . . . instructors took it as a matter of course.

"Since I was a cadet in 1925 and McAllister an officer, I had no opportunity of getting to know him well, but this morning I found him to be an interesting and pleasant friend. If he ever held any resentment toward me, as I was told was the case, there was certainly no trace of it remaining. And all during the day he went out of his way to be as considerate and helpful as possible."[14]

McAllister served as a B-24 wing commander in Africa, Sicily, and Italy during the war. He also flew the P-47. He retired from the military in 1948 but continued to fly. He bought a single engine Beachcraft Bonanza and even flew it to South America in 1960.

The last time Lindbergh and McAllister got together was in April 1954. McAllister was retired in Florida, and Lindbergh visited Orlando on a tour to inspect potential sites for the new Air Force Academy. McAllister was asked to assist his home community of Orlando because of the relationship he had with Lindbergh, but competition for the Academy was intense and the winner was Colorado.

Beginning as a young man and continuing through his life, Lindbergh advanced aviation on a path it continues today. He died in 1974 at the age of seventy-two.

McAllister died in 1997 at the age of 101.

"He was very confident. He was an optimist," says his daughter, Jean Elrod. "I think every pilot has to be an optimist. Otherwise, they wouldn't go up. He always tried to look on the good side of everything. He always tried to see things from a positive perspective."[15]

In spite of a lifetime of flying, McAllister, one of the first members of the Caterpillar Club, never again had to parachute out of an airplane after the March 6, 1925, accident.

Lindbergh had to parachute to save his life three more times. On June 2, 1925, while doing a test flight for the Robertson Aircraft Corporation in St. Louis, Lindbergh's plane spun out of control and fell to earth, twisting and turning all the way. Lindbergh jumped in the last minute, the plane nearly hit him, and he had to take evasive measures to keep from landing on high-tension wires.

On September 16, 1926, he made his third emergency jump on a mail run when his engine died at five thousand feet in a blinding storm of snow and rain.

His fourth emergency jump occurred on November 3, 1926, just six months before his trans-Atlantic flight. Again on a mail run, again in snow and rain, his plane ran out of fuel. Realizing what was about to take place before his fuel was completely spent, Lindbergh took his plane higher to accommodate a safer jump. He landed on barbed wire.

When he took off for Paris on May 20, 1927, the *Spirit of St. Louis* carried 451 gallons of gasoline that weighed 2,750 pounds. He carried 140 pounds of oil. Lindbergh himself weighed 170 pounds and he had forty miscellaneous pounds on board. The empty plane's basic weight was another 2,150 pounds.[16]

Everything had been weighed and calculated to precision for the dangerous flight. Some items, including his radio, were left behind to save weight and space and because Lindbergh thought they would not help him accomplish his goal. He left another item behind at Roosevelt Airfield in New York state: his parachute.

Roy Bridges Jr.

"10 . . . 9 . . . 8 . . ."

Roy Bridges was strapped to the pilot's seat in the Space Shuttle *Challenger.* To his left was Commander Gordon Fullerton. Five other astronauts were placed behind them and on the level below.

The sky was clear and systems were "go." Bridges had been an astronaut for five years—five years of hard work and waiting leading up to this moment. It was really more like a lifetime—a lifetime working and waiting.

"7 . . . 6 . . . 5 . . ."

Bridges monitored the controls in front of him and listened to the countdown for STS-51-F as the shuttle's three main engines began to burn as planned. His heart rate accelerated. His concentration focused. His body prepared for launch.

"4 . . . 3 . . . We have main engine shutdown."

The shuttle attached to its booster and rockets swayed back and forth. Looking out the window, it appeared to him that they were standing still and the tower was swaying. Five years of waiting. Five years of work.

There would be no launch today.

Roy Bridges was born in Atlanta, Georgia, in 1943, long before the space age, only sixteen years after Charles Lindbergh flew the Atlantic. Bridges's father served in the Army Air Corps during World War II. And years after the war, an uncle was an engineer working on the B-58, a supersonic Air Force plane, part of the Strategic Air Command. It could carry a single nuclear weapon.

"When I was in the seventh grade, I visited my uncle in Texas, and I saw the plane," Bridges says. "I was thrilled. It was quite impressive. I was very intrigued."

His uncle graduated from Georgia Institute of Technology, and Bridges planned to follow in those footsteps until he read an article about the new U.S. Air Force Academy in Colorado. He decided the Academy was the place for him.

The year he finished high school, Alan Shepard and Virgil "Gus" Grissom launched into space. President John F. Kennedy made a speech at Rice University: "I believe this nation should commit itself to achieving the goal, before this decade is out, of landing a man on the Moon and returning him safely to Earth."

Bridges left for the U.S. Air Force Academy with the immediate ambition of becoming a pilot and test pilot, but with thoughts of space firmly planted in his dreams.

He studied aeronautical and astronautical engineering at the Academy during the Mercury and Gemini space programs. “It was a very exciting time,” Bridges says. “I followed very closely what was taking place. I really wanted to be an explorer. This was very intriguing. I felt very blessed to be alive at this time. I was at the Air Force Academy, learning to fly. All of the astronauts were being taken from the corps of test pilots. I kept my eye on the possibility of doing this. It was very much a long shot. But I kept my eye on the astronaut program.”

He was accepted into the master’s degree program that had been set up for Air Force Academy graduates at Purdue University.

“Purdue is a great engineering school,” Bridges says. “They had great professors who were interested in the space program and everything that was going on. They gave us sound guidance about how to conduct ourselves in life so that we could be successful individuals. I found that Purdue has always been a good family. It’s more than a school where you just go, pay some money, learn something, and get a diploma. To me Purdue has always been a lot more than that.”

He met his wife, Benita, at Purdue. That event changed his life for the better. They remain happily married and have two grown children and two grandchildren.

From Purdue, Bridges went to Williams Air Force Base for pilot training and arrived in Vietnam for his one-year tour of duty in January 1968. He flew 226 missions in an F-100.

When he returned to the United States in 1969, he was sent to Oklahoma to train pilots. That’s where he was when Neil Armstrong landed on the Moon.

“I had just arrived at Manns Air Force Base to be an instructor,” Bridges says. “We had no furniture in our house. We did not even own a TV at the time because I’d been over in Vietnam. So I went out and rented a black-and-white TV. I actually constructed an antenna. We were eighty miles from Oklahoma City, and this was in the days before cable. So I had wires and everything hanging out on the trees in the back yard just to get a fuzzy picture of Neil Armstrong stepping out on the Moon. After that, we bought a TV. Right after that, I told my wife, ‘I can’t miss this. You know, I want to watch every one of these lunar landings.’”

He applied for test pilot training and was accepted. In 1978, when NASA announced it would name a new class of astronauts, Bridges applied. He was given an interview. It went well, but he didn't make it.

"It was a big disappointment," he says. "But less than 1 percent of the people who applied got selected."

Two years later, NASA was ready for another class. This time he made it. "I was thrilled," he says. "It was my dream come true." He reported to Houston in July of 1980 and his training began.

On July 12, 1985, he was strapped in at the Kennedy Space Center, listening to the countdown reach the final seconds. It was Benita Bridges's birthday. It was exactly one week before Bridges's forty-second birthday.

"We got to 2.8 seconds before liftoff," Bridges says. "After the engines had started, they all shut down. That's not something you want to have happen. It was a great disappointment. We were ready to go fly. And to get that close to flying and then have it abort, was a great disappointment."

They tried again on July 29. This time the shuttle lifted off the launch pad and Bridges felt himself forced back into his seat. He saw the blue sky turn back and watched readings on the instruments before him. They had an eight and half minute flight to reach orbit. At five minutes and forty-five seconds, a main engine failed. It was the first time that had happened. It has never happened since.

Bridges likes to tell people if the engine had stopped thirty seconds sooner, they would have set a trans–Atlantic Ocean flight record. They would have been forced to make an emergency landing in Spain about thirty-seven minutes after liftoff from Florida. Instead, they were able to do an "abort to orbit," which saved the mission.

"We were very fortunate," Bridges says.

Life is different on the shuttle. Bridges's bed was on the "floor" of a rack of bunks. But his sleeping bag was actually tied to the ceiling of that bunk. Because of weightlessness, the up and down orientation didn't really matter.

"You don't need quite as much sleep up there," Bridges says. "I need seven hours down here, but I was feeling pretty rested with four or five hours up there."

The landing is very busy, Bridges says. It's like a ballet with the tempo getting faster and faster.

"You start out by burning your engines about halfway around the world, and it's going to take you about an hour from the engine burn until touch down. So we burned our engines over Africa. We hit about 400,000 feet somewhere over Guam, and then we landed in California at Edwards, where I had been a test pilot. As you begin to slow down, things happen faster and faster. Time seems to compress as the rate of deceleration increases. The G-forces build up again. And then all of a sudden you're over the west coast of California. We were coming right down the Harbor Freeway at about Mach 3. And then we were over Edwards and making our turn for the landing. It all builds up into quite a crescendo of activity."

After the Shuttle *Challenger* was lost, the Air Force reassigned Bridges to commander of the 6510th Test Wing at Edwards Air Force Base. Later, he was the commander of Patrick Air Force Base in Florida, and then commander of the Air Force Flight Test Center at Edwards Air Force Base in California. He retired from the Air Force in 1996 as a major general. In 1997, he was named director of the Kennedy Space Center. And in 2003, he was named director of NASA's Langley Research Center.

"Being in space made me more optimistic," Bridges says. "I think you always have to be an optimist to be an explorer. And I think it's a great philosophy for life. I certainly could not conceive of having done what I've been able to do if I were not an optimist. Being in space and seeing more of this magnificent universe that God created for us to explore is just awesome. It's inspirational, and it makes you want to get up in the morning and go out and see what else you can find out there that might help us out on Earth even more. Space has changed my thinking.

"It has reinforced my basic philosophy of life and helps me get a lot of joy out of living."

Chapter Seven

In the 1930s, if the insurance companies found out someone was going to fly in an airplane, they would threaten to cancel the policy. That was a handicap we had to overcome in the airlines.

—Ralph Johnson

It was an exciting time and Ralph Johnson remembers it all with hearty laughs and a gusto never lost for a job he still loves. It was a great time to be young. It was a great time to be flying airplanes in an industry that was just getting off the ground and held so much promise for those visionary enough to see the future.

The 1930s were Depression years, but they were also the years when commercial airlines were emerging in the United States to carry passengers from Detroit to Chicago or San Francisco to New York. Doors were opening and dreams were coming true.

Charles Lindbergh's solo flight across the Atlantic had impacted the entire world and the potential for airplanes was growing each day as people actually came to believe they could travel by air and reach their destination safely and quickly.

Lindbergh's world-shaking flight had been in 1927. Only 5,800 passengers flew in 1926. Four years later the number was 417,000.[1]

One of the first airline services in the nation had started in 1914 when Thomas Benoist transported people from St. Petersburg, Florida, to nearby Tampa. The two communities were separated by Tampa Bay and people were forced to commute by train or travel on a once-a-day boat. Benoist's airline offered an alternative and it flourished during the winter tourist season but went out of business with the arrival of spring.[2]

In 1913, Silas Christofferson is reported to have carried passengers from San Francisco to Oakland, and in 1920, Aeromarine Airways began international flight service between Cuba and Miami. It was soon extended to include a destination in the Bahamas and connections to Cleveland and Detroit. More than two thousand flights were completed carrying almost ten thousand people, but a crash off the coast of Florida in 1924 killed four people and destroyed Aeromarine Airways.[3]

Since 1910, aeroplanes had excited the public during air shows from coast to coast. Aviation had shown enormous potential during the World War I, but with railroads crisscrossing the country offering people convenient, fast, economical transportation from city center to city center, there was little need for anyone to travel by air in the days immediately before and after the war.

This was the world Ralph Johnson was born into. Ultimately, with a Purdue University engineering degree, Johnson would help to reshape the thinking of this nation, and the world, as airlines grew into a major industry in the twentieth century.

Johnson was born on a Goodland, Indiana, farm in 1906 just three years after the Wright brothers' first flight at Kitty Hawk.

"My dad was a farmer," Johnson says. "When I was growing up there was only one time that I remember when we even saw an airplane. My family learned that there was a pilot at George Ade's property in Brook. . . . My father loaded up all us kids and took us over to Brook, which wasn't far, to watch that airplane."[4]

They didn't fly. There was a charge for rides and Johnson lived in a family that had ten children—too many fares for one farmer to pay.

"The pilot was a lady, and that really surprised me," Johnson says. "Her name was Ruth Laws. We thought what she was doing was quite interesting. Of course at that time, we didn't know much about airplanes. Automobiles interested us much more."[5]

If there weren't any planes in Goodland in the days before, during, and after World War I, there weren't that many automobiles, either. The number of cars was growing quickly, and Johnson had a natural born love for motors that led him to learn for himself how internal combustion engines worked. He eventually set up his own mechanic business.

In 1924, Johnson put enough money together to enter nearby Purdue University. He took jobs on campus to pay his room, board, and tuition and also took a lengthy time off from his studies and worked full time to earn more money, so he could go back and work on his dreams. Johnson had enrolled in an aeronautical engineering program that had only started at Purdue during the 1921–22 academic year. It was part of the School of Mechanical Engineering. In 1930, Johnson was among the university's—and the nation's—first aeronautical engineering graduates.

He was lured into the exciting new field by the opportunity to work on airplane engines and by the potential he could see for aviation. If this was going to be a new industry, he wanted to be part of everything that was going to take place.

"Really, Purdue's aeronautical engineering program at that time was very minimal," Johnson says. "I guess I just had a curiosity about airplanes. And we got a chance to design crankshafts and that sort of thing."[6]

Johnson was on campus in 1929 when George Haskins arrived to take over the program and began to build and move it forward rapidly.

"Haskins was a very nice person," Johnson says. "He taught the courses himself, but in those days I think he was kind of wondering himself where aviation was going."[7]

In addition to his engineering studies, Johnson took part in the university's military training program.

He graduated in 1930 during one of the hardest economic times of the twentieth century. The stock market had crashed in the fall of 1929, and by the following June, the Great Depression was on, although it was not yet as bad as it would become. There were no jobs for young college graduates.

When Johnson learned that some of his classmates were traveling to Chanute Field in Illinois for physical exams in hopes of joining the Air Service Corps, he decided to give it a try himself. "I thought, 'I'm in good health. I'll give it a try,'" he said. "The next thing I knew I was on a train heading for March Field in California."[8]

From March, Johnson was sent to Kelly Field in San Antonio, Texas, where Charles McAllister and Lindbergh had both trained. Johnson flew in open cockpit, trainer biplanes.

"We were being trained by West Point graduates. They were really quite strict and by the book, and we were just a bunch of dodos," Johnson says. "The planes weren't particularly difficult to fly, but some of the concepts were a little difficult to handle. Some of the boys were a little afraid of the ground when they came in to land. We started with a lot of pilots and ended up with relatively few because so many washed out."[9]

Johnson graduated as a second lieutenant in 1931 and was assigned to San Antonio, flying in one of the best airplanes of the day: the Ford Tri-Motor. (It also happened to be a plane that was flown by Purdue graduate Jimmie Johnson.)

The Ford Tri-Motor had a corrugated aluminum body and wings. It had three motors, one in front and one on each wing and, because it was built by the Ford Motor Company who had revolutionized automobiles, the public trusted its performance, and so it became a popular plane for early passenger transportation.

"It handled well and was a very good airplane," Johnson says. "Of course, none of the planes from that time were modern in any real sense as we think of aircraft today. There weren't many instruments in those planes. We did not have the instruments to fly 'blind.' That would come later."[10]

By 1932, Johnson had served two years, the maximum allowed in the Army Reserve. He left the military and found work in Muncie, Indiana, giving flight lessons at an airport opened by the Ball brothers who had founded a canning jar corporation. He also worked out of Lake Wawasee in northern Indiana, flying a Sikorsky S-39 amphibian boat plane, a big plane with pontoons on each wing and a floating fuselage, to take passengers to the Chicago World's Fair during the Century of Progress. He made his landings there on Lake Michigan.

On one of those flights to Chicago in 1933, Johnson met a man named Walter Addems, chief pilot for National Air Transport, one of the major commercial airlines of the day.

"When I landed he was there, and he came out to look at my airplane," Johnson says. "I inquired about a job with National Air Transport. He said, 'That's quite an airplane. If you can fly that, I believe you can fly with us.'"[11] Ralph Johnson, a young man from the farming community of Goodland, Indiana, was in on the ground floor of the emerging airline industry. It had all started with airmail.

There were many individual mail deliveries between 1910 and World War I. These were mostly stunts for publicity and did not include any continued service. The first official, regularly scheduled airmail in the United States began on May 15, 1918. Unfortunately, airmail had not advanced far from the days when the *Jupiter* balloon left Lafayette bound for the eastern Seaboard and landed in the next county south near Crawfordsville.

According to the U.S. Centennial of Flight Commission, on May 15, 1918, "U.S. Army Air Service Lieutenant George Boyle, picked because he was engaged to marry the daughter of a powerful man whom the post office wanted to impress, made the first official [airmail] flight. Boyle had been told to follow the clearly visible railroad tracks north from Washington, D.C., to Philadelphia, but in a rather ignominious start to the service, he flew south instead and crashed into a field. Postal managers let him try again, but he went even farther off course, flying almost out over the Atlantic Ocean 150 miles. Other pilots managed to get the first airmail through between Washington and New York, and Boyle retired in embarrassment."[12]

While airmail started by using U.S. military airplanes and pilots, that practice was quickly discontinued. In August 1918, the post office took over from the Army and ran its own civilian airmail service.[13]

The planes they used were mostly World War I surplus, for example the deHavilland DH-4 that only had room for the pilot and his bag of mail.[14] There was no shortage of problems. In its first year, the post office airmail service recorded 1,208 missions. Out of that, there were ninety forced landings, "fifty-three due to weather and thirty-seven to engine failure." The post office started with forty pilots. By 1920, at least half were dead.[15]

In the beginning, airmail was moved mainly by short-hop flights, but in September of 1920 cross-country service began.[16] At least it was a partial coast-to-coast airmail system. In those early days, Johnson says, airmail was only flown during the day. When night arrived the pilots could not navigate by sighting familiar buildings, landscapes, and railroad routes on the ground. So they landed, and the mail was loaded onto trains. The railroad then advanced the mail until morning when it was reloaded on an airplane. In the early 1920s, the government began installing powerful beacon lights along the main airmail routes and the planes soon started flying at night.[17]

Regularly scheduled airmail coast to coast began in 1924, the same year Harold Turner "Slim" Lewis, who would later become a friend of Ralph Johnson, flew the first night airmail on a run between Omaha, Nebraska, and Cheyenne, Wyoming.[18]

All of this was cutting into the mail profits of the powerful railroads. The railroads lobbied Congress saying a government-owned and operated airmail service was unfair competition. In response, Congress approved the Airmail Act of 1925 requiring the government to get out of the flying business and contract with private companies. A number of airline companies emerged to bid for the work. In an attempt to protect their mail profits, the railroads had unwittingly helped create an airline industry that would eventually take away their U.S. passenger service.

Small "feeder" airline routes were put under contract first. Among the first set up was a St. Louis to Chicago route handled by Robertson Aircraft Corporation. Robertson employed Lindbergh to fly the mail before his famous flight. National Air Transport was given the Chicago to Dallas run.

In 1927, the transcontinental airmail route was split into two segments and taken over by private companies. The Boeing Company flew the western route from San Francisco to Chicago. And National Air

Transport, where Johnson would work, flew the route between Chicago, Detroit, Toledo, Cleveland, and Newark.[19]

The system was successful, but the new airlines were quick to learn how they could increase profits. The carriers were paid for airmail by the pound and according to a U.S. Centennial of Flight Commission report, "They sometimes sent postcards to themselves using registered mail, which required a heavy, secure lock. The lock added weight and the government had to pay more."[20]

Everything began to change with the election of Herbert Hoover as president of the United States in 1928. Hoover's postmaster general, Walter Folger Brown, changed the method of payment and regulations for airmail. Among Brown's initiatives was a provision that paid airlines for maintaining a large cargo capacity. He also granted air carriers guaranteed routes.

According to a U.S. Centennial of Flight Commission report, "The main provision changed the way mail payments were computed. Now airmail carriers would be paid up to a dollar and twenty-five cents per mile for having a cargo capacity on their planes of at least twenty-five cubic feet, whether the planes carried anything or flew empty. If they had less capacity, the per-mile rate would be less. There was no incentive to carry mail since the airline would receive the same amount for a plane of a certain size whether it carried anything or not. But an airline could easily get additional revenue by carrying passengers. Thus, there was an incentive to use larger planes that were suited to carrying more passengers."[21]

That was the government's goal: to push the airlines into the passenger business, ultimately reducing the cost of airmail. It worked. Airlines used the extra space to sell tickets to passengers as they carried the mail around the nation in their new "big" planes. Passenger flight was an exciting idea for people who had the money. Advertisements talked about the speed of the service and the breathtaking view from the air.

Airline passenger service was just emerging when Ralph Johnson began work as a copilot with National Air Service. Before he even started, National Air Service had become part of a conglomerate known as United Aircraft and Transportation Corporation. It owned companies that did everything from assembling airplanes to manufacturing engines to flight service.

In about 1930, a National Air Service direct flight from Chicago to Cleveland cost twenty-eight dollars and took about three hours. Buses took passengers from downtown locations to the airport. The planes

Johnson flew at this time were usually Ford Tri-Motors with room for ten to fifteen passengers, and it wasn't easy to fill those seats.

"In the mid-1930s, if the insurance companies found out someone was going to fly in an airplane, they would threaten to cancel the policy," Johnson says. "That was a handicap we had to overcome in the airlines. It was a tough go.

"And it was dangerous. We were all new in the business and there were a lot of things we didn't understand. For instance, we didn't understand that when you had an east wind at Newark you would probably be fogged in. There were hazards. It was not unusual for us to lose our friends. That was part of the challenge. This was a new industry, and I expected to stay with it and see it develop."[22]

When Franklin Roosevelt was elected president and took office in 1933, he set about making changes to the Hoover, Republican airmail policies. According to the U.S. Centennial of Flight Commission, "When the Democrats returned to Washington with Franklin Roosevelt in 1933, they lost little time in declaring that Brown's actions amounted to scandal. He had used his powers in high-handed ways and Democrats declared that he and the airlines together had committed fraud. Roosevelt responded by turning the airmail over to the pilots of the U.S. Army. It didn't work. They were unprepared and a number of them crashed."[23]

Johnson says copilots with his company were sent home and were put out of work by the action. "The military attempted to fly the same routes we were flying, and their aircrafts were not equipped for it," he says.[24]

In fact, during an eighteen-day period in late February and early March 1934, twelve military pilots were killed in sixty-six separate accidents.[25]

Roosevelt put airmail back in the hands of commercial airlines, but there were changes when commercial carriers returned to the airmail contracts under the Roosevelt administration. The government payments were reduced. This meant the airlines had to look even more aggressively for passengers. Also, the huge airline conglomerates that did everything from manufacturing to flying airplanes were broken up by the Roosevelt administration. Air transfer companies emerged with new names. According to the U.S. Centennial of Flight Commission, "American Airways became American Airlines; Northwest Airways became Northwest Airlines; EAT/Eastern Air Transport [became] Eastern Air Lines, and TWA changed to TWA, Inc."[26] Boeing Air Transport,

National Air Transport, Pacific Air Transport, and Varney Speed Lines emerged as United Air Lines.

Johnson was in on the ground floor of one of the world's major air carriers, and as a copilot, Johnson's responsibilities included feeding the passengers. "We were responsible for stowing the luggage and the co-pilot went back and served box lunches to the passengers. It was usually fried chicken,"[27] he says.

The first stewardesses were actually nurses responsible for taking care of the well-being of passengers, in addition to feeding them. When stewardesses came onboard, Johnson was happy to focus on his flying responsibilities instead of taking care of passengers.

"As co-pilots we were supposed to help fly the planes and learn from the captains," he says. "Most of the captains were nice and they'd discuss the flight with us, but they didn't know too much themselves."[28]

It was rough flying and sometimes cold. "We couldn't fly over the weather," Johnson says. "We had to fly in it—whatever the weather might be. If it was turbulent, we were turbulent right with it. About 10,000 feet is as high as we could manage. We had some dandy storms. I remember one time coming out of Toledo, I was flying the airplane and we got into a thunderstorm and the airplane bounced around so hard the pilot couldn't even grab hold of the wheel. Imagine the airplane holding together in those conditions. But it did."[29]

"With the Ford Tri-Motor planes," Johnson says, "we were just taking heat for the cabin off the exhaust pipe. It would get pretty cold. Later the planes were heated with steam heating systems, but we had a terrible time with them because they would freeze up."[30]

Johnson eventually found something he liked even better than commercial flying: becoming a test pilot for United Airlines, at a major maintenance center in Cheyenne, Wyoming. When Johnson learned that the test pilot there had been killed in a crash, he applied for the job and, being a Purdue graduate with a degree in aeronautical engineering, he was exactly what United wanted as they worked to upgrade the airplanes purchased from manufacturers.

According to a biography in the *Retired United Pilots Association News*, "During [this] time, aviation began to grow. More powerful engines were being developed and planes were able to fly faster and higher. As chief test pilot and an innovative engineer, Ralph helped develop propeller de-icing systems, pulsating de-icing boots, heated leading edges, a hooded approach light system that became today's

VASI, and the stabilized three-degree landing approach. In 1938, United loaned Johnson to Douglas Aircraft to help improve the new DC-3."[31]

The DC-3 was a major step forward in commercial air transportation. Much more comfortable than earlier planes, some models even had sleeper compartments for long, cross-country flights. They were far more quiet and warm. The seats were comfortable, and the planes could fly above turbulent weather. The DC-3 had taken over about seventy-five percent of all passenger service by 1939, and they remained in service for many years.[32]

Johnson tested every airplane that United flew from the mid-1930s until 1947, and when World War II began, Johnson and United played a major role.

"During the war, United just like all companies, joined in to help in any way they could," Johnson says. "Boeing produced 6,000 B-17s. Those planes were flown to Cheyenne, and at the United facility we would install things like the armaments and electronics. Before they left Cheyenne for the front, we test flew every one of them."[33]

The B-17 was one of the major airplanes in the U.S. war effort. "It was a wonderful, wonderful, amazing airplane," Johnson says.[34]

There are many amazing stories associated with the B-17 and one of them belongs to Johnson. It is a story that the Cheyenne newspaper once summed up perfectly in this single headline about Johnson: "He Landed a B-17 Backwards." It happened during the war when Johnson and Captain Woddy Woodruff were assigned to fly a B-17 from Cheyenne to Minneapolis for a research test.

"They had a hangar there where they could reduce the temperature to below zero, and they specified that we had to have the plane there on a certain day and it was urgent," Johnson says. "It was winter. We got over Sioux City, and they told us Minneapolis had freezing rain during the night and was completely iced over. That presented a problem for us.

"I called back and said, 'Are you certain there are no dry spots?' They came back and said they were absolutely sure. It was all ice. I decided to continue."[35]

He had formulated a plan in his head, and when he reached Minneapolis, he landed the plane on the ice and applied a little extra power to one of the engines. That caused the B-17 to slowly go into a spin. With the plane reaching the point at which it was sliding fully backwards, he applied full forward power, which countered the skid, and the plane came to a halt.

"Years later, I learned they did the same thing quite regularly in Alaska on frozen lakes, but I didn't know that at the time," Johnson says.[36]

In 1947, United moved its facility from Cheyenne to San Francisco. Johnson stayed behind and opened his own flight services. He also served as Wyoming's civil aeronautics director, was elected twice to the Wyoming House of Representatives, and was selected by President Richard Nixon to serve on the U.S. Export Expansion Council.

The *Retired United Pilot's Association News* says, "Ralph Johnson was born three years after the Wright brothers flew when many people still owned horses and buggies. His pioneering can-do spirit helped propel aviation into the massive, reliable industry it is today. His inventions, no doubt, saved countless lives."[37]

In 1991, the National Aeronautical Association presented Johnson with its Certificate of Honor. The award says, "Johnson is widely acknowledged as the father of the 'stabilized approach,' a technique that is still being used and saving lives fifty years later."

In presenting the award, W. Walker of America West Airlines said, "The stabilized approach procedure is the largest single factor in achieving the success realized today in reducing approach-landing accidents. It is, in fact, the biggest contributing factor in surviving wind shear encounters during the landing approach phase in swept-winged jet aircraft."

"I lived in the most magnificent century of all times," Johnson says. "I don't see how anything could possibly match it in the future. But of course, something will."

In 1988, Ralph Johnson retired at the age of eighty-two. He was also eighty-two the last time he flew his own airplane.

"But I could fly again today," he says at the age of ninety-seven. "As long as you have good eyes and good nervous control, you can fly. It's not a mystery."[38]

Jerry Ross

No one knows what a shuttle launch feels like better than Jerry Ross, who has flown into space seven times, more times than any other person.

"As you might guess," he says matter of factually, "getting strapped into a space shuttle that is full of fuel and ready to launch is a pretty exhilarating thing. Quite frankly, it's also pretty scary. You know you're about to be pushed off the surface of this earth by about seven million pounds of thrust. And you also know everything was built by the lowest bidder."

Ross could not even imagine spending his life doing anything else. Space flight has been his goal since he was a boy growing up in Crown Point, Indiana. And now that he holds the record for launches, his dreams haven't changed. What Ross wants next is to launch into space again.

Born in 1948, when commercial air flight was still in its infancy, Ross grew up with the space program. His memories extend back long before there were manned space flights to the days of rockets and satellites.

"For a young kid growing up in Indiana, that was the kind of stuff that really captured your imagination," Ross says. "I started reading all the magazine and newspaper articles about space that I could get my hands on. I made scrapbooks about it."

His father worked in the steel mills in northern Indiana. The family had a house on a farm owned by Ross's grandparents.

"Since we were living in Indiana, a lot of the articles I read focused on the fact that many of the engineers and scientists and management in our early space program had Purdue backgrounds—Purdue engineering degrees for the most part," Ross says. "So in the fourth grade, I decided that I was going to go to Purdue. I was going to become an engineer. I was going to get involved in our country's space program. Everything that I did from the fourth grade on was pretty much to support those decisions. Every dollar I made, working on farms, baling hay or whatever, was put into a savings account for college."

"Purdue was very challenging," he says. "I think anyone who goes through a Purdue engineering curriculum knows that they have to put in some pretty hard labor, a lot of sweat and worry."

He still remembers details of Neil Armstrong walking on the Moon. That was the summer day the earth stood still.

"I was working in Gary that summer," Ross says. "I remember very distinctly a whole bunch of us crowded around our black-and-white TV watching it happening. I was stunned. I understood what I was watching, but it still basically seemed unbelievable that we had actually done it.

"After that," Ross says, "I was even more motivated. I was in college. I was getting close to realizing the dream of getting my engineering degree. And by that point, I had signed up for Air Force ROTC, and I had received a scholarship from them. Quite frankly that was another decision that was made as a way of maybe helping myself get experience, since the Air Force was the chief proponent, user, and operator of rockets and missiles for the military."

Ross received a bachelor of science in mechanical engineering in 1970 and earned his master's degree in 1972. He met a young woman named Karen at Purdue and they married. From Purdue, Ross went to Dayton, Ohio, where he was stationed at Wright-Patterson Air Force Base doing engineering work.

In 1976, he graduated from the Air Force Test Pilot School's flight test engineer course and was assigned to Edwards Air Force Base.

"I wasn't an Air Force pilot," he says. "I was an Air Force engineer who flew in the back seats of the airplanes with the test pilots. Together, we worked as a team to plan and execute flight tests and then to evaluate the data and make reports on what we learned, trying to understand how these airplanes performed, whether or not they met specifications.

"In 1977, NASA was taking applications for the first class of astronauts to be hired to support the Space Shuttle Program. I applied. I think, close to nine or ten thousand people applied. I was fortunate enough to be one of 210 that were brought to Houston for a series of interviews and medical examinations over a one-week period. I was not fortunate enough to be one of the thirty-five selected. When I saw all my friends who had been selected leaving Edwards to move to Houston, and I wasn't going with them, I was really disappointed and frustrated. But I didn't let it stop me.

"I called and talked to the people who had been on the selection board," Ross says. "I was trying to figure out whether or not I had any hope for another opportunity, or if I should figure out what I would do with the rest of my life. Fortunately, they said, 'No, we didn't see anything we didn't like about you, and in fact, we hope you apply again.' They said, 'Why don't you come down to Houston and work with

NASA as an Air Force officer helping to integrate military payloads into the space shuttle.'"

He accepted, and in 1980, Ross was admitted into the astronaut program. His first mission launched on November 26, 1985.

"Launch is very dynamic," Ross says. "There's a lot of vibration and a lot of noise—a real sensation of getting shoved off the surface of the earth by a tremendous amount of energy. And of course, that's exactly what happens. The first time—I had dreamed of doing this for close to thirty years. I had listened to members of the crews that flew before me and they told me what it was like. I had put all that into my data bank and my imagination, and I had lived that moment many, many times over. And yet, with all the expectation and imagination I spent on it, it wasn't anywhere close to the real thing. The real thing is so much more dynamic and so much more exciting, and at the same time, a somewhat frightening experience, that it caught me by surprise."

Ross holds the records for space walks. He's done nine.

"It is the ultimate experience of being in space, there's no doubt about it," he says. "If you can imagine, being in your own little pressurized cocoon, stepping outside of the space shuttle and looking at the surface of the earth passing by at five miles a second below you. And all that you hear is a little crackle over the radio and there's a little bit of a hum from the fan circulating air in your suit. You can see the earth from ear to ear. You can see over a thousand miles north and south of your track. That's the ultimate, as far as I'm concerned.

"When I had a little bit of time, I just paused and reflected on what I was doing," he says. "I had this really weird sensation that I was in unity with the universe, and I was doing exactly what God had designed me to do. I know for an engineer that sounds very ethereal. But that's exactly what I felt."

His wife, Karen, works for a company that contracts with NASA to provide the food services for the space shuttle and the space station.

"Since my wife helps make the food for space, I have to tell you it's pretty good," he says. "Most of the foods we have are what you would consider to be commercially available foods. It's all repackaged into containers that are compatible with our food servicing system in the orbiter. Most of the foods are dehydrated. We have fuel cells in the space shuttle that provide our power. They combine oxygen and hydrogen gas in a catalytic way that generates electricity, and a byproduct of that electricity generation is water, distilled water. So we use that water to rehydrate our foods before we eat them. We also have thermally stabilized foods.

We have some fresh foods. We have snack foods, like cookies and candy, nuts and things like that."

Ross has a daughter, Amy, who has a bachelor's and a master's from Purdue in mechanical engineering. She helped to finish the design, manufacturing, and certification of the space gloves that Ross wore on two missions. She is now involved in the design of new, advanced space suits that could be used when NASA returns to the Moon and goes to Mars.

Ross serves as astronaut office branch chief for Kennedy Space Center Operations Support. Part of his job is getting the astronauts on board the shuttle before launch.

"I feel exceptionally fortunate and honored to have these opportunities," he says. "I know people say that just to be nice, but I really feel that way. I feel extremely blessed that I've had the opportunities to do what I've done and that I have been able to serve my country in such a fascinating endeavor.

"I love what I do. It's just incredible."

Chapter Eight

I have been most impressed by the enthusiasm of the Purdue aeronautical students, faculty, and airport officials, not only for practical knowledge, but for the furthering of aeronautical research. . . . In fact, I have become so impressed that I have become enthusiastic myself over the possibilities of the present Purdue tie-up of an aeronautical department with an airport on the campus.

—Wiley Post, April 1934

The solo flight across the Atlantic by Charles Lindbergh had a huge impact on flight in the United Sates and throughout the world. With that accomplishment, the average person began to consider the possibility of taking a ride in an airplane someday, even if they were saying they would only fly with Lindy.

There was a great deal of excitement about the possibilities of flight in the fall of 1929 when George W. Haskins, the Purdue University alumnus who ten years earlier had flown into campus with a petition calling for an aeronautical engineering program, again arrived in West Lafayette. This time he came as an assistant professor of mechanical engineering assigned to head the aeronautical engineering program.

The program at Purdue had grown rapidly. In June 1929, the *Purdue University Alumni Record and Campus Encyclopedia* reported that Purdue aeronautics was the largest program in the nation. It said, "Aviation and aeronautical work at Purdue were given decided impetus by Colonel Lindbergh's successful flight to France. Since 1926, there has been an increase in the enrollment figures of the School of Mechanical Engineering with the study of aeronautics standing out as the principal major subject. Today, Purdue has the largest number of students enrolled in aeronautics of any university in the United States."[1]

Since Haskins had flown in with that petition in 1919, an aerodynamics laboratory had opened at Purdue. In 1928, two courses for graduate students had been added, and there were three airplanes at the university along with nine operating engines. Much of the equipment had come from the Navy because they were not using it after World War I.[2]

There was also a great deal of excitement in aviation taking place off campus, and developments in the community were having a huge impact on Purdue in flight. Lafayette finally had an airport.

The first airfield in Lafayette opened in May 1928. It was named Shambaugh Field, and it was south of Lafayette in an area along Teal Road and South Eighteenth Street that would later be occupied by Lafayette Life Insurance. Lafayette businessman Charles Shambaugh leased eighty acres at the site and opened it for commercial and private air service after leveling the area, seeding it with grass, and building a metal hangar.[3]

The field was immediately put to use by Purdue students who took streetcars from campus as far as they could and then walked the rest of the way to get their flight training.[4]

Purdue Engineering historian H. B. Knoll describes Shambaugh as "one of the mechanical enthusiasts of his time, an early builder and driver of racing cars, a longtime automobile dealer, and a contributor to automobile design. Aviation represented another step onward for him, and though his airport had but limited success, his enthusiasm for mechanical matters was not one whit diminished."[5]

Supporting Shambaugh in the venture was another Lafayette aviation enthusiast, Dr. A. C. Arnett, a physician, founder of the medical clinic that carries his name, and president of the Lafayette Chamber of Commerce in 1928.

Shambaugh Field was a first-class operation for a community the size of Lafayette. It was large enough to accommodate almost all planes being flown at that time. It met with enough success that the hangar, originally built to hold three planes, was enlarged to service even more.[6]

It could even accommodate night landings and takeoffs in the days before electricity was extended to rural sites. Shambaugh purchased one hundred lanterns and hung them on fence posts to mark the field. In the evening, a young man named Leland Reynolds lit them and received flying lessons for his work instead of pay. The lanterns enabled Shambaugh Field to qualify as an emergency landing strip for airmail planes, an important designation toward gaining recognition in those early days of flight.[7]

Wiley Post—an internationally famous pilot who would later make a stop at Purdue that would make headlines from coast to coast—used Shambaugh on at least one occasion.

Shambaugh Field also attracted other well-known flyers. At the dedication of the field in August 1928, ten thousand people attended a stunt-flying demonstration by the World War I Flying Ace Eddie Rickenbacker. There were parachute jumps and plenty of excitement. The landing field did prove too small for at least one airplane of the day. Amelia Earhart was a scheduled guest, but she said the field was too small for her fourteen-seat Fokker. She dropped a note apologizing to the people who had waited to see her. She would come back several years later for a much longer stay.[8]

During the next five years, airplanes using Shambaugh Field carried fifteen thousand passengers and flew 300,000 miles without an accident. The field hosted an air circus that drew ten thousand people, proving again that the people of Lafayette were fascinated by airplanes. Seventy pilots were trained at Shambaugh, many of them—perhaps even most of them—Purdue students who eagerly traveled from campus.[9]

Among the students, says Knoll, was Mike Murphy, who came from a farm along the Wildcat Creek. "He later proved to be the world's foremost aerobatic flier, and on D-Day in Normandy his glider aircraft was the first to land in enemy-occupied territory."[10] In fact, Murphy's D-Day story, using fictitious names, was recounted in the movie *Saving Private Ryan.*

Murphy was a lieutenant colonel and the senior glider officer in the ninth troop carrier command on June 6, 1944. On his glider, which was specially reinforced because of its important passenger, was Brigadier General Don F. Pratt, the assistant division commander of the 101st airborne division.

Murphy landed his glider, the *Fighting Falcon,* on a wet field of tall grass at 3:45 A.M., although some accounts say it was seconds after 4:00 A.M. Murphy was unable to break the glider in the tall, wet grass, and it crashed into a tree-lined hedgerow at sixty to eighty miles per hour. Pratt was killed along with the copilot, John M. Butler. Murphy survived with two broken legs.

According to a Wright-Patterson Air Force Base history, Murphy was a prewar stunt pilot who later became director of the AAF glider-training program. "He developed new tow techniques, assisted in the planning for the D-Day invasion of France, and led the gliders into Normandy. He received a Purple Heart."[11]

In his book *D-Day June 6, 1944: The Climatic Battle of World War II*, writer Stephen Ambrose says, "Colonel Mike Murphy had the controls of the lead glider. It [took] hits from a German machine gun—General Pratt was killed, the first general officer on either side to die that day—and Murphy crashed into a hedgerow breaking both his legs."[12]

Murphy was probably the most famous pilot who ever learned to fly at Shambaugh, although the field would be the training site for many great pilots who would make a name for themselves before and during World War II.

The stock market crash of 1929, followed by the Great Depression, brought an end to Shambaugh Field. Beginning in 1930, the financial losses started to mount, and in 1933, Shambaugh closed the airfield and started farming the land. At the same time, the mayor of Lafayette announced the city had no plans to build an airport.[13]

After a great early history in aviation, it appeared Lafayette was closing its doors to flight, but that did not happen. A major factor in keeping Lafayette and Purdue University focused on the potential for aviation was the pilot manager at Shambaugh field, Lawrence "Cap" Aretz.

Aretz had learned to fly in the Army Air Corps during World War I. A Minnesota farm boy, he did his flight training in 1917 at Chanute Field in Rantoul, Illinois. He never went overseas, but he was nearly killed by the flu epidemic that swept through the world during the war. After the war, he barnstormed around the country doing stunt flights and selling rides until the airplanes he was flying were destroyed in a fire. He next flew for Standard Oil but quit when he felt he was being asked to take risks that were unacceptable to the by-the-book pilot. It was then that he found work more to his liking with Shambaugh.[14]

During his career, Aretz would teach four thousand people to fly, among them Joe Halsmer. In 1931, Halsmer opened an airfield on forty acres near what is now I-65 and 38 East in Indiana. The field was run by brothers Joe, John, and Francis, and during World War II, they had a government contract to teach flying at Purdue. Halsmer Field continued until 1986 when it was closed for industrial expansion. Other pilots trained to fly by Aretz, who later went into the airfield business in and around Lafayette, included Frank Reimers and Bob Wellborn.[15]

The major development in Lafayette area airports came when Shambaugh closed his field and Purdue University stepped in. In 1922, Purdue had hired a progressive new president. His name was Edward

Elliott, and he would become a major advocate for promoting flight at Purdue. Elliott was a man of chiseled features with deep character lines on his face. He was a man of principles. He set high standards, met them, and expected other people to do the same. He stood straight, and people often believed he was taller than his real five-foot ten-inch stature. When he arrived, he had the feeling Purdue was a "sleepy and staid" place. He said so publicly. Privately he thought, "The university was dead."[16] He had a mind to change that.

Elliott was strict. Since students were not allowed to smoke on campus, he informed the Purdue University Board of Trustees, to their displeasure, that they would also have to follow the rules.[17]

According to Knoll, "There was an air of buoyancy and drama about him, even when he dealt with routine affairs like when he received a faculty member in this office. He would be busy with papers at his desk, would thump his desk lightly, and would talk roughly, almost in a bark. Things were moving fast, his manner seemed to say. Regularly, he walked the two and a half miles from his home on Seventh Street to the university in the morning and home again in the evening or five miles in all—the minimum he said every university president should walk outdoors every day for communion with his better self. He strode up State Street Hill as if there were no grade at all, rugged in physique and powerful of countenance. From the State Street Gate he advanced purposefully on his office Eliza Fowler Hall, seeming to announce by his manner that the university would have another great and wonderful day."[18]

He was a progressive man who had strong theories on education, who advocated opportunities for women, and who believed in the possibilities of flight and the need for Purdue to take leadership in all great potentials. He was convinced once and for all about the future of flight through a meeting with Aretz, probably during the winter of 1929.

Knoll found that, "Aretz earned a large share of the credit for getting aviation started at Purdue. He was at Shambaugh Airport one blustery winter day when someone who said he was President Elliott phoned to ask if he could be flown to Indianapolis to make a speech. The highways were impassable because of snow and ice. Aretz thought that he was being kidded but said that of course he would make the trip. To his surprise, a car pulled up a few minutes later and out stepped Elliott. The two of them worked together to clear the snow away from the plane, and the flight down and back was a total success. Elliott said afterward that the trip had sold him on aviation." Aretz also later did a selling job on

David Ross, president of the Purdue Board of Trustees, taking him on a flight to view his farmland from the air.[19]

Elliott and Ross had ideas for an airfield at Purdue. In the late 1920s, the plan being developed for Purdue included a great transportation proving ground for trains, airplanes, and lighter-than-air ships. Railroad tracks for the testing of locomotives were to be in a huge figure eight on a large field south of campus. The area inside one loop of the figure eight was to be for airplane departures and landings. The other loop was for lighter-than-air ships such as big dirigibles. The plan crumbled with the Great Depression,[20] but the idea for airplane field did not. Ross and Elliott were determined that Purdue would have an airport.

Years later Shambaugh's wife, Gertrude, said Ross and Elliott sought out her husband for advice on the airport. Shambaugh, she said, responded it would cost at least $250,000 to do what they wanted to accomplish. "Why don't you have an airport at Purdue," Shambaugh asked. "I'll close mine, and you can have Captain Aretz."[21]

In 1930, Ross made the first of several donations of land to the recently established Purdue Research Foundation for the creation of an airport. A committee was formed to draft the plans, and by November 1, 1930, Haskins was on the site. With him were representatives of the U.S. Coast and Geodetic Survey and the U.S. Department of Commerce.

According to Knoll, "The site, it was agreed, would be placed on government maps as the Purdue University Airport when a wind sock was installed and the landing area [was] marked by a ring of light colored limestone. Before the day ended, the wind sock was hung from a dead tree, the stone ring was in place, and the government representatives were notified by wire that the requirements had been met."[22]

Purdue had the world's first university airport. It happened less than three months after Neil Armstrong was born in Wapakoneta, Ohio. It wasn't much of an airport. Knoll says, "the sock hung lonely and forlorn over empty farm land. One summer the airport, such as it was, had to be closed because, by pure inadvertence, some of the land was plowed and planted."[23]

What got things moving was the federal Works Progress Administration (WPA), an agency designed to foster development and put people to work. With WPA money along with additional donations from Ross, the airport land was drained, a rotary beacon was put into place along with other markers and a hazard lighting system, and a laboratory-hangar was constructed. On September 4, 1934, the improved airport was officially open for business.[24]

The airport was leased to Aretz "with a pledge that he would operate it in a manner consistent with the needs of the university," Knoll says. "He became the figure most readily brought to mind when the airport was mentioned and was responsible for much of the rapid growth that occurred."[25]

Elliott personally promoted flight training among the students, although some members of the engineering faculty were opposed to it, believing it was beneath the standards of their profession. According to Knoll, "one professor said that he could not see why an engineering school should train 'chauffeurs for airplanes.' Another felt that as soon as a student showed an interest in becoming a pilot he disqualified himself from becoming an engineer. In his opinion, the drive that took a man into the clouds above the earth was incompatible with the drive that took real engineers into the rarified atmosphere of engineering thought. Elliott's presidency seems to have had much to do with the presence of the course in the curriculum."[26]

The charge to the students for flight training was a high $600, a point Knoll credits in explaining the early low enrollment. Students took their classroom, technical instruction through the university, which had an arrangement with H. Weir Cook of the Curtiss-Wright Corporation for flying lessons.[27]

Progress at the airport was steady, and on April 14, 1935, an unexpected visitor dropped in at the Purdue Airport bringing the new facility considerable national attention and notoriety.

One of the most famous aviators of the day was Wiley Post. A small man, he was born in Texas in 1898 but grew up in Oklahoma. His education was limited. As a youth he was convicted of car theft and spent a year in prison before being paroled. After prison he went to work in the oil fields and in the mid-1920s lost his left eye in a job accident. For the injury he received a $1,800 cash settlement and used that money to buy an airplane. A dashing man who wore a white eye patch that only added to his mystique, Post went to work as the pilot for a wealthy Oklahoma oilman, F. C. Hall. Hall financed many of Post's record-breaking flights. He also owned two of the planes used by Post, both named for Hall's daughter Winnie Mae. The second *Winnie Mae* was a specially designed and built blue and white Lockheed Vega.

In 1930, Post flew the *Winnie Mae* Lockheed Vega from Los Angeles to Chicago in nine hours, nine minutes, and four seconds. It was the first record for Post and the airplane.

In 1931, Post set a record for flying around the world in eight days, fifteen hours, and fifty-one minutes with fourteen stops. Aviation had come a long way since Frederick Martin's world flyers and their 175-day trip. Two years later Post flew around the world again, this time in seven days, eighteen hours, and forty-nine minutes making only eleven stops.

Post next turned his attention to long duration, high-altitude flights that would allow him increased speed. He used a supercharger on this plane to accomplish this—the same equipment that was being researched at Purdue by Haskins and his students.

At the heights Post was flying without a pressurized cabin, he needed a special suit to protect him. He also needed to carry oxygen. According to the Smithsonian Institution Air and Space Museum, this was the world's first practical pressure suit. It put the United States on an ever-developing course for space exploration that has never ended.

Post had help developing the suit from Russell S. Colley, of the B. F. Goodrich Company. It had three layers: the innermost layer was a pair of long underwear used to help protect the pilot from the cold at the elevations he was flying; the second layer was a black rubber pressure bladder; and the third layer was an "outer cloth-contoured suit" covering the pressure bladder.[28]

Post also had a specially designed helmet that was bolted to the suit. The helmet was more rectangular than circular and rose high above his shoulders. There was a round facemask in the front and breathing tubes were connected to it. When he put it on, Post had the appearance of something straight out of Jules Verne. And there was more.

For his high-altitude, high-speed flights, Post included special landing gear on the *Winnie Mae.* After takeoff, Post pulled a lever in his cockpit that dropped the wheeled landing gear. The result of this was reduced weight and drag on his plane. He would land using a specially designed skid attached to the fuselage.[29]

Post could fly at amazing speeds for the day. According to the Smithsonian Institution Air and Space Museum, which houses the *Winnie Mae,* on at least one occasion Post reached speeds of up to 340 miles per hour flying in the jet stream.

In 1935, Post attempted four transcontinental flights, and they all failed. The third attempt ended at the Purdue University Airport and brought the young, up-and-coming facility a great deal of attention and publicity. For an early twentieth-century comparison, it was like the space shuttle making an emergency landing at Purdue.

Post's third attempt started in Los Angeles on April 9, 1935. His target was New York, and he carried enough oxygen to supply him for eight hours.[30]

He was flying at speeds of up to 290 miles per hour when his plane developed trouble. Before landing at Purdue, Post flew above Lafayette and word of what was happening shot through the community. By 3:40 P.M. on a Sunday afternoon when he attempted his final approach at the airport, a crowd of people had gathered to watch, although it wasn't until the last minute that they were aware an actual aviation celebrity was landing. They just knew something was wrong and something exciting was about to happen.

According to Knoll, hundreds of "spectators held their breath as they half-expected to witness disaster, hardly able to believe that Post could get down safely. They saw a landing [on skids] made with such skill that they could hardly believe their eyes. Post looked like a man from Mars in his stratosphere suit and demanded of the student fliers who rushed to his plane, 'Get me out of this.' About forty wing nuts had to be loosened before they could remove his helmet."[31]

He had actually flown all the way to Ohio before he discovered he was in trouble and made the decision to return to Lafayette for the landing. He never explained why he didn't land in Ohio. He was close to Cleveland when he turned back. He apparently was looking for Shambaugh Field, which had long been closed, but when he saw the Purdue Airport from the air, he liked what he saw.

Before landing, Post circled the airfield several times apparently checking things out. He then shot thousands of feet into the air again to begin his approach. He had to stall his engine and lock the propeller into a horizontal position to keep it from spinning into the ground when he landed on his short skids.

In Lafayette, Post received the celebrity reception he was due. He in turn was impressed after getting a tour of the Purdue facilities. He met with Elliott for photographs and then asked for a copy of the picture "so he could prove to his friends that he had been to college."[32]

Post's unexpected touchdown at Purdue on Monday, April 15, was received with World War II–size headlines across the top of the *Lafayette Journal and Courier,* "Post Rests after Forced Landing:"

Resting in bed at the Fowler Hotel Monday morning after his stratosphere flight from California and his forced landing at the Purdue Airport Sunday, Wiley Post, world famous airman, informed a Journal and Courier reporter that he was not disheartened by the failure of his latest attempt, but did not contemplate a fourth trial with his present equipment.

The intrepid flyer whose marvelous performance in landing his plane without mishap at Purdue with the landing gear missing won him the admiration of the thousands who milled about the scene after he dropped down out of the skies and settled the ship down on the field, was dejected over the failure of his latest flight, but said it was "all in the game."

I am tired of having to make landings without landing gear, he said, but he intimated he does not contemplate abandoning his stratospheric flights. It is apparent that he intends to improve his equipment and try again.

"I don't feel so hot," he said Sunday night when interviews were sought at the hotel. Monday morning he was feeling better, but not inclined to talk much. . . .

"I want to thank all the Purdue University Airport boys, the Purdue students, and anyone and everyone who helped me yesterday afternoon at the Purdue field. They're all regular fellows and took good care of me and my ship," Post said.[33]

According to the newspaper report, Post had been flying at about thirty-six thousand feet for most of his trip when he developed supercharger trouble."[34]

After takeoff from California, he told Lafayette newspaper reporters he had released the landing gear and let it drop to the ground to improve the aerodynamics of the airplane. Pressed about exactly where the landing gear fell, he said, "I hope it didn't kill any movie people."[35]

"Post circled the city for nearly thirty minutes before bringing his ship to earth," the *Journal and Courier* reported. "He first started to land at the old Shambaugh Airport where he had stopped several years ago and then apparently discovered the location of the Purdue field by observing a number of planes which were aloft at the time."[36]

Hundreds of people pressed around the *Winnie Mae* and some of them chipped off paint to take home as souvenirs. An article on the front page of the *New York Times* on April 15 said traffic was jammed around the Purdue Airport for blocks. When the emergency landing took place at Purdue, the *Times* said people had already started gathering in New York, awaiting Post's arrival.

"Over this college community the sturdy ship, which has set around-the-world marks, failed him," the *Times* said. "After circling the university field the flier came down on a six-foot skid attached to the bottom of his plane's fuselage in what airport [personnel] termed a 'sweet landing.'"[37]

The stories continued until April 17 when Post finally was able to fly the *Winnie Mae* back home to Oklahoma.

On April 16, the *Lafayette Journal and Courier* said Post had appeared at a meeting of the Indiana National Guard Observation Plane Squadron in Indianapolis. At that meeting, more information surfaced about the flight. According to the *Journal and Courier*, "Post . . . was reported to have told a friend that he had trouble with his nose while locked in his stratosphere suit and head-piece. It seems that an automatic valve started pouring oxygen into his rubber suit faster than the release valve could carry it away. As a result, the windshield in his aluminum headpiece became fogged. In order to see, he had to stretch out his neck and wipe off the glass with his nose. Finally, aches crept into his nose and neck, and when a clutch on the supercharger stripped, he set his globe-girding monoplane down on the Purdue Airport."[38]

Post declined to speak to the Indianapolis group. "I don't think I have anything to say," he said. But Aretz, who escorted Post to the dinner, did give a talk. Aretz said, "It was the most beautiful bit of maneuvering I ever saw. I had been up with a student and had run out of gas and had to make a dead-stick landing. I bawled out the help for failure to put in enough fuel. . . . Then I saw Post shooting the field. I got out of the way and let him go up again to get ready to shut off the motor and slide in. And in he came, dead stick, no landing gear, and made me ashamed of myself. The ship hit the ground, skid about fifty feet on the grass, and it was all over. That man doesn't need wheels."[39]

Before he left on Wednesday, April 17, Post did have something to say. "Since I had to land, I certainly feel now that I was fortunate in my choice of a landing field," he said. "During my three days here at Purdue, I have been mightily impressed with the institution's facilities for aeronautical training, both theoretical and practical. The primary purpose of my stratosphere flights has not been to establish speed records but to further scientific investigation of the possibilities of practical high-altitude flying. I have been most impressed by the enthusiasm of the Purdue aeronautical students, faculty, and airport officials, not only for practical knowledge, but also for the furthering of aeronautical research, which after all is really my first love. In fact, I have become so impressed that I have become enthusiastic myself over the possibilities of the present Purdue tie-up of an aeronautical department with an airport on the campus."[40]

"My ship is all right," Post said, "but she's six years old and only has a top speed of 150 miles per hour at sea level. But at 28,000 feet up, I've attained speeds of more than 300 miles per hour, which gives you an idea of the possibilities of operating ships in the stratosphere."[41]

Before leaving, Post also talked about upcoming plans for a flight in Alaska using a different airplane—not the *Winnie Mae.*

The last thing he did before taking off was to shake hands and thank two people he had been praising in his assessment of what was taking place in aviation at Purdue: Aretz and Haskins.

Four months and one day later, an airplane Post was piloting crashed near Point Barrow, Alaska. He died, along with his passenger, one of the best-loved humorists of all time: Will Rogers. But before that tragedy, the Purdue Airport had been placed "on the map" after hosting one of the world's greatest pilots and most sophisticated planes.

It was a great moment and more was coming, very quickly. Another of the world's most famous flyers had already visited Purdue, and she would soon become a regular part of campus life.

Her title was counselor on careers for women, and it was at West Lafayette that she would first conceive and then receive substantial funding from the Purdue Research Foundation for her flight around the world. At Purdue, she would first see and pilot the airplane in which she would fly off into history. He name was already known around the world when she landed at Purdue. Her name was Amelia Earhart.

Guy Gardner

Guy Gardner uses four words to sum up the experience of flying in space: *exciting, fun, meaningful,* and *awesome.* He could add one more: *fulfilling.* Gardner is a man who has been given the opportunity to fulfill his greatest dream.

"I don't remember a time in my life when I didn't want to go into space," he says.

Born in Virginia, Gardner first became interested in space when he was a boy in the 1950s. He was in the eighth grade in May 1961 when Alan Shepard became the first American in space. By that time, he knew the common thread between all of the original Mercury 7 astronauts: they all were test pilots.

Gardner's career path was mapped: the military, flight school, test pilot school, astronaut training.

He was accepted at the Air Force Academy and graduated with distinction in 1969, having majored in astronautics, mathematics, and engineering science. Gardner then took part in the special Purdue University-Air Force Academy master's in astronautics program.

He arrived at Purdue in June 1969, one month before Neil Armstrong and Buzz Aldrin walked on the Moon.

"I shared an apartment with three others guys from the Academy," Gardner says. "All four of us sat and watched the moonwalk on a little nine-inch black-and-white TV. That's all we had. I made a moon cake. It was a two layer, round cake with yellow icing. I thought it would be ten or fifteen years before I was an astronaut, and so I'd get to go to Mars. I was wrong. But I did get to fly in the shuttle, so I'm not complaining."

From Purdue, Gardner went to flight school and soon found himself based in Thailand, flying F-4 fighter jets in Vietnam. He flew 177 combat missions. He returned to the United States in 1973, was an instructor and operational pilot, and in 1975 was selected for USAF Test Pilot School at Edwards Air Force Base.

Next, he applied to be an astronaut in the class of 1978. He was a Distinguished Graduate of the Air Force Academy, top graduate in pilot training, and top graduate from the U.S. Air Force Test Pilot School. He was Test Pilot School Outstanding Academic Instructor and Test Pilot School Outstanding Flying Instructor. He had done everything necessary to accomplish his dream.

He was not accepted into the program.

"That was a pretty big blow," Gardner says. "Because they didn't pick me, I assumed that meant I would never be picked. So I had to reorient my career and think about other things I might do. Actually, this was very healthy for me. It gave me a broader perspective on life. Two years later when I was selected, I was better prepared mentally for the actual job of training as an astronaut."

Gardner went in with a large group of Purdue graduates that included Roy Bridges, Jerry Ross, and John Blaha.

Gardner was the pilot on STS-27, December 2–6, 1988. It carried a Department of Defense payload. In December 1990, he flew on *Columbia* and carried the ASTRO-1 astronomy laboratory into space.

"It's tough to describe a space shuttle flight in words," Gardner says. "Words don't do it justice. But I've kind of boiled it down to four aspects of flying, and I use four words.

"The word I use for launch is *exciting*. I mean, it's just incredibly exciting to have that physiological experience. You're pushed back in your seat from the G-forces, there's a lot of vibration and shaking and noise during the first two minutes. And on top of that, there's the knowledge that you're bolted down to four million pounds of high-explosive rocket fuel, and it's hopefully burning in a controlled fashion. The shuttle leaps off the pad, and you are up in space before you know it. It's just an incredibly exciting experience.

"The seats are small. The astronauts launch in space suits and carry a parachute.

"There's not a lot of room," Gardner says. "And you're on your back for on the order of two and a half hours before launch. So they actually have a little inflatable pad that you lie on that you can pump up or let the air out just to give you a little bit of change of feeling under your back."

The suit is bulky, cumbersome. Astronauts get out of those suits as soon as possible once in orbit.

"It's a blast to be weightless," he says. "But we don't spend all those tax dollars just for excitement and fun. We do meaningful work while we're up there. And that's my third word—*meaningful*. All the shuttle missions have a purpose.

"The fourth word I use to describe looking down at Earth from space from a couple hundred miles up, going around Earth every ninety minutes at 17,500 miles an hour. The word I use is *awesome*. It's just an incredible experience. I love maps, and I love geography. It was just a great thrill to be able to pick out the different parts of the earth. It's amazing how different the topography is. After a few days up there, you can almost get to the point where you can just float to the window with no clue about where you are. You can look out and see the colors and textures of the ground below, and say—'Oh, we're over China.' You see a sunrise every ninety minutes and a sunset every ninety minutes. And they're pretty spectacular."

Gardner has spent a great deal of time lecturing since his space flights. He's talked to a lot of children. It's always the young children, he says, who ask the question that everyone wants to know, but most are afraid to mention.

How do astronauts use the toilet in the weightlessness of space?

"Very carefully," Gardner says. "Since everything is weightless, you use airflow to make sure everything goes where you want it to go."

Gardner's original, long-term plan was to go on three shuttle missions. The third flight he would be a commander.

"My wife said she'd put up with me flying three times, so that was my plan," Gardner says. "But then Roy Bridges called and asked me to command the Air Force Test Pilot School. I thought and prayed about that. It was probably the one job back in the Air Force that would take me out of flying the shuttle again. But after I looked at the options, I decided I would love to head up the Test Pilot School. So off I went."

In 1992, he retuned to NASA as a civilian to head the U.S.-Russian Shuttle-Mir Space Station Program. As the Mir program transitioned into the International Space Station, Gardner left NASA. He has done a variety of work since, including lecturing, working for the Federal Aviation Administration, and teaching high school.

"I love teaching," he says. "I love being in the classroom with the kids."

Does he miss the space program? No. Would he like to fly in space again?

"If NASA were to call me up and say, 'Hey Guy, would you like to go fly in the next shuttle flight? I'd say, 'You betcha. I'll be there,'" Gardner says. "As long as I don't have to train for two years, I'd love to go fly again. But, on the other hand, that's what I did when it was time for me to do that. And since then, I've had other things that I was supposed to be doing.

"I just have an appreciation for the uniqueness of the experience that I happened to have. It certainly was awesome."

And exciting, meaningful, and a blast.

 Chapter Nine

by Jo Ellen Meyers Sharp

Miss Earhart represents better than any other young woman of this generation the spirit and the courageous skills which may be called the new pioneering.

—Edward Elliott

For months in 1937 and 1938, ships from at least three countries scoured the Pacific Ocean in search of Amelia Earhart and her *Flying Laboratory*, a specially equipped, twin-engine Lockheed Electra paid for, in part, by the Purdue Research Foundation.

The searches proved fruitless, and in 1939, Earhart was declared dead. However, the declaration did not end the public's interest in the world's most famous female pilot. In death, Earhart's spirit haunts the imagination, and the mystery of her disappearance still draws ships to the Pacific nearly seventy years later in search of clues to her fateful flight.

The relationship between Earhart, Purdue, and her family did not die, either. Her husband, George Palmer Putnam, donated materials to Purdue that relate to Earhart's life, career, and disappearance shortly after her death. In 1964, the university renamed the women's residence Earhart Hall to honor her work on campus, and in 2002, Putnam's granddaughter, Sally Putnam Chapman, rounded out the collection with the donation of personal and private papers including Earhart's poems, flight log, prenuptial agreement, and other memorabilia. Purdue now holds the world's largest, most comprehensive collection of Earhart materials.

It was the bold action of Purdue President Edward C. Elliott that started the university's relationship with Earhart. Elliott met the pilot in New York in September 1934 when they both addressed the fourth annual Women's Conference on Current Problems sponsored by the

Herald Tribune. He spoke about "New Frontiers for Youth," and she spoke about the role of women in the development of the field of aeronautics.

"She had just completed her notable flight over the Atlantic, and her comments were of great interest to Elliott. That evening Elliott began to mull over the possibilities that could come about if Amelia Earhart and Purdue University could be related in some way. The next day at a luncheon arranged by Elliott, he, Miss Earhart, and her husband, George Palmer Putnam, discussed some possibilities. Elliott later reported that it was at this time that he learned that 'her primary interest in life was not in this career of adventure upon which she had embarked, but rather in an effort to find and make some additions to the solution to the problem of careers for women.' She was interested primarily in the education of women in order to qualify them for their place in the world, Elliott observed. He asked her to come to the campus and state her philosophy; she was delighted at the prospect. Within an hour after the luncheon was over, Elliott had made several phone calls, Miss Earhart had rearranged her schedule, and in less than a month Miss Earhart was on the Purdue campus to address faculty members and women students on 'Opportunities for Women in Aviation.'"

Earhart was quite pleased with the opportunity to visit Purdue. Purdue Airport was the first in the country to be operated by a university. Purdue was one of the few universities to offer aeronautics, an interest of hers that started as a teenager.

"I believe it was during the winter of 1918 that I became interested in airplanes," Earhart wrote in her autobiography, *The Fun of It.* She was working as a nurse's aide at Spadina Medical Hospital in Toronto, caring for wounded soldiers who had returned from World War I. Her autobiography, as well as most of her other writings, is written in a clipped, notes-like style.

"Though I had seen one or two [airplanes] at county fairs before, I now saw many of them, as the officers were trained at the various fields around the city. Of course, no civilian had opportunity of going up. But I hung around in my spare time and absorbed all I could. I remember the sting of the snow on my face as it was blown back from the propellers when the training planes took off on the skis," she wrote.

Her work as a nurse's aide prompted her to take up the study of medicine at Columbia University in New York, but she soon left for California where she found her true calling. "It took me only a few months to discover that I probably would not make the ideal physician. Though

I liked learning all about medicine, particularly the experimental side, visions of its practical application floored me. For instance I thought, among other possibilities, of sitting at the bedside of a hypochondriac and handing out innocuous sugar pellets to a patient with an imaginary illness. . . . . When I left New York I intended to follow up on medical research that, at least, still greatly appealed to me in the field of medicine, but somehow I did not get into the swing of the western universities before aviation caught me."

Drawn to the popular flying circuses in the Los Angeles area, the twenty-one-year-old Earhart's first flight was with Frank Hawks, a man who held more records than anyone for fast flying. "As soon as we left the ground, I knew I myself had to fly. Miles away I saw an ocean and the Hollywood Hills seemed to peep over the edge of the cockpit, as if they were already friends. 'I think I'd like to learn to fly,' I told the family casually that evening, knowing full well I'd die if I didn't. 'Not a bad idea,' said my father just as casually. 'When do you start?'"

Earhart took lessons whenever she could afford them from whoever would take her up and teach her. Her first instructor was Anita "Neta" Snook, and Earhart trained in a Curtiss Canuck, similar to the fighting Jenny of wartime. After she had flown alone and got her pilot's license in 1921, her mother helped her buy a used plane, a Kinner Canary. "If mother was worried during this period, she did not show it. Possibly, except for backing me financially, she could have done nothing more helpful. I didn't realize it at the time, but the cooperation of one's family and close friends is one of the greatest safety factors a fledgling flyer can have."

Family support and a can-do attitude nurtured Earhart from her birth on July 24, 1897, in Atchison, Kansas, to her last flight in June 1937. No one reined in her tomboy activities as a young girl, growing up in the home of her wealthy grandparents and attending a private school in Atchison. After her parents moved in 1908 to Des Moines, Iowa, she began to travel frequently with her father, a railroad man. The journeys led to new places and meeting new people, something she relished throughout her life. She liked sports of all kinds and was not afraid to play. "There is a thread of liking to experiment . . . and of something inside me that has always liked to try new things. There they all are, weaving in and out and here and there through the years before aviation and I got together."

President Elliott was attracted to Earhart's sense of adventure, and he could see that she would be a tremendous asset in attracting women to higher education and Purdue. Discussions about Earhart becoming affiliated with Purdue began March 22, 1935. A few months later, Elliott announced Earhart would be a visiting faculty member. She was to serve as a consultant for Purdue's flight programs and as a counselor for careers for women.

"Miss Earhart represents better than any other young woman of this generation the spirit and the courageous skill which may be called the new pioneering," Elliott said.

Earhart was just as pleased. "There is plenty of opportunity for pioneering in fields other than aviation and that is what we are doing here," she said in an interview with the Purdue *Exponent* on November 8, 1935. Purdue was the first university in the country to have a specific position to counsel women about careers, she said. "Things are changing so rapidly and the field is broadening so much for women that the opportunity from college is better than it ever has been and promises to expand even more," she said in her first campus interview. "We shall have to feel our way along because nothing like this has ever been done before."

Although seldom on campus for more than a few weeks at a time from 1935 to 1937, she lived in the women's residence hall near State and Russell streets. The campus always knew when she was coming "because of all the flowers and boxes that came first," wrote Miriam Beck in an article about Amelia Earhart at Purdue for *Airlines* magazine in April 1937. The article speculated that Earhart might have been problematic for the campus because she attracted too many students.

Beck observed that the famous pilot, known for her mannish style and also as a designer of a line of clothing sold at Macy's, had not influenced dress on the campus. "In the 1930s, there were about 800 women enrolled at Purdue and none of the women were allowed to wear trousers, so it's easy to see why Earhart did not influence dress," said Louise Schickler Rogers. However, she did influence other things on campus. Earhart liked buttermilk and in efforts to emulate her, many girls started drinking it with their meals. When on campus, Earhart almost always ate dinner with the 120 women in the hall, quietly slipping her shoes off under the table and resting her elbows on top.

"I'll never forget that first evening when she was here at dinner," Frances Merritt, a nineteen-year-old student from Frankfort, Indiana, told the *Indianapolis Star* in a story published on November 23, 1935. "Gee, I felt as if I were eating sawdust, until she started to talk, then I was so engrossed that I got along fine. She's so darned sweet and charming. She talks right into your eyes and you forget who she is. Now, she says 'Hello, there' when I meet her on the campus or in the hall here, and I nearly pop my buttons with pride. I even managed a big wink at her the other night at dinner. And when she goes by in that big crate of hers [referring to Miss Earhart's motor car] and waves, do I feel like somebody! She doesn't ride to her office, though; she walks with some of us, takes big strides like a boy, and often goes bareheaded."

The men in Cary Hall invited Earhart to dinner, too, said Virginia Kelly Karnes, a 1935 Purdue graduate who was running the office in the men's residence hall. "She talked to the boys, engineering students, about things pertinent to their work. But she didn't stay very long. Her husband called every night at 8 P.M.," Karnes said.

Earhart seemed at ease with the students. "After dinner, as many students who could would follow Miss Earhart into my room and sit around on the floor and talk and listen. She sat on the floor, too. She was adaptable, easy, and informal. It was during these times especially that we got to know some of the underlying beliefs and hopes and dreams that motivated our distinguished guest," wrote Helen Schleman in her 1975 memoir which appears in *The Sound of Wings: The Life of Amelia Earhart.*

"The conversations invariably centered around Miss Earhart's belief that women should have and really did have choices about what they could do with their lives. She believed and said that, of course, women should be engineers or scientists; they could be physicians as well as nurses; they could manage businesses as well as be secretaries or managers. She believed in women's intelligence, their ability to learn, and their ability to do whatever they wanted to do. She saw no limitation on aspirations," Schleman wrote.

Marian Frazier of Oak Park, Illinois, told the *Star* in the November 23 article that she was proud to be in the room next to the flyer's. "One night I was sitting in my room studying and she stuck her head in and asked if she could borrow my pen. She promised to bring it back in a 'sec,' just like the girls do. Well, I guess I couldn't keep it to myself because when she did bring it back, there were a bunch of girls in my room just to get another glimpse of her."

The friendliness extended beyond the residence hall, too. Earhart frequently chauffeured students around in her tan Ford coupe with red leather upholstery.

"This afternoon, as I was standing on the corner in front of the hall, waiting for a street car, you zipped past me in the car. Half a block away, you stepped on the brakes, put her in reverse, and crawled back again," wrote Alice Price in an unmailed letter to Earhart dated July 15, 1937. Price, a nursing student at Purdue from 1935 to 1937, included the letter in *The Sound of Wings*, a memoir she wrote January 5, 1939, upon learning her friend had been declared dead.

> *"Going places, Nursie?"*
>
> *"To the city."*
>
> *"Climb in."*
>
> *I did. You informed me that you were on your way to buy gasoline, asking me to suggest one of the better filling stations. Seeing a chance to ride to Lafayette, I began a voluble discussion of the superior class of filling stations that were located on the other side of the river.*

Price wrote in the letter that she wondered aloud during the ride what would happen if Earhart confused the car with a plane.

> *You remarked that you didn't worry too much about consequences of an accident, either plane or car, and delighted me by adding, "now that I know about good nursing care, all I need do about getting banged up is remember your telephone number." You stopped at the corner . . . and I left the car, but before you could get started, the red light caught you. As I stepped to the sidewalk, a woman who was standing nearby grabbed my arm, pointed to you, and asked so that people within the next block could hear, "Isn't that Amelia Earhart?" I was unprepared for such a sweeping interruption to my train of thought and glanced confusedly back at you. You grinned at me as much as to say "serves you right for riding with me," and with a wave your hand, went on your way.*

Not all of the student's experiences were on the ground. Price recalled the day she played hookey from chemistry lab. "You had just come from the dining room, dressed in brown slacks, shirt, leather jacket, and shoes, the only other color in evidence was the gray scarf which you wore 'round your neck," Price wrote in her memoir of the unexpected encounter.

> *"Where to, Nursie?"*
>
> *"Look," and I held up the text for you to see. "Where to for you?"*
>
> *"I'm going over to look at my pet."*
>
> *"No fair. There's absolutely no justice when you can play around at the airport and I have to spend a morning like this in the classroom and I haven't even seen your plane yet. . . . I wanted a personally conducted tour by the owner."*
>
> *"Oh, well, why not play hookey and come along with me this morning?"*
>
> *"Do you mean it?" Already the sun was brighter. The day gave promise of being satisfactory after all.*
>
> *"Of course I mean it. I was never especially interested in classes on a morning like this either. If you're not sissy enough to be afraid to skip a lecture, we can have fun."*

It was October 8, 1926, and the two women explored the *Flying Laboratory*, pretending to fly it while Earhart demonstrated the controls. Earhart convinced the head of the airport to take the student up in a "two-seater, open-air, puddle-jumper with a whole flock of idiosyncrasies," Price wrote. "I had suspected you of using a small amount of child psychology in getting me in the mood for a flight and when you were reluctant to wait until we could get another plane, I was sure of it."

While up in the air, Price "lost the sensation of speed and was surprised to learn that we were traveling at a rate which, had I been in a car, would have been grounds for screaming with fright. [The pilot] pointed out several of the key buildings in Lafayette, and I was able to locate others for myself. The Wabash [River] was a narrow ribbon separating Lafayette from the West Side."

If trousers, a red upholstered car, elbows on the table, and stocking feet at dinner weren't controversial, Earhart's mere presence on campus was for some, despite Elliott's endorsement and support. Some professors took issue with Earhart and her appointment, calling attention to the fact the pilot had no college degree and was not qualified for her post. Some of the male students didn't like Earhart's feminist message, said Dorothy Stratton, dean of women at the time the pilot was on campus. Men were upset with the notion women that could do other things besides get married, Stratton recalled in *The Romance of Flight*, a Purdue-produced videotape about Earhart's life.

Earhart was not deterred by such talk. She said Purdue was her type of school. "It is a technical school, where instruction has practicality and where a progressive program for women was being started," she told the *Star*.

"Amelia was a feminist, but never resorted to the extremes of blatant feminism, nor did she need to do so," Mary S. Lovell wrote. "Her thinking, her entire philosophy, was based on her certain knowledge that she was the equal of anyone, and in her marriage to George, she was able to live in harmony with her concept of life. She actually denied being a feminist, disliking the connotation, saying that her opinions were merely 'modern thinking.' Her constant speeches on the subject, however, were made because she could see discrimination, even if she did not experience it herself."

When told frequently that aviation was no field for a woman, Earhart said she didn't see where people got such notions, saying, "After all, it is an individual matter. Of course, all women are not suited to aviation any more than all women are suited to be lawyers, or even housewives," she told an unidentified newspaper in the Earhart collection at Purdue. "Some day," she said, "people will be judged by their individual aptitude to do a thing and [society] will stop blocking off certain things as suitable to men and suitable to women."

One of Earhart's first acts as counselor was to survey the female students, asking them why they were in college and if they wanted a career. She also asked them if they wanted a career because "your aunt says you ought to do it? Or because you think it is the thing to do? If you are married, how does your husband fit into the picture? What do you expect of him? What part does he play in your life?" Ninety-two percent of the women students who answered wanted a career.

"Education does not start soon enough to discover aptitudes or to help the individual develop what he [or she] is best able to do; it fails to bridge the gap between training and the practical aspects of employment; and it is making very little effort—certain it is not leading the way toward remedying the present economic situation in which neither the ability to work, or the desire to do so, nor the necessity for having a job, will provide one," she told the *Exponent.*

Stratton, who shared office space with Earhart and considered the pilot a close personal friend, said Earhart was a person of considerable stature and that students watched her every move. Earhart was a captivating speaker who could "hold an audience in the palm of her hand."

Marguerite Call, the only female at Purdue enrolled in electrical engineering at that time, recalled for the *Star* article how she and two female chemical engineering students benefited from their conference with Earhart. "Well, she explained to us very clearly what some of the obstacles were in the way of women who went into what has always been known as a man's field. She was encouraging, too. She didn't see why, if a woman has special talents along that line, she couldn't go out and show 'em! She realized that there was radio work, for instance, that didn't require hard, manual labor and that a girl could do quite as well as a man. She told us about opportunities in television and in radio operation."

Florence Sequartz of Indianapolis, secretary for the women's residence hall, told the *Star* that Earhart was "for women in everything and that's why I think she's so grand. Even for me, a freshman in home economics, which leads, you might think, directly into home and marriage, she sees a hundred opportunities, even in marriage. She doesn't believe that a woman's career has to stop with her marriage, necessarily, and she also believes that you can make a real career out of being a homemaker. I asked her about what she thought of keeping one's own name, if one had won distinction. She said she thought it quite permissible, and that her own husband introduced her as Miss Earhart and usually referred to her as A. E."

In another unidentified newspaper article in the collection, Earhart spoke about the future, in which "we may find an ideal state when both husband and wife work and when both share equal responsibility for the home."

Earhart, who was paid about $2,000 a year, took her responsibilities at Purdue seriously. Shortly after arriving on campus, she typed some notes about Purdue's system of education, based on her observations and impressions. In the draft, Earhart said students complained about there not being enough electives to satisfy their desire to explore topics not related to their majors. "Lowering the fortress walls between schools would serve to eliminate some of the condescending attitudes on the part of men students toward girls. Today it is almost as if the subjects themselves had sex, so firm is the line drawn between what girls and boys should study."

In a biography, Putnam wrote that his wife never quite adjusted to her title at Purdue, yet she found her job at the university one of the most satisfying adventures of her life. Earhart took the job immediately because Purdue was a premier institution and one of the few to have an airfield and a program in the field of aeronautics. Earhart told the *Star* that she had "high regard for the educational theories of Dr. Elliott, whom I have met frequently in a social way.

"Timing is everything," said Sally Putnam Chapman, Earhart's step-granddaughter, in an interview at Purdue on March 10, 2003. "No one had offered her a job," she said of Elliott's offer. Earhart had a "deep sense of pride" about her Purdue connection. "It filled a void in her life, and it was a gift from Purdue that gave her the chance to expand her horizons."

The gift, of course, was the Lockheed Electra, which, along with the support of Purdue and its benefactors, has linked forever the university and the world's most famous female pilot.

As George Putnam told it, Elliott "asked him what he thought most interested Miss Earhart in the field of research and education beyond immediate academic matters. Putnam said he told Elliott that she was 'hankering for a bigger and better place, only one in which she could go to far places farther and faster and more safely, but to use as a laboratory for research in aviation education and for technical experimentation.'"

Discussions among Elliott, Putnam, Earhart, and David E. Ross, a Purdue graduate and benefactor, led to the establishment in April 1936 of the Amelia Earhart Fund for Aeronautical Research within the Purdue Research Foundation. Among the chief contributors were Ross, Josiah K. Lilly, and Vincent Bendix. "The fund purchased the $80,000 Lockheed Electra which became known as the *Flying Laboratory*. After a number of test flights, Miss Earhart brought the *Flying Laboratory* to the Purdue University Airport and to other major cities over the country getting various pieces of equipment and support for her projected round-the-world flight. Her last official visit to the university as a coed counselor was in November 1936."

"Your generous cooperation and that of your associates is making a dream come true," Earhart wrote to Elliott in a letter dated March 25, 1936. "I am exceedingly grateful to President Elliott and the friends of Purdue who are making possible my new plans. I hope its use may result in constructive accomplishment—both for Purdue and for women in general. For it is not often we of the feminine persuasion are given such opportunities to pioneer in our chosen fields."

Earhart prepared for her 27,000 mile, round-the-world trip with navigator Fred Noonan. Her Lockheed Electra was outfitted with a soundproofed cockpit, special instruments, de-icing appliances, stabilizers, a radio honing device, and a two-way radio. Passenger seats were replaced with gasoline tanks. Among the research projects on which Earhart was to work during the trip was the effect of high altitude and long distance on the human physique. Fatigue, eyestrain, and alcohol were part of the experiments. "I am the guinea pig," Earhart once said.

The *Flying Laboratory* took off from Oakland, California, on March 17, 1937, but it crashed in Hawaii, delaying the trip for weeks. Earhart and her crews decided to fly east to west and took off from Miami on June 1, 1937. The trip was relatively uneventful until Earhart and Noonan left New Guinea for Howland Island in the Pacific.

There's no doubt Earhart was fully aware of the hazards she faced, but she told family and friends that flying was what she wanted to do. Flying was like poetry, she said. Still, few were prepared for the radio transmission in which Earhart said she had a half-hour's fuel and could not see land. "We are on the line of position 157-337. We are running north to south." The last radio contact was July 2, 1937. A radio signal was heard for several days but to no avail. Eighteen months later, Earhart was declared dead. No wreckage or bodies have ever been found. Elliott, upon hearing that Earhart was missing and presumed dead, said, "Flying owes a great debt to her courage, skill, and intelligence."

Price, in her memoir, was more passionate. "The printed [newspaper] paragraph stated briefly that 'Amelia Earhart, missing eighteen months in the South Pacific on her round-the-world flight, is now declared legally dead.' The terse explanation for such an action is to the effect that 'the ruling of the court, although not in accordance with the seven-year law, will probably stand unquestioned because of the abundance of evidence pointing to her death.' I like to believe that the abovementioned 'abundance of evidence' is misleading, as evidence so often can be. I like to think that Miss Earhart's disappearance had nothing whatever to do with the South Pacific Ocean. Her element was air—not water. She had no medals won in aquatic sport, she was not an enthusiastic sailor, and she loved flying. The blue sky was her playground, a pair of wings her prized medal of achievement.

"I like to believe that on the morning of July 2, 1937, while riding through the clouds, she knew and was able to describe so vividly, she inadvertently came upon a world which enchanted her, that, like Alice in *Through the Looking Glass*, she entered in. Here, she discovered a world of blue sky, white tumbled clouds, glowing sunsets, a world peopled with mechanics and equipped with all the machinery and tools of which she had dreamed, a veritable paradise for aviators with fingers that itch to tinker. I like to imagine that even now, her tousled, curly head is bent with interest over a gadget, which she is fashioning in her own particular dream shop. In my mind, I can see her busily engaged in doing the things she had long wished to do. I know that her hearty, unbounded enthusiasm and her contagious friendliness has already made her beloved in this, her new world."

That kind of romantic view persists in 2003. Two expeditions are searching for any sign of what may have happened to the famous pilot, according to *Time* reporter Tim McGirk. "Two rival groups of Earhart enthusiasts are convinced that they can at long last solve the riddle of her crash. Their hypotheses are wildly different—and yet both are plausible. One group, led by Ric Gillespie from Delaware-based The International Group for Historic Aircraft Recovery (TIGHAR), believes that Earhart and Noonan wandered far off course. After running out of fuel, they crash-landed on Nikumaroro, a tiny crust of an atoll far south of their intended destination. The searchers believe that Earhart and Noonan, injured after ditching the plane, survived for at least several days before perishing on the deserted atoll."

A twelve-member group has been searching the atoll since August 27, 2002. "The team members speak of searing heat, voracious bugs, and possible gravestones that, so far, have turned out to be chunks of coral. But their four previous expeditions on the island between 1989 and 1997 unearthed several tantalizing, though far from substantiating, clues: aircraft debris and a leather sole that could have belonged to Earhart's shoe," McGirk wrote.

"Meanwhile, David Jourdan, founder of Nauticos, the Maryland-based outfit that plumbed many of the secrets of the sunken *Titanic*, is heading in another direction. In January, Jourdan and crew will utilize the latest sonar technology and fiber-optic cables to explore a roughly

5,200-square-kilometer area of the ocean floor northwest of Howland Island. The sensors will dangle below Nauticos' ship, picking up sounds bounced off any odd shapes on the flat ocean floor. The Nauticos team selected the search area based on new, high-tech analysis of the radio-beam strength of Earhart's last messages, wind speed, and just how far her 42,000 liters of fuel would have taken her," McGirk wrote.

And so, the romance and spirit of Earhart and what she represented still pull people to the Pacific in search of answers to her mystery.

Janice Voss

As a girl, Janice Voss loved to read science fiction. There are books she can still remember, such as *A Winkle in Time* from the sixth grade. She thought it was the neatest thing she had ever read.

It's a story about two children whose father disappears. Beings from outer space come and visit them and say their dad is trying to save the universe, and he needs their help. And so, they go wandering about the universe assisting out their father.

"I just started reading science fiction, and I thought it was the most interesting kind of thing that I had ever heard about," Voss says. "And if anybody was doing anything—anything even close to that—I wanted to be part of it."

She made it. She has flown on five space shuttle missions and is one of the most experienced NASA astronauts.

Born in South Bend, Indiana, she considers Rockford, Illinois, to be her hometown. She graduated from Minnechaug Regional High School in Wilbraham, Massachusetts, in 1972. She knew she was interested in engineering, but had not decided where she wanted to focus. She applied to Purdue University, where her parents had graduated. She also applied to the University of Illinois and the University of Michigan.

"I ended up at Purdue because they had by far the friendliest services people," Voss says. "They just sent you all kinds of information that you didn't know you needed and were very helpful and friendly."

Voss was a straight-A student in high school. She would graduate from Purdue in December 1975 with a degree in engineering science.

Shortly after arriving at Purdue in 1972 she applied for a co-op program at the NASA Johnson Space Center. She alternated semesters between Purdue and Houston where she did computer simulations in the Engineering and Development Directorate. Her first semester at NASA began in January 1973. Eugene Cernan and Apollo 17 had returned to Earth on December 6, 1972. Voss was immediately launched into the coming big program—the Space Shuttle Program.

"The shuttle was already a very solid program at that point," Voss says. "There were lots of people working on it. There was a commitment to fly it."

When she graduated from Purdue, Voss went to MIT and received her master's degree in electrical engineering. She would return to MIT and receive her Ph.D. in aerospace engineering in 1987. After completing her master's degree, she went to work with NASA doing training. She wrote and taught a class in shuttle entry guidance and navigation.

In 1978, Voss applied to be an astronaut. She was not accepted.

"I just decided to keep trying," she says. "I just didn't get that job. I could do some other job, and I'd keep trying."

After finishing her Ph.D. at MIT she went to work for Orbital Sciences Corporation. Her responsibilities there included mission integration and flight operations support for an upper stage called the transfer orbit stage (TOS). TOS launched the Advanced Communications Technology Satellite from the space shuttle in September 1993, and *Mars Observer* from a Titan in the fall of 1992.

She was accepted to the astronaut program in 1990 on her fourth application.

Her first mission was STS-57, June 21–July 1, 1993. Among the highlights of the mission were retrieval of the European Retrievable Carrier with the shuttle's robotic arm and a space walk by two crewmembers.

There is a little, but not a lot of, relaxation time once in orbit and everything is underway.

"It's expensive to go up there," Voss says. "But they recognize that if they work you too hard you won't be very efficient, because you'll get tired. On a typical day, you might have half an hour to an hour that you can do personal stuff like write E-mail to home. We have what is effectively an E-mail connection. Or, you can use that time to look out the window or write in a diary or listen to music."

Voss enjoys writing messages to family and friends.

"I think that's a really fun way to share the experience of flying in space, so I don't look out the window as much as some," she says. "I'm probably in the lower 10 percent of window gazers."

Voss flew on STS-63 February 3–11, 1995, and had a rendezvous with the Russian space station, Mir. She was payload commander on STS-83, April 4–8, 1997. The mission was cut short because of problems with one of the shuttle's three fuel cell power generation units.

The entire crew and payload flew again on STS-94, July 1–17, 1997. Her next flight was STS-99 February 11–22, 2000. This was an eleven-day flight during which the international crew aboard the Space Shuttle *Endeavor* worked dual shifts to support radar-mapping operations. That shuttle radar topography mission mapped more than forty-seven million square miles of the Earth's land surface.

Voss has logged more than forty-nine days in space, traveling 18.8 million miles in 779 Earth orbits. And as for her love of science fiction — she re-read *A Wrinkle In Time* during one of her space missions.

Chapter Ten

Thanks for the memories
Of moment, lift, and drag,
Along with Coke and fag
Of lab reports and drafting sports
And metatarsal sag.
Oh thank you, so much!

—Purdue Curtiss-Wright Cadettes song

Amelia Earhart was lost somewhere in the Pacific Ocean, and the winds of war were blowing throughout the world. They would eventually reach all way to Purdue University, where the new airport and aviation programs would play a significant role in the fight for freedom.

On September 1, 1939, Germany invaded Poland. While the overwhelming sentiment in the United States was to stay out of this fight, there were those who knew what would inevitably occur. The worst fears that had been voiced since the end of World War I by people such as Billy Mitchell were coming true.

From the end of the war to the start of the new hostilities in Europe, the United States had only a minor aviation program. In 1938, the nation had only five thousand Army pilots. Worse, it had only one thousand planes for them to fly. The Army Air Corps had one location in the nation where it could train only five hundred pilots a year: Randolph Field in San Antonio. The Navy could train about five hundred pilots a year at its facilities in Pensacola. In the civilian ranks, there were about twenty-one thousand pilots, but many of them had allowed their licenses to expire. There were fewer than ten thousand civilian planes, only about four hundred of them in scheduled operation. At the same time, Germany was training sixty-five thousand pilots and technicians and Italy was preparing a flying fighting force of 100,000.[1]

The United States was behind, and it would have to catch up quickly. One of the first efforts to accomplish this came in 1938 when Congress passed the Civil Aeronautics Act. This legislation created, for the first time, "an independent government agency for the control, supervision, and furtherance of aviation in the United States to foster and develop all areas of civil aviation."[2]

The act authorized funding for what would become the Civilian Pilot Training Program. On December 27, 1938, President Franklin Roosevelt announced the program at a White House press conference. If the Germans and Italians were preparing thousands of young people who could be pulled into military air service, the United States could and would do the same.

The Civilian Pilot Training Program (CPTP) was created to provide flight training for twenty thousand college students every year. The programs would be set up through universities. No school would have more students than Purdue, which already had the unique combination of an aeronautical engineering program and flight training at a university-owned airport.

Soon, Purdue would also have Grove Webster, one of the top officials from the CPTP. Grove Webster was a native of New York State and another of those twentieth-century men whose lives flowed with the birth and growth of aviation.

He was born in 1896, the year that Wilbur Wright was first beginning to take an interest in the possibilities of powered flight. Webster was probably fourteen years old when he saw his first flying machine. It was love at first sight, and he came to play a major role in helping build United States air power for World War II. With that accomplished, he would arrive at the Purdue University Airport and oversee its development until retiring in 1973.

Webster joined the Army Air Service during World War I and served in France. The war ended before he flew any combat missions, but he knew immediately he wanted to spend his life around airplanes.

After the war, he continued his involvement with aviation in the private sector and in 1930 established an airport directory that covered most of the United States. The directory filled a void, providing important information on major airports in every state including photographs of each field. It was an enormous help to early flyers.

Webster continued this work until 1938, when he was summoned to Washington, D.C., by Robert Noble, the new chairman of the Civil Aeronautics Authority. Webster was asked to join the new agency to develop the program for civilian aviation training that would be announced at the end of year by Roosevelt. He agreed on the spot to take the position and on September 1, 1938, was named chief of the private flying section. He had a secretary, a budget of $20,000, and a lot of work to do.[3] He had to work fast.

His instructions were to put together a program that used the nation's universities for training civilian pilots, and Webster decided to build on what he had learned observing flight training during World War I.

In a 1979 article for *Aerospace Historian* magazine, Webster wrote, "The World War I program was set up to send the enlisted cadets to one of the participating colleges or universities for an eight-week ground school and, upon successful completion, to a military flying school for flight instruction. [I] . . . suggested we follow a similar pattern. The ground school would be taught in a college or university, and the flight training would be given by a fixed-base operator at an airport convenient to the institution."[4] The program was almost tailor-made for Purdue.

A decision was reached creating a seventy-two hour ground-training program followed by a thirty-five-hour flight-training course using airplanes with a minimum fifty-horsepower engine. Roosevelt was quickly sold on the program and announced it that December.

It was slated to start in the spring of 1939, just three months away. This first, experimental start-up program would consist of 330 students. The program was funded with $150,000 from the National Youth Administration—part of Roosevelt's New Deal.[5] Although the president was quickly on board, the military moved slower. According to a U.S. Centennial of Flight Commission report, "The military establishment was initially unenthusiastic about the concept, quite unimpressed by any program initiated and administered by civilians. Also, Congress was split along mostly party lines as to the value of the [program]. Isolationists branded the program as provocative saber-ratting that threatened the nation's neutrality; others slammed it as a New Deal pork barrel waste of tax dollars, while supporters touted the positive impacts on the aviation industry and the defense value of a vastly enlarged base of trained pilots."[6]

With funding lined up, Webster's private flying section split with the technical development division. Webster's new title was chief of the private flying development division, and he and his staff started outlining the course.

The universities that were chosen and the target number of students at each institution for the first programs were the following: Purdue, 50;

University of Michigan, 30; North Carolina State, 30; Georgia Tech, 30; University of Alabama, 30; North Texas Agricultural, 30; Pomona Junior College, 15; San Jose State Teachers College, 15; University of Washington, 30; University of Minnesota, 20; University of Kansas, 20; New York University, 30.[7]

Webster visited each university before the program was started. He received a warm reception from Purdue President Edward Elliott. Elliott, who had a strong interest in aviation and the backing of David Ross from the Purdue University Board of Trustees, told Webster if he ever decided to leave the government, there would be a place for him at Purdue.[8]

Purdue not only had the largest initial class, it was first to get its program going. At precisely 1 P.M. on February 16, 1939, a Purdue student took to the air and became the first person in the United States to receive instruction through the CPTP.[9]

By June 1939, when the spring semester was completed at universities across the country, 313 of the original 330 students had earned their private flight certificates. Webster and others began gearing up for the fall semester with increased numbers of both students and instructors.

Then the world quickly changed. When Nazi Germany invaded Poland, and World War II began.

According to the U.S. Centennial of Flight Commission, "After the invasion of Poland, the military value of the Civilian Pilot Training Program became obvious even to the program's detractors. The United States started to evaluate its ability to fight an air war and the results were appalling. Pilots, instructors, and training aircraft were all in short supply. Acknowledging the shortage of trained pilots, both the U.S. Army and Navy reluctantly waived certain 'elimination' courses for Civilian Pilot Training Program graduates and allowed them to proceed directly into pilot training."[10]

Funding for the program skyrocketed. Webster wrote, "President Roosevelt appeared before a joint session of Congress on May 16, 1940, and asked for $1 billion for defense and an Air Corps of 50,000 aircraft. One obvious question was, 'Where are you going to get the pilots?' The immediate result of this action was a greatly expanded Civilian Pilot Training Program. The budget for fiscal year 1940–1941 was increased from five million to thirty-seven million dollars. The number of participating schools was increased from 400 to over 700."[11]

There were two other interesting developments from the CPTP that were not originally anticipated. It had the impact of opening aviation to African Americans and women.

While there were women pilots dating back to the days before World War I, they were always very few in number. It was even harder for African Americans. The few who did become pilots were often self-trained, trained by the few other African American pilots, or they received their instruction overseas. In 1939, African Americans were not accepted into military flight training. Since that was the major route to flying, the doors of aviation—one of the twentieth century's most important opportunities—were closed to them. The CPTP opened the door, if only a crack, that later would swing wide open.

The CPTP did not discriminate based on race or sex. Six African-American colleges participated in the program: Tuskegee, Delaware College, Hampton Institute, North Carolina A&M, West Virginia State, and Howard. The CPTP at Tuskegee Institute began in 1939, offering African Americans a new opportunity.

"Tuskegee, besides participating in all civilian pilot training courses, later was a contractor for the training of [Army] Air Force pilots," Webster wrote. "And on January 17, 1941, the War Department announced that henceforth, blacks would be accepted in the [Army] Air Force. Civilian pilot training was the key that opened the door for these young men. The Navy did not train black pilots during this period."[12]

While the Army accepted African American pilots, the military in 1941 was racially segregated, and the training of these pilots was focused at Tuskegee, where the famed Tuskegee Airmen were formed. Between 1941 and 1945, Tuskegee trained more than one thousand African American aviators for the war effort.

They initially had difficulty being assigned to overseas combat duty, but once into action, the Tuskegee Airmen greatly distinguished themselves. Called the Black Bird-Men by the Germans, they completed 15,500 missions. Tuskegee Airmen destroyed more than 260 enemy aircraft and facilities fighting in the Mediterranean theater. Several of the airmen died in combat, but they never lost a bomber to enemy fighters.

Medals awarded to the airmen included the Distinguished Flying Cross, the Legion of Merit, the Silver Star, the Purple Heart, the Croix de Guerre, and the Red Star of Yugoslavia. The entire 332nd Fighter Group of Tuskegee Airmen received a Distinguished Unit Citation for "outstanding performance and extraordinary heroism."

In addition to Tuskegee, Willa Brown ran a Civilian Pilot Training Program at Harlem Airport in Oak Lawn, Illinois. Brown, an African American woman who became an aviator and aviation entrepreneur, was truly a trailblazer.

She was born in Kentucky in 1906 when the Wright brothers were perfecting their flying machine in Dayton, Ohio. She moved with her family to Terre Haute, Indiana, where she graduated from high school. She enrolled at Indiana State in Terre Haute, where she successfully completed her studies and graduated.

In 1927, she moved to Gary where she taught school and, at age twenty-one, was the youngest teacher in the district. She later moved to Chicago, became involved in social work, and was lured by the adventure of aviation. She received flight training from Cornelius Coffey, one of only two African Americans who had civil service credentials in mechanical aviation at that time. Brown was attracted to more than aviation. She was attracted to Coffey, and they soon married.

Four women's colleges were included in the CPTP: Lake Erie, Adelphi, Mills, and Florida State. In addition, a quota was established for all Civilian Pilot Training Programs requiring that one out of every ten pilots had to be female.

According to Webster, by July 1941 more than three thousand women had participated in the program, but as the war opened flight opportunities for African American men at Tuskegee, the door was closed for women. On July 1, 1941, with war growing in Europe, women became ineligible for civilian pilot training because of budget pressures and because the government wanted to focus on training men who would be needed to fight.

Webster cites eleven major contributions of the CPTP. It "created the rating of flight instructor; standardized civil flight instructions; created ten volumes of flight and ground instruction manuals; established the standardization center; opened the program to all regardless of race, color, or sex; cooperated in the training of pilots for scheduled airlines and ferry and glider pilots for the military; produced 10,000 flight instructors for civil and military aviation; provided a pool of over 400,000 partially trained pilots for military aviation; established schools for aviation training of inter-American nationals for airline companies south of the border; established five schools for the training of Navy flight instructors; [and] turned in a remarkable safety record."[13]

At its peak, the Civilian Pilot Training Program was working with 1,132 colleges and universities and 1,460 flight schools.[14] At Purdue, Lawrence "Cap" Aretz helped train 639 students in the Civilian Pilot Training Program.[15]

After December 7, 1941, and the attack at Pearl Harbor, the CPTP became the War Training Service. The war training service continued until the summer of 1944 as a screening program for potential military pilots.

In a report for the U.S. Centennial of Flight Commission, Roger Guillemette said, "The Civilian Pilot Training Program/war training service was phased out in the summer of 1944 but not before 435,165 people, including hundreds of women and African Americans, had been taught to fly." The CPTP admirably achieved its primary mission, best expressed by the title of aviation historian Dominick Pisano's book *To Fill The Skies With Pilots.*[16]

Even before the attack on Pearl Harbor, Webster could see changes coming in the program. It was heading more toward military control. He resigned from the civil pilot training service on October 8, 1941, to form his own consulting service. One of his first accounts was Purdue University. As part of his consulting work, he drafted an air transportation plan for Purdue. It impressed university officials and on July 1, 1942, Webster came to work at Purdue on temporary duty. That temporary assignment lasted thirty-one years.

When he arrived in 1942, the Purdue University Airport was closed to the public and being used only by the military.[17] It was a busy place. Purdue engineering historian H. B. Knoll says, "During the war the airport became a training center, and planes buzzed around it like bees around a hive."[18]

With the arrival of Webster, Elliott and Purdue University Board of Trustees President David Ross moved to create the Purdue Aeronautics Corporation. It was started in 1942 with Webster in control. Overseeing the corporation was a board that included Elliott, Ross, and other members of the board. The purpose of the corporation was to advance aeronautical engineering at the university and improve the use of the airport.

Elliott had a great vision for the role of universities in aeronautics. In *Edward Charles Elliott: Educator,* Frank K. Burrin writes, "Shortly after the Purdue Aeronautics Corporation was established, Elliott testified before a senate subcommittee that he thought land-grant colleges could perform the same services to aviation that had been rendered to agriculture—indicating that perhaps aviation, in the years to come, was going to be just as important to the nation as agriculture had been in the last two generations. The Purdue Aeronautics Corporation, without question, has had a major role in the development of airport facilities and equipment."[19] That statement was key to what was beginning to develop at Purdue.

Webster became director and general manager of the Purdue Aeronautics Corporation and served as manager of the Purdue Airport. He also directed flight-training programs such as the Inter-American program, which was sponsored by the U.S. State Department. In this program, young men from eight countries in South America and Central America came to Purdue for training in airline and fixed-base operations. About eighty-five completed the ten-month program.[20]

According to *A Record of A University In The War Years*, three groups of pilots were trained at the Purdue Airport between June 1942 and the summer of 1944. "Twenty-eight pilots from the Army Enlisted Reserve Corps; 534 from the Navy V-5; and 166 from the War Training Service flight instructors school." There were about sixty planes at the airport and as many as forty civilian instructors and another forty ground personnel were employed.[21]

E. F. Bruhn arrived at Purdue in January 1941. In *A History of Aeronautical Education and Research at Purdue University for the Period 1937–1950,* he wrote about meeting with a group of students in the Air Corps cadet aeronautical engineering program. The meeting took place in June 1941.

The students were being trained for flight operations and aircraft maintenance first at Purdue and then at Chanute Field in Rantoul, Illinois. Bruhn said, "As I entered one of the larger classrooms in the mechanical engineering building, the group as a whole appeared to be terribly downcast. When I asked the reason for all the gloom, they replied, 'Professor, the way the Hitler war machine is rolling to victories, we are fearful this war will be over before we finish at Chanute Field and get our commission.' Little did any of us realize at that time that the Pearl Harbor catastrophe was less than six months away. Years later, I learned that several of them had died in the great Pacific air campaign."[22]

By mid-1941, the dean of engineering at Purdue, A. A. Potter, was convinced that air power was going to be a significant factor in the war and the years that followed. He recommended a four-year course of study leading to a bachelor of science degree in aeronautical engineering. The course work appears in the 1941–1942 Purdue catalog, and in 1942, the name of the school was changed to the School of Mechanical and Aeronautical Engineering.[23]

While women had been removed from the Civilian Pilot Training Program before the war even started, a new opportunity arose in late 1942 when the Curtiss-Wright Corporation started a program. With men serving in the military, there was a need for women to step into factories, building the machinery the war effort needed—including airplanes. Curtiss-Wright decided to train between 700 and 1,000 women for engineering jobs in plants located in Buffalo, New York, Columbus, Ohio, and Louisville, Kentucky. Seven universities, including Purdue, went to a meeting where the program was outlined, and all of them decided to participate.[24]

The program was scheduled to start on February 12, 1943. The women, who were called "cadettes" in the Curtiss-Wright cadette training program, were recruited from throughout the United States. Curtiss-Wright paid them ten dollars per week during the training period in addition to all their living expenses.

Says Bruhn, "The 100 cadettes for the first program arrived on the Purdue campus on February 12, 1943. I definitely remember that day as there was over six inches of snow on the ground and still snowing. . . . As this very attractive group of cadettes filled the hallways of the aero building, it appeared the aero school men students were very pleased and readily assisted the girls in getting registered and oriented, so to speak. The aero staff seemed to appear in smiles or quite happy with the sudden turn of events."[25]

On July 4, 1944, 116 cadettes started in the second program and 98 successfully completed the work.

The Purdue cadettes wrote their own songs to popular tunes of the day. They tell a great deal about what their experience was like. The following song is sung to "Thanks For the Memories:"

Thanks for the memories
Of moment, lift, and drag,
Along with Coke and fag
Of lab reports and drafting sports
And metatarsal sag.
Oh, thank you, so much!

Many are the times that we've calculated,
And many are the times that we've estimated;
But still we're never dated
Still we are without any beer.

Oh, thanks for the memories,
Of torsion, torque, and shear,
Of sailors with a leer,
Of walks on Intramural Field
Along with you, my dear
Oh, thank you so much! [26]

Bruhn had high regard for Webster. He said, "His extensive flight operations necessitated the building of the large west hangar at the airport, with two story north and south wings for housing, shops, laboratories, classrooms, offices, etcetera. His practical experience, his broad knowledge of every aspect of civil aviation, and his broad acquaintance with leaders in the aviation world, definitely indicated that if Purdue decided to establish a long range, postwar program in the broad field of air transportation, Purdue already had possibly the best qualified person in the United States to help develop and present such a program, and also already had operating facilities that could be used in such a program."[27]

On July 1, 1945, a separate School of Aeronautics opened at Purdue with Bruhn as head. An air transportation program was initiated, including airport management and operations, flight and flight operations, and traffic administration options. But that was all after the war because on December 7, 1941, the focus at Purdue and throughout the country was on more immediate needs.

John Blaha

"Our *Discovery* spaceship currently is moving across India as I look north into China. The panorama before me is beautiful. Two-thirds of the planet is dominated by white clouds. Movement over the terrain is quite rapid as we orbit the earth at 17,500 miles per hour. We currently have our right wing pointed forward; the spaceship is upside down.

"I stop what I'm doing to pause and think just how incredible this experience is. . . . How can anyone adequately describe this unbelievable and exhilarating panoramic view that I have of . . . our unique, beautiful planet. How lucky we are to be here. Wow!

"This is God's country. God built all of this. I wish I had the proper words to describe my feelings and the beauty in front of me."

John Blaha, recorded orbiting Earth on the *Discovery*,
—Sunday, November 26, 1989

Selected as an astronaut in May of 1980, John Blaha has spent a lot of time in space—161 days, on five missions. Through it all, he has never got bored with the beauty of Earth as seen from space, he has never got tired of the thrill of exploring.

Born in San Antonio, Texas, where he lives today, Blaha grew up with his dreams in the sky.

"I always wanted to fly airplanes, so I went to the Air Force Academy," Blaha says.

He started at the Academy in June 1961 and was there when the Soviets and the United States were launching people into space. He had gone to the Academy to fly, but a seed of space was planted in Blaha that would grow in the years ahead.

"I started thinking, maybe once I stop flying airplanes, maybe I'd like to fly spaceships," Blaha says. "There were the Mercury missions and then the Gemini missions, and I started feeling like I strongly wanted to fly in a spaceship. It sounded more exciting than flying airplanes. The Academy had an astronautical engineering major, and that sounded very neat to me because it was things that the astronauts do."

Blaha graduated in 1965. He worked to take part in the Purdue master's degree program.

"I wanted to be in that program. I competed to be in it," Blaha says. "I was selected to do it, and I was very excited because to me that was a check mark along the path to achieving the goal. I was interested in increasing my knowledge of electrical engineering, astronautical engineering, propulsion engineering—all those kinds of things. To me, Purdue was a way to improve my competitiveness to be an astronaut.

"And I'll tell you another thing," he says. "I learned that there were a number of Purdue graduates who were already astronauts. So it seemed like if you wanted to be an astronaut, Purdue was the school."

From Purdue he had jet pilot training and then Vietnam. He was there for one year and flew 361 combat missions. After reading the bios of astronauts, Blaha knew what he needed to do after Vietnam—go to the Air Force Aerospace Research Pilot School.

"So, I started understanding what it took to become competitive to get into there," he says. "And I made sure that I was building a competitive bio to be accepted into that school. I wanted to go to that school to learn how to be a test pilot."

After graduation he worked as a test pilot instructor at the school.

"Buzz Aldrin had come back to the Air Force, and he was the commandant of that school," Blaha says. "Of course, I was asking him, 'What should I do? I want to be an astronaut.' He said, 'John, stay right here in this school, and teach low lift to drag approaches and rendezvous.' There was no question I was always focusing on what I could do to be prepared for the day when NASA said they wanted to hire more people."

He made it in June 1980.

"I remember the day I got the call," Blaha says. "I was working in the Pentagon. I went and told my boss what I was going to do. He took me up to see the vice chief of staff of the Air Force. The vice chief of staff said, 'John, why are you doing this? You have such a good career in the Air Force right here. We really like you.' He even made a call over to the NASA administrator, put him on a squawk box. He said, 'I have a good guy here, who's coming to you. Why don't you tell him what he's going to do for the first five years?' He was trying to tell me that it would be more exciting staying in the Air Force.

"I will say this, the NASA administrator, what he said on the squawk box that day, was the truth. It's exactly what occurred."

Blaha was assigned to a crew in January 1985—four and a half years after being selected for training. The launch was set for December 1985. But there were changes in the schedule. The flight was rescheduled for June 1986. In January 1986 *Challenger* exploded, and the program went into a holding pattern while the accident was investigated.

Blaha finally flew his first flight in March 1989, almost nine years after his selection. He flew again very quickly, on STS-33, November 22–27, 1989.

It was an incredible experience for him after waiting all that time.

"I will always remember that Thanksgiving eve when I felt our three main engines start," he said into a recorder as he orbited Earth on his second mission. "Six seconds later, the solid rocket boosters ignited, and off we went, rocketing into space. On board, inside our space suits, it was very quiet. We could feel the vibrations from all the engines as our vehicle accelerated towards space while fighting the gravity of Earth. Two minutes after liftoff, flames from the separation motors engulfed the forward windows as the solid rocket boosters separated. After separation, the spaceship ride became very smooth and quiet as we continued to accelerate. Without a doubt, this is the best elevator ride in the world. We experienced a force of three times that of gravity near the end of powered flight ascent, and I felt like a gorilla was sitting on my chest.

"Eight and a half minutes after liftoff, the main engines cutoff, and we were in space—in zero gravity. My arms floated up to chest level, and I noticed my ascent procedure reference book floating in front of me at eye level. We were in heaven. This is it, I thought. This is the space program! Unbelievable! With a busy day ahead of us, we immediately went to work."

NASA prepared him so well, Blaha says, that there were no surprises—other than the spectacular view out the window.

"That surprised me," he says. "It was much more than I thought it would be. It was pretty incredible."

Blaha was commander of flights in August 1991 and October–November 1993. So after waiting nine years, he had four flights in a four-year period.

His second launch as commander of STS-58 was recognized "as the most successful and efficient spacelab flight NASA has flown." Flying with Blaha on that mission was Purdue graduate Dave Wolf.

But Blaha wasn't through yet. He had picked up a new interest: the *Mir* space station.

"I was at an Association of Space Explorer's Conference in Berlin in 1991," Blaha says. "I was watching some cosmonauts, through interpreters, show a video about *Mir* space station. I thought, boy, we keep talking about a space station, and here's a real one that someone's operating. I came back to the states, and I said to a number of people at

NASA, why don't we get a program with the Russians, where we go fly with them, so that we can get some experience on the operations of a space station."

NASA did, in fact, start a program putting Americans on *Mir.* Two people were selected to go. They were both mission specialists.

"One day at a pilot's meeting, I raised my hand and I said, 'Is *Mir* a 'mission specialist's only' club? Why can't we have pilots go?' A little bit later, they came to me and said they wanted me to go to Russia to do this. It turns out, I was the only pilot of the seven [Americans] that flew on *Mir.*"

Blaha started Russian language training in August 1994. In January 1995, he and his wife, Brenda, moved to an apartment in Star City on the outskirts of Moscow for a one and a half year training course at the Cosmonaut Training Center.

He launched for *Mir* in mid-September 1996 and returned January 22, 1997.

"I was surprised by a number of things on that mission," Blaha says. "Having flown the four missions with NASA, I thought I understood spaceflight. During our training, the Russians kept telling us, in effect, there were some differences to a long flight. And of course, being an American, I was thinking, 'You know, they're just telling us that because they want us to think they know something about this that we don't.' Well it turned out they were right. The long mission is quite a challenge."

Blaha sent emails to his wife Brenda during the mission:

> *When we were 20 miles from the Mir (approaching in the shuttle), it appeared as a bright, glowing star. From five miles out to docking I looked at this absolutely beautiful, shining Mir Space Station . . . I (had) really misjudged the beauty that was now in front of me. It looked like a very new space station . . .*
>
> *I will always remember the incredible sight as the Atlantis undocked [after dropping him off] and flew around the Mir. The views of Atlantis silhouetted against the darkness of space, the horizon of the earth, or zooming over the top of Russia and China will never leave my memory. Wow, what an incredible space ship America built. Boy, was I proud to see that. . . .*

I am very impressed with the Russian engineering that built this beautiful space station. This has been in orbit for almost 11 years and is functioning—incredible. [Russian cosmonauts] Valeri and Sasha spend about 50 percent of their day maintaining the Mir. They are fascinating people—working tirelessly 16 hours a day . . .

I wake to an alarm clock every morning at 8:00 A.M. By 8:30 I am talking to folks all around the world on the Ham radio. This is a great way to meet folks and receive news from planet Earth. I usually am finished with breakfast at 9:30 A.M. I have a lot of exciting experiments that I perform until 12:30 P.M. Then I run on the treadmill and use expanders to maintain my muscle strength. After cleanup, we eat lunch together, talk about what we have been doing in the morning and what we will be doing in the afternoon. We do science experiments for another four hours; then have another hour of riding the bicycle before dinner. After dinner I usually spend one to two hours preparing for the next workday. It now is 10:00 P.M.

I spend the next two hours looking at our beautiful planet, looking at the stars, finding planets, and watching movies. I have 50 fantastic movies, a few Dallas Cowboys games, etc., as selections.

I am really enjoying this mission. The work is very challenging. This Space Station is amazing. The views from the different windows are fantastic. . . .

Before I launched I had many questions related to boredom, or what I would do to pass the spare time. There is no boredom here. There is always something to do. . . .

Living in space was not as difficult as the return to Earth. “When the human body gets away from gravity for four and half months, it really knows it did something,” Blaha says. “You have soft bone tissues loss in your joints. You have muscle loss. You have to go through a pretty good recuperation period, using water initially, with an individual trainer helping you get going again. Overall it takes about three months until you feel normal again."

While Blaha felt normal after three months, it actually takes six months for the body to return to normal.

He is now retired from NASA and working as a corporate vice president in charge of the business continuity program at USAA, a financial services business that serves people in the U.S. military.

He sees the future of space eventually returning to the Moon or reaching for Mars.

"NASA will figure out what went wrong with the *Columbia* accident," he says. "NASA will get the other three space shuttles flying again, and continue the Space Station. That probably will be complete between 2015 and 2020. After that, I think the next time we talk about a space flight, we need to leave low Earth orbit.

"We need to expand our exploration mission to the solar system and the universe."

Chapter Eleven

George and I became close friends because we thought we were pretty good at aerial combat. We figured ourselves the top guns and the rest of them could take a crack at us if they wanted. We happened to have a very good day together on the seventh of December, 1941.

—Ken Taylor

George Welch was twenty-three years old the day his life changed forever. He was in step with his times. It was the day the world changed forever, too.

Fires were burning at Pearl Harbor; U.S. Navy ships lay in ruins and black smoke billowed in the blue sky as Welch stepped out of a P-40 fighter plane at Wheeler Field the morning of December 7, 1941. The attack was over, but in less than two hours, the U.S. military had suffered 3,435 personnel casualties and the loss of or severe damage to 188 planes, 8 battleships, 3 light cruisers, and 4 other vessels.

Welch, who had left Purdue University to pursue a military flight career, was stunned. Two hours earlier he had been at the officer's club trying to get some sleep after a Saturday night on the town. Now men and women lay dead and dying everywhere—ships, airfields, military bases—on this island paradise. Welch's plane had been hit by enemy fire four times, maybe five according to some people. It was a miracle he had survived.

American losses were enormous. As he walked away from his plane that morning, Welch had no idea exactly how bad it was, but at that moment he had a better idea than most people in the world. He had seen it from the air as it happened—up close and very personal.

When the reports were completed and the records published, Welch would be credited as one of only a handful of American pilots able to get their planes off the ground and into the sky to fight the enemy on that morning. He would be credited with shooting down four—some accounts say six—Japanese airplanes, about 14 percent of the twenty-eight planes the Japanese lost that day. His friend Ken Taylor had two confirmed kills on the day of the attack and later was credited with two more.

Welch and Taylor shot down more Japanese planes during the December 7 attack on Pearl Harbor than any other individuals, thereby becoming instant heroes around whom people could rally and cheer. In the disaster, fear, and anger that followed Pearl Harbor, twenty-three-year-old George Welch was a source of national pride. He arrived on the world scene at a time when America needed heroes, maybe more than at any other time in history.

The attack on Pearl Harbor was a major victory for Japan. There was little about that morning that Americans could use to build confidence for the future. Welch was just what America needed. He and Taylor received the Distinguished Service Cross "for extraordinary heroism in action."

A lot of people, including Air Service Commander General Henry "Hap" Arnold, thought Welch should receive the congressional medal, but no Medals of Honor would emerge from December, 7 1941.[1]

Welch's heroism has been recounted in every major book on the attack at Pearl Harbor. His story was featured in the movie *Tora, Tora, Tora* and part of the popular 2001 movie *Pearl Harbor* was based on his story.

The attention that swirled around Welch was not limited to the days following the Pearl Harbor attack. He was cited for heroism several more times during World War II and, after the war, became one of the nation's top test pilots. He was among the first to break a speed the public had come to know as "the sound barrier." Some people say Welch was the first to reach that mark.

If fame came quickly to Welch, it did not surprise the people who knew him. He was always one to stand out from the crowd. In his 1939 photograph in the *Debris,* Welch is seen standing with forty-eight other members of Delta Upsilon Fraternity and one great dane dog. Forty-seven of the young men pictured are wearing suits and conservative ties. Welch stands at the back in a signature bow tie.

Layton Allen, a childhood friend, remembers a meeting with Welch in their hometown of Wilmington, Delaware, in 1943.

"He was brought back for a bond tour," Allen says. "George, my new wife, and I spent an hour together in the cocktail lounge of the DuPont Hotel in Wilmington. He never mentioned a word about his combat heroics in the South Pacific. That was a George I never knew. My remembrance of him as a boyhood friend was a likeable, friendly, sometimes mild-mannered, sometimes hell-raising, nice guy."[2]

Welch grew up at 906 Blackshire Road, Wawaset Park, Wilmington, Delaware. He had one young brother, Dehn. Their parents were George Lewis Schwartz and Julia Welch Schwartz. Maybe his childhood home, the site of the first airplane flight in Delaware, spurred Welch's interest in flight.[3]

George, the oldest boy in the family, was born May 18, 1918, at the close of World War I, when anti-German sentiment remained high. According to his birth certificate, his given name was George Louis Schwartz Jr.[4]

"The boys were later given their mother's maiden name, Welch, because of the prejudice against Germans as well as Jews," says Allen. "The parents felt the name Schwartz might, mistakenly, be taken for either—or both."[5]

George's father had grown up in Seattle where he earned a degree from the University of Washington. George Schwartz, Sr. was a chemist and worked for DuPont in Wilmington and had been the victim of anti-German sentiments. Welch's parents had good reason to worry.

"During World War I and later, as the war in Europe was heating up for a second time, the German name and his sensitive position in a premiere defense industry made him an easy target for paranoid spy catchers," Al Blackburn says in *Aces Wild*. "He was often accosted and, on one occasion, even jailed for a brief period before his credentials could be clearly established."[6]

The family lived a prosperous life and the parents pushed to provide the best for their children. "Young George's mother hoped that he would become an accomplished musician," Allen says. "He was made to practice an hour every day on the bass violin. I can still hear the terrible scratching sound coming out of the Schwartz residence while waiting outside for George to come and play. George detested every second of those dreadful sessions. He just wasn't cut out for it."[7]

What George liked was riding his bicycle around Wawaset with other boys in the neighborhood and playing war games that emerged from the Air Service stories of World War I. The boys made rubber band machine guns out of two-by-fours and clothespins. These weren't rubber bands found in the kitchen drawer. They cut them from the inner tubes of discarded auto tires. The boys mounted the "guns" on the handlebars of their bicycles.

"We would split up into two teams and ride into the open court at the foot of Blackshire Road from different directions and try to get on an opponent's tail and hit him with a rubber band 'bullet'—shades of World War I aerial dog fights," Allen says.[8]

As they grew into teenagers the games required more speed. The neighborhood boys bought an old, one-cylinder Indian Prince motorcycle for fourteen dollars. "Ownership passed from one [boy] to another as horrified parents discovered that their son possessed a gasoline powered vehicle," Allen says. "Each boy, in turn, was told to 'get rid of it now!'" The motorcycle issue was finally resolved when one boy proved he could ride it standing on the seat without using his hands. He did it, but with limited success. The stunt ended with the motorcycle hitting a parked car. "The front end of the cycle became somewhat bent," Allen says.[9]

Adventures in the neighborhood ended for Welch when he was sent to St. Andrews, an Episcopal boarding school in Middletown, Delaware, where he "mingled with DuPonts and the sons of other affluent families from along the Eastern seaboard."[10]

There were only fourteen students in Welch's high-school class of 1937, so everyone was required to play the eleven-player sport of football.

"George was only five-nine and quite slender," Blackburn says. "Still, agile, and fit, he was told to suit up for the team. An earlier childhood trauma induced him to complain, 'I'll break my collar bone.' In his first play from scrimmage, he met the team's hard-charging fullback head on and retreated to the bench holding his left arm. 'I just broke my collar bone,' he reported rather matter-of-factly and without a grimace. Clinical examination proved that to be the case. Thereafter, George was assigned water boy duties. . . . In his senior year he was the team's manager."[11]

Voted the laziest member of his class, his nickname was "cowboy." He was a good student, particularly in physics and chemistry. He was a chain smoker.[12]

Welch entered Purdue as a freshman in the fall of 1937, majoring in mechanical engineering. No matter what his major, Welch's intentions were clear. He needed two years of college to be accepted for Army Air Corps flight training. And that is what he wanted to do. He wanted to fly, and the best way to fly was through the military. Purdue had a large and active ROTC program. In fact, all male students were required to take either two years of ROTC training or perform in the All-American marching band," which dressed and functioned as a military unit.

Away from Delaware, a legend quickly emerged about Welch. Perhaps it was the result of his wealthy background. Whatever the reason, reports emerged and continued for many years, wherever he lived, that he was part of the Welch's Grape Juice family. There was no connection, but it's hard to imagine how the rumors persisted unless Welch decided not to argue them.

At the end of his sophomore year at Purdue, he applied for the Army Air Corps but was put on a waiting list. As the fighting in Europe spread, increasing numbers of young men were enlisting for flight training, sensing war on the horizon.

Welch came back to Purdue as a junior in the fall of 1939 and switched his major to science. Within several months he received his orders to report for military training. At the end of the first semester during his junior year, he was off. He completed his education in the military, became a pilot, and was commissioned a second lieutenant in late 1940. He was not promoted to first lieutenant until March 1942, after Pearl Harbor.

In February 1941, Welch was assigned to the Forty-seventh Fighter Squadron at Wheeler Field in Oahu, Hawaii. To most people in the United States in 1941, Hawaii was on the other side of the world. It would be nineteen years before Hawaii became a state. December 7, 1941, is the first time many people even heard of Pearl Harbor, one of the Navy's major bases in the Pacific.

Welch found the island of Oahu to be a great assignment. Twenty-three years old, thin, good looking, and a great pilot, he fit right in with the military routine and the Hawaiian lifestyle.

Francis S. Gabreski, a fellow fighter pilot who would later become a World War II Ace, described Welch as "a rich kid . . . and we couldn't figure out why he was there since he probably could have avoided military service altogether if he wanted to."[13]

"Welch settled into the slow pace of study typical of pre-war Hawaii," Corey C. Jordan writes in an article. "Working days were short. There was an abundance of time off and parties were the favorite pastime, frequently lasting from sunset to dawn. George was never the wallflower type and took to the social scene with his typical self-confidence."[14]

"Fighter pilots, especially bachelor fighter pilots, were generally in great demand for the social whirl that the residents of Oahu used to mask their uneasiness at being on the ramparts for stopping further Japanese expansion in the Pacific," Blackburn writes in *Aces Wild.* "The recently concluded Battle of Britain had greatly burnished the image of all fighter pilots as a romantic, devil-may-care band of brothers who jousted with death from dawn through sunset. George was certainly not one to jeopardize such a view. He entered into the social activities on the island with an enthusiasm only slightly less energized than his determination to maximize his flying skills."[15]

Blackburn tells one Welch story about a party at the Royal Hawaiian Hotel on Waikiki Beach. Welch was not invited. "Undeterred, he donned his flight suit, drove his car to Waikiki Beach, buckled on his parachute, and slid quietly into the surf just west of the party. When he reached a point abreast of the Royal Hawaiian, he popped his 'chute and, silk canopy cradled in his arms, strode out of the breakers and onto the beachside dance floor. . . ."[16]

Whether true or false, another Welch story centered on old BT-2B two-seat biplanes that had no practical use for defensive or offensive purposes, but which pilots were required to fly as part of their training in Hawaii.

In the spring of 1941, Welch's Forty-seventh Fighter Squadron was training at a remote airfield near a beach. One afternoon, while pilots were sitting around complaining about having to fly the BT-2B, Welch handed his watch to a friend and told another pilot to join him in a flight. Welch took the plane out over the water and then flew back toward shore, but instead of getting safely back to the airfield, Welch landed the plane in the water, nearly tipping it upside down in the process. The plane went down fast as the pilots rushed to free themselves and swim to shore.

The pilots didn't have to worry about flying that BT-2B anymore, and Welch apparently escaped any punishment for the "accident."[17] In fact, his legend grew.

Welch's best friend in Hawaii, Ken Taylor, tells a little slightly different story.

"He was a loner, really shy," Taylor says. "I wouldn't say he was a 'hail, fellow well met' but the two of us got along fine. George and I became close friends because we thought we were pretty good at aerial combat. We figured ourselves the top guns and the rest of them could take a crack at us if they wanted. We happened to have a very good day together on the seventh of December, 1941."[18]

Being based in Hawaii, life was good for Welch. But that was about to change, dramatically and forever.

On December 6, 1941, Welch and Taylor along with others in their group were assigned to temporary duty at Haleiwa Field. It wasn't a desirable place. Welch described Haleiwa as "a very short, sandy field originally used as an emergency landing field and probably about six months before the war started they had chopped down a few trees and were allowing fighter squadrons to operate out of there . . . to practice short-field landings. . . . A month before the war started, the Fifteenth Group, of which the Forty-seventh Squadron is a part, was sending each squadron out there for two weeks in rotation to operate . . . in simulated combat conditions."[19]

It was tough duty for men accustomed to life an Oahu. They had to bring their own tents.[20] On Saturday evening, December 6, Welch and Taylor were off duty. They decided to leave the remote airfield for a better time. They "made the rounds" in Honolulu, Hickam Field, Wheeler Field, and Pearl Harbor. At Wheeler's Officer Club, Welch joined an all-night card game that did not break off until almost 8 A.M.—moments after the attack began.[21]

Welch apparently left the game early. According to Taylor, they separated when they reached Honolulu and didn't meet up again until back at the Officer's Club. There were facilities there for them to spend the night.[22]

Awakened from a short sleep, Welch, Taylor, and the other men in the Officer's Club that morning had no idea of the chaos and horror that was emerging. They thought the first sounds they heard were nothing more than the usual noises at a huge military base, but when Welch and Taylor met in the hallway they could see the Japanese planes in the air, and they knew an attack was on.[23]

Welch and Taylor grabbed their clothes. Taylor ended up wearing the military tuxedo paints he had worn the night before.[24]

"I called [Haleiwa] and told them to arm up a couple of our planes," Taylor says. "Then I went for my car—a Buick hardtop. I drove out there. George's car had been confiscated by his commander for speeding."[25] No one was going to stop them from speeding this time.

In *December 7, 1941: The Day the Japanese Attacked Pearl Harbor,* Gordon Prange quotes from official Pearl Harbor attack reports and says, "They [Welch and Taylor] reached Haleiwa to find that the attackers had 'passed right over it'. . . . This was just as well for Haleiwa because the planes 'were lined up in a perfect line right down one side of the field, . . . we parked them there just to look nice and also to keep them bunched so we could guard them easier.' Evidently, someone at Wheeler had alerted Haleiwa because crewmen were already loading the fighters [planes] when Taylor and Welch pulled up."[26]

Welch noticed another lieutenant, Robert Rogers, arriving from Wheeler at the same time. By the book, Rogers was the ranking officer on the scene at that moment. But Welch and Taylor waited for no one to give them any orders. They had seen enough. They were in a hurry. They knew what they needed to do. They jumped into their planes equipped with wing-mounted machine guns and took to the air. All they had was .30 caliber ammunition on board.[27]

"We jumped in our planes and started the war," Taylor says.[28]

Blackburn says this: "Donning soft helmets with earphones and goggles, they fastened their seat belts. Experience would later teach them that a few deep breaths of 100 percent oxygen does wonders in clearing the cobwebs of late-night overindulgence. On the morning of December 7, youth, adrenaline, and raw courage would have to do."[29]

As he flew off, Welch believed between four and six other fighters were able to take off, in addition to he and Taylor.[30] Welch and Taylor flew to nearby Barber's Point to patrol and see if any Japanese planes were in the vicinity.

Welch's Distinguished Service citation describes what happened next. "Upon arrival at Barber's Point [Welch] observed a formation of approximately twelve planes over Ewa, about one thousand feet below and ten miles away. Accompanied by only one other pursuit ship [Taylor], he immediately attacked this enemy formation and shot down an enemy diver bomber with one burst from three .30 caliber guns. At this point he discovered that one gun was jammed. While engaged in this combat, his plane was hit by an incendiary bullet, which passed through the baggage compartment just in the rear of his seat.

"He climbed above the clouds, checked his plane, returned to the attack over Barber's Point, and immediately attacked a Japanese plane running out to sea, which he shot down, the plane falling into the ocean."[31]

Seeing no more planes, Taylor and Welch flew to Wheeler where they expected to find more action and could find .50 caliber ammunition and more fuel. When they reached Wheeler there were no Japanese planes. So they landed to take on the ammunition.

"The field was a mess," Blackburn says. "The big hangars were ablaze and a number of parked aircraft had been torched, but for a moment there was a lull in the action."[32]

They worked on Welch's jammed gun but couldn't fix it. Refueled, Welch restarted his engine and, along with Taylor, blasted down the runaway just as the airfield came under attack once again. Welch's plane was hit three times during takeoff.[33]

Here is how Prange describes it in *December 7, 1941:* "[The] second wave of fighters came back while Welch's and Taylor's P-40s were still taking ammunition. The attackers came in at such a low altitude that their faces could have been recognized had anyone on the ground known them. The crews loading Welch's and Taylor's aircraft ran for shelter, but the two fliers promptly took off, their planes rolling over dollies and running into boxes of ammunition. As they soared skyward, loose rounds lying on their wings fell in all directions."[34]

Both pilots flew right into the attacking Japanese formation. Taylor found one enemy fighter on his tail firing at him. He pulled up and Welch shot it down. Welch's plane was hit three more times during this attack—once in the motor, once in the propeller, and once in the cowling. He kept going.[35]

Welch's medal citation says, "He returned to the vicinity of Ewa and found one enemy plane heading seaward, which he pursued and shot down about five miles off shore."[36]

The Japanese planes in the area decided they had accomplished enough and the leader signaled them to leave. "He rocked his wings to signal the other pilots and they tore off for the rendezvous," Prange says in *At Dawn We Slept.* "As a result, they did not stop to attack any combat planes at Haleiwa as had [been] planned. Thus, Haleiwa became the only field of any consequence on Oahu which escaped Japanese attention, not because they did not know of its existence, as some Americans later assumed, but because two men from Haleiwa and their comrades chased off the attackers."[37]

Welch patrolled the skies for forty-five minutes after the fighting ended, looking for more. Finding nothing, he returned to Haleiwa. Welch's flight report for the day in his personal flight log simply stated "The real McCoy."[38]

Welch officially received his medal on January 8, 1942. He told news reporters, "All hell broke loose and before we knew it, the air was full of Japanese planes. I picked the nearest thing and went after him. . . . It was a funny feeling. I was plenty excited, and I know I was mad because they caught us on Sunday morning. So we went up and fixed them."[39]

Meanwhile, government and military officials were taking two courses of action. First, they needed to build up the military in preparation for war that had been declared on December 8. And second, high ranking officials were looking for someone to blame for the disastrous and deadly attack. Among the complaints was that airplanes at the

Hawaiian air fields had been lined up close together in rows, making them sitting duck targets for the attacking Japanese.

The commander of the Hawaiian Air Force on December 7, 1941, had arrived thirteen months earlier. In *At Dawn We Slept*, Prange describes his arrival. "On Saturday night, November 2, 1940, a tall gentleman walked down the gangplank [of the Army transport Leonard Wood]. He had wavy gray hair and thick brows shadowing pleasant eyes. His thin face with its oblong jaw, big nose, high forehead, and large ears looked more scholarly than military."[40] He was Frederick L. Martin, Purdue class of 1908, who in 1924 crashed while commanding the first around-the-world flight. Now a major general, Martin was moving to the forefront of aviation history for the second time.

Since the Flight Around the World, Martin had held a series of command positions. In 1937, he became commander of the Third Bombardment Wing at Barksdale Field, Louisiana. By the time he reached Hawaii to take over his new command, he had two stars and was the senior pilot in the Air Corps with two thousand hours of flight time.[41]

"Martin was not in the best physical condition," Prange says. "[He] appeared older than his fifty-eight years. He had earlier developed a severe, chronic ulcer condition, which required surgery and undermined his health. As a result, he had not touched an alcoholic drink in years."[42]

There were differences of opinion between the various air, naval, and land commands in Hawaii, and Martin arrived as a peacemaker. Like several other high ranking officers on the island, Martin also answered to several different commanders—a structure which caused problems.

Prange says: "[Martin's] assignment placed him in an ambiguous position. As commander of the Hawaiian Air Force, he had direct access to Major General H.H. 'Hap' Arnold, chief of the of the Army Air Corps, but he remained under the command of [Lt. General Walter] Short, a foot soldier to the soles of his boots. The situation could not have been more delicate, and indeed, Martin had received specific instructions from Arnold to end the undeclared civil war which had raged on Oahu between the Army, its Air Corps, and the Navy. . . ."[43]

One of Martin's chief concerns was expressed in a written statement to Arnold on December 17, 1940, not long after he arrived on the island. "It is my purpose to provide an outlying field for each of the combat squadrons," he said. Prange explained, "Martin did not want his planes huddled together so that an enemy would have easy pickings if he swooped in on them."[44]

Martin's counterpart in the Navy was Real Admiral Patrick N. L. Bellinger, commander of the U.S. Navy Air Force. Like-minded in their concern about defense of the island, on March 31, 1941, Martin and Bellinger issued a report. Confidential when it was issued, it was made public in inquiries that followed the attack on Pearl Harbor. It became known simply as the *Martin-Bellinger Report.* And it simply predicted the Japanese attack with stunning insight.

Referring to Japan with the code word "Orange," the *Martin-Bellinger Report* began with a "Summary of the Situation:"

> Relations between the United States and Orange are strained, uncertain, and varying.
>
> In the past Orange has never preceded hostile actions by a declaration of war.
>
> A successful, sudden raid, against our ships and Naval installations on Oahu might prevent effective offensive action by our forces in the Western Pacific for a long period. A strong part of our fleet is now constantly at sea in the operating areas organized to take prompt offensive action against any surface or submarine force which initiates hostile action.
>
> It appears possible that Orange submarines and/or an Orange fast raiding force might arrive in Hawaiian waters with no prior warning from our intelligence service.[45]

Next in the report came a summary of "Possible Enemy Action:"

> A declaration of war might be preceded by:
>
> A surprise submarine attack on ships in the operating area,
>
> A surprise attack on Oahu including ships and installations in Pearl Harbor, or
>
> A combination of these two.

> It appears that the most likely and dangerous form of attack on Oahu would be an air attack. It is believed that at present such an attack would most likely be launched from one or more carriers which would probably approach inside of three hundred miles.
>
> A single attack might or might not indicate the presence of more submarines or more planes awaiting to attack after defending aircraft have been drawn away by the original thrust.
>
> Any single submarine attack might indicate the presence of a considerable undiscovered surface force probably composed of fast ships accompanied by a carrier.
>
> In a dawn air attack there is a high probability that it could be delivered as a complete surprise in spite of any patrols we might be using and that it might find us in a condition of readiness under which pursuit would be slow to start. . . .[46]

The *Martin-Bellinger Report* recommended steps that could be taken, including the use of patrol planes, but there was not sufficient air power in Hawaii to carry this out, a point that was clearly stated in the report.

Martin and Bellinger recommended daily air patrols "as far as possible to seaward through 360 degrees to reduce the probabilities of surface or air surprise. This would be desirable, but can only be effectively maintained with present personnel and material for a very short period and as a practicable measure cannot, therefore, be undertaken unless other intelligence indicates that a surface raid is probable within a rather narrow time limit."[47]

As the year 1941 progressed toward its world-changing end, another command came out of Martin's headquarters. Planes were to be lined up along the airfield at Wheeler in neat rows. There were two reasons for this. First, there was considerable fear of sabotage on the island and the orders had come from above Martin's command that the best way to guard these planes was to keep them together.

In December 7, 1941, Prange says Wheeler was very exposed. A public road ran next to the base. Protective storage areas for the planes at Wheeler had been constructed.

"About 125 protective bunkers had been built for Wheeler's v-shaped aircraft walls made mostly of earth, eight to ten feet high, enough for the main elements of the fighter force," Prange says. "Unfortunately, by direct orders of General Martin's headquarters, the planes had been removed from these bunkers and 'concentrated so they would be easier to guard against sabotage.'"[48]

A second reason for the way airplanes were positioned on the fields showed up in congressional inquiries following the attack. Admiral Husband Kimmel, commander in chief, U.S. Pacific Fleet, felt he was under orders not to alarm the public by taking defensive positions.

The Congressional Investigation Report states, "In his testimony Admiral Kimmel has suggested that one can appreciate the 'psychological handicaps' that dispatches he received placed upon the Navy in Hawaii. He stated: 'In effect, I was told:

'Do take precautions'

'Do not alarm civilians'

'Do take a preparatory deployment'

'Do not disclose intent'

'Do take a defensive deployment'

'Do not commit the first overt act.'"[49]

However, the report noted that had Kimmel taken some defensive precautions, it would not have had the impact of alarming the public.

But Martin had his orders.

The attack on Pearl Harbor occurred at 7:55 A.M. That Sunday morning Martin was preparing for breakfast at his base home when he heard the first explosions.

"The action was taking place less than a mile from his home, and Martin immediately recognized the attacking aircraft as Japanese," Prange says.[50]

He grabbed his telephone and began giving orders. Next, he rushed to his headquarters.

"Martin's ashen face and grim expression showed how deeply the attack had shocked him," Prange says. "The General had but one burning ambition at the moment—'to get to the [Japanese] carriers.' So he called Bellinger on the field phone that connected their offices. The bombardment was so heavy the two men could scarcely hear one another; however, Bellinger told Martin that he 'had no information whatever . . . as to which direction to go to find the carriers.'"[51]

Martin was described as "looking like a walking corpse" that morning. The attack was shock enough. But he was also physically ill. He was having continued problems with his ulcer.[52]

On December 16, 1941, Short, Kimmel, and Martin were relieved of their commands. Subsequent reports placed heavy blame on Kimmel and Short, although there are continued efforts to clear their records. No blame was placed on Martin.

President Franklin Roosevelt appointed a commission to investigate what happened at Pearl Harbor, and he released the findings to the news media on Saturday, January 24, 1942. The report cleared Martin of any failures in command. It said, "Subordinate commanders executed their superiors' orders without question. They were not responsible for the state of readiness prescribed."[53]

While Martin was relieved of command in Hawaii, his war service was far from finished. He was given command of the Second Air Force, responsible for defending the northwest section of the United States. In continued poor health, he retired from active duty in 1944, before the war ended. Martin did remain active in military activities, however. He attended reunions of the around-the-world flight crew members.

On February 24, 1954, he died at West Los Angeles Veteran's Hospital following an illness of only several days. He was seventy-two years old.

At Pearl Harbor after December 7, George Welch kept very busy flying patrols but without any combat. By May, the military decided that, for the time being, Welch could do more good returning to the mainland as a war hero until the nation was better prepared for combat with the enemy. Welch—whose national fame was established in newspapers from coast to coast after Pearl Harbor Day—was used to help sell war bonds.

More than eight thousand people cheered him when he returned to Wilmington for a celebration in his honor. An Associated Press photo featured his mother and father sitting on their family living room couch holding a large model plane glider which Welch had made as a boy. The tag line said, "An aviation enthusiast since he was a child, Lt. Welch made hundreds of model planes, including the glider shown here, which ironically is covered with tissue paper made in Japan."

On May 25, 1942, he was in Washington, D.C., where he met with President Franklin Roosevelt in the Oval Office. A photo the next day in the *New York Herald Tribune* shows a smiling, confident Roosevelt seated at his desk, reaching to one side to shake hands with Welch who was standing straight and proud in his Army uniform. Next to Welch stood his mother and father along with Mrs. James H. Hughes, wife of the U.S. Senator from Delaware.

The *Herald Tribune* reported, "Lt. George S. Welch of Wilmington, Delaware, twenty-three-year-old pilot who downed four Japanese planes over Pearl Harbor on December 7, received a warm handshake from President Roosevelt. . . . Told that Lt. Welch had eaten three large beefsteaks after downing the Japanese planes, the President looked over the lean flyer and remarked that he probably could stand three more." [54]

"It was a strenuous three months, that established at least two things," Blackburn says. "George Welch was not the Air Corps' most effective public speaker, and there is a limit to the amount of adulation that even a virile twenty-four-year-old fighter pilot can gracefully absorb."[55]

In August, he was back in Hawaii and by mid-October his Forty-seventh Fighter Squadron had been sent to New Guinea where they began to see regular action. According to some of the men who were with him, Welch didn't always take credit for enemy aircraft he shot down, especially if there was only one. On December 7, 1942, he did take credit for what he accomplished. On the anniversary of the surprise attack at Pearl Harbor, Welch shot down three enemy planes, giving him a total of seven and making him an official World War II Ace.[56]

According to Blackburn, in spite of their success, Welch and other pilots in the group were unhappy with their planes. They wanted the much better Lockheed P-38 twin engines airplanes that some other U.S. forces in the area were flying. When Welch asked superiors when they would get the new, better planes, he was told when they ran out of the ones they were flying.

"Wrong answer," Blackburn says. "George Welch was becoming an expert at meeting the challenges of getting rid of inferior aircraft." According to Blackburn, after Welch received that answer, it became more common for fighter pilots in his unit to report last minute problems with their "old" planes and bail out not far from the beach. Within a few months, Welch and others were flying the Lockheed P-38.[57]

During the last week of February, 1943, Welch—by this time a captain—went to Australia for a thirty-day leave. There, in Sydney, he met

Janet Williams, a young woman Blackburn describes as "short, trim, with dark brown hair, and sparkling dark-brown eyes topped by heavy eyebrows, and beneath a mischievous smile that seemed to say almost anything you wanted it to say."[58] They quickly fell in love and married on October 23, 1943.

During a trip to the Australian Great Barrier Reef, Welch fell quickly into trouble. He failed to report for active duty on time and was listed as AWOL. When he reported late, officers on duty in Australia were prepared to place him in the stockade.

"George . . . explained that the boat that was to have picked them up from their island on the reef was two days late, etcetera, etcetera," Blackburn says. "As the problem drifted higher up the chain of command, cooler heads came into play. The war was still young, experienced fighter pilots were at a premium, and bona fide heroes were not to be dumped unceremoniously into the brig."[59]

Welch escaped discipline. In fact, he was assigned to remain in Australia for three more weeks training pilots. He could not have created a better assignment if he had written the orders himself, Blackburn says.

Returned to the war, Welch extended his record. On June 21, he shot down two enemy planes and possibly a third. On August 20, he shot down three more; in early September there were an additional four. With sixteen kills, Welch was considered a triple World War II Ace. He had flown 348 missions. In September 1943, the war for Welch came to end when he contracted malaria.

He was sent to a hospital in Sydney and gradually recovered. Before long, he was back to his old ways. "As flesh returned to his frame," Blackburn says, "George regained his penchant for mischief. Although not yet discharged as a patient, he felt good enough to sneak away from the ward one day, borrow an old biplane trainer from the Aussies, and beat up a nearby beach where Jan was getting a bit of sun."[60]

Now a major, Welch was returned to the United States with his bride and began making war bond rally appearances once again.

His medals included: The Distinguished Service Cross, the Silver Star, the Distinguished Unit Badge, the Distinguished Flying Cross with two Oak Leaf Clusters, and the Air Medal with two Oak Leaf Clusters. In addition to the sixteen enemy planes he was officially credited with shooting down, he had eight more "probables."[61]

But the war was far from being finished. Walker "Bud" Mahurin had come to Purdue from Fort Wayne to study aeronautics. He left in 1941 to join the Army Air Corps. Stationed in England flying a P-47 fighter plane escorting bombers, Mahurin became an Ace on October 4, 1943. He was a double Ace by the end of November. Promoted to major, in March 1944, he was shot down over France and escaped back to England with the help of the French underground. The leading Ace in Europe, he could no longer fly over France because of his knowledge of the underground and a fear, if he were captured, information might be obtained by the Germans.

Mahurin was transferred to the Pacific front where he successfully shot down a plane and was shot down again himself. He was officially credited with twenty and three-fourths planes shot down in World War II.

In 1949, Mahurin finished his degree at Purdue and returned to active duty in Korea. He was given credit for three and a half planes shot down in Korea, then was shot down again and spent sixteen months as a prisoner of war. After being released, he spent time at the Pentagon and eventually went to work in the aerospace business. Bruce Stockdell from southern Indiana finished only one semester in engineering at Purdue before leaving for the Army Air Service. Near the end of the war, he was selected as a pilot in the classified Atomic Bomb Group. He was trained at Roswell, New Mexico, and told his next assignment would be Tinian Island, the launching point for planes that carried nuclear weapons to Japan. The war ended before his training was finished. After the war, Stockdell entered air intelligence work, often infiltrating behind enemy lines.

In the spring of 1944, the war was officially over for George Welch. He received an offer he could not refuse. General "Hap" Arnold had recommended Welch to North American Aviation, which was looking for top pilots to help them design their airplanes. Welch and his wife, Jan, moved to Los Angeles where he started work on the new P-51 Mustang planes.[62]

George Welch was now a civilian test pilot with North American. Every day he was flying some of the hottest experimental planes at Muroc Army Air Field, which later would be renamed Edwards Air Force Base. In September 1947, Welch got a great new assignment. He was named project engineering test pilot for the new XP-86 Sabre jet.

At this same time, from Washington, D.C., to the hangars at Muroc, there was a single challenge that dominated thinking and conversations: break the sound barrier.

The plane assigned to do it was the Bell X-1, built by the Bell Aircraft Company. It was designed to be taken aloft beneath a B-29. It would be released, fire its engines until all the fuel was spent, and then glide back to the dry lake bed runways at Muroc. The pilot chosen for this plane, Chuck Yeager, would become a legend.

Every day, Yeager pushed the barrier which had come to be called Mach 1, but in an amazing story on the first to conquer supersonic flight, Blackburn, in *Aces Wild*, says that before Welch even flew his new XP-86 Sabre, he had started asking questions about how fast the new airplane could fly. He had a particular speed in mind: the sound barrier.

According to Blackburn, in conversation after conversation, Welch was presenting a scenario to North American engineers. What if he took the plane to Mach 0.9 in level flight, which they knew it could do, and then, at thirty-five thousand feet, went into a twenty-five- to thirty-degree dive? He got the answer he wanted to hear: he would go supersonic. The engineers estimated the risks from attempting this were small. Welch estimated they were zero.[63]

Welch and Jan, who was seven months pregnant with their first child, lived in Brentwood near the famous Sunset Boulevard and one hundred miles from Muroc. Welch drove an MG roadster from their home to the airfield, covering the distance in about ninety minutes. When it came time to test the Sabre, he decided to stay near Muroc at a place known as Pancho's Fly Inn, later named the Happy Bottom Riding Club.[64]

"It comprised some 400 acres bordering the Muroc Air Base on the south," Blackburn says. "In addition to rooms, there were suites, a restaurant, bar, swimming pool, riding stables, and an air strip."

Pancho's Fly Inn and its owner, female Pancho Barnes, both became legends. It was the place where the pilots and engineers involved with the top planes of the day—including the Bell X-1 and the XP-86 Sabre—gathered to talk about the work of the day and to listen to rumors about what everyone else was doing.

Blackburn says, on the evening of Monday, September 29, 1947, Welch talked to a friend, Miller Palmer, during dinner at Pancho's. He told her he might take his plane supersonic during its first test flight on Wednesday, October 1, but since it was not on his list of objectives for the day, there would be no instruments in use to measure his airspeed relative to the speed of sound.

According to Blackburn, "If [tomorrow morning] you hear a sharp boom like a clap of thunder, be sure and write it down—what it sounded like, what time, reaction from others, stuff like that," Welch said. Palmer told him to be careful.

"Not to worry," said Welch.[65]

According to Blackburn, on Wednesday, October 1, Welch flew the plane, going into several high speed dives just as he had described to Palmer, but when it finally came time to end the flight, the nose landing gear would not snap into place. It was hanging down at a forty-five-degree angle.

Welch talked with the ground crew about what to do. A number of options were considered, including bailing out. It was decided he would land and deal with it as best he could. At the last minute the gear slipped into place, locked, and the plane landed safely.[66]

Later that day, Welch called Palmer. "She was more excited than he'd ever known her," Blackburn says. "[She said] it was just like you said, Ba-boom! It nearly bounced me out of bed. And I wasn't the only one who heard it. Pancho is really [angry]. You know how nuts she is about Yeager. Her story is that the boom stuff happens all the time. Says it comes from some mining operation up in the hills, but nobody else recollects ever hearing one. Not like that boom you lowered on Pancho's habitat this morning."[67]

According to Blackburn, there was further evidence. The airspeed indicator on Welch's plane had seemed to be stuck at 350 knots during his dive. Then, it suddenly bounced to 410. They didn't understand this on October 1, 1947, but Blackburn says "this was a signal the XP-86 was going supersonic."[68]

On October 9, Welch took the Sabre up again, this time with the nose landing gear locked into place. The problem had not yet been repaired, but the safety measure also prevented Welch from trying any supersonic speeds. On completion of the flight that day, Welch learned Jan had gone into labor. He rushed back to Los Angles shortly after their son, Giles, was born.[69]

Blackburn says, when Jan called her family back in Australia to tell them the news abut the baby, she had another big story to tell. She told her mother her husband had broken the sound barrier.[70]

Meanwhile, Welch was not allowed to fly his plane without the landing gear bolted down pending an investigation. Welch felt this was intended to stop his supersonic flight attempts. Blackburn recreates a conversation between Welch and Jan in which Welch said, "The government has spent a bunch of bucks on this Bell X-1 rocket ship for the sole purpose of exploring the challenge of going supersonic with a man along. . . . Suppose a new fighter comes along, say a Sabre, which is the greatest fighter of the decade, carries six guns, bombs, and makes the United States numero uno in the world of air combat. Incidentally, this

Sabre can also take its pilot supersonic and does it even before the supposedly advanced technology rocket ship—or even a day or two later, or a week or two later. It still makes the government look like a bunch of spend thrift idiots."[71]

On October 14, the Sabre flew again.

Blackburn says, during this flight, Welch pulled up the landing gear and went into his dive. His sonic ba-boom thundered below once again. He landed and at 10:30 A.M., near the hangar where he was working, he heard another large ba-boom. Yeager had just officially broken the sound barrier in the X-1.

Officially, Blackburn says, Welch denied even pulling up his landing gear, but unofficially, people at Muroc knew. At Pancho's that evening, people said they heard two sonic bombs that morning about twenty minutes apart. The first, Welch's, had broken some windows.[72]

According to Blackburn, Welch had broken the sound barrier twice before Yeager accomplished it officially for the first time. But Welch's mark came without the sophisticated equipment used to measure the speed of Yeager's X-1.

The military kept Yeager's record a secret and did not confirm Welch's supersonic booms. But on November 13, the military allowed the same high-precision equipment that had confirmed Yeager's flight to be used by Welch in the Sabre. The supersonic flights by the Sabre that day were officially clocked at a low of Mach 1.02 and as high as 1.04. Now two men had officially passed through the sound barrier, but the government was still keeping it all a secret.[73]

"Between November 3, 1947, and the end of February, 1948, Welch flew twenty-three flights in the XP-86," Blackburn says. "Almost certainly, each flight included at least one incursion into the realm of the supersonic. The average is more likely two or three per flight."[74]

In December 1947, *Aviation Week* reported that Yeager had become the first person to break the sound barrier on October 14, a statement confirmed by the military. When the military finally publicly released information about Welch's supersonic flight, it reported he was the second person to break the sound barrier. They set the date at April 26, 1948.

Blackburn is no novice to flight. He was a test pilot during the Korean War and later for North American, the company which built the Sabre Jet. Blackburn knew Welch personally.

"He was very bright, extremely smart," Blackburn says. "One time he picked up a newspaper, looked at it for a short time, and tossed it in a corner. I said, 'come on George, you can't have read that paper that fast.' He tossed it to me and said 'ask me a question.' No matter how obscure a story I picked, he had it."

Blackburn says it was common knowledge among people who were around North American in 1947 what had happened. "The crew chiefs and all the guys on the line, they knew," Blackburn says. "They all knew what he was doing."[75]

His Pearl Harbor Day friend Ken Taylor, who stayed in the military and eventually worked at the Pentagon, agrees.

"What George did [with the sound barrier] was well-known among people who did this kind of thing," Taylor says.

"North American was a government contractor, says Taylor. There was no way they were going to risk future contracts by trying to place a claim on a record the military was working to accomplish. Yeager has denied that anyone beat him.

"There's no question that Yeager's plane was designed for this purpose and did the job," Taylor says. "So be it, but I think George and North American should have gotten some of the credit for the sound barrier."[76]

In the years that followed, Welch continued as a legendary test pilot for North American. Some people considered him eccentric. He sometimes wore loud coats and checkered pants. In the 1950s—the era of the crewcut—he wore hair down to his shoulders. He liked to drive an English sports car convertible wearing a scarf and a beret. He and Jan had another son, Jolyon.[77]

Some people had started calling him "Wheaties," although the exact reason for this is unclear. Stories vary widely. Maybe it's just because he was a champion.

On October 12, 1954, Columbus Day, in a structural demonstration flight for the U.S. Air Force, Welch took an F-100A jet to its limits, more than one and a half times the speed of sound.

That very day Ken Taylor was traveling from Washington, D.C., to California for a meeting with Welch. Lee Atwood, of North American, had asked Taylor to intercede with the test pilot.

"I was asked by Lee to see if I couldn't talk him out [of further F-100 test flights]," Taylor says. "Lee just thought he had done his share [of flying]. They were going to move him up in the company. Flying is a dangerous business."[78]

The F-100A had stability problems. And that October day, Welch ran into difficulties at a critical moment. The plane went out of control.

"The nose structure, not designed to fly sideways, broke and folded back, with the canopy bow crushing Welch's chest before separating from the rest of the fuselage," Blackburn says. "By some miraculous instinct for survival or as a consequence of the structural failure, the ejection seat was fired and the parachute deployed, but at such high speed that several panels of the 'chute were torn out, making the rate of descent quite high."[79]

When they reached Welch, he still had a pulse, but within minutes, it was over. With one final sonic bomb, George Welch was gone.

John Casper

Orbiting Earth in a space shuttle, John Casper looked out a window and saw a sight that took him back many years. He called someone over to share the story.

"You see that?" Casper said to his fellow astronaut. "You see that water right off Vietnam there? I spent the longest night of my life in that water waiting to be rescued in 1969."

It's interesting what your eye can land on from space. It finds important places in your life. In Vietnam, Casper flew the F-100 fighter jet, an improved version of the airplane George Welch was testing when he crashed and died.

John Casper was born July 9, 1943, in Greenville, South Carolina, and grew up in the military. His father was an Air Force pilot.

"My father never really pushed me to go into flying," Casper says. "But it was something I was always around. And I wanted to do it. It looked pretty exciting and adventurous. Plus, I think, from the time I was eight years old, I really wanted to fly in space. I wanted to be an astronaut."

Casper considers Gainesville, Georgia, to be his hometown. He graduated from Chamblee High School in Chamblee, Georgia, in 1961 and wanted to go to the new Air Force Academy.

"But I didn't make it in the first year I applied," he says. "So I went a year to Georgia Tech. And then I applied the following year, and was accepted. The academy was just very competitive. I needed to do a little more work. It was just an obstacle I had to overcome. I always had going into the Academy and being a pilot and maybe an astronaut as my goals, so I just worked my hardest at Georgia Tech and kept my goals out there in front of me."

After the academy, Casper came to Purdue on the master's degree program.

"Purdue was very intense, very difficult," he says. "I was impressed with the professors, the quality of the program. It was tough. I mean, it was really tough.

"I really came to love Purdue. We were welcomed there as kind of full-fledged graduate students, even though we were on this short program. We went to football games and parties and student activities, and it was great for us because we'd been in this military academy environment for four years, so seeing the other side was fun."

Casper received his master of science degree in astronautics from Purdue in 1967. He went straight to Reece Air Force Base in Lubbock, Texas, for flight training and by January 1969 was in Vietnam for a twelve-month tour.

In July 1969, when fellow Purdue graduate Neil Armstrong landed and walked on the moon, Casper was in Vietnam flying an F-100 fighter-bomber.

"In fact, I was on a bombing mission," he says. "I was just rolling in on the bomb target, and I had the radio on. We had a radio in the airplane. I had it tuned to a military station, and they announced that we had landed on the Moon. There I was, I thought, this is really weird. This is wild. Here is someone walking on the Moon, and I'm rolling in on a dive bomb pass about to deliver my bombs.

"I knew then that space was what I really wanted to do.

"I was glad to get out of Vietnam alive," Casper says. "I lost of a lot of good friends, including two very good friends who had been through the Purdue program with me. So it was tough. War is not glamorous, you know. There is nothing about war that's glamorous."

On one mission he lost his plane. He doesn't think he was hit. He thinks it was engine failure. He ejected from the jet at about 2:00 A.M. and landed in the ocean.

"There were some North Vietnamese boats that were trying to pick me up with their search lights," Casper says. "We always flew in pairs, and my wingman flew overhead, and I vectored him in, talking to him on the radio. I vectored him in overhead, and he lit his afterburner, and I think that's what helped scare the North Vietnamese.

"Once they had cleared, the wingman had to go home. He was running low on fuel. Then the first rescue chopper came out to pick me up. It was still nighttime, and the helicopter was making a spiral approach down to pick me up. I was talking to them on the rescue radio, and they flew right into the water. It was a black night out there, and I was, I don't know, five or ten miles off shore. They all got out okay, and we were yelling to each other for a while there. But then, during the night, we all drifted apart. I talked to somebody on the radio, and they said they were going to wait until daylight to make another pickup attempt. But they sent a gun ship overhead, with lots of searchlights and guns on board, and they flew an orbit overhead for the rest of the night to keep the North Vietnamese away. Then, in the morning, some Navy boats came and picked up the chopper crew, and another helicopter from the base came out and picked me up. So I spent four or five hours in the water.

"The water was fairly warm. This was July in Vietnam, but I had gotten rid of my life raft because I was about to be picked up by the helicopter. So I just had my life preserver. From my shoulders down, my body was in the water. So yeah, I was pretty cold, pretty chilly. It just sucks the heat right out of you."

From Vietnam he went to England and spent four years flying F-100s there. Next, he was accepted for flight school at Edwards Air Force Base in California. He spent six and a half years flying at Edwards.

While at Edwards, in 1978 he applied be an astronaut, but he didn't make it. He reapplied in 1984. He was forty-one and working in the Pentagon.

"Everyone said I was crazy to reapply," Casper says. "They said I was too old, and it would never happen. NASA would never accept a guy my age. So I went to Houston, and I talked to a few folks at NASA about my chances. They said I should go ahead and apply. They'd look at me.

"The first time when I didn't get accepted, I really felt devastated," he says. "I had been promoted early, I was in charge of a test squadron, and I thought I was at the top of the pack. I was really discouraged. But perseverance counts for a lot. That's been my story. It's really been one of perseverance, and try again. When I was accepted, it had been six years since I first applied. In fact, at the time I was accepted, I was the oldest astronaut to ever enter. Since then, we've had two or three that have been older than me. Once I got into NASA, I found out that over half of the astronauts don't make it the first time, sometimes it's two, or three and four or five times. Persistence counts for a lot."

Casper has flown four shuttle missions. He was pilot on STS-36 in February 1990, carrying a classified Department of Defense payload. On his next three flights he served as commander. He flew STS-54 in January 1993, along with a number of experiments they launched a satellite. In March 1994, he commanded STS-62, a two-week microgravity research mission on the Shuttle *Columbia.* His next flight, STS-77, was in May 1996, performing a record number of rendezvous with satellites.

He has logged more than 825 hours in space and is currently working on NASA's team to return the space shuttle to flight safely. "Flying in space is incredible," Casper says. "It's just the most awesome, scariest, most exhilarating, experience you can imagine. The launch can scare you to death."

The landings are equally exciting.

"It's a real thrill," Casper says. "You know, pilots like to hold the stick and make the landing. We train for this. We have shuttle training-airplanes so we make over a thousand approaches. The first time I actually grabbed the stick of the shuttle, it felt like the shuttle training-plane I'd been flying.

"The big difference between the shuttle and a regular airplane is that you're a glider in the shuttle. You have to make that first landing a good one, because, you don't get a chance to go around and try it again. There's a lot of pressure on you.

"You come down very fast. Things are happening quickly, and the pace of events is accelerating as you make the re-entry, so there's a tendency to get behind what's going on. You have to push yourself to catch up, catch up, get ahead, get ahead of the shuttle, get ahead of what's happening. It's not an easy vehicle to land. It takes a lot of training to land it right. It has those big delta wings, and it's very sensitive on the controls, and of course, there's no engine."

It is a life changing experience to fly in space.

"One thought I've had up there is that it's amazing that all of mankind has lived and died on that one tiny planet," Casper says. "It makes you feel more connected to the continuation of mankind and how determined we are as people. It's in our spirit to explore. This is what drove the great sailors of the sixteenth and seventeenth centuries to sail out in their little boats, to discover the New World. It's the spirit of wanting to learn, wanting to explore. I think God has put that in us, and it's part of our makeup to learn about what's out there, to find out what's out there, and learn more about it.

"Having the opportunity to experience all this, is just part of God's plan for me," he says. "I wish everybody could go up there and see the earth. It makes you feel more connected to everyone else. You see that we're all one planet. From space you can't see the political boundaries. What you see is one planet, one Earth—one human species."

Chapter Twelve

The next generation of professional pilots may very well come out of the halls of ivy, both sheepskin and license in hand, ready to take their places in the world of flight. Graduates of Purdue University could be leading the way. For that university is the only place in the nation where a youngster without any flying experience can enroll as a freshman and in four years earn a B.S. degree with a major in professional pilot technology.

—*FAA Aviation News,* February 1966

In 1969, Jerry Goldman sat in the captain's seat of a brand new DC-9 jetliner, flying it home to Purdue University from Douglas Aircraft Company in Long Beach, California. It was a dream come true.

Purdue had been the first university in the nation to have its own airport. It was the first university in the nation selected for the Civilian Pilot Training Program and the first to offer bachelor of science degrees to students majoring in professional pilot technology.

In 1969, Purdue had entered the jet age with a brand new 104-seat DC-9. It was painted blue and white with "Purdue Airlines" written across the fuselage and a stylish "PA" logo on the tail. To Goldman, it handled like a dream sailing above the clouds over the western United States and flying to West Lafayette where it would become part of a unique charter program in which students worked as copilots receiving incredible experience.

This was one of two DC-9s Purdue Airlines had just purchased. The company would lease a third, and there was a fourth DC-9 parked inconspicuously at a hangar back on campus. That one was painted jet black with a white Playboy bunny on the tail. It was only used by one man and his guests. When Hugh Hefner called, Purdue Airlines was ready with this airplane.

There had been a huge celebration at Douglas when Purdue Airlines took possession of the new DC-9. Fifty Purdue alumni who worked for

Douglas lined up beside the airplane. They posed for photographs and applauded as Grove Webster, chairman of Purdue Airlines, accepted a model of the plane from J. J. Dysart, a Douglas vice president. The fifty Douglas employees had all graduated between 1931 and 1968—thirty-seven years of Purdue engineering dating back to the days when the university first cleared a field, put up a wind sock, and called it an airport.

In the mid-1940s, then-Purdue President Edward Elliott had testified before a U.S. Senate committee in Washington, D.C., to suggest that land-grant universities could do for aviation what they had done for agriculture.

It was a bold statement, and it had come true. Purdue was not only supplying engineers for the manufacture and design of aviation and space vehicles, it was also graduating pilots and mechanics and professionals for the nation's airlines and airports.

Nineteen sixty-nine was a big year for Purdue. On Sunday, March 9, Purdue Airlines put the sleek new DC-9 jetliner on public display. Lafayette area people jammed the road to the airport to take part in the tour. Grandchildren of the men and women who had gathered in 1911 to watch Lincoln Beachy and George Witmer in their flying machines on the old Stuart Field were now gathered at Purdue to witness the university in the age of the jet.

Just four months later, a Purdue graduate would walk on the Moon.

As Goldman, who was Purdue Airlines director of flight operations and engineering, flew the new plane back to West Lafayette, he couldn't help but think he had come a long way from his boyhood days in Camden, New Jersey, sneaking through a fence to get a closer look at the hottest plane of the day: a Ford Tri-Motor with such a large body they nicknamed it the "Tin Goose," because that's what it looked like.

Goldman played a unique role in the development of pilot training at Purdue, a program that grew enormously following World War II as the aviation industry became larger and larger and demanded more professionally-trained people.

Born in 1922, when the first aeronautics classes were being introduced at Purdue, Goldman's father took him to the Camden County Airport on Sunday afternoons to watch the planes coming and going. It was an exciting way to spend an afternoon for a father and son. Soon, Goldman was sneaking off to the airport on his own.

"There was an area where they kept private planes, and there was a hurricane fence around it," Goldman says. "A sign said, 'no admittance.'

I would go in all the time, right through the gate. They'd put me out and I'd go back in. Pretty soon they just started saying, 'Okay kid. If you're going to come in here, just don't touch anything. Just stay over there.' Well, I'd go into the hangar and climb on a wing of a plane and look inside."[1]

They finally decided they would never be able to stop this boy, so they let him have the run of the place and even took him up for rides. As a high school student, Goldman would have his first experiences flying a plane with those friendly pilots in Camden.

Even as a young boy, he knew what he wanted to do. He wanted to become an aeronautical engineer and a pilot. A family friend had graduated from Purdue, and after a conversation with him, Goldman knew where he wanted to go: Purdue University.

He arrived on campus in 1940 in time to take part in Grove Webster's Civilian Pilot Training Program.

"I was a second-semester freshman," Goldman says. "You weren't supposed to get in until you were a sophomore, but I went over to the administration building and complained. I said, 'You're training people to fly who are majoring in science and pharmacy. I'm majoring in aeronautical engineering. It's ridiculous not to take me.' I won my point. I got in. I got my pilot's certificate."[2]

One of the men who taught him was John "Pop" Stair who owned an airport in the nearby town of Mulberry and came to Purdue to help out. In a few years, another of Stair's students would be Roger Chaffee. Born in 1890, Stair was an aviation pioneer. He learned to fly in 1928 and opened his twelve-acre airstrip in Mulberry that same year. He was hired to help handle flight training at Purdue.

In 1940, Lawrence "Cap" Aretz was the Purdue Airport manager. He gave students their proficiency flight checks.

"He was so big, with huge, broad shoulders, he'd sit in the front seat of the airplane, and I'd sit in the back where I couldn't see anything," Goldman says. "When you landed, he usually didn't say anything. He just got out and walked away. I guess that meant you passed."[3]

The year 1940 when Goldman arrived was a significant time for Purdue and flight. Dean of Engineering A. A. Potter had recognized the increasing importance of aeronautics, and he was taking steps to meet a growing interest from students. Purdue students had been taking aeronautics courses in mechanical engineering for nearly twenty years, but in mid-1941, Potter decided it was time to establish an official four-year bachelor of science curriculum in aeronautical engineering. The coursework appeared in the 1941 to 1942 catalogue and the name of mechanical engineering was officially changed to mechanical and aeronautical engineering in 1942.[4]

World War II began while Goldman was on campus, and the nation's tremendous need for educated young men put all students at the university on accelerated schedules. Goldman enlisted in the Army Air Corps after Pearl Harbor and was called into the service at the start of his final semester in 1943. He served in the Pacific with the Twentieth Air Force, flying B-29s out of Saipan and Guam.

In the spring of 1946, Goldman returned to Purdue. He received his degree in February 1947.

A great deal had changed at the university in a very short period of time. The seeds for everything that would come were planted on May 12, 1942, when a certificate of incorporation was filed with the state of Indiana for a new company called Purdue Aeronautics Corporation. This was a not-for-profit corporation created by the university to help develop the potential for flight. It had emerged from a proposal created by a consultant who would become a major figure in Purdue aviation.

In October 1941, Grove Webster left his position in Washington, D.C., as head of the Civilian Pilot Training Program to begin a private flight consulting business. One of his first clients was Purdue where President Elliott and others were pursuing a vision for aviation. Webster did a study of the university and its airport and drafted a plan for the future. It included a proposal to use the university's airport and equipment to train military personnel. It also included a plan for the new not-for-profit corporation that could support airport activity and education.

Webster officially began working at Purdue on a half-time basis on July 1, 1942, but he wasn't really just working part time. From the records of what was taking place at Purdue, he was probably working double time or triple time for part-time pay until the program he envisioned got off the ground.

The foundation for everything he envisioned would emerge from the new Purdue Aeronautics Corporation. The incorporation papers defined a purpose for the company broad enough to fit any possibility that might come along: "To promote education and research in aeronautical engineering, aviation, airport construction, management and operation, and related subjects either in connection with Purdue University or otherwise; to encourage foster and conduct education, instruction, investigation, and research relating to any or all of the above mentioned fields; to acquire and provide facilities, equipment, and personnel for any such purpose; to acquire by purchase, lease, or otherwise and to manage, control, and operate an airport; to acquire by such lease, contract, gift, devise, bequest, or otherwise property, real, personal, or mixed; and to hold, use, control, operate, lease, sell, convey, mortgage, or pledge the same for any lawful purpose."[5]

Incredibly, during the next thirty years Purdue Aeronautics would do just about everything on that list.

On Tuesday, July 7, 1942, just six days after reporting for work, Webster started putting his plans into action. He laid out his proposal at a meeting of the Purdue Aeronautics Board of Directors, which included the president and university trustees. The plans were accepted and flight at the university sailed into new heights.

The program Webster advanced used Purdue Aeronautics to purchase equipment and hire people for the purpose of training military pilots. The training would be done under contract with the government and profits from the program would be invested in the airport and flight facilities.

Webster initiated five immediate areas of training, mostly for Navy cadets and a small number of Army cadets. He initiated a primary flight course, a secondary course, a cross-country program, an instructor's course, and a fifth program using a Link instrument trainer.

The bill for training military men in these programs would be sent to the Civil Aeronautics Administration. Estimated income when everything was up and running totaled $191,286. To do this, the corporation would need to invest about $18,000 in equipment.[6] The numbers added up.

On January 1, 1943, Webster's status officially became full-time. He was given the title General Manager of Purdue Airport. "Cap" Aretz, who had previously operated the airport under contract with the university, was put in charge of aircraft maintenance—a major job with the large number of aircraft flying in and out during the war.[7]

As military flight training at the airport grew, business for Purdue Aeronautics boomed. More airplanes were purchased.

By June 30, 1943, at the end of the first fiscal year of business, Purdue Aeronautics had done far better than expected. It reported $433,562 in operating revenue, $279,345 in costs, $27,576 in administration and other expenses. Total assets were listed at $204,434, and there was a $20,000 bank note.[8]

Profits were re-invested in the airport—more land, new and bigger runways, a new hangar.

As the war approached conclusion, it was apparent that military pilot training would be reduced. New needs were arising and Purdue began preparing for the next era. Millions of young, former G.I.s would be arriving at the nation's universities in the years immediately following the war. They would need immediate training and education in the technologies of the day. New industries would be emerging during the second half of the twentieth century and young people would be needed to run them.

In 1944, Dean Potter along with Harry Solberg, then head of the mechanical and aeronautical engineering program, asked for a study of postwar aeronautical needs at Purdue. Placed in charge of the study was E. F. Bruhn, head of Purdue aeronautics. He was assisted by Webster and Joseph Liston, a professor of aeronautics. They began to look at a broader curriculum than traditional engineering. They began to examine the entire field of air transportation education including flight, traffic and maintenance, airport management, and mechanics.[9]

Some other universities were also looking at this broad area of needs—but not many. Near the end of the war, the American Council on Education for the Civil Aeronautics Administration polled 1,500 colleges and universities. It revealed that only 399 universities "offered or were planning to offer education in aviation, while 844 reported no aviation courses. 257 failed to respond. Of the 399 institutions with aviation programs, only eighteen offered a B.S. degree in aeronautical engineering and only eight provided graduate work. Furthermore, only two universities, Purdue and Southern California, had recognized the need to expand beyond the traditional limits of engineering and to consider the broader field of air transportation."[10]

Bruhn and his team reached several conclusions. First, since more than two million men had served in the Army Air Service, many of them would want to continue their education and careers in aviation. Second, since the government predicted that more than 500,000 small, privately owned airplanes would be built after the war, there would be a huge need for trained people to run them. There would be a need for new mechanics and an increase in new opportunities for pilots. And third, a drop in the immediate need for aeronautical engineers as war production stopped would soon be offset by new opportunities that would be emerging in areas such as jet and rocket technology.[11]

Aviation had a promising future.

According to *One Small Step: The History of Aerospace Engineering at Purdue*, the Bruhn-led team further identified four important facts about the university that all pointed toward a broad, expanded program in flight:

Purdue had an airport close to campus within easy reach of students and had the potential for growth.

The university had Purdue Aeronautics Corporation, an operation that had the legal capability of performing many nontraditional functions to support aviation education. It also had Webster who had a wealth of experience in aviation, training programs, and air transportation.

Purdue already had a four-year bachelor of science program in aeronautics.

Combining all the aeronautical engineering programs at the Purdue airport was a logical use of space and equipment. Some of it had been located in a small building next to the mechanical engineering building.[12]

A plan emerged: create within aeronautical engineering a four-year curriculum in air transportation and consolidate all aeronautical work at the airport.[13]

It was a brilliant plan. There were three options available to students in the new air transportation program: airport management and operations; flight and flight operations, which included flight instruction leading to certified professional pilots and certified engine mechanics; and third, a traffic administration option that included airplane maintenance.[14]

Purdue's plans were presented to experts in the United States and abroad in an effort to seek out outside opinions. The minister of education for Great Britain who was visiting Purdue said, "I have visited practically every leading Aero school in the United States to see what their postwar plans were, but this proposed postwar Aeronautical and Aviation Education and Research Center at Purdue is by far the most interesting and comprehensive."[15]

After explaining the plans to the head of the aeronautical engineering program at MIT, Bruhn said, "I came back to Purdue with an aviation pioneer feeling that we were starting to develop and build something really worthwhile for the future of aviation in the broad field of aviation education and research."[16]

In 1945, it all went into effect. The School of Mechanical Engineering was split, and a separate School of Aeronautics was formed. The air transportation program began as part of the new School of Aeronautics.

Meanwhile, aeronautical engineering was moving into the study of jet engines and rockets with research at Purdue being led by Professor

Maurice Zucrow.

In May 1945, Webster told the Purdue Aeronautics Board that in order to support the new air transportation program they would need additional equipment including these: 10 Piper Cub trainers; 10 Waco trainers; 4 VKS-7-F Cabin Wacos or the equivalent; 3 C-78 Cabin Cessnas; and 2 Link trainers. The total cost would be $75,000.[17]

The program became a quick and huge success.

In October 1945, Purdue's air transportation program was featured in *Flying* magazine—a magazine with national circulation. As a result, in the next four months the program received more than two thousand letters of inquiry for sixty positions in the fall class.[18]

When he returned to Purdue after the war, Goldman became a pilot instructor for Purdue Aeronautics, but he had his eye on something bigger. It was an idea that was floating around the university but had not yet taken hold. Goldman hoped Purdue would start a new program featuring a certified airline which would provide education and experience for the professional pilot degree.

When that didn't happen, he left West Lafayette in 1948 to take a job flying for United Airlines out of New York. Webster, Goldman's boss at Purdue, helped him find the new job, but there was a catch.

"Before I left, Grove told me he was only lending me to United," Goldman says. "He said, 'You'll come back someday.' I thought that was the biggest joke of the year. I went to work for United flying New York, Chicago, and Denver."[19]

He married and lived in Jackson Heights, New York, for several years before he and his wife bought a house in Hicksville, New York.

"We'd only lived in the house for ten months and Grove came out to see me," Goldman says. "He looked around our house and said, 'Well, you won't have any trouble selling this.' I said, 'Sell it? We just moved in.' He said, 'You're coming back to Purdue. We're going to start an airline.'" They were starting the new program Goldman had hoped for before moving on to United.

The new air transportation program was attracting a large number of students, but the university was having difficulty finding funds for new equipment and airport improvements. Contracts for training military pilots had diminished after the war, so Purdue Aeronautics had lost its major source of income.

According to the Purdue Aeronautics Board of Directors minutes, "The corporation had to look to other fields of endeavor in order to provide operating revenue."[20]

Then they found the new endeavor. They bought an airline.

Purdue Aeronautics worked closely with the Purdue Research Foundation. This was the same foundation that had helped to finance Amelia Earhart's final flight. Many of the directors of the Purdue Research Foundation were also on the board of Purdue Aeronautics. The Research Foundation provided money to advance the endeavors of Purdue Aeronautics.

In December 1951, the Purdue Research Foundation Investment Committee approved the purchase of Midwest Airlines headquartered in Des Moines, Iowa. The airline had very little in terms of equipment—mostly single engine planes that Purdue was not interested in using. What the university wanted was the airline's operating certificate and routes. The Purdue Research Foundation acquired the airline as an investment by purchasing Midwest's notes (debts) totaling $58,000 plus 493.54 shares of stock.[21] The total investment came to $73,436.[22]

In addition to buying the airline, the Purdue Research Foundation Investment Committee made arrangements for a $900,000 loan and an additional $900,000 line of credit for Midwest.[23]

Owning an airline that operated commercial routes would allow the university to place its students as interns in a variety of fields including flight, mechanics, maintenance, and operations. The company would be a laboratory where students could get real-world experience working side-by-side with professionals. Airline income received from paying passengers and freight would defray the cost of the training. It was an ideal program for air transportation students.

Goldman, who returned in 1953, says the plan was to operate the airline out of state using a name that made no reference to Purdue so that people would not mistakenly think the tax-supported university had gone into the airline business as a for-profit venture.[24]

Since Midwest needed new equipment, the Purdue Research Foundation Investment Committee reached an agreement to purchase ten DC-3 aircrafts from Eastern Airlines for $35,000 each. Two of the planes had already been delivered when the Federal Civil Aeronautics Board voted three to two against renewing the Midwest Airlines flight certificate. The Purdue Research Foundation decided against appealing, liquidated the airline, and sold nine of the DC-3 planes—all for a profit.[25]

With new engines and propellers and after a complete overhaul, the airplanes were sold to Wisconsin Central Airlines for $90,000 each. Other terms of the sale brought Wisconsin Central Airline's total obligation to Purdue to about $1 million. To secure the debt, the Research Foundation put a lien on all the company's airplanes. Also, Purdue's R. B. Stewart was named to the company's board and Webster was named a vice president. Wisconsin Central eventually became North Central Airlines and paid off the debt.[26]

Goldman says the one remaining DC-3 was kept by Purdue and used to launch a charter airline service with students working in the business, much like the university had planned to do with Midwest Airlines. A major feature was allowing students who had their commercial license to fly the big planes as copilots, gaining experience that would eventually help them land jobs.[27]

By this time, Elliott had retired as president of Purdue. He was succeeded by Frederick Hovde who shared Elliott's enthusiasm for flight. Like Elliott, Hovde was a member of the Purdue Research Foundation and Purdue Aeronautics Boards.

Hovde explained the benefits of the charter service program at an Aeronautics Board meeting. "Its maintenance shops provide a live laboratory for [Purdue] transportation students, its planes provide necessary equipment for the training of airline pilots, and it will cooperate . . . in training of airline technicians and professional pilots."[28]

Hovde continued, "Aviation is one of the fastest growing industries in the country, and Purdue should be prepared to serve this industry in the fields of education and research. Without live laboratories, such as the airport and Purdue Aeronautics Corporation, the university would be severely handicapped in its endeavors. Since the airport cannot be operated without funds, the manager has been given the task of operating the airport with charter service of DC-3 planes as the main source of income."[29]

In addition to the DC-3 aircraft, Purdue Research Foundation also supplied the funds to purchase a C-47 transport for cargo hauling and additional equipment was added over the years.

Many of the first customers of the charter service were university athletic departments that wanted the speed of air travel to take teams on trips to away games. At one time or another Purdue Aeronautics flew various teams from all the Big Ten schools and Notre Dame, as well as other universities such as Ohio University and Western Michigan. For two years, Purdue Aeronautics flew the Chicago White Sox baseball team and painted an airplane with the Sox logo. They flew military charters, cargo for the auto industry, and once a Danish ballet company.

"We got a contract with Frankenmuth Brewery in Michigan," Goldman says. "We painted "Frankenmuth" on the side of the plane. We flew all over Michigan taking bartenders and waitresses on rides. The plane was called "The Flying Beer Can." We flew AAA baseball clubs. We flew a team from Columbus, Ohio, in the International Baseball League to Toronto, Syracuse, Richmond, Miami, and Havana. This was before Fidel Castro. We had a lot of fun."[30]

They also provided students with incredible flying experience. The air transportation program, working in cooperation with the Purdue Aeronautics Corporation, was a tremendous success.

In 1949, Bruhn, who initiated the air transportation program, announced he was stepping aside as head of aeronautics and returning to the classroom. He was replaced in 1950 by Milton Clauser. Clauser immediately let it be known he believed air transportation did not belong in the School of Aeronautics, and shortly after he left Purdue in 1954, the air transportation program was discontinued as a part of the aeronautics program. To replace it, a program in airport operations emerged in the new Department of Industrial Management which would become the School of Management. The flight and maintenance options from the air transportation program were terminated as degree options.

Purdue had the resources for flight training and maintenance and there was also an established need, made clear by the continued enrollment of new students. So flight and maintenance training programs were started in the division of technical institutes. This was the beginning of what eventually would become the Purdue aviation technology program.

A two-year nondegree program in aviation maintenance technology was created in the Division of Technical Institutes in 1954. In 1955, James Maris arrived at Purdue to head this new program. In 1956, he started a new professional pilot technology program, also a nondegree training opportunity.

These were two-year programs. They were located at the airport and used Purdue Aeronautics Corporation training opportunities but were not considered part of the standard university. Academic subjects were taught in special courses. Aviation students paid extra fees. For the next twenty-five years, Maris was to head this training, eventually building it into four-year bachelor of science degree programs considered among the top in the nation.

"When I arrived in 1955, Grove Webster was Mr. Aviation at Purdue," Maris says. "He was running the operation at the airport. There was quite a bit of activity out there and Grove was the daddy of it all. He sort of looked at me at first as competition. He didn't know what this new, young upstart was at Purdue to do. But we became good friends and supported each other."[31]

When they met in 1955, it was a veteran who had flown open-cockpit biplanes in World War I meeting a veteran of the World War II who had piloted B-24 missions over France and Germany. Maris's second World War II mission was on June 6, 1944, over the beaches and towns of Normandy.

Born in Lafayette, Colorado in 1919—the year George Haskins flew into Purdue with a petition for an aeronautics program—Maris's family moved to Champaign-Urbana, Illinois. As a boy, he filled his bedroom with model airplanes. One of his first large flying models was Wiley Post's *Winnie Mae* that had landed at Purdue.

During his high school years, Maris would ride his scooter to the Champaign Airport and wash planes in exchange for rides—and sometimes a chance to fly himself with licensed pilots. Like Goldman, one of his first airplane rides was in a Ford Tri-Motor.

He completed two years at the University of Illinois before enlisting in the Army Air Corps after Pearl Harbor. Trained as a B-24 pilot, he found himself stationed in England in June 1944. They were just going to bed on the evening of June 5 when they were told to report to operations.

"They usually didn't come and get pilots for a mission until two or three in the morning," Maris says. "We thought, 'Wow! This is ridiculous.' They told us this was something special. We got to operations and they put the map up. Immediately we knew what was happening."[32]

The planes took off in thick weather using only a lamp shining out of the back of each plane to provide a target for the next pilot to follow. But the darkness and the weather left the flyers unable to see one another.

"We went into the clouds at 300 feet and did not see another plane after that," Maris says. "As we were climbing at about 5,000 feet there was a brilliant burst and a horrendous explosion. Two of the planes had collided, loaded with fuel and bombs. It was just tremendous! A little later there was another explosion. Well, somebody broke radio silence and said, 'The hell with this. Turn on your lights.' Everybody turned on their lights. It was like flying in a Christmas tree. As we were crossing the channel, dawn came up. When you looked down at the water there were what seemed like just thousands of boats—even fishing trawlers, little boats. You could see a thousand wakes in the sea"[33]

Maris flew over the coast of France at 6:25 A.M. and believes he was one of the first four-engine heavy bombers to reach Normandy. His crew hit their targets—bridges and railroads—and returned safely.

They weren't always so lucky on future bombing missions into Germany. On one mission, they returned to England with eighty-four holes in their plane, some of them in the wing big enough for a man to drop through.

"Most of our missions were long, eight to ten hours," Maris says. "When you reached the coast you usually had to fly through anti-aircraft fire. And when you got near your target in Germany, they were trying to intercept you with fighters. There was a lot of stress. I went in weighing about 220 pounds. I came out weighing 140. There was one incident when we got near our target and saw planes go in ahead of us. Boom! We'd see four, five, six B-24s spinning out on fire, wings coming off. Another element would go in. Boom! B-24s spilling parachutes out all over the place. We flew into that knowing, most probably, we would not come out. But in the military you follow orders. This was one time I was so afraid I vomited in my mask. We came out the other side, but we were badly shot up."[34]

Maris finished his thirty maximum missions in ninety days. He was separated from the military in 1946 and went to Curry's School of Aeronautics in Galesburg, Illinois, to obtain his flight instructor and airframe and power plant mechanic certificates and then stayed on to teach mechanics. He was recalled to the military during the Korean conflict.

In 1952, he returned to the University of Illinois to complete his degree in education. "Since Champaign was my home, I wanted to go to work at the University of Illinois," Maris says. "They were starting an aviation program, and they were going to have a maintenance program. Everything was all set. I was employed. But I graduated at mid-year and my contract didn't start until August. To survive and to support my wife and new baby daughter, I started selling Buick automobiles. The director of the aviation maintenance program at the University of Illinois Airport was driving a Buick, and he came into the dealership where I was working to have his Buick serviced. We were talking, since I was contracted to start teaching in his maintenance program with the start of the fall semester. He told me that I should check at Purdue where they were looking for a properly trained individual to start a new aviation maintenance technology program in the fall. But the chance to create a new program at Purdue was such an opportunity that I should look into the position. I checked the program opportunities, and after an employment interview, I was hired immediately."[35]

The Purdue aviation maintenance technology program led to civil aeronautics administration airframe and power plant mechanic certification. The professional pilot program started a year later made use of the Purdue Aeronautics charter service. Students were required to have a commercial pilot certificate prior to being admitted to the program. In addition to using Purdue Aeronautics airplanes, they used equipment left behind by the air transportation program. Academic subjects were available to the students for an extra fee.

Maris started with twenty-eight students that first year. When he arrived, Purdue Aeronautics had finished its contracts with ROTC for flight training and was working on its charter service with the big DC-3s. Maris was able to get the smaller training planes from Purdue Aeronautics for his new flight technology. He eventually used these planes to teach flight to pilots.

"I taught the ground school classes as well as organized the program," Maris says. "I was working ten to fifteen hours a day. I had to redo the coursework that was from air transportation to meet our educational goals. That first year, I was only a day or two ahead of my class."[36]

Jill McCormick came to Purdue in 1957. She had been a woman air service pilot (WASP) pilot during World War II, flying and ferrying many of the World War II fighter and trainer aircraft. After the war she was an instrument instructor in Link trainer for several airlines. McCormick was hired by Professor Maris as the first full-time academic instructor for the professional pilot program and taught most of the classes. She had retired as a major in the Air Force Reserve. She retired from Purdue in 1981 and died in 1989.

Maris's programs continued to grow as more and more students applied. It became highly selective. By 1960, all academic subjects in the program were being taught within the regular university course structure. Effective in 1961, aviation students no longer had to pay the extra fee. Also in 1961, a third option was started: aviation electronics technology. Students graduating in 1962 received associate degrees.

Charles Holleman came to Purdue to teach in the aviation program in 1960. He had been a civilian instructor at Spence Air Force Base in Georgia before deciding Purdue was the best place for him to move when the base was being closed. Holleman retired in 2000 and is professor emeritus of aviation technology.

Holleman says when he arrived they were looking at moving the program to the bachelor's degree level. "It wasn't so much an immediate goal, but we realized the potential for it was there," he says. "Everything was done by a committee, but I was the primary writer for the professional pilot's degree program."

In 1964, Purdue created a School of Technology. The Department of Aviation Technology was established as the first department in this new school.

Maris says he was able to accomplish a great deal because he had the ear of President Hovde. "At that time when President Hovde had to go to Fort Wayne, he didn't have any transportation except to drive," Maris says. "So I would fly him in one of our Cessna-172s. We were making these trips with President Hovde all over the state, and we decided maybe he should learn how to fly. He thought that would be challenging and worthwhile. Whoever was flying with him would teach him the fundamentals of how to take off, land, and navigate. We prepared him to qualify for his license, but he never had the time to take the FAA tests. One time he was coming back from Fort Wayne, and he went off the runway and bent the propeller. So we put it on a mahogany base and gave it to him. He kept it on display in his office."[37]

While they flew with Hovde, the president not only had an opportunity to see the aviation program first hand, but Maris also had an opportunity to explain what they needed to teach their students.

Both Purdue aeronautics and aviation technology advanced rapidly with strong support from Hovde.

On October 15, 1959, Purdue Aeronautics took center stage in the announcement of an exciting new idea called the Midwest Program on Airborne Television Instruction or (MPATI). On October 16, the *Indianapolis Star* reported on its front page that MPATI would impact up to five million students. The newspaper said, "Purdue and Indiana universities joined eight other educational groups yesterday in a bold new space-age plan for broadcasting education television programs from Purdue's West Lafayette campus to high-altitude airplanes for broadcast to classrooms in a half a dozen Midwest states.

"The program, viewed by some experts as a forerunner to manned space platforms, was announced in Chicago by the Midwest Council on Airborne Television Instruction."[38]

The purpose of the program, as explained in an MPATI brochure, was to beam educational television programs to elementary and high school students in Indiana, Ohio, Kentucky, Michigan, Illinois, and Wisconsin. The programs were taped and then broadcast from specially-equipped Purdue Aeronautics planes flying in a wide figure-eight pattern over Montpelier, Indiana. The broadcasts were transmitted over an area that included thirteen thousand schools in the six states. The first demonstrations took place in the spring of 1961. By fall, the program was up and running with a Ford Foundation contribution of $4.5 million.

MPATI records are now archived at the National Public Broadcasting archives at the University of Maryland Libraries. According to a University of Maryland overview on MPATI, the technology for the program dated to World War II. At that time television stations were having a difficult time transmitting signals from tower to tower. Westinghouse discovered that a plane flying at twenty-five thousand feet could transmit a signal over an area twenty times larger than ground transmitters. The system was called Stratovision, but it was not put into use.

By the late 1950s, commercial TV stations had overcome their problems, but Westinghouse saw a need to improve educational TV transmissions. A conference was held at Purdue, and the Ford Foundation offered the $4.5 million to fund the first three years of the program.

Purdue Aeronautics acquired two DC-6AB aircraft that were specially equipped as UHF-TV stations transmitting in flight. Goldman was among the pilots, spending up to eight hours a day flying the big figure-eight patterns. A twenty-four-foot antenna hung from the bottom of each plane in flight and was retracted during ground operations.

"That was the granddaddy of big things that we did," Goldman says. "It was very important. We flew at about twenty-three thousand feet. Westinghouse had equipped these airplanes as flying television stations. It took us almost an hour to get up to our altitude because we were so heavy."[39]

The program ended in May 1968. It had never become fully self-sufficient. Schools participating were charged a dollar per student. To be self-sufficient, the program needed participation from 5,600 schools out of the 15,000 that could receive the signal. Top membership was 1,770 in 1967.[40]

By 1966, Maris had moved his program to the full, four-year bachelor's degree level. Before and after World War II, many airline pilots had received their training in the military. With the Purdue program, a new age was emerging.

"Little by little, the number of military pilots within the airlines began to diminish, and they began to take more and more civilian trained pilots," Holleman says, "and our people competed very well with military pilots. They were trained specifically for commercial programs."

An article in *FAA Aviation News* from February 1966 says, "The next generation of professional pilots may very well come out of the halls of ivy, both sheepskin and license in hand, ready to take their places in the world of flight.

"Graduates of Purdue University could be leading the way. For that university is the only place in the nation where a youngster without any flying experience can enroll as a freshman and in four years earn a B.S. degree with a major in professional pilot technology. In addition to the conventional sheepskin diploma, he'll have a commercial pilot's certificate and instrument rating with hundreds of flight hours, including copilot time in advanced transport aircraft. All students received flight engineer training in DC-6, only two per class were checked out as first officers [copilots].

"Universities have not previously offered four-year baccalaureate degrees in pilot technology because officials who determine policy, for schools such as Purdue zealously maintain high academic standards and do not confer degrees lightly. Also, conservative forces in the education field regard flying as something just for fun and find it hard to relate to higher education."[41]

Purdue students in the four-year aviation program were required to take a basic university curriculum in addition to their flight studies.

According to *FAA Aviation News*, in the winter of 1966 Purdue Aeronautics was operating four DC-3 airplanes, including three that had been completely rebuilt by Purdue. The company also had two DC-6 airplanes and two more that were used for MPATI.

"Purdue students had to meet all FAA requirements to serve as DC-3 copilots," the magazine says. "They logged some 200 hours in that capacity carrying cargo and passengers for Purdue Aeronautics. Also, students were logging flight engineer time in the DC-6 and qualifying for a flight engineer's certificate if they were twenty-one years old."[42]

The first graduate in the bachelor of science program was Jack Brown in 1967. Brown went on to become chief pilot with World Airline.

Holleman says one of the major points that moved the Purdue program above others was the ability of students to fly as copilot on Purdue Aeronautics DC-3 and flight engineer trainees on the DC-6 airplanes. Professor Holleman wrote and received Federal Aviation Administration

(FAA) approval of Purdue's first flight engineer curriculum. At this same time, the program was also acquiring from the military its first DC-6 simulator—a major step for students. While preparing space in a corner of the Aerospace Engineering Laboratory at the airport for the new simulator, the equipment was loaned to United Airlines and used by its pilots. The aviation technology staff provided both pilot and flight engineer training to students and initial training to newly hired Purdue Airlines pilots in the "new" simulator.

Contract training in the DC-6 simulator was provided to outside organizations, such as the Ambassador Travel Club in Indianapolis and a forest fire fighting organization in California that operated DC-6 aircraft.

As the four-year program got underway for aviation technology and MPATI ended for Purdue Aeronautics, a new era was beginning. Organizations that had used Purdue Aeronautics charter services were starting to expect faster travel times. Goldman says it became clear that in order to compete, the company would have to purchase new jet airliners, but the cost was huge, about $4.5 million per plane.[43]

Purdue Aeronautics found a friend in Jack Stephens of Stephens, Inc., an investment banking firm in Little Rock, Arkansas. Goldman says the connection to Stephens came through Hovde.

In 1967, Purdue Aeronautics transferred its assets to a new corporation named Purdue Airlines. Stephens acquired 80 percent of the new company for $800,000. Stephens's company provided the funds needed to purchase two DC-9 twin engine jetliners. The company leased a third.[44]

When the first new planes arrived in 1969, students continued to be offered the opportunity to serve as copilot once they had been certified in jet flight. Three students, Bill Arnold (now with Delta), Jim Rice (now with Southwest), and Mike McIntyre (now with TWA) were the only students fully qualified as first officers on the DC-9. All other students flew as second officers.

Meanwhile, Purdue also operated a DC-9 for Hugh Hefner, founder of Playboy. Hefner had a home in Chicago at that time. Goldman says under contract with Playboy, Purdue Airlines operated and maintained the plane and flew it exclusively for the company, protecting Hefner and Playboy from liability. The plane was kept in a Purdue Airport hangar and taken up to Chicago to pick up Hefner when he wanted to travel.

It was a luxurious airplane, including Hefner's signature round bed and a deluxe bath and shower. Stewardesses prepared gourmet meals on board. Hefner wanted every passenger to have a choice between steak, prime rib, and chicken, so if there were ten passengers on board, Purdue Airlines had to be prepared with thirty meals. The plane flew as far as Africa.

On March 22, 1971, Purdue Airlines announced it would cease operations effective April 30. According to the *Lafayette Journal and Courier,* "Six months of agonizing reappraisal ended with the announced decision by Purdue Airlines, Inc. to end its DC-9 jet operation.

"The announcement came nearly two years to the day after the first [Purdue Airlines] flight.

"Reasons for the sale of the two 104-passenger twin-jet planes included general economic conditions in the Midwest, cutthroat competition from major airlines that also are caught in the economic squeeze, and a lack of adequate return on investment."[45]

Goldman says while income from the airline was sufficient for a nonprofit operation owned by a university and employing 102 people, the new private partners were not receiving a large enough return on their investment.[46]

Goldman stayed on until December 1972. He fulfilled the contract with Playboy. He also tried to restart the airline but was not successful and closed the doors.

In thirty years of operation, company personnel were involved in two major accidents.

Two men were killed in Dallas on April 18, 1962, when a twin-engine executive DC-3 owned by Purdue Aeronautics crashed on a routine maintenance test flight. Killed were Paul Maisonneuve of Lafayette, a maintenance worker with Purdue Aeronautics who was flying the plane, and Tom Cogburn of Dallas, an engineer for Dallas Aero, which was making modifications on the recently acquired plane.[47]

The FAA determined Maisonneuve should not have been authorized to fly the plane. Goldman said Maisonneuve was not a company pilot and the test flight was not under the authority of Purdue Aeronautics.

On November 29, 1963, a Purdue Aeronautics DC-3 crashed attempting to land in bad weather at Morgantown, West Virginia. The plane, which was scheduled to pick up the University of West Virginia basketball team, was empty except for the crew. A flight attendant was killed. The pilot and copilot were injured. The Civil Aeronautics Board initially ruled the probable cause was "the pilot's execution of an instrument landing approach in an aircraft not equipped with navigational instruments appropriate to the ground facilities being used."[48]

However, Goldman—who was not the pilot—said the Civil Aeronautics Board later reported a proper alternative landing process had been used and there was an error in the FAA published approach procedure issued to pilots who used it at Morgantown. The error was subsequently corrected and the Civil Aeronautics Board did not find Purdue Aeronautics at fault.[49]

On March 21, 1973, Purdue Airlines transferred $1,031,702.20 to the university for further airport development.

Many of the company's more than one hundred pilots, flight attendants and mechanics found new jobs with an emerging company in Texas called Southwest Airlines. The closing of Purdue Airlines/Purdue Aeronautics also resulted in lost training opportunities for students in aviation technology. These opportunities were picked up through other options created in aviation technology.

"When Purdue Airlines closed, we struggled," Holleman says. "We didn't have a good multi-engine lab for our students, except our own Twin Beech and later a Piper Navajo. We soon added a couple of Cessna 310s, which were obtained as excess property from the Air Force by Dick Gelzleichter of the Extension Service in the Ag School."

These ex–Air Force aircraft were manufactured in the late fifties, but had an obsolete instrument panel arrangement that was used in WWII aircraft. The general flight section maintenance personnel modified the instrument arrangement to the modern ALPA-T configuration and put a second set of instruments on the right side for the instructors. These airplanes had the best instrument panels of any Cessna 310s in the country for training purposes.

The Navajo was primarily used for trips with the president, upper level administration, and the coaches, with students flying as copilots. The 310s were primarily for the agricultural extension agents, though there was some cross-over in the use of the aircraft. The students flew in the left seat as captains in the 310, and a staff instructor normally flew in the right seat as their copilot. These trips allowed those students, who already had copilot trip experience in the Navajo, to act as captains and obtain more multi-engine left seat pilot-in-command time.

Purdue also was able to set up an arrangement with Vermilion County Aviation (Vercoa) in Danville, Illinois, to provide copilots for their regional airline operation, which was an Allegheny Commuter Airline. They operated turboprop Beechcraft 99s. Purdue provided the academic systems and operations training for the aircraft, and Vercoa provided the flight training for the copilot checkout.

This operation started with the 1972 seniors and continued through the 1973 and 1974 classes. One exceptional student of this operation was Rosemary Merims, the first female accepted into the Purdue professional pilot training program. She graduated with a bachelor's degree in December 1972. Merims was accepted in the first Navy class that included women pilots. She was one of eight. She was the first female Navy pilot to fly fighter, or attack, type aircraft. She was the first woman assigned to an aircraft carrier and then was among the first women to land on a carrier. Merims was also the first woman to command a flying squadron.

Bill Britt, the owner and president of Vercoa, wanted to move his base of operations into the now vacated former DC-6/DC-9 hangar at the Purdue Airport, as he needed more space than was available at Danville. He also indicated that he could use more of our students as copilots, due to his expanding operation. The airport administration turned down this request because they were trying to lease the hangar out to a larger operator.

Shortly after this, Air Wisconsin regional airline started operating into Purdue, and the hangar remained empty for a good while.

Vercoa then moved their operation from Danville, Illinois, to Terre Haute. It was then felt that it was too long a commute for the students, and the program was dropped.

Prior to Purdue Airlines being shut down, the department had been working on obtaining a Boeing 707 simulator, which had been in use by American Airlines. Fortunately the acquisition of this simulator came at exactly the right time. Purdue Airlines shut down on April 30, 1971, and the simulator arrived in Lafayette the same day.

This moved the Aviation Technology simulator program into the jet age! This was the beginning of the post–Purdue Airlines period and set the basic mold for the future of the professional pilot program.

Bill Turner, a former naval aviator and furloughed Pan American flight engineer, had been hired to instruct in the DC-6 simulator and teach the DC-9 systems course. He and Holleman went to American Airlines to train on the Boeing 707 aircraft, and when they returned, Turner started converting the flight engineer program from the reciprocating engine DC-6 to the turbofan engine Boeing 707.

The first graduates to receive 707 flight engineer training completed the program in 1972. Three of those graduates actually went down to American Airlines to take the flight engineer check ride in American's Boeing 707 aircraft.

American hired all three of these graduates, Joe Halsmer, Dave Johnson, and Bill Weatherspoon and their instructor, Bill Turner. Turner and Haismer have retired from American as a Boeing 757/767 captains. The other two are still flying as senior captains with American.

Most of the seniors went to American Airlines for their turbojet flight engineer check rides during the following ten years.

Fairly early in this program with American Airlines, an American vice president came to visit Aviation Technology while some of the students were in Fort Worth taking their airplane check rides. He was asked how the previous students had been performing on their check flights. With that he called his office, and it was obvious from his end of the conversation that something had gone wrong! As it turned out the nose gear on the airplane had collapsed on landing!

There was a procedure in the emergency manual extension of the landing gear on the 707 where the flight engineer had to go into a compartment below the cockpit and perform part of the operation. Purdue could not teach this in its simulator because the simulator did not have that compartment. It was only taught in class. Our first reaction was that one of the students had messed up and had caused the nose gear to collapse. The initial feeling was that the program with American was over.

As it turned out, the nose strut had a crack in it and broke off when the airplane landed. The student had nothing to do with it.

Prior to this arrangement with American, only six professional pilot graduates had been employed by American Airlines, the smallest number employed by any major airline. By 1997, American was the largest employer of the graduates, at least partially as a result of having a close look at their performance on these checks.

As the airlines phased out the 707 aircraft, the 707 simulator became a less viable trainer and there were no longer 707 aircraft available for the check rides.

Normally, the staff transportation flights were scheduled well in advance, but occasionally one would come up without warning. Such was the situation early one afternoon in April 1980. The secretary that scheduled the airplane trips called Holleman to see if he could fly a trip that night. He asked where the trip was going. She said she couldn't tell him then, but to call her back later. When he called, she said she couldn't talk to him on that phone, but would have to move to a more private one in an office. He was to go to Bowling Green, Kentucky, to pick up the new basketball coach, Gene Keady. When they arrived back at Purdue he was to be let out of the airplane at a different location from the normal one on the airport. This was almost a CIA-type operation. Purdue and several other schools had been "scooped" before on announcing new coaches, and Purdue was not about to be "scooped" on this one.

In 1980, United Airlines donated a DC-8 simulator. Professor Dick Ortman, who had been an Air Force fighter pilot during the Korean War and was also a retired American Airlines captain, rewrote the flight engineer program for the DC-8 aircraft. The 1982 and 1983 classes were trained on the DC-8.

Nineteen eighty-three was a major change year for the program. Purdue's new president, Dr. Steven Beering, had approved the purchase of Purdue's first King Air. This was the first "brand new" corporate transportation aircraft to be put into aviation technology's operation. All of the previous aircraft had been surplus or excess from the military, used or donated. Holleman and McCallister went to Wichita, Kansas, for training and returned to soon start flying trips in that aircraft. After a few trips together in the aircraft, and after the students had completed their ground school on the aircraft, students were used exclusively as copilots.

Purdue purchased Beechcraft's course outlines and 35mm slide program for the airplane and provided this training to all of the junior professional pilot students. This enabled all junior and senior students to fly a turboprop powered, pressurized, color radar and flight director equipped aircraft — free. The passengers in the back were paying for the trip.

Also in 1983, Purdue obtained its first Boeing 727 simulator. This was the "entry level" airplane with most airlines and placed the program exactly where it needed to be at that time.

Ortman rewrote the flight engineer program again, for the second time in three years, this time aided by Professor Don James, a retired Air Force colonel who had also flown fighters in Korea and had later flown the U-2 and SR-71 (the world's fastest jet aircraft).

Ortman, and later Professors James, John Young, and Ron Beyers, obtained FAA approval as designated flight engineer examiners. Beyers was a former Indiana Air National Guard colonel and TWA pilot. These certifications enabled Purdue to examine its own students, and issue a flight engineer certificate following a simulator check. The airplane check ride was no longer required. This reduced the cost of the certificate considerably, since the students didn't have to "rent" time in a 727 airplane. It also showed the confidence the FAA had in simulator training.

John Young had been a student in the program, and after graduation in 1974, had been employed as a flight engineer by Braniff Airlines. Young was later furloughed from Braniff following a downturn in the industry and came back to Purdue as a faculty member. Though he had several chances to return to Braniff, he remained at Purdue. Ortman, who was an excellent systems instructor himself, once made the statement that John Young was the best airline systems instructor he had ever run into.

Purdue had long recognized a need for aerobatic training as part of any comprehensive pilot training program. All military pilots receive acrobatic training. Many foreign countrys' civilian airlines had already incorporated this training in their curricula. Purdue had no airplane suitable for this type training. Professor Steve Rans had placed some recoveries from extreme unusual altitudes in the simulator program, but it was felt that this training was not complete unless some of it could be accomplished in an airplane. Simulator training is great for learning systems and procedures, but no matter how exotic a simulator is it cannot adequately simulate changing positive, negative, or zero G accelerations.

Holleman, while visiting with John T. Venaleck, a Painesville, Ohio, industrialist, who employed several Purdue graduates, was asked what the plans were for the program and what the immediate needs were. Holleman answered that at that time Purdue needed a visual system for the 727 simulator and an acrobatic airplane. Venaleck asked why the university needed an acrobatic airplane. He owned a number of ex-military aircraft and acrobatic airplanes, and it is suspected he already knew the answer. He was told of the perceived deficiency in the training. His response was "If you want an acrobatic airplane, I'll buy you one."

The search began for a suitable airplane and several of the more popular ones were eliminated for various reasons. A British deHaviland "Chipmunk" was selected because of its beautifully balanced controls, acrobatic training capability, visibility, ease of tail wheel transition for tricycle gear pilots, maintainability, and low initial and operating costs. At first Venaleck was resistant to buying an old military airplane for the job, but after being convinced that it was what the staff wanted, he bought it and also a spare engine for it.

Holleman developed a training syllabus for the course, with emphasis placed on recovering from extreme, unusual altitudes, and started teaching the course, as an elective, in December 1989. Approximately 250 students (about half of the graduates during this period) chose to take the course and were trained in the aircraft over the next eleven years.

In 2001, the course became a required course, but the time was reduced from five hours to a little over one hour. Instead of including a basic acrobatic course, it became primarily training to recover from extreme, unusual altitudes, which is minimally what the students needed. The big improvement was that now all of the students must take the course.

"We have always offered more advanced training than anyone else," Holleman says. "We've always had great people teaching. At the junior and senior levels of the program, virtually all of the instructors/professors had either airline or military flight experience or both. Our students were well prepared when they graduated."

Benefitting from Purdue's strength in preparing students for the space program and serving on the Aviation Technology Industry Advisory Committee, Dr. William Ross Hamman is Purdue's unknown astronaut. Hamman graduated from the professional pilot program in 1975. After graduation he served as a corporate pilot and then decided on a career change. He attended medical school at the University of Wisconsin and became an M.D. He was later employed by United as a pilot and also became United's quality assurance manager. Along with this and assisting United's medical department, he became an aviation medical consultant to NASA. Hamman trained with NASA as a payload specialist and after several delays in being assigned to a scientific space flight, due to the need to equip the space station, he was assigned to a ground position taking medical data during the STS-107 flight, which became the *Columbia* tragedy. Hamman and astronaut/payload specialist Dr. Laurel Clark were looking for methods to reduce the amount of bone density loss that occurs during extended space flights.

Mark Brown

Mark Brown grew up in Valparaiso, Indiana, the son of an electrician who worked construction projects around the Lake County steel mills. He grew up with a love for flight, and a father who took him to the airport to watch the planes and feel the excitement. All his life, Brown knew he wanted to be a pilot, but he thought anything more than that was probably beyond his dreams.

"I was born in 1951, and starting in the late 1950s, early 1960s, it was all about the space program," he says. "The astronauts were portrayed as bigger-than-life people, and becoming one was, quite frankly, beyond my expectations. It was beyond any concept of reality that a kid from Valparaiso could aspire to be an astronaut. I mean, it was just beyond reality. When you grow up in Valparaiso, you just don't watch Neil Armstrong on TV, and say, 'Oh yeah. I can do that.'"

You actually can. In high school, Brown told counselors he wanted a career in flight with the military, so they advised him what he needed to do.

"They said, 'You're going to need to go to college or to one of the military academies. You're going to have to get a degree in either engineering or the technical sciences, and then you go to pilot training.'"

They were right on all but one count.

Brown applied to the Air Force Academy and also applied for an Air Force ROTC four-year scholarship at nonmilitary institutions. He was not accepted at the military academies, but he did win the ROTC scholarship and was admitted to Purdue University in the fall of 1969 to study engineering.

"I had been there about two weeks doing the whole freshman orientation thing, getting acclimated," Brown says. "And I got called into the ROTC commander's office. He said, 'I've good news for you. Somebody has already resigned from the Air Force Academy, and if you'd like to go, we've got a slot for you.' I said, 'No thanks. I like it right where I am.' So I made a conscious decision to stay at Purdue and loved every moment of it."

He fell in love with engineering. As a high-school student, he hadn't really understood what engineering meant. But when he got to Purdue, he got more than a taste of it and liked what he was experiencing.

"Not only did I fall in love with the discipline, but also the way the whole technical community nurtures you at Purdue," Brown says. "It was just wonderful for me. I had great instructors. I had a lot of encouragement. Yeah, there were struggles in a lot of the classes, but the nice thing about it is, besides just getting the theory on how things do what they do, there was also the practical application."

The ROTC program at Purdue was especially helpful to Brown.

Brown was succeeding, but he wasn't giving the program all that he could due to the demands of an engineering course load. At the end of his junior year he was pulled into the commandant's office. He wondered what he did wrong.

"The commandant looked me straight in the eye, and he said, 'You're it.' I said, 'What do you mean?' He said, 'You're the commandant of cadets for next year.' I felt all the blood run out of my face. They did it intentionally. They thought I had promise but needed to be forced into a leadership position as part of growing and development before I left the university. It was probably the best thing that ever happened to me, next to getting the educational foundation that I got at Purdue.

"That leadership experience, the organizational skills, how to deal with people, just the simple self-confidence that I could do this, has stayed with me for my entire life. When I left the university, I felt I could do just about anything. I had not only the technical background, but I had the managerial skills and the self-confidence to go at it. I use all of that even today."

He went into aeronautical and astronautical engineering at Grissom Hall and every day saw a picture of Gus Grissom.

"Every day you're reminded that not only did Neil Armstrong walk these paths around Purdue, going to class every day, but so did Gus, and so did a whole lot of others. It started to very slowly turn science fiction into reality. By that I mean, even though the Moon program was going on, and all these great and glorious things were going on, I was able to see that this whole space business was more than just something we see on TV. They weren't movie stars. They were real people who had walked a lot of the same paths that I was walking.

"And that also meant that there was a possibility that one day I could have the same aspirations and hopes. It was actually after I left Purdue and had gone through pilot training and was flying airplanes around the country that I bumped into some of the astronauts and got to talk to them and get to know them a little bit. I was very delighted and surprised to find out that they were no smarter or dumber than I was. And that, quite frankly, was a big turning point. That finished this last piece of an inferiority complex that was simply the result of the way that the media and NASA had portrayed astronauts as bigger-than-life people."

Brown graduated from Purdue with an aeronautical and astronautical engineering degree in 1973.

After flight training he entered the Air Force Institute of Technology and earned a master's degree in astronautical engineering, following that up in 1980 with an assignment to Houston, where he worked as an engineer in the early days of the Space Shuttle Program.

"I loved it," Brown says. "I was actually enroute to another assignment in the Philippines, to fly airplanes with the Air Force, when I got called back to be an astronaut."

He was selected for the program in 1984. It had taken eleven years of hard work following graduation from Purdue.

Brown was in the tenth astronaut class. There were seventeen in the group. In addition to Brown, there were two other Purdue graduates—John Casper and Michael McCulley.

It sounds easier than it was for Brown. He had applied once before and was rejected.

"Those of us in the military service, you have to go through the military competition first," he says. "And then, if you're selected, you go into the NASA competition. I didn't even make it out the Air Force competition the first time. The second time, I made it through both, so that was a big deal. I was told there were fifteen thousand qualified applicants, and I was one of seventeen selected. When I attended the first meeting for applicants selected for interviews they handed out a package with short bios of everybody, and I was totally intimidated. It seemed like there were people there that, you know, found cures to cancer, invented water. It was just absolutely unbelievable. I was just an engineer who happened to fly airplanes."

But NASA needed people like Brown, people who had the skills to fly jet airplanes, even if they weren't being selected to pilot in the space program. Brown became a mission specialist.

After one year training, Brown was quickly assigned to a flight in 1985. *Challenger* in January 1986 changed all plans. Brown worked on the team that investigated the cause of the accident.

"It was a very hard time," he says. "It was a tremendous shock to the NASA community for two reasons. One is, obviously, we lost people that we knew and loved and worked with everyday. But the second thing was the failure mode in the vehicle was totally unknown to all of us. We thought the shuttle and the solid rocket motors and all that were just as safe as they could be. We weren't aware that there was a history of problems with those things that were directly related to cold temperatures. It was a real shock to be surprised like that. One of the reasons that we went into the investigation with such vengeance is we wanted to know not only what happened in that specific case, but was there anything else that was lurking in the weeds that was going to step out and bite us later on. And that's why we went through the entire vehicle from one end to the other, looking for absolutely anything that could be a potential smoking gun."

Brown also was a member of the redesign team, and he had a technical role in the first shuttle launch after *Challenger.*

They did further analysis after *Challenger.*

"We did a risk analysis," Brown says. "And the calculations showed that there was about a one in fifty chance of a major catastrophe anytime we flew. That's about two flights in every hundred. *Challenger* went down on flight twenty-five. We did make a lot of changes to the vehicle, the equipment, and so on. And although I never saw it in print, I was told that the statistics had changed to about one in every ninety-eight and a half flights—so just a little bit better than what it was before. But then STS-107 *(Columbia)* went down. So, it makes you think that roughly one in fifty flights was pretty darn close."

Brown's first flight was on STS-28 in 1989. It was a secret Department of Defense mission. Brown, who flew as an astronaut mission specialist, was responsible for the primary satellite payload and deployed a satellite. The launch was absolutely thrilling, he says.

"Every now and then I hear people talk about how afraid they were at launch. I think that's a little bit of a discredit to the astronauts and also the way the program is set up. Before you ever go out to the launch pad, there are so many things that you do to make sure that you're prepared before the flight—and not just the training that you go through, but also the personal affairs you take care of as well. Everything has to be put in order before you get out there, whether it's life insurance or letters to your family members. All that personal data needs to be squared away so that when you finally do get out to the launch pad, your mind is not elsewhere; your mind is focused on the event of the day. It certainly worked out that way in my case. When the engines finally started, I was totally absorbed in the experience, and I found it to be a great thrill."

He did write letters to his family before launch.

"Everybody does it a little differently," Brown says. "We go through sleep shifting during that quarantine period right before we fly. On my first flight, ironically, it worked out to where my office hours were in the middle of the night, like three or four o'clock in the morning. I sat up there one evening, and planned to write letters to my wife and each of the kids. I went in with this preconception that it was going to be page after page after page of things that I wanted to say just in case I didn't come back.

"I was very surprised by two things. First off, it turns out that you can say just about everything you need to say in about a page and a half. That sounds incredible, but it's true. The other thing that surprised me is how emotional an experience that was. When I got it all down, and wrapped them up, and put their names on, and put them in my desk drawer, I knew that the only way those would ever be read, is if I didn't come back. So those would be the last words I would have to my family. It was a pretty amazing thing."

Brown was not at all frightened at launch time.

"The liquid engines start off and that takes about six and a half seconds for all three of them to come up to full power," he says. "The vibration inside the shuttle feels very much just like sitting in your car with the engine starting. It's just a very minor vibration. You can feel the sway in the orbiter from the force of the motors pushing the stack over to one side . . . what they call the *twang*. And then when the solid rocket motors ignite, you really do jolt off the launch pad. And they burn very rough, so it shakes you as you head straight up. By the time you clear the top of the launch tower, you're already going over one hundred miles an hour. By the time you get to fifteen thousand feet, you're going faster than the speed of sound. It is a very dynamic event. You're not pulling, you know, eight to ten Gs coming off the launch pad. It's one and a half to two, depending on what they're doing. It's the shaking that is very attention getting and the realization that this is not a simulation—that you really are going to go from the ground to space in eight and a half minutes.

"After two minutes, when the solid rocket motors are jettisoned, it gets very smooth again. The next three or four minutes, as you basically go up above Earth's atmosphere and then pitch over to follow the curvature of Earth, is a very smooth ride. But the last minute and a half or two, the shuttle accelerates out to three Gs acceleration because there's no air to pull at the wings to slow you down. And wearing a seventy-pound pressure suit and life raft and parachute and all that stuff—it's a very strenuous experience to be pushed into your seat at three Gs for that length of time. So when the engines finally do shut down, at main engine cutoff, you basically go from three Gs acceleration to weightlessness in about a second. And that is quite a shock on your body, and it induces a head-over-heels tumbling sensation from your inner ear. Then you literally just sit there for a few seconds and kind of get your act together before you start getting on with your business."

On that first flight, Brown was in the mid-deck and didn't have an opportunity to glance out a window at launch. When they reached space, he was busy helping everyone get out of their space suits.

"It was a very funny time, too," he says. "You have to make this mental adjustment of going from Earth to weightlessness in space. When I first unbuckled myself from my seat, I went drifting off across the room and hung myself on my oxygen mask because I'd forgotten that I was weightless. So you laugh at yourself and do things like that. You do it all with a big smile on your face. When I first got up there and the engines stopped, I sat there for a moment, took a pencil out of my sleeve, and just watched it float in front of me, in the air. It was really cool. I mean for an individual like myself that was the realization of a dream come true. And when I finally did get up on the flight deck and looked out the window in the daytime, I was just overwhelmed by the beauty and the scope and the colors. That initial feeling then gives way to the fact that you don't see the lines between the countries and the cities. They're not labeled. It's very difficult to see major roads. And then you finally realize, kind of in the third take, that you don't see the people. Where are all the people? I know there's six and a half billion people down there, on the ground. And I can't see one of them! You get a little sense of separation from humanity."

About the time Brown started feeling that separation, the shuttle passed into sunset on Earth and darkness.

"All the lights come on below," he says. "You can see every city and town on the ground. You can see just about every highway lit up by streetlights and headlights. You can see that the earth is alive and teaming with humanity. That is really a cool feeling."

Brown flew a second time as a mission specialist on STS-48 in September 1991. In 1993, he retired from the Air Force and left NASA.

Brown and his wife, Lynne, a Purdue graduate in art education, met at Purdue, and they married in 1974. They have two daughters—Karin, a high-school junior in 2003, and Kristin, who in the fall of 2003 entered her senior year at Purdue.

"It's very hard being married to an astronaut," Brown says. "Some of it's comical, and some of it's not. When you're on active duty as an astronaut, you do roughly two personal appearances a month. So you go off to Oshkosh, Wisconsin, or, Dayton, Ohio, and you're doing speeches at the high schools or colleges or Rotary Clubs. And you're treated very well. You're basically king for a day when you show up and do these events. Well back home, you know, the spouse is dealing with kids and dogs and groceries and lawn mowers and all the normal routine of everyday life. And you kind of walk in the door after playing king for a day, and she's [or he's] there looking for help in the reality of life. So, you very much end up living two lifestyles: the high-profile one and then reality. A lot of people have trouble making that adjustment."

When you do fly, it becomes a major family event, Brown says. The launch is like planning for a wedding.

"In addition to everything, just the psychological aspects of a spouse going into space, your wife [or husband] is expected to host a reception for all the friends and family that are going come to the launch and the landing," Brown says. "The spouse has to coordinate all of that. There are invitations to be written, halls to be rented, menus to be sorted out. Everybody wants shirts, pins—you name it. Your phone just rings constantly. People that you haven't talked to in twenty years call and act like it was just yesterday because they want to get in on the fun. So it's quite a burden for the spouse in addition to the emotional aspects of it."

Brown would like to see some changes in the space program.

"I think this is a good time to get our strategy adjusted," he says. "I think we've kind of veered off course of late. The primary mission of NASA should be research and exploration. And the exploration, I think, has lost emphasis. We need to put together a program that results in a very step-by-step evolution to exploration of the solar system. And by that I mean let's get back to the Moon. Let's go to Mars. And I would change the use of the space station from a research laboratory, that's focused on pure science, to one that's focused instead on helping to develop the systems and engineering tools that will be required to support long-duration space flight. So, what I would advocate doing is let's go ahead and take development systems up to the Space Station, and try them in a very nearby environment to develop the technologies we need. Then we need to establish an outpost on the Moon, which is three days away, where we can try stuff for a longer duration. We need to refine the skills and the vehicles that we need for that kind of exploration.

"And then ultimately, let's go to Mars and the other planets."

Chapter Thirteen

Question: Someone has said that a person has to be a bit strange or abnormal in his mental makeup to want to explore space. Do you agree with that?
Iven Kincheloe: Not at all. If that is the case, then we have a great number of such people in this world. Here at the Flight Test Center, we have some thirty pilots involved in flight test phases of everything we're got in the United States in the way of aircraft, and every one of those individuals is expecting and hoping for a chance to get into a program of this nature.

—*U.S. News and World Report,* January 17, 1958

The stunning news screamed in three lines across all eight columns at the top of the *New York Times.* "Soviet Fires Earth Satellite Into Space; It Is Circling the Globe at 18,000 M.P.H.; Sphere Tracked in Four Crossings Over U.S."[1]

The headlines might just as well have shouted, "The Space Race On! The World Will Never Be The Same."

On October 5, 1957, the Soviet Union announced that the day before it had successfully launched a 184-pound satellite. It was only twenty-two inches in diameter, but it was big enough to shake the world.

"The official Soviet news agency *Tass* said the artificial moon . . . was circling the earth once every hour and thirty-five minutes. This means more than fifteen times a day," the *Times* reported.[2]

It did not take a general in the Pentagon to calculate the potential threat this posed to the United States. Although government and military officials tried to downplay the significance of *Sputnik,* as the satellite was named, the average U.S. citizen readily picked up on the concerns. Public worries were reinforced by a news media that was very willing to speculate on the possibilities.

The *Times* on October 5 stuck to the facts. "The Soviet Union said the world's first satellite was 'successfully launched' yesterday. Thus, it asserted that it had put a scientific instrument into space before the United States. Washington has disclosed plans to launch a satellite next spring. The Moscow announcement said the Soviet Union planned to send up more and bigger and heavier artificial satellites during the current International Geophysical Year, an eighteen-month period of study of the earth, its crust, and the space surrounding it. The Soviet Union said its sphere circling the earth had opened the way to interplanetary travel. It did not pass up the opportunity to use the launching for propaganda purposes. It said in its announcement that people now could see how the 'new socialist society' had turned the boldest dreams of mankind into reality."[3]

Another *Times* article on October 5, 1957, stated, "The Soviet launching of an earth satellite followed by less than six weeks the announcement in Moscow that a Soviet intercontinental ballistic missile had been fired a great distance. Both announcements appeared calculated to impress the uncommitted nations. The Soviet Union is thought to be making a conscious effort to persuade people, especially in Asia and Africa, that Moscow has taken over world leadership in science."[4]

That was a frightening thought for Americans in the late 1950s.

As *Sputnik* sailed through space, people on Earth with amateur radio equipment could listen to its "beep, beep" signals which were also carried by television and radio news reports. Everyone knew the "beeps" from space.

"What sort of information is being transmitted to the earth from the Soviet earth satellite?" the *Times* asked on October 7. "American scientists disagreed yesterday over whether there was any secret code concealed by the unearthly radio beeps from the satellite as it circled the earth. . . . Dr. Fred Whipple, director of the Smithsonian Astrophysical Observatory in Cambridge, Massachusetts, charged Saturday that the Soviet satellite was transmitting scientific information in code. . ."[5]

The news did not get better.

On November 3, the Soviets announced they had launched a second satellite. This one weighed 1,110 pounds and, even more startling, it carried a dog named Laika.

By November 5, the *Times* was reporting, "Scientists in many lands speculated yesterday that a Soviet rocket might already be en route to strike the Moon with a hydrogen bomb in the midst of its eclipse Thursday. They noted that the launching of a satellite Saturday with a payload of more than a half-ton showed that a trip to the Moon was within Moscow's capabilities. The explosion of a bomb on a moon darkened briefly in eclipse would create an illumination on the earth brighter than the light of a full moon in the view of one American scientist. It was thus seen as a 'firework' that would provide a spectacular display for the fortieth anniversary of the [Russian] October revolution."[6]

The lunar eclipse passed without incident, but concerns continued to mount.

On December 6, a U.S. Vanguard rocket carrying a satellite lifted off from Cape Canaveral, Florida. The seventy-two-foot vehicle, only forty-five inches in diameter at its widest point, rose two to four feet and burst into flames, crashing to the ground.

This was not the reassurance American people were waiting to witness.

Finally on February 1, the U.S. Army successfully launched a satellite into orbit. The United States was now in the race, and it was clear that this was going to feature more than sending hardware into space, more than sending dogs into space. It was going to mean sending people into space.

The U.S. Air Force quickly put together plans for a program aptly named "Man In Space Soonest." It would ultimately become the NASA Mercury program.

The first task of Man In Space Soonest: pick the Americans most qualified for space flight. In 1958, only a handful of men were deemed candidates.

A government-briefing chart stamped *secret* and now declassified was seen at the time only by those in the top echelons of the Air Force and the administration of President Dwight Eisenhower. That document contained a list of nine test pilots who were deemed eligible for the space program based on their background, skills, and weight. Weight was an important consideration for the rocket technology of the day.

At 150 to 175 pounds, the Air Force list of candidates included four men: Joseph Walker, Scott Crossfield, Robert Rushworth, and Purdue University graduate Neil Armstrong. At up to 200 pounds, which was considered the maximum limit, were Bill Bridgeman, Alvin White, Bob White, Jack McKay, and Purdue graduate Iven Kincheloe.[7]

Eisenhower knew what he was looking for in candidates to become the first American in space. He wanted a military man. Eisenhower's interest in space was not exploration. He was interested in the use of space for military purposes—offensive and defensive. The potentials were huge.[8]

In an article for *Air & Space Magazine* in the fall of 2000, Tony Reichhardt wrote, "For Ike, it was a natural decision. He had zero interest in the romance of space travel and was only intrigued by the prospect of military men spying on the Soviets from orbit. 'Eisenhower was not picking the first humans to go to the moon,' says American University Space Historian Howard McCurdy. The people he had in mind 'were more in the legacy of Francis Gary Powers (a spy plane pilot) than Lewis and Clark.'"[9]

That ruled out a number of the candidates who were not in the military, including Armstrong who was then a civilian test pilot.

Among the military pilots who remained, one was already being called Mr. Space in the news media. He had piloted a Bell X-2 rocket plane to 126,200 feet, the highest any human being had ever flown. He had already entered the edge of space.

Handsome, young, and articulate, this man was already the designated prime pilot for the next generation plane: the X-15. He had a Purdue engineering degree. He was a Korean War hero. He was appearing in TV shows such as *I've Got A Secret,* and his story was being told in newspapers and magazines across the country. Everyone wanted to interview him: Walter Cronkite, *U.S. News and World Report,* the *New York Times.*

In June 1958, when candidates were being considered for space, one man's name was at the top of everyone's list. He had everything they were looking for. He had everything anyone could hope to find, including that intangible quality Thomas Wolfe would later call "the right stuff." This man was Iven Kincheloe. Many of his friends just called him "Kinch."

In a biography of Kincheloe, author James J. Haggerty Jr. simply called him the First of the Spacemen. Before the shuttle program, before the Apollo Moon shots, and before the Mercury 7 astronauts, there were a handful of test pilots who were pushing the limits of technology, science, and space. The most famous of them all was Iven Kincheloe.

In his book *Test Pilots: The Frontiersmen of Flight,* Richard P. Hallion says, "Iven Kincheloe, a Korean jet ace, fitted the popular physical image of the test pilot, with ruggedly handsome good looks and a friendly personable nature. Articulate, brimming with confidence, he was an Air Force public relations dream come true—and it was all true. The blond pilot was a superlative airman, a fine engineer, and held in the highest esteem by his peers." He spoke calmly and in simple terms that people could understand. He used understatement and never boasted.[10]

He talked about himself and his airplanes or rockets as "we," a clear appreciation that neither man nor machine was capable of incredible feats separately. To Kincheloe, it took man and machine working in perfect harmony to reach the new unknown barriers, to explore where no one and no thing had ever been before.

The fact that Kincheloe was at the top of the list of military test pilots in 1958 is made apparent by the fact that he was named the prime Air Force test pilot for the hottest, most advanced project the United States had in development: the X-15.

This is how Tony Reichhardt summed it up in an article for *Air & Space Magazine:* "Already dubbed 'Mr. Space' by the press for piloting the Bell X-2 rocket plane to a world's record of 126,200 feet in 1956, two weeks before his name appeared on a Man In Space Soonest weight chart, [Kincheloe] had tested a science-fiction spacesuit called the Mark I in a simulated flight to 100 miles. If anyone was primed to be the first space pilot, Kincheloe was."[11]

In the summer of 1958, it seemed as though everything that had happened in his thirty years of life had taken Kincheloe to a pinnacle. He had arrived at a breathtaking moment in his life from which a thousand dreams could be launched.

He was born in Detroit, Michigan, on July 2, 1928, only one year after Charles Lindbergh made a solo crossing of the Atlantic Ocean that changed aviation forever.

His father worked in engineering for Graham-Paige Motors in Detroit, but in 1929 when the Depression began and spread a dark cloud over the nation and world, auto industry jobs disappeared.[12] So the Kincheloes moved to a farm that had been owned by the family for generations in the small community of Cassopolis, Michigan, northeast of Niles near the Michigan-Indiana border when Iven was three years old.

With little to do and little money to spend on anything, the family enjoyed Sunday afternoons at a nearby airport at Grosse Isle watching the airplanes. It was there that flight—and everything associated with it—captured the imagination of the World's First Spaceman.

In his biography of Kincheloe, Haggerty says that the tipping point came in April 1933. "On the Kincheloe farm was a small landing strip, built years earlier by the government as an emergency field for its airmail pilots. One day, a barnstorming pilot dropped around to see the senior Kincheloe to ask permission to use the field for a flight exhibit that would include selling two-dollar rides to the locals. Kincheloe Sr., as interested in airplanes as anybody, agreed readily and waived his rental fee in exchange for a plane ride for young Iven. It was a never-to-be-forgotten experience. Iven's baby face was a study in ecstasy as the biplane lifted off the ground. His waving parents grew smaller and smaller and the familiar farmland took on a new magic as he viewed it from above. When he was lifted out of the cockpit half an hour later, he was speechless with the thrill of this great experience. From that day on, airplanes were uppermost in Iven's thoughts."[13]

He began assembly model planes—typical enough for a boy growing up in the 1930s—but he took his interest to new levels. When a fifth grade school Christmas play featured Santa being flown on his important mission by airplane, Kincheloe sought and won the role of the pilot.[14]

"He read and read," Haggerty says, "until he almost exhausted the stock of aviation literature [in his home town]. He built up his own library, ranging from juvenile air fiction like *The Daredevils of the Air* and *The Airship Boys* to highly technical trade magazines. He haunted the [nearby] Dowagiac public library until he had read every aviation book on its shelves and then pestered the librarian to find new ones. Impressed by the youngster's ambitious reading program, the librarian entered into the spirit of the game and took delight in coming up with volumes of which even young Kincheloe had not known. He read all of them."[15]

In high school, Kincheloe was allowed to drive a car at the age of fourteen because the distance he lived from school was too far to walk in days when rural areas didn't supply bus service. Kincheloe decided if he was old enough to drive, he was also old enough to fly and he convinced his parents to allow him to take flight lessons. The instructor was so impressed at how quickly Kincheloe took to flight that he said the fourteen-year-old was ready to solo after only two hours of instruction. In fact, before long he was landing in snow using pontoons and doing aerobatics such as spins and diving turns, but legally, Iven couldn't fly alone until he reached the age of sixteen.[16]

By the time he soloed on his sixteenth birthday, July 2, 1944, Kincheloe had several hundred hours of flight experience behind him.[17]

Kincheloe's seventeenth birthday fell in 1945 near the end of World War II. He knew he wanted to attend college and his interest was aeronautical engineering. His first option was a military academy, but he was too young. To enroll at West Point, Annapolis, or the Coast Guard

Flight came to Purdue in 1911 when Lincoln Beachy and George Witmer put on an airshow at Stuart Field. Seven thousand people watched from Stuart Field and ten thousand more from other vantage points as the "birdmen" brought flying machines to Tippecanoe County.

Purdue opened the first public university airport in 1930. *Photo taken in 1937.*

James Clifford Turpin helped the Wright brothers with their engine and control designs and was a member of the Wright exhibition flying team, introducing flight to America. He was the first Purdue graduate to set a flight altitude record.

Amelia Earhart, aviator and counselor to women students at Purdue, is working with George Haskins, who helped start aeronautical engineering at Purdue and later headed the program.

Jimmie Johnson (right), among the nation's first test pilots, is congratulated after an air race victory by a man he taught to fly—General Billy Mitchell.

Frederick Martin, commander of the 1924 Around-the-World Flight

Charles McAllister led one of the military's first precision flying teams.

Ralph Johnson, as a United Airlines pilot, helped advance commercial air travel.

Grove Webster (left), chairman of the board of Purdue Airlines, accepts delivery of the firm's first McDonnell Douglas DC-9 from the Douglas Aircraft Company, in Long Beach, California, 1969. Douglas Vice President J. J. Dysart hands Webster a model of the plane in a ceremony that included fifty Purdue engineers who worked for the company.

Wiley Post brought national attention to the Purdue Airport when he made an emergency landing in 1935. His first words after landing: "Get me out of this [helmet]!"

George Welch, World War II Ace, is officially the second man to break the sound barrier.

Iven Kincheloe—the first "spaceman"

Jerry Goldman, Purdue Airlines, director of flight operations and engineering

Purdue graduate Malcolm Ross (right) with Victor Prather perparing for liftoff of Strato-Lab V from the aircraft carrier *Antietam* in the Gulf of Mexico, May 1961. They set a balloon altitude world record of 113,740 feet—more than 21 miles.

Virgil "Gus" Grissom—astronaut in Mercury, Gemini, and Apollo programs

Neil Armstrong (left) and Eugene Cernan are two of the twelve people in the world who have walked on the Moon. *Photo taken in 1967.*

Roger Chaffee believed strongly that "you have to *want* to dedicate your life to a worthwhile cause."

Charles Walker

Loren Shriver

Gary Payton

Donald Williams

Richard Covey

Roy Bridges Jr.

Jerry Ross

Guy Gardner

Janice Voss

John Blaha

John Casper

Mark Brown

Michael McCulley

Gregory Harbaugh

David Wolf

Mary Ellen Weber

Mark Polansky

Andrew Feustel

Academy, he would have to wait one year after gradating from high school, and he was not a patient young man.

He picked Purdue University. It was fairly close to home and had an excellent aeronautical engineering program along with a strong Air Reserve officer's training program. In fact, in 1945 the aeronautical engineering program at Purdue was spinning off from the School of Mechanical Engineering to become its own separate school. Adding to the luster of Purdue was that it had its own university airport.

At Purdue in the postwar period, Kincheloe attended classes with a number of veterans who were overflowing college campuses across the country on the G.I. Bill. He made many friends among these veterans—especially the pilots. "Iven sought them out and picked their brains . . . encouraging them to talk about planes and combat technique," Haggerty writes. "He learned a great deal from them, and they occasionally learned something from him, for hastily-trained men of the Army Air Forces knew surprising little about their aircraft. Iven could contribute to the conversation by telling them intricate details of the construction of the B-17 or the involved workings of its power plant, things they have never learned in the helter-skelter quick-and-dirty war-training programs."[18]

He pledged Sigma Phi Epsilon Fraternity and took part in ROTC, which was required of male students.

As far as Kincheloe was concerned, about the only thing Purdue lacked was an airplane for him to fly. So he set about finding one on his own. He formed a flying club composed of a dozen pilots who pooled their money and bought a surplus PT-19—an open-cockpit, two-seat Army trainer.[19]

In April 1946 while flying the PT-19 home to his family farm in Michigan, he had his first accident. Flying into the airfield on the family farm—the same field he had used on his first airplane ride in 1933—he forgot the location of an REA power line. At the last second he dove his plane beneath the line but didn't make it completely. The wire tore his right wing tip and ripped through the rudder. He landed safely but somewhat embarrassed. A friend had taken the trip with him, and the two engineering students were able to repair the plane sufficiently for the flight back to Purdue.[20]

When he returned to campus, his friends found the accident great material for teasing. But Kincheloe had a ready comeback. "I'm a test pilot for the REA. I was testing the strength of that wire," he told them.[21]

While at Purdue, Kincheloe began to develop an interest in not only being an aeronautical engineer, but a test pilot, a flyer who takes new and experimental aircraft up to see firsthand how well it works—or doesn't work.

Following his junior year in 1948, he did a six-week ROTC summer program at Wright-Patterson Air Force Base in Dayton. There he had a chance to meet Chuck Yeager who less than a year earlier had officially broken the sound barrier in the Bell X-1 over California. A Bell X-1 was also at Wright-Patterson, and Yeager, who was impressed with Kincheloe, allowed the young college student to sit in the cockpit.[22] There were no longer any questions about what Kincheloe wanted for his future.

Back on campus in the fall of 1948, Kincheloe was a college student again, showing his love for pranks. Haggerty writes, "[Kincheloe's] flying ability came in handy in the fall of 1948 on the eve of the Old Oaken Bucket football game. In the pregame hijinks between students of Indiana University and Purdue, a group of IU students raided the Purdue campus, let all the air out of every auto tire they could find, and littered the university grounds with pamphlets telling of Purdue's absolute inability to muster a football team worthy of winning the bucket. The student council called [Kincheloe] and his PT-19 into action. Hastily they prepared a counter-leaflet predicting slaughter of the inept Indiana squad. [Kincheloe] flew to the Indiana campus, did a startling low buzz job over the grounds, and when he had attracted sufficient attention, let go ten thousand leaflets. It was acclaimed as a masterful job of morale destruction."[23] And the Boilermakers trounced the Hoosiers 39-0.

In June 1949, Kincheloe received his bachelor's degree in aeronautical engineering and set out to fulfill his dream to become a test pilot. Commissioned a second lieutenant upon completion of ROTC, he was sent to Perrin Air Force Base in Texas.

Kincheloe was in his element. He soon was training on jet aircraft at Williams Air Force Base in Arizona. Every step of the way, he was enjoying his flight experience more and more. He was not deterred when flying at thirty thousand feet on a training mission his cockpit canopy blew off. "The pressurized air in the cockpit escaped in a blast, which the Air Force medics call explosive decompression, and left him exposed to the thin, rarefied upper atmosphere," Haggerty writes. "He became giddy and started to black out, but he had enough presence of mind to put the plane into a steep dive. [He] managed to retain consciousness and keep control . . . until he pulled out at 6,000 feet. He felt weak and dizzy and his head was pounding, but he was able to guide the plane back to Williams for a landing. The experience left him ill for several days. 'It kind of raised hell with the blood vessels in my head,' he wrote home, 'and apparently caused some damage to the sinuses. I have had terrific headaches since.'"[24]

Kincheloe graduated from his jet-training program at Williams on August 4, 1950. About five weeks earlier, war had broken out in Korea and there was little doubt where Kincheloe was heading. He was anxious to go, but first, there would be another year of training.

He was sent to Chicago and O'Hare Air Force Base where he was put to work on a new plane, the F-86 Sabre, the same jet that had been tested and taken past the speed of sound by George Welch in 1947 and 1948.

For a short time Kincheloe was loaned from his work at O'Hare to a group at Edwards Air Force Base in California where Welch was working. In 1950, Muroc had been renamed Edwards. At Edwards, Kincheloe was assigned to fly a new version of the Sabre Jet called the F-86E. In the summer of 1951, Kincheloe was back at O'Hare.

He arrived in Korea that September and was stationed at Kimpo Field, Seoul. A year later he had flown sixteen missions and had only seen the enemy three times, never even getting close enough for real battle.

In November, he was transferred to Suwaon. He flew four missions in the first two weeks of December in an F-86E he had named *Iven.* He came in contact with the enemy in all of them. On January 25, 1952, he shot down his first enemy plane. By April 6, he had shot down four more and by official Air Force Standards was classified an Ace—the tenth pilot in Korea to receive that designation. By mid-May, Kincheloe was a double Ace, having destroyed ten enemy planes and damaging eleven others.

"His last mission was as uneventful as his first," Haggerty writes. "He landed, gave *Iven,* his airplane, a last pat on the nose. . . . He was going home with a chest-full of ribbons: a Silver Star . . . a Distinguished Flying Cross, the Air Medal with two oak-leaf clusters, the Korean Service Medal with three bronze stars, a Distinguished Unit Citation Emblem, the Republic of Korea Presidential Unit Citation, and the United Nations Service Medal."[25]

His war record was so outstanding the Air Force promoted him as a national hero and his exploits received coverage in newspapers from coast to coast.

He had been out of Purdue for only three years. He was twenty-three years old. He knew what he wanted to do next. It was what he had wanted since his days on the Purdue campus. He wanted to be a test pilot, but that would take some time. First, he was assigned to Nellis Air Base in Nevada where he became a fighter-gunnery instructor.

He also lost his rank. While serving in Korea he had been promoted to captain, but there was less need for captains back home, and he was dropped all the way to first lieutenant. It was not uncommon for the times, but Kincheloe didn't like it.[26]

Those were hard days. His career seemed to be stalled. He had gained national acclaim as a war hero, but Haggerty says some of his superiors were jealous. Only sixteen pilots were chosen for each session of test pilot school. To be accepted a candidate was required to be an aeronautical engineer with considerable flight experience. Kincheloe fit those requirements, but time again he was passed over. He suspected the reason was petty jealousies.[27]

"When he was not flying he was a frequent visitor to the night spots of the Vegas 'strip,'" Haggerty writes. "Handsome as a movie star, famous to a degree, and full of personality, he was a popular favorite with the Vegas female colony. To entertain them properly, he bought a big, black convertible Cadillac with money he had saved from Korea."[28]

He visited Edwards Air Force Base and he knew that's where he wanted to be, testing the latest aircraft.

By spring of 1953, he had regained his rank as captain. His applications for test pilot training continued to go nowhere. He had several job offers in the private sector and was finally considering leaving the Air Force. Then, just before Christmas of 1953, he got the word that he would be part of a special exchange program with the British. Two British flyers were sent to the United States for test pilot training. And Kincheloe, along with one other flyer, was sent to Empire Test Pilot School in Farnborough, forty miles outside of London.

Kincheloe's first love in England was on the ground—a twenty-five-year-old "retired" London taxi that he named *Lizzie*. He loved to drive the car around the English countryside. He loved flight school. He enjoyed the British people.

There was only one thing about England Kincheloe didn't love. Every morning he was brought a cup of tea, every morning he threw it down the drain, and every morning when his cup was spotted empty again, they poured him some more.[29]

It wasn't long before Kincheloe and the other pilots in the program had completed the preliminary classroom work and were in the air. But being a test pilot was much more than flying.

Haggerty explains: "[Kincheloe] would be given an assignment to fly one of these planes in a specific series of maneuvers and write a report on his findings. . . . The report was more important than the flying . . . You had to tell the engineers what was wrong and what was right about the airplane you were testing, and you had to do it in clear, lucid technical language. Although a flight might only last half an hour, the report might take several hours to write—and it had better be a good one if you wanted to complete [the] course."[30]

The pilots were being judged in three areas: skill in the airplane, academics, and aptitude. Haggerty says Kincheloe rated tops in aptitude and showed it on the ground by loading all his friends into his London taxi for an evening of pub-crawling. Kincheloe put signs on his vehicle that read, "Caution, ejection seat," "only qualified operators may handle," "emergency exit," and "hot exhaust."[31] Those were the warning signs posted on the airplanes Kincheloe was flying, and he liked to make his experiences in his London taxi every bit as exciting as his flights.

Kincheloe also picked up a taste for some of the finer things in life while training in England. He found that he loved both art and music. He studied painting and enjoyed traveling to London to hear concerts featuring Bach and Beethoven.

He also loved pranks. One evening he and two other students rolled the group captain tightly into a rug, stood it up in a corner, and occasionally poured beer down the open end to keep the officer from getting too hot under the collar.[32]

By the end of 1954, Kincheloe had successfully completed test pilot school. He prepared to leave England and head home to the United States. He would leave behind *Lizzie*, but that didn't matter. He had found something much more an important to him—Dorothy, an American from Oakland, California. Kincheloe met her while she was touring Europe with friends. Before she went home from her three-month tour, Kincheloe proposed, and they arranged to be married back home.

They were married August 20, 1955, at the Carmel Mission in Carmel, California. By that time, Kincheloe was already deeply involved his new job as a test pilot at Edwards Air Force Base. All his dreams were coming true.

His new wife quickly faced the dangers of her husband's career.

"Dorothy shared Kinch's own philosophy about accidents," Haggerty writes. "They were bound to happen, but he had spent years preparing for emergencies and felt when something went wrong, he had the skill to handle it. There was, however, always the possibility of the type of accident that no amount of skill could forestall—the swift visitation of death, which was ever present on a test flight of a new, untried plane. Dorothy thrust that possibility to the back of her mind."[33]

Kincheloe's lifestyle changed after his marriage.

"He gave up his nightly visit to the officer's club for a hangar-talk session and came straight home from the flight line each evening," Haggerty says. "He liked to change into a pair of shapeless slacks and a t-shirt and loll about the house, listening to his favorite Mantovani-style dreamy music, which had supplanted Bach and Beethoven. He loved to entertain and, with his flair for storytelling and his big, booming, ready-laugh, he was always the life of the party. He had a constant stream of visitors coming to the house because he was proud of Dorothy and wanted everybody on the base to meet her. To each of them he made a standard introduction. 'This is my lovely wife, Dorothy.'"[34]

Edwards was the epicenter of everything that was happening in flight technology. In addition to the Air Force, the civilian National Advisory Committee for Aeronautics did testing at Edwards. The NACA would later emerge as the National Aeronautics and Space Admission—NASA. But that would come several years later.

Testing new airplanes was a very precise job that was broken into four steps. First, the company that designed and built the new airplane had its own test pilots. They were the first to take the new technology into the air to test its performance. Next, military test pilots would take the aircraft up for a test. Changes would be recommended and made by the contractor. The civilian pilots would then take the planes up again to check out the changes. Finally, the military test pilots, such as Kincheloe, got another go at it.[35]

Chuck Yeager, the first man to officially break the sound barrier, had flown a rocket plane at more than 1,650 miles an hour. It was called the X-1A. An X-2 capable of flying 2,000 miles per hour was due to arrive at Edwards within months for testing. There was never any doubt what Kincheloe wanted to do. He wanted to fly the farthest, the fastest, and the highest. He wanted to be a rocket man.

Kincheloe did everything he could to get more work and the most important jobs as a test pilot. He moved up the ladder quickly and was soon considered one of the most experienced and best pilots at Edwards.

"It was fascinating work, just what he had been after for years," Haggerty writes. "It had the thrill and adventure which he had sought since his earliest flying days and he reveled in every moment of it. But he had fixed his eye on a still more distant goal."[36]

The X-2 had arrived at Edwards. It was a thing of beauty to any pilot and to any aeronautical engineer who saw it. To a man who was both a pilot and an engineer, it was irresistible.

"It was so fast, it had no ordinary ejection seat," Haggerty says. "The wind blast in a high-speed ejection would be severe enough to kill the pilot. The X-2 had a system wherein the whole cockpit could be blasted away from the fuselage and lowered by parachute."[37]

"X" stood for experimental, and that's precisely what the X-2 was. It was designed to be the first airplane to go well above the measurable atmosphere, right to the edge of space. Engineers wanted to study stability and control at those heights and at supersonic speeds.

There were many dangers. Before the X-1, there had been a "sound barrier." Now, with the X-2, they were beginning to explore a "thermal barrier"—the point where an aircraft is flying so fast severe heat created by aerodynamic friction threatens the pilot and plane.

Like the X-1, the X-2 did not take off from the ground. It was fastened beneath a big, specially outfitted, B-50 Boeing Bomber. It was flown up to thirty thousand feet and released from the mother ship. Its rocket engines were fired, and the X-2 flew upward to record heights. Its fuel spent, it then fell back to earth in a controlled glide landing on the dry lakebed at Edwards.

Only two X-2 planes were built. Jean "Skip" Ziegler was the first man to pilot the X-2 during a test at Edwards on June 27, 1952. During another test in 1953, while still attached to the mother ship, there was an explosion. The X-2 broke into pieces and the aircraft crashed into Lake Ontario where it remains today, killing Zielger and an observer, Frank Wolko.

The last remaining X-2 had its first powered flight at Edwards in November 1955. The pilot was Lt. Col. Frank K. "Pete" Everest. In subsequent flights, Everest took the X-2 to a speed record of 1,900 miles per hour—Mach 2.87. However, Everest reported the X-2 was dangerously close to spinning out of control.

Everest had his last flight in the X-2 in May 1956 before being transferred from Edwards by the Air Force. That meant a new primary pilot for the plane would be named. It was the moment Kincheloe had been preparing for since he first started to fly as a boy back in Michigan.

Kincheloe immediately volunteered to take over the X-2. So did every other test pilot at Edwards. Competition was intense with every pilot working to promote his own cause.

"There was a tense period while the center bosses mulled it over," Haggerty says. "They called in Everest, who as immediate chief of the test pilots best knew his crew, and asked for his recommendations. Everest, who had been anticipating a transfer for some time, had given it a lot of thought. He named Iven Kincheloe as primary alternate and little balding Mel Apt, Kinch's friend, as secondary."[38]

But Kincheloe had a problem to overcome—a big problem. He was too big. The X-2 was famous for its tight cockpit. It was filled with so many controls they had to be miniaturized to squeeze everything in. When fully equipped, there was just room in the cockpit to squeeze in Everest, who was five feet, eight inches. Kincheloe was six feet, one and a half inches tall.

Apt, who was smaller than Everest, was no problem. Engineers took Kincheloe to the X-2 to see if he could fit into the cockpit. Wearing nothing but his military uniform, Kincheloe barely squeezed in. It wasn't good. In flight he would wear a bulky pressure suit.

"We'll have to shrink him if he's going to fly this plane," said Jim Powell, the Bell Company's flight test engineer.

"Okay, then. I'll shrink myself," Kincheloe answered.[39]

Kincheloe insisted he could do it, so he was told to report to the X-2 later that same day wearing his flight suit for further testing.

The schedule that afternoon called for a ground check of the X-2 power control system. Kincheloe would have to sit in the plane through the entire test wearing his pressure suit. It would be tremendously hot and cramped for Kincheloe. Perhaps he actually would shrink during the long test.

"They pressed him into the seat and it took two men to clamp down the canopy, forcing his head down into the cockpit so that he had to sit hunched over and look up to see the instrument panel," Haggerty says. "The control-system was started and the cockpit got hot, then unpleasant, then downright torturous. To onlookers watching and listening on the intercom, expecting a plea for release from the cockpit furnace, there was never a peep from Kinch. They all watched in admiration. . . . Just toward the end of the run, Kinch's voice came weakly over the intercom, not begging for a shutdown, just trying to make a gag out of it.

"'Hey, you guys, I'm nearly drowned in my own juice. The cockpit is nearly half full.'"[40]

When the power system check was finished and Kincheloe stepped out, he was soaking wet. But he had done it. He was happy. "Told you," he said.[41]

It was unanimous. This was the guy everyone wanted to fly the X-2. Miraculously, engineers suddenly had a few ideas on how they might find more room in the cockpit to fit Kincheloe's tall frame.

On May 25, Kincheloe got his first ride in the X-2. Pilot and plane dropped from the big mother ship at thirty thousand feet, and Kincheloe ignited the rocket engine. At forty-one thousand feet he leveled off slightly to pick up speed, but the engine quit and would not restart. Remaining fuel was jettisoned, and Kincheloe glided down to the dry lakebed. The day was not a total success, but Kincheloe had flown past Mach 1 and had started a new era in his life. In his postflight report he wrote, "Without a doubt, it was the greatest flight of my life."[42]

Now it was time for greater flights. The engineers decided they were going to exceed 100,000 feet in the X-2. It was an important milestone, another barrier. Most experts of the time considered 100,000 feet to be the edge of space.

There were several more flights leading up to the first 100,000-foot attempt. Kincheloe handled them with ease, but control problems continued to slow progress. He reached a top speed of Mach 2.57 and a height of 87,750 feet—just short of the record. Before the big attempt, the X-2 was taken out of service for an overhaul and to work on its control difficulties.

The big date was finally set for September 7, 1956. When the day arrived, everyone, including Kincheloe, was excited—and nervous. This was extremely dangerous work. They were going where no man and no machine had ever been before. They hoped their calculations were all correct.

At thirty-three thousand feet, Kincheloe and the X-2 were dropped from the B-50 mother ship.

"It was an exciting moment for Kincheloe," Haggerty says, "the start of a venture into an altitude realm that man had never before explored. . . . As he described it later, he had a sinking feeling in the pit of his stomach, like the gnawing of a hunger pain. He knew only too well the dangers of the mission he was about to start, but the knowledge was crowded into a back corner of his brain. Through his conscious mind whipped the long list of things he must do in the next few minutes, and do perfectly. He was tense but exhilarated."[43]

Once he fired his rockets, it was only a matter of seconds before he reached Mach 1, the huge barrier that had been surpassed less than ten years earlier. He did 75,000 feet, 90,000 feet, and then he got the word over radio that he had passed the 100,000-foot barrier. He was higher than anyone had been before, and he was still climbing. The fuel was all burned 133 seconds into the flight, but Kincheloe continued to climb, carried forward by momentum.

Haggerty says, "Kinch was in space, the first of the spacemen if you accepted the arbitrary borderline of 100,000 feet set by some experts. At that altitude almost 100 percent of the Earth's atmosphere was beneath the X-2. There was no air to support flight; it was climbing on momentum alone. The sun's rays, unfiltered by the atmosphere . . . were intensely bright, so blinding that he could not see the pad affixed to his knee on which he was scribbling notes. Away from the sun, the sky was a deep purple."[44]

From the incredible height, Kincheloe looked down toward Earth at a view no human being had ever seen. At a point that was later determined to be precisely 126,200 feet, the X-2 reached its maximum height and began its descent to the ground.

There was a wild celebration when Kincheloe and the X-2 slowed to a stop on the dry lakebed. Kincheloe kissed his wife, Dorothy, who was on hand to witness the event. He celebrated with the engineers, flight crew, and officials who had gathered for the moment.

The next day he wrote his report about the first space flight. It was only two paragraphs long. The final sentence stated, "The aircraft was pleasant to fly throughout the flight and the achievement as anticipated."[45] The space age had begun. And so, perhaps, had the practice of American astronauts understating their accomplishments.

The next X-2 flight went to Apt, and it would be the last by the Air Force before the plane was turned over to the NACA. A record height had been accomplished. Apt's flight record would be for speed.

Apt, on his first X-2 flight, was to take the plane to seventy thousand feet and dive to reach the top possible speed. With Kincheloe coaching Apt from a chase plane, everything went according to plan. Apt passed Mach 3—the fastest anyone had ever flown. He had reached 2,060 miles per hour—well over twice the speed of a bullet fired from a rifle.

At 140 seconds into the flight, Apt ran out of fuel and began the job of getting the X-2 home. But the plane suddenly started rolling. It was out of control. Apt pulled the ejection lever. That was another first. No one had ever ejected at these speeds before. The cockpit and the X-2 separated. The plane crashed into the earth. Apt was knocked unconscious in the separation, and his cockpit crashed hard to the ground. Mel Apt was dead. The last X-2 was gone.

The news of Apt's tragedy did not dim the star status that was surrounding Kincheloe. The Air Force had already sent him to appear at the premier of a Hollywood movie about test pilots called *Toward the Unknown.*

The next X-plane was already well into development. It was the X-15 designed to reach speeds in excess of four thousand miles per hour, twice what the X-2 had accomplished.

The Air Force used Kincheloe's star status and movie star looks to its advantage. He was the subject of newspaper and magazine articles around the nation. When he appeared on *I've Got a Secret,* hosted by Gary Moore, they had little trouble guessing who Iven Kincheloe was. They had all read about him in the newspapers.

"His travels kept him constantly broke, for although the Air Force paid a small per-diem allowance for trips away from Edwards, this rarely covered half the actual cost," Haggerty says. "For Christmas 1956, he could buy Dorothy only a wine bottle opener, a kitchen stool, and a pair of earrings."[46]

On March 31, 1957, Dorothy Kincheloe gave birth to a boy they named Robert. Kincheloe liked Sam better, but Robert was the name.[47] It was a big year.

In July, Kincheloe was given the Mackay Trophy "for the most meritorious flight of the preceding year." The first winner of the Mackay Trophy in 1912 had been H. H. "Hap" Arnold who was taught to fly by Purdue graduate Cliff Turpin. Arnold would win it again in 1934. In 1924, the trophy went to the around-the-world pilots, but not Purdue graduate Frederick Martin who had crashed in Alaska.

Finally in September 1957, one of the best years in Kincheloe's life was topped off when he was officially named the primary Air Force pilot for the X-15 which would be ready for flight in 1958. He went into intense training, which included a centrifuge to duplicate the enormous acceleration forces he would experience piloting the X-15. He was tested on "weightless" flights, a "phenomenon about which little was known," Haggerty says.[48]

In a lengthy question and answer article in *U.S News and World Report* in the January 17, 1958, issue, Kincheloe said the X-15 potential was classified but it would be "space equivalent."

"I am the Air Force pilot of the program," he said. "However, there are three other pilots who are NACA pilots here: Mr. Walker, Mr. McKee, and Mr. Armstrong. The four of us have been working on various portions of this investigation for high-altitude flying. I have done the work on the X-2 and the other three persons have been doing work on X-1 series and reaction-control series."

He was asked if he felt his work got more difficult as he aged. "Let's put it this way," Kincheloe said. "I think it gets extremely interesting."[49]

In June 1958, he got the first look at his airplane. He was ready. The X-15 was not. There would be a delay before his first flight.

But Dorothy was pregnant with their second child, and the world was looking brighter for Iven Kincheloe.

On Saturday, July 26, 1958, Kincheloe reported to Edwards for an assignment. He was to fly a Lockheed F-104 which he had piloted a number of times. "Kinch generally liked the airplane's performance, but there were a couple of things he and the other pilots did not especially like," Haggerty says. "For one thing, the plane had a glide angle like the Washington Monument; if it lost power, it would drop like a rock. . . . For another thing, its ejection seat fired downward instead of upward, which was fine at high altitude, but not so good for a low-altitude ejection."[50] To eject at a low altitude, the pilot would actually have to roll the plane on its back so he could shoot upwards—not an easy maneuver in an airplane that is about to crash.

Shortly after takeoff, Kincheloe reached a height of two thousand feet. His airplane suddenly lost all power and began dropping like a rock. He was too low to eject downward. He reported his problems to base and rolled the plane on its back but only finished three-fourths of the maneuver before he ejected at the last possible moment.

"The F-104 smashed into the ground with a terrific impact," Haggerty says. "The fuel ignited and burst into a billowing cloud of black smoke. Kinch, his 'chute streaming and not fully opened, followed the plane right into the deadly cloud. In the calm wind, the telltale cloud rose straight up for a thousand feet . . . bringing its tragic message."[51]

Iven Kincheloe, age thirty, the world's first spaceman, was gone.

President Dwight Eisenhower wrote a letter to the president of the United States in 1972–1976 asking that Kincheloe's son be given an appointment to a military academy.

An Air Force Base in Michigan was named for Kincheloe. A Kincheloe Trophy was established, and it is still awarded annually for outstanding professional accomplishment in the conduct of flight testing.

Purdue graduates Virgil "Gus" Grissom and Neil Armstrong are among the winners. There is a Kincheloe Flight Wing at Purdue where the graduate is also part of the ROTC Hall of Fame.

"Kinch was, to use his own term, a 'space bug,'" Haggerty says. "He knew before *Sputnik* that man would penetrate farther into space. And when that came about, he was determined that he would be one of the penetrators."[52]

Iven Kincheloe did not live to fulfill that destiny, but everything that was to follow built on what he and others had accomplished.

One of the men who worked with him and knew him very well was Neil Armstrong. "He was a very good pilot," Armstrong says. "He was an excellent engineer, thanks, no doubt, to his education at Purdue. He was a good man, a good friend, his wife is a grand lady. And I'm sorry we lost him. Had he survived, he might very well have been asked to join and accept astronaut activity."[53]

Michael McCulley

Twenty-one years after Iven Kincheloe graduated and left West Lafayette, Michael McCulley received his Purdue degrees. McCulley followed in Kincheloe's footsteps. He did training at the Empire Test Pilot School as part of the exchange program with Great Britain. And like Kincheloe, McCulley would ultimately pursue his dreams in space. McCulley not only reached the U.S. astronaut program. He ultimately became one of the top executives in the private space industry.

McCulley was born in 1943 in San Diego, but considers Livingston, Tennessee, his home. His father was killed when he was nine years old, and his mother moved back home with family in Tennessee.

In 1961, McCulley graduated from Livingston Academy, in Livingston, and pursued his career plans. He joined the Navy and was assigned to submarines, beginning a military career that was to take him from the depths of the ocean to outer space. But all that would come later.

"I got out of high school on Friday night," McCulley says. I was seventeen years old. The next Monday, I was in boot camp. You know, the Navy recruiting posters in those days said, 'Join the Navy and See the World.' I just wanted to go, explore the world, and get some training. I ended up training as a missile electronics technician. My original plan was to spend three or four years in the Navy, and come out with a skill. Nothing more complicated than that.

"But after I'd been in the Navy for about a year or so, I decided I really liked it," he says. "Then I decided, if I was going to stay in it for a long time, I really wanted to be an officer. I wasn't even flying at the time. I was in submarines. But I wanted to be a commissioned officer, and you had to get a college education to do that."

He competed for a Naval Enlisted Science Education Program Scholarship intended to provide enlisted personnel an opportunity to advance themselves and their careers. Competition was tough. He won. Twenty-one universities were part of the program, including Purdue. The scholarship winners had the opportunity to select from the twenty-one participating schools.

"I went to Purdue because a naval officer that I worked for had a very, very high esteem for Purdue," McCulley says. "When I was selected for the program, he said 'You need to go to Purdue.' And I said, 'Yes sir!' I showed up in West Lafayette, and saw the campus for the first time when I was checking in."

He had a plan. And it had nothing to do with aviation. But all that would change at Purdue where the university was already celebrating its astronauts—Virgil "Gus" Grissom, Roger Chaffee, Eugene Cernan, and Neil Armstrong.

"My plan was to go back to submarines in the nuclear power program," McCulley says. "Then one day in my junior year a Navy recruiter showed up out at the Purdue Airport with a T-34 trainer, and you could sign up for a flight. So I signed up to go on a flight with this guy. He let me fly it. We went upside down and did aerobatics. I had never been in a small airplane before. And that afternoon, I went over and signed up for flight training. It was one of those defining moments in life—you know, something happens and everything changes directions.

"I found out that I'd been selected to go to flight training at about the same time that Neil Armstrong walked on the Moon in July 1969," he says. "Neil was a Purdue engineer and a naval aviator. So when I was watching Neil walk on the Moon on July 20th, of 1969, I knew where I was going. I was a Purdue engineer heading for Pensacola, for naval aviator flight training."

McCulley graduated in January 1970 with a bachelor's and a master's degree in metallurgical engineering.

From Purdue, McCulley went to Pensacola, earned his wings and moved on to flying on and off aircraft carriers. Four years later he decided he wanted to be a test pilot.

"I wanted to be like Neil Armstrong and Gene Cernan and all those guys," McCulley says. "The first time I applied, I was selected as an alternate. The next time I got picked. I was very fortunate. Every year an American does an exchange with the Royal Air Force of Great Britain. In 1978, I was fortunate enough to be selected as the one American. I spent 1978 at the Empire Test Pilot School in Great Britain."

It was the same school where Iven Kincheloe had trained.

By 1980, his sights were focusing higher. He applied for the space program. "But because I had been an enlisted man for all those years before I entered Purdue, I was about four or five years older than all my contemporaries," McCulley says. "And in 1980, the Navy had an age limit on who could apply to become an astronaut? I was outside that age limit. I think it was thirty-six or thirty-seven at the time. So I was rejected for being too old in 1980. But when the 1984 selection came around, and they had removed the age criteria, I was able to apply and then got selected."

In October 1989, McCulley was the pilot on STS-34. He logged 119 hours and 41 minutes in space.

"It was everything I expected and more," McCulley says. In 1990, he left the astronaut corps and the Navy. "I went to Lockheed first," he says. "I went down to the Kennedy Space Center, and I eventually became the launch site director for Lockheed."

In 1996, United Space Alliance (USA) was formed out of Lockheed and Rockwell. Today it is as a Limited Liability Company equally owned by The Boeing Company (which bought Rockwell) and Lockheed-Martin Corporation, employing about ten thousand people in Texas, Florida, Alabama, California, and Washington, D.C. It is one of the world's leading space operations companies

On its website the company explains its roles: "USA manages and conducts space operations work involving the operation and maintenance of multi-purpose space systems, including systems associated with NASA's human space flight program, space shuttle applications beyond those of NASA, and other reusable launch and orbital systems beyond the space shuttle and space station.

"As the prime contractor for NASA's Space Shuttle Program, United Space Alliance is responsible for the day-to-day operation and management of the U.S. space shuttle fleet and brings a broad range of expertise to the job, including:

- Mission Design and Planning
- Flight Operations
- Software Development and Integration
- Payload Integration
- Integrated Logistics
- Astronaut and Flight Controller Training
- Vehicle Processing, Launch and Recovery."

McCulley is chief executive officer of USA. He is looking forward to getting the shuttle flying again. "After *Columbia*, we have to get through this one more reminder that this is not a low-risk business," he says. "One hundred years from now, people are going to look back and see that Mercury, Gemini, Apollo, Skylab, Apollo-Soyuz, the shuttle and the space station were all just steps in the journey. What scares me is that if we ever stop human space flight, that we may never start it back up again, as a country. So I want to continue to go out there and explore. I think it's in our nature.

"The weak-willed and faint-of-heart will say, 'It's too risky. We can't do this.' Our forefathers didn't feel that way about risk and exploration. And neither should we."

Chapter Fourteen

Until the day of the manned satellite, a balloon is by far the best means we have for studies, using human observers.

—Malcolm Ross, 1957

At the crest of their nine-hour balloon ride, twenty-one and a half miles high, Malcolm Ross and Victor Prather Jr. sat for more than two hours in a nearly open gondola with the world spread out before them. It was a view like no one else had ever seen before.

People in experimental airplanes had flown higher than Ross and Prather. A select few people flying at supersonic speeds had viewed the world momentarily from greater altitudes looking through tiny windows that offered limited and halting glimpses of the colorful Earth and the deep blackness of space. But no one else had been allowed the time to see what Ross and Prather were viewing.

They had a wide-open, picture-window view of the world from their vehicle, a field of vision that allowed them to see a half million square miles of Earth from Texas to Florida in one big gulp.

Their vehicle rotated allowing them to see 360 degrees, and they could clearly identify New Orleans, Mobile, Vicksburg, and Savannah. Ross even thought he could pinpoint Cape Canaveral, Florida, off on the distant shores of the Atlantic.[1] They could see the horizon shining above the blue gulf water, clinging to the gentle curvature of the world they had left behind. Immediately above the horizon, they saw the whitish-blue light that glowed in the troposphere—the portion of Earth's atmosphere that extends eight to ten miles high. Above that, in the stratosphere, they saw a band of luminous, darker blue, which disappeared into the deep blue-blackness of space.[2]

Ross, a 1941 Purdue University graduate, was overwhelmed. He was so awed by what he was seeing that he forgot the significance of what was taking place until a voice crackled on his radio. "Mal," Otto Winzen radioed from Earth. "Do you realize you have already broken the record?" On the intercom Ross responded to his partner, Prather, "I had forgotten all about the record. Somehow it seems rather insignificant."[3]

If the view they were seeing was so enormous that it made everything else in life seems less important, the record Ross and Prather set that day was hardly insignificant. More than forty years later in the twenty-first century, it remains unbroken.

On May 4, 1961, Ross and Prather reached a height of 113,740 feet above the earth—twenty-one and a half miles—and they did it sitting in an aluminum gondola with Venetian blinds, suspended beneath a balloon that Ross described as a "ten million-cubic foot gasbag [that] swelled to the diameter nearly the length of a football field."[4]

It was a potentially deadly journey. They depended entirely on their space suits and helmets with clear plastic visors. Any failure in the suit meant instant death. In fact, one of the primary objectives of the mission was to tests the suits for future space flights.[5]

As Ross and Prather sat suspended above the world, transfixed by the incredible view, they had no idea what awaited them. Their fate lay less than seven hours away. One of them would not survive the day.

Ross, a mild-mannered, slightly balding man, was not a jet pilot. He was not an engineer. He was not cut from the cloth of space adventurers who thrilled at tremendous speeds. He was an explorer. He was among the first spacemen, the first astronauts who probed the unknown before NASA sent any of the initial Mercury 7 into space.

He was part of a program that helped advance science by developing and testing technology that the U.S. space program would need for its race to the Moon. He was also part of a military program that spawned reports of flying saucers that gripped the nation in the 1940s and 1950s, including the reported UFO crash at Roswell, New Mexico, which reached mythical proportions.

In addition, the U.S. military ballooning program produced one of the most spectacular, dramatic moments in the first century of flight.

On May 4, 1961, when Ross and Prather set a new balloon altitude record, they were breaking a mark set in 1960 when Air Force Captain Joe Kittinger reached 102,800 feet. At the crest of that flight, Kittinger unhooked the belt across the opening to his gondola and jumped out to set a high altitude parachute jump and freefall record that might never be broken.

"Lord take care of me now," Kittinger uttered softly as he left the gondola.[6]

At one point the speed of his fall reached 614 miles per hour, close to the speed of sound. The temperature outside his space suit reached ninety-four degrees below zero. When he hit the ground thirteen minutes and forty-five seconds later, medical personnel jumped out of a helicopter that had been tracking his fall and ran to help.

"I'm very glad to be back with you all," Kittinger told them.[7] His work was important in proving that aviators flying at high altitudes could return safely to Earth in an emergency.

Malcolm Ross was born in 1919 at Momence, Illinois, but he grew up in and around West Lafayette, Indiana, the home of Purdue University.

His recollections of the 1920s and 1930s show an idyllic childhood and certainly no thoughts of traveling into space. "My earliest memories are of pleasant Sunday afternoon drives in the country with my parents," he wrote in his own short biography. "I also recall terminating those trips with an ice cream cone before returning home."[8]

He was smart enough to skip from the sixth to the seventh grade. He sang, for ten cents per Sunday, in the St. John's Episcopal boy's choir and men's choir in Lafayette and finished high school in nearby Linden where the family had relocated.[9]

Ross received a scholarship to attend Purdue University and study civil engineering. He also pursued an interest in radio and worked at the campus station as a sports announcer where he was soon hooked. He later changed his major from engineering to creative writing, communication, and radio.

Ross graduated in June 1941—six months before the attack on Pearl Harbor. The winds of war were blowing and like many other young men of the time, his career and his life would forever be altered by the rush of world events.

After graduation he married his high school sweetheart, Marjorie Martin, and took broadcasting jobs in Anderson, Chicago, and Indianapolis before being commissioned in the Navy in January 1943. When he received word of his commission, Ross was so excited he immediately went out and bought himself a uniform. He wore it out of the store and was saluted by passing sailors. He was also embarrassed when he realized his shoes and socks were not yet military—and not even the right color.[10]

After two months of indoctrination school at Quonset Point, Rhode Island, Ross's career took a life-changing swing. He was sent to the University of Chicago for nine months of graduate school in aerological engineering—the study of total atmospheric meteorology. He earned a professional certificate in meteorology and atmospheric science.

His World War II Naval assignments included Fleet Weather Center at Pearl Harbor. He also served as aerological officer aboard the USS *Saratoga* during strikes on Tokyo and Iwo Jima.

Released from the military in 1946, Ross opened his own business in Pasadena, California, where his wife had settled during the war. With experience in engineering, broadcasting, and meteorology, he had his choice of good fields. He picked none of them. He decided to enter a whole new career and opened an advertising agency.

It was a good business. He enjoyed it and was doing well. His wife, Marjorie, was office manager. They had a small staff, a good and diverse list of clients. Everything was going great until the Korean conflict began in June 1950, and Ross was quickly recalled to active duty.

He wasn't sent far. For a short time he was based in San Francisco and commuted home on weekends to see his wife and work the business. But in the summer of 1951, the Navy moved him. Ross and his wife closed the ad agency, sold their house, and he became involved in a new career: high-altitude balloon flights. High-altitude balloon research and development had become very active following World War II. The efforts included espionage.

"In 1946, the Research Division of New York University undertook the development of a constant-level balloon to be used in monitoring acoustically the Soviet development of nuclear weapons," says Charles B. Moore, who would later work with Ross and was part of this effort. He would later become professor and professor emeritus at New Mexico Institute of Mining and Technology.[11] The work was so secretive that Moore did not even know the military code name for the project. It was "Mogul."[12]

The New York University group launched three experimental projects from Bethlehem, Pennsylvania. These efforts used fourteen to twenty-three balloons tied together. For the fourth test they moved to an Army Air Base in Alamogordo, New Mexico, where there was less air traffic.[13]

On June 4, 1947, they launched twenty-eight balloons connected in a train carrying a container of equipment. It was all tracked by radar along with a B-17 airplane. "But when transmissions from the airborne microphone ceased because of battery failure, the balloons and electronic equipment were lost over New Mexico," Moore says.[14] According to Moore, it all later turned up outside of Roswell, New Mexico, where it was promoted as the wreckage of a flying saucer—"which has provided the city of Roswell with its main tourist attraction" ever since, Moore says.[15]

As years passed and the military filled the skies with more and more balloons flying at such high altitudes that they still reflected sunlight after nightfall on Earth, UFO sightings became frequent. "During the 1950s, these sightings increased in frequency along with the Navy's and Air Force's balloon operations," Craig Ryan writes in *The Pre-Astronauts: Manned Ballooning on the Threshold of Space.* "Air Force studies showed a direct connection between balloons in the stratosphere at dusk and dawn and reports of UFOs."[16]

According to Moore, "military interest in the use of these balloons increased with the U.S. Air Force Project Gopher, beginning in 1950, which was aimed at floating high altitude balloons carrying reconnaissance cameras over the Soviet Union."[17]

In 1951, Ross was named resident Office of Naval Research liaison officer in Minneapolis. Minneapolis was an active area for balloon research and development, including the University of Minnesota and General Mills. The Navy Project Skyhook, an unmanned balloon program, was based in Minneapolis.

In 1953, "Federal coordination of the many military applications that developed for balloons was transferred to the air branch of the Office of Naval Research in Washington to which Ross was transferred," Moore says.[18]

According to Ross's official U.S. Navy biography, "In that position he directed many high-altitude balloon projects to obtain cosmic ray and meteorological data from unprecedented heights."[19]

While working on Skyhook, Ross lobbied hard to move the Navy into a manned balloon program for astronomical research. In 1954, he received the go-ahead and established Project Strato-Lab. Strato-Lab was a Navy manned ballooning program in which astronomers were carried aloft to make astronomical measurements above much of Earth's atmosphere. Ross served as administrator, and in 1955, Moore trained and certified him as a balloon pilot.

In a pre–Strato-Lab flight on August 10, 1956, Ross and Navy Lt. Morton Lee Lewis flew in an open gondola to a height of forty thousand feet, high into the troposphere just below the stratosphere. "It was a remarkable flight in an open gondola near the top of the troposphere," Moore says.[20]

On November 8, 1956, again with Ross and Lewis onboard, Strato-Lab I was launched from Rapid City, South Dakota. A natural 500-foot canyon outside of town was ideal for balloon launching and was called the Stratobowl.

In Strato-Lab I, Ross and Lewis reached seventy-six thousand feet, a new manned balloon record in a closed gondola. Ross believed the record-breaking height of the mission was secondary in importance. "Far more important than a record is the fact that the feasibility of penetrating the stratosphere with a light, relatively inexpensive man-carrying balloon of polyethylene plastic has now been demonstrated," Ross and Lewis wrote in an article for *National Geographic Magazine.* "This, we believe, marks a new era of exploration of the great frontier just a few miles above our heads—a region now being invaded more and more by rocket planes and missiles, and soon by man-made satellites."[21]

They believed balloons provided the best technology of the day to accomplish research that was needed for the manned rockets that would follow. "A gondola suspended from a bubble of gas provides a stable viewing platform that can hang at a given altitude for hours," Ross and Lewis wrote. "Research rockets with automatic instruments and even manned rocket aircraft go higher, but they remain only brief minutes on the fringe of the great void. Thus the purpose of the Navy's balloon program is strictly scientific; altitude records are incidental."[22]

This balloon flight in a completely sealed gondola did not go quite as uneventfully as Ross and Lewis indicated. "The ascent went smoothly and the two balloonists sipped coffee and chatted with their ground crew as they rose," Ryan says in *The Pre-Astronauts.* "Ross and Lewis had enough room to stand up and exchange seats. They marveled at the view and struggled to describe the strange coloring of the sky."[23] They felt isolated, separated from Earth.[24]

The beauty of the view and the excitement of the altitude record were abruptly broken when the balloon began an unexpected and rapid descent.

"Suddenly the descent rate quickened," the men wrote in *National Geographic.* "Our stomachs seemed to rise and float around within our bodies. It's the same initial sensation one gets in a fast elevator descent, but greatly enhanced and prolonged."[25]

They radioed their situation to the ground crew, but when they finished speaking all they heard in response was a hearty "congratulations" on a great mission. They had been speaking on the radio at the same time the ground crew was talking. No one heard what anyone else was saying.[26]

Again they radioed distress. Lewis said to the ground crew, "We are in an emergency situation. We hit seventy-six thousand feet and now we are descending rapidly. We are standing by to pass seventy thousand. We are buckled in with our seat belts. No shoulder harness. We have our faceplates on but not down. We are rotating and have a decided elevator feeling."[27]

They were dropping at about four thousand feet per minute.

They released ballast to slow the fall. It did not help. Beneath the balloon, the gondola was suspended from an unopened parachute. They considered letting the balloon go and taking their chances with a parachute drop, but the ground was so uneven they decided against that.

Lewis radioed to the ground crew again. "We are cool, calm, and collected. We think we will stay with the balloon as long as we can."[28]

According to Ryan, "Once the balloon fell back into the survivable region of the atmosphere, Lewis and Ross opened the portholes on the gondola and began jettisoning whatever they could get their hands on in order to slow their descent—all together some two hundred pounds of hardware. Out went the oxygen tanks and converters, the air regenerators, the instrument panel, the radio. 'We will be out of communication for some time,'" they radioed to the ground crew.[29]

They actually stopped working and watched as the air regenerator fell to the ground—perhaps visualizing what was about to happen to them. They were seven thousand feet high and dropping at one thousand feet per minute.[30] Somehow, they landed safely.

"Injuries—not so much as a scratch," they reported. "The descent rate at impact, about 800 feet per minute, had been double the normal landing speed, but a thick Styrofoam pad beneath the gondola cushioned shock."[31]

"It was a smooth, uneventful landing on a relatively level stretch of land," Ross told reporters.[32] That sort of understatement did not surprise his wife, Marjorie, who actually had little idea about the risks her husband was taking. He rarely discussed them within the family—or with anyone else.

"He was a quiet, unassuming person who was not too interested in relating stories of his unusual experiences in balloon flights," she wrote a friend. "Very few people were aware of his accomplishments."[33]

For their work on Strato-Lab I, Ross and Lewis were given the 1957 Harmon International Aviation Award for the outstanding lighter-than-air flight of the previous year. A Harmon Award was also given annually to the outstanding heavier-than-air flight of the previous twelve months. It was an award that had been given to Charles Lindbergh in 1927. Vice President Richard Nixon presented the Harmon Trophy to Ross and Lewis on behalf of President Dwight Eisenhower.

It was given not only for their world record altitude, but also for "making detailed scientific studies of the effects of weightlessness, drastic temperature complications, and psychological complications during their trip."[34]

A photo in the *New York World* featured Nixon holding the trophy with Ross's two-year-old daughter, Jane. In presenting the award, Nixon said in the very near future the Harmon Trophy would probably also be awarded for exploits of travel in space in addition to the two existing categories.[35]

The trophy is now on display at the Smithsonian Air and Space Museum.

In 1955, the Air Force initiated its own balloon program called Project Manhigh. It sent up three high-altitude balloons during 1957 and 1958 reaching 96,000, 101,516, and 99,700 feet.

Ross continued his balloon flights for the Navy. Strato-Lab II went up on October 18, 1957, and reached a height of eighty-six thousand feet. By this time, Manhigh had accomplished a height of 101,516 feet. The Soviet Union had launched *Sputnik* on October 4, 1957. But Ross and Lewis did set the world balloon altitude record for a two-man crew on Strato-Lab II.

During the October 1957 mission, Ross carried camera equipment to photograph *Sputnik*. However, they did not make visual contact with the satellite.

The United States' first satellite, *Explorer I,* was launched January 31, 1958. The balloon program was continuing and setting records even as the space race heated up and rockets were launching from Cape Canaveral, Florida.

On May 6 and 7, 1958, Ross and A. H. Mikesell went up in an open gondola to a height of forty thousand feet. It marked the first time an open gondola balloon had remained aloft at that height after sunset. Mikesell and Ross also made the first astronomical observations from a balloon at that elevation.

On July 26 and 27, 1958, Ross and Lewis again joined on Strato-Lab III. This time they stayed in the air for thirty-four hours and forty minutes. They reached eighty-two thousand feet, and their time in the air was a duration record for a "stratospheric" balloon flight. They carried television equipment with them and produced a broadcast that was carried live by NBC.[36] After the flight, Ross received the Distinguished Flying Cross. That was Lewis's last flight with Strato-Lab. He left and transferred to Project Manhigh. He was later killed in an accident while testing a gondola.

Ross believed strongly in what they were accomplishing. "The manned balloon laboratory can be an important stepping stone or bridge to manned earth satellites and space ships," he wrote in 1958. "Certainly it is not a space vehicle. There are a number of dissimilarities. But in many important aspects related to the occupants, a sealed cabin suspended from a stratospheric balloon is remarkable comparable to future sealed cabins in orbital vehicles. The flights and tests conducted to date can be extended to answer knotty problems facing the scientists and engineers who will design and build true space cabins in the not-to-distant future."[37]

"In October of 1958, Ross and Charlie Moore ascended in a nylon and plywood gondola into a storm cloud that was developing over Mount Withington in central New Mexico in order to observe firsthand the formation of rain and the generation of electricity," Ryan says.[38]

The Navy was pitching its program to the scientific community in an effort to try and to encourage researchers to put the balloon program to even more extensive use.

Ross said, "The visionaries dream of satellites and space ships for [these applications]. Some day their dreams will materialize. But why wait?"[39]

Balloons were already available for the research work.

On August 10, 1959, Ross and Robert Cooper flew in an open gondola to thirty-eight thousand feet. They were the first to make observations from a balloon with a coronagraph—a telescope used to examine the sun's corona.

Ross and Charles Moore launched on Strato-Lab IV on November 28 and 29, 1959. They reached eighty-one thousand feet. They succeeded in using a sixteen-inch telescope system to make the first high altitude observations of a planet Venus. "This marked the cross-roads," Ross said. "It demonstrated for the first time—literally for the first time—that man can take an observatory off the ground."[40] Not only could it be done, but also the observations are far clearer than what can be done on Earth.

They made a discovery that hit newspaper headlines around the nation. "Evidence Hints Water on Venus, Does Balloon Data Mean Venus May Support Life?"

On December 1, 1959, the *Washington Daily News* reported, "New evidence of water vapor in the atmosphere of Venus has raised the possibility that some form of life may exist on that planet. Scientists reported yesterday the evidence was uncovered by instruments carried fifteen miles into the stratosphere . . . by balloonists Malcolm Ross and Charles B. Moore. Dr. John Strong of Johns Hopkins University, who designed the instruments, told reporters, 'The experiment in our opinion indicated there is water vapor on Venus. How much there is will take some time to determine.'"[41]

This balloon had launched from Rapid City, South Dakota. The 4,000-pound gondola finally landed at Manhattan, Kansas. Ross told reporters the landing was "very nice."[42] "Anyone could do it," he said.[43]

Ross's famed understatement was at work again. The "very nice" landing was followed by a near disaster. Ross and Moore had jettisoned their balloon as the gondola hit the ground, but an emergency parachute still attached to the gondola filled with wind. The seven-foot aluminum sphere that carried the two men was dragged about a quarter mile over rough pasture. The episode lasted about two minutes and seemed to Ross and Moore to have been much longer.

Moore was not hurt. Ross was "shaken up" according to newspaper accounts and flown by helicopter to a hospital at Schilling Air Force Base in Salina, Kansas. He was released the next day. Newspaper accounts included photographs of a badly battered, fully enclosed gondola.

Ross was a keen observer of the world from high altitudes. "The outstanding sight of all was at sunset Saturday," he said after Strato-Lab IV. "We could see it was getting dark on Earth and all the lights were coming on in the little towns and it was still daylight where we were. There were the most vivid colors imaginable both in the sunset and in the sunrise Sunday morning. The whole sky was streaked with vivid browns, purples, rose colors, and shades of yellow. The sun shining on extremely high clouds produces these colors. Anyone would enjoy it. While the sky is streaked with color, the earth takes on pastel shades of green and brown. You can still see the rivers and mountains and at night, the lights of town."[44]

This was a man who shrugged off near-death experiences and went into great detail to describe sunsets and sunrises. He loved balloon flights. He loved his work.

By 1961, Ross was at the top of the world among balloonists. He had spent more time in the stratosphere than any other person. He would soon have more than one hundred hours in the stratosphere.

"Yet, in his own mind, he was never the intrepid explorer or space hero," Ryan says. "He described his role, instead, as manager, planner, the seeker of funds, operational organizer, project engineer, then finally, and anti-climatically, pilot, medical subject, and sometimes semi-scientist."[45]

The research completed by programs such as Strato-Lab was essential to NASA and its effort to reach the Moon and return safely. Ross and others performed countless tests that speeded NASA's progress.

Of all Ross's accomplishments, perhaps that last ascent to a record height of 113,740 feet will most be remembered—for what it accomplished, for how it ended, and for what followed immediately after.

Strato-Lab V was the most ambitious balloon flight of all time. It started when the "pre-astronauts," Ross and Vic Prather Jr., boarded the aircraft carrier *Antietam* at Pensacola, Florida, and headed into the Gulf of Mexico where the mission would be launched—from sea instead of land.

The morning of May 4, 1961, Ross and Prather underwent medical tests and sensors were attached to their bodies so their heartbeat, temperature, brain wave, respiration, and other important medical data could be transmitted to medical personnel on the ship.

The captain of the ship kept the *Antietam* perfectly in sync with the wind so the elongated balloon, followed by a parachute attached to the gondola, stood perfectly straight and tall, rising from the flat deck of the carrier. The entire assembly rose taller than an eighty-story skyscraper into the air above the calm gulf waters.

The two men donned space suits and climbed into the gondola for launch at 7:08 A.M. There were several last minute problems: holes in the plastic balloon and tangles in the lines attached to the parachute. As Ross sat in the gondola and observed the repair work taking place, he had a sinking feeling in the pit of his stomach. He did not feel as ready as he thought he should have. But then, he always had a sinking feeling at the start of every flight. Each time before he went up a moment would arrive when he would ask himself, "How did I get myself here?"[46]

The feeling didn't last for long. The tie downs were cut and the gondola carrying Ross and Prather rose smoothly from the ship. The Venetian blinds that covered the gondola were painted silver on one side, black on the other. When the gondola cooled, they would put the black side out to absorb energy from the sun. When they wanted to cool their compartment, they turned the silver side out to reflect the rays.

At twenty-six thousand feet Ross and Prather focused their eyes on the altimeter. If their suits did not begin maintaining artificial pressure on their bodies after twenty-seven thousand feet, the results could be fatal. They passed twenty-six thousand feet. The suits did not begin pressurizing. Twenty-seven thousand feet. Nothing. Finally, their suits started to inflate with pressure values giving off a pulsating sound Ross thought sounded like a foghorn: "ah-oooom ah-oooo."[47]

Temperatures around them reached ninety-four degrees below zero. At the peak of their ascent, the air pressure was so low that without the artificial pressure their blood would boil, and their blood vessels and organs would rupture.[48]

There were many more concerns. When they reached fifty-two thousand feet their balloon became brittle, "as brittle as a glass Christmas tree ornament," according to Ross. "A sharp change in wind speed, a wind shear, could shatter it into confetti. I have seen this happen to unmanned balloons; I shall not forget the sight."[49]

Ross also worried about the jet stream carrying the balloon and gondola into storms where they could be hit by lightening. To top everything off, the facemasks on their helmets fogged during the ascent and built-in warming devices created to deal with the problem were turned on. But these were dangerous. If they heated too much, they could melt the shields. A red light was rigged to flash when the faceplates reached 135 degrees so the device could be turned off. As a backup, crew at the control center on the *Antietam* also had a red light to warn when the danger was present.

Near the boundary of the stratosphere, Ross heard a hissing noise. He thought his suit had started leaking. He also spotted a cloud of vapor rising from behind him, but he could not bend sufficiently to see what was going on. He tried to alert the *Antietam* control center and discovered his radio was not working. Ross and Prather raced through different radio frequencies and tried to contact an airplane that was monitoring their progress. Nothing worked.

That's when Ross noticed more trouble. His instruments indicated their ascent had slowed first to 750 feet per minute, then 600. To Ross, this meant one thing only—that the balloon was leaking.[50] The balloon was not leaking as it turned out. A small pocket of warm air had caused the problem. Once past it, the balloon began rising at the proper rate once again.

As quickly as that crisis ended, the radio came back. And the hissing sound and vapor cloud disappeared—never to be explained. Ross was beginning to feel very lucky.

At seventy-one thousand feet, a call from the ship alerted Prather that his face shield was overheating. The red light on the gondola had failed. Had it not been for the backup light below on the *Antietam,* the result would have been deadly for Prather.[51]

As the men topped 100,000 feet they pulled up all the blinds to improve their view. Ross was breathless with the sight. It was "magnificent," and for long moments they gazed at views no one had ever seen.[52]

They could have remained there for hours, but they carried a limited oxygen supply with them. Timing was essential. After a little more than an hour, Ross began releasing helium to initiate the descent.

A half hour later, Ross did the math in his head. He computed how long it would take them to reach the earth at the current pace. He knew how much oxygen they had left. The results were startling. They were descending far too slowly.

Ross released helium steadily for fifteen minutes. They began to drop more rapidly. The oxygen problem was solved, but another crisis had emerged. Now they were dropping too rapidly.

They were falling at a rate of 1,140 feet per minute. They jettisoned ballast. They threw overboard batteries and 125 pounds of steel shot. Next went equipment—a power supply unit, an oxygen converter.[53]

They reached an elevation where they could breathe with their facemasks open. They tore down their Venetian blinds and tossed them overboard along with other heavy equipment no longer needed including their boots. Feeling safe as the gondola finally gently floated toward the Gulf, Ross and Prather settled back in their seats and lit cigarettes.

They hit the water at 4:02 P.M., almost exactly nine hours after they lifted off the deck of the ship. The final descent had been accomplished with the parachute. The huge balloon had already been released before they hit the water.

As they joked and waited for rescue crews to reach them, another emergency arose. They could not release the parachute from the gondola. If a gust of wind filled the parachute, it would tip the gondola that would sink as it was dragged along the Gulf like a giant spoon scooping up water.

Ross had already been dragged once across the land by a parachute. He didn't want to try it again on the water. As Ross grabbed a knife to start cutting the parachute lines, a helicopter from the *Antietam* appeared. The helicopter crew lowered a cable with a hook at the end to the gondola. Ross told Prather to take it and head home. But Prather declined saying Ross should be first. Rather than sit there arguing over who should leave first, Ross finally grabbed the line and shouted, "See you later."[54]

He stepped on the rescue cable hook, the helicopter lurched forward, and Ross slipped off into the Gulf water, still wearing his space suit. Miraculously, he was able hang on to the cable with his hands and arms so he did not fall completely into the water. He pulled himself back up, and the helicopter lifted him away. Prather watched the entire scene.

With Ross safely on the helicopter, the cable and hook was dropped for Prather. The same problem occurred. Prather slipped and fell into the water. His desperate effort to grab the line and hang on failed. He sunk beneath the waves. His suit started filling with water. Divers jumped in for a rescue. But it was futile. Prather had become tangled in the parachute. Prather drowned.

At Pensacola the next morning Ross met with news reporters. In a true testament to the ethics of the day, reporters never asked Ross how he felt about losing his partner so close to complete success.

"Commander Ross was so obviously grieved by Commander Prather's death that he was not questioned about the accident," the *New York Times* reported. "'We had a wonderful flight,' [Ross] said. "The basic objectives we had in mind—testing the capabilities of the suit and further acquisition of physiological data—were met."[55]

He would later write, "Vic saw my mishap. He had been sitting happily in his seat, secure in the knowledge that we had accomplished all our objectives and thanks to our suits, had survived prolonged exposure to the deadly stresses on the doorstep of space. The Navy had made a major contribution toward outfitting the men who will walk on the Moon."[56]

He termed the mission a success, but by the end of the month, Ross had left the Navy and went to work on space research for General Motors.

Dr. James Van Allen, who had discovered the Van Allen Belts, wired him concerning his retirement. "We are honored to have been associated with you over a fifteen-year period during which your personal devotion and courage have been major factors in giving U.S. Navy ballooning world leadership in cosmic rays, astronomy, and other scientific fields, as well as in the art of manned balloon flights."[57]

On October 17, 1962, his name was again added to the Harmon Trophy. Prather's was added posthumously. The *Lafayette Journal and Courier* reported,

> West Lafayette's Malcolm D. Ross received the Clifford B. Harmon trophy from President Kennedy at the White House Thursday for flying higher in a balloon than any man alive. . . .
>
> "Those who have traveled this great ocean of space have our admiration," the president said. Standing at Ross' side were his wife and their two small children, Jane, seven, and John, five. . . .
>
> "Naturally I'm very pleased to win it a second time," [Ross] said. "At the same time, I feel keen sorrow that Dr. Prather isn't here with me today." . . .
>
> [Ross] stood rim-rod stiff in civilian clothing as he accepted the parchment scroll. From the neck down, Ross and the president looked like identical twins. Both wore blue-gray suits, black shoes, and diagonally striped neckties.
>
> Asked if Prather's death was the reason he gave up ballooning, Ross told newsmen, "No. I had decided before that to start a new career. . . . I'm getting too old."[58]

He was forty-two. He never ascended in a balloon again but believed in the work that he had done. He said, "The balloon business has helped in a real way to pioneer the space program, starting with the plastic balloons of 1946 and 1947. The balloon was being used when people were not interested in space, but would accept a certain amount of basic research by this invention that dates back to Montgolfier in the late eighteenth century.

"When the space age finally started moving, it rushed on by the balloons. No one bothered to pick up this aid and boost it along, also. The glamorous programs are missiles and rockets—they get the large funds. The balloon projects, which could make major contributions to our overall space program, have received pitifully small financial support. And actually, as programs go, they are an extremely inexpensive means to proceed with the acquisition of basic information, which we need. There are definite scientific objectives that balloons can accomplish for, perhaps, $100,000 that a satellite, costing millions, cannot do as well."[59]

Among the people who knew and respected Ross was fellow Purdue graduate Neil Armstrong. Armstrong was a test pilot flying the X-15 when he knew Ross. "He was a very erudite fellow," Armstrong says. "He was a good guy. We went to the Seattle World's Fair in 1962 together as two of the few people in the world who had flown above 100,000 feet. I went for winged aircraft. He went for balloon."[60]

What Ross and those who worked with him accomplished ultimately helped to move America forward in the space program and the moon landing. "It was a component and an important one," Armstrong says.[61]

Malcolm Ross died in his Birmingham, Michigan, home on October 8, 1985. He was sixty-five years old, and his interesting career had turned again. He had become a stock brokerage executive for Merrill Lynch Pierce Fenner and Smith, Inc. Ross served as assistant vice president and account executive at the Bloomfield Hills branch. He is buried at Arlington National Cemetery.

His record balloon ascensions remain an important part of space and aviation history. But his final mission, ending at 4:04 P.M. on May 4, 1961, was overshadowed by events of the following day. About seventeen hours after Ross landed—at 9:34 A.M. on May 5—Alan Shepard, another Navy man, launched from Cape Canaveral and traveled more than 116 miles into space on a fifteen-and-a-half-minute ride aboard Freedom 7.

America officially had a spaceman.

Twenty days later on May 25, 1961, President John F. Kennedy said, "I believe that this nation should commit itself to achieving the goal, before this decade is out, of landing a man on the Moon and returning him safely to the earth. No single space project in this period will be more impressive to mankind, or more important for the long-range exploration of space; and none will be so difficult or expensive to accomplish."

The race to the Moon was on.

Gregory Harbaugh

Malcolm Ross loved his work with balloons, but Gregory Harbaugh is living Ross's dream: Harbaugh has flown on four shuttle flights. He's walked in space on three occasions.

"A space walk is an incredible experience," Harbaugh says. "It's just sensory overload. There is just so much to see and take in as you watch Earth go by. It's not like you're passing over the earth so much; it's as if you're standing off from it, and watching it turn in the distance. That's the way it struck me."

Harbaugh was born in Willoughy, Ohio. He had two choices upon graduation from high school. He could play football at Yale, or he could study aeronautical and astronautical engineering at Purdue. Purdue was an easy choice and one he's never regretted.

"I became interested in flying when I was nine years old," Harbaugh says. "My father, who was a commercial artist, rented a Cessna 172 with an instructor, and the instructor flew us to my grandmother's house in Beaver Falls, Pennsylvania. It was about a forty-five-minute flight. I got my logbook that day. I actually logged my times because I got to sit in the front right [copilot] seat. It was just wild. I loved every second of it, and I just knew I wanted to fly from that point on."

At first, he thought he would become a commercial pilot. His eyesight failed him, and he started looking at other possibilities.

"The opportunity to go to Purdue and get into the aeronautical engineering, to use my math and science skills, seemed like a logical progression," he says. "And Purdue had a great aviation technology program. So, I got my pilot's license at Purdue."

Harbaugh developed an interest in space while at Purdue.

"I remember as a kid watching Neil Armstrong walk on the Moon," Harbaugh says. "That left a lasting imprint. But initially it was something that was improbable for me to consider. It just seemed so far fetched."

While at Purdue, he became involved in the Old Masters Program, a student event in which successful people from various fields are invited to the university to talk and exchange ideas.

His first year of involvement in Old Masters he was a host for one of the invited guests—Rusty Schweickart. Schweickart was not a Purdue graduate. But he was an astronaut and had flown on Apollo 9—two flights before the moon landing.

"By spending two and a half days with Rusty, I came to see astronauts as real, live human beings, with their strengths and their weaknesses," Harbaugh says. "He made it real for me. He made it a possibility. Because of him, I started thinking more seriously about it. I could see myself, in my mind's eye, answering the questions he was being asked. And Rusty was very encouraging to me. He remains a friend."

The next year at Old Masters he was cochairman of the event and one of the professionals invited to the university was astronaut Joe Allen—a graduate of DePauw University and an Indiana native. Allen's first mission would come several years later on the shuttle.

"He was a great, great guy and also remains a friend," Harbaugh says. "And so, in the course of those two events, the idea of working in the space program and maybe even becoming an astronaut became real to me."

When he was a senior in 1978, the Johnson Space Center sent representatives to Purdue to interview students.

"I was fortunate to get an interview," Harbaugh says. "And then I was even more fortunate to get an offer. It was the lowest paying job offer I received—by quite a bit. But that was no surprise. And I knew where I belonged. I just knew in my heart that NASA was the right place to go."

In 1978, NASA was getting ready to fly the shuttle, and Harbaugh went right to work on it. He supported shuttle flight operations from mission control for most of the flights from STS-1 on April 12, 1981, to STS-51L on January 28, 1986.

There were many high points in the shuttle program. The *Challenger* and *Columbia* accidents have been the tragedies.

"*Challenger* was awful," Harbaugh says. "It was the result of us pushing too hard, and trying to do too much with too little. That morning I was with one of the senior NASA managers, briefing him on our inability to meet our training requirements. The shuttle flights were being scheduled too close together. We were too schedule-driven, and, as a result, we were building up this training deficit. In the middle of that briefing, we took a break to watch the launch. Everybody remembers where they were when *Challenger* happened."

Harbaugh was out of NASA when the *Columbia* tragedy happened. "My sympathies extend to the families of the crew as well as to the folks within NASA who face the challenge of recovering from the accident and continuing the work of human space flight."

In 1987, he applied to be an astronaut along with two thousand other people. There were fifteen positions. Harbaugh was accepted.

"I just thought it would be so much fun to be an astronaut," he says. "It seemed like the logical extension of everything that I had done to that point. It just seemed like the natural evolution. By that time, they had selected several classes of the newer guys that included mission specialists. I came to believe that I had what it took to do that job. It was also a personal challenge. I didn't know whether I had what it took, but I wanted to test myself and see if I could do the job and do it well. It was sort of a personal mountain to climb."

He was a mission specialist aboard STS-39, April 28–May 6, 1991, an unclassified Department of Defense mission. He was flight engineer on STS-54, January 13–19, 1993. During this mission he experienced a four-hour, twenty-eight-minute walk in space.

From June 27 to July 7, 1995, he was flight engineer during the first docking with the Russian space station, *Mir*, and an exchange of crews.

His last flight was STS-82, the second Hubble Space Telescope servicing mission. The flight launched at night on February 11, 1997, and returned to the Kennedy Space Center on a rare night landing February 21. During the flight, the crew secured the Hubble Telescope in the shuttle payload bay. Then, in five space walks, the crew installed two new spectrometers and eight replacement instruments and placed insulation patches over several compartments containing key data processing, electronics, and scientific instrument telemetry packages. Harbaugh participated in two of those space walks, totaling fourteen hours and one minute. Following completion of upgrades and repairs, Hubble was redeployed and boosted to its highest orbit ever.

Harbaugh has spent a total of 818 hours in space, including eighteen hours and twenty-nine minutes in space walks.

After that fourth mission Harbaugh became the manager of the EVA (Spacewalk) Project Office. He was the senior NASA manager in charge of all aspects of the safe and successful execution of all space walks performed by American astronauts, including those performed on the Russian *Mir* space station and the International Space Station. Harbaugh remained in that position for four years, leading the EVA team through Hubble Telescope missions, *Mir* missions, and the initial phase of the International Space Station assembly missions. All told, Harbaugh has overseen twenty-seven space walks in his four-year tenure, nearly as many as had been performed in the history of the Space Shuttle Program prior to his assignment as EVA Project manager.

In March 2001, Harbaugh retired from NASA and accepted the postion as vice president of Sun 'n Fun Fly-In, Inc., as well as museum director of the Florida Air Museum at Sun 'n Fun. Sun 'n Fun is a nonprofit organization dedicated to bringing the joy of aviation, in all its aspects, to children and adults. Sun 'n Fun's signature event is an annual Fly-In in April of each year, which attracts hundreds of thousands of visitors, exhibitors, and media representatives and provides over $100,000 in donations and fund-raising to surrounding charities, including the Boys and Girls Club of Lakeland, Florida. As museum director, Harbaugh has instituted educational programs for children and adults that provide opportunities for anyone who is interested to learn about aviation. Programs include a youth summer camp, a lecture series that brings true aviation heroes and pioneers to the Sun 'n Fun campus, and competitive aviation activities for children, among many others. This summer, Sun 'n Fun also hosted the World Aerobatic Championships—this was only the third time this "Olympics of Aerobatic Flying" has been held in the United States.

Space flight is not an experience he can forget. "Being able to have done what I have done and seen what I have seen has been a wonderful gift," Harbaugh says. "I am truly blessed to have been given such an opportunity. I am grateful to the people that selected me and to the people all along the way who helped with advice, counsel, and wisdom. And I'm certainly in debt to Purdue for being the education foundation from which I could pursue such a career path.

"It's been a wonderful, amazing career, and my space flight experiences still echo in my soul."

Chapter Fifteen

At Purdue we have a unique gathering of expertise and facilities. We've got an outstanding aeronautical engineering program and related programs, and I think we have the best aviation technology program in the country. Plus, we've got a university-owned airport, and we have great faculty and students, and outstanding laboratories. When you put all these things together, we are almost without peer.

— Thomas Carney,
Head of Purdue Department of Aviation Technology

At the dawn of the twenty-first century, flight at Purdue University is positioned to launch into a new era. Generations of visionary people worked for more than 125 years to put their dreams into practice. Now, a new generation is prepared to forge an exciting future.

At the start of the twenty-first century, Purdue engineering and specifically aeronautical and astronautical engineering [AAE] are ranked among the top programs in the nation. Aviation technology [AvTech] is considered one of the top three programs in the United States.

Tom Carney, the man who momentarily thought his near-perfect 3.9 grade point average would not be good enough for the Purdue aviation technology program he now heads, believes more than a century of visionary, hardworking people have been the key.

"As is so often the case with institutions, we had some really key people—bright, very focused people with a passion who were here at the right time, doing the right things," Carney says. "Some of us who came along afterward further developed that same vision, the same passion for flight. And that has resulted in the excellence we see today. We've had great leadership from Presidents Ed Elliott, Fred Hovde, Art Hansen, Steve Beering, and Martin Jischke."

Purdue University graduates working in aviation and space come from all fields of engineering, as well as other disciplines. A large number of them have studied in a program that since 1973 has been titled the School of Aeronautics and Astronautics.

Tom Farris is head of this program with about 450 undergraduate and about 170 graduate students. It is one of the largest aeronautical and astronautical engineering undergraduate programs in the nation. The number of aeronautical engineers Purdue has graduated is one of the largest in the nation.

With twenty-three faculty members, *U.S. News and World Report* ranked Purdue's aeronautics/astronautics program seventh in the 2002 survey. "Purdue has an outstanding and well-deserved reputation in engineering," Farris says. "And the fact that there has been a flight program and airport here for so long has contributed to the excellence of the program and the recruitment of students. Recently, I think a big part of what's happening here is the excitement among students about space. An overwhelming majority of our undergraduate students are here for their interest in space—most both in manned space flight and satellites."

The aeronautical/astronautical faculty is deeply involved in research, generating about $5 million in sponsored program grants each year. That support comes from a variety of sources including the U.S. Department of Defense, the Air Force and Navy, NASA, the National Science Foundation, and many partners from industry such as Boeing and Lockheed-Martin. The program receives research grants from aerospace companies such as Northrup-Grumman and Ball Aerospace. There are ongoing research programs with propulsion companies such as General Electric, Rolls-Royce, and Pratt & Whitney. Purdue's University Technology Center (UTC) in high-Mach propulsion is the first UTC established by Rolls-Royce in the United States. AAE Professor Steve Heister is the UTC director.

Large numbers of Purdue graduates work for these companies in aeronautics and astronautics. While people often associate Purdue with its twenty-two astronauts, thousands of the university's graduates work in the some part of the aerospace industry. Purdue has about 433 alumni currently working for NASA, the Jet Propulsion Lab, and other associated entities. If you include those currently employed, the total number of alumni who have worked at some time directly for NASA is about 524. In addition, Purdue has at least 5,695 alumni currently employed with fourteen of the largest private contractors doing business with NASA.

"We've given more than seven thousand degrees, and our graduates have gone off and accomplished wonderful things in all parts of the aerospace industry," Farris says. "For example, Boeing is the world's largest aerospace company. At Boeing there are four people in the executive office, and two of those are Purdue graduates. There's David Swain, a graduate AAE, and Mike Sears, who graduated in electrical engineering.

"Another of our graduates, Roy Bridges, has been director of the Kennedy Space Center and is now director at Langley. Mark Craig is the associate director of the Johnson Space Flight Center. Purdue graduates play a major role in the Joint Strike Fighter Program, which is the largest Department of Defense acquisition program ever for aircraft." Purdue AAE alum, General Jack Hudson currently directs the JSF Program.

One example of a Purdue graduate is James Raisbeck, president of the Raisbeck group in Seattle, Washington, who has devoted his career to the application of aerodynamic research in transport and private aircraft. Through his leadership and understanding of the modern aerodynamics of wings and high-lift technology, the firms he led or founded have succeeded in making it economical to replace existing wings with his innovative designs, markedly improving the safety and efficiency of a wide variety of general aviation aircraft. He also created one of the first secure cockpit doors. James Raisbeck and his wife, Sherry, celebrated the combined contributions of AAE and AvTech by establishing the Raisbeck Engineering Distinguished Professorship for Engineering and Technology Integration. Professor A. F. Grandt Jr., former head of AAE, currently holds the Raisbeck Distinguished Professorship.

The list could go on forever. Some recently honored alumni include:

Paul Bevilaqua. Much of his career has been devoted to the development of vertical takeoff and landing aircraft. He played a leading role in creating the Joint Strike Fighter program. Bevilaqua is the chief scientist for advanced development programs at Lockheed-Martin Aeronautics Company.

Steven E. Lamberson, the chief scientist for the Airborne Laser System Program office, Space and Missile Systems Center at Kirtland Air Force Base. He is responsible for the overall technical functioning of the $11 billion Air Force Airborne Laser Program.

Brigadier General David A. Wagie, dean of the faculty at the U.S. Air Force Academy in Colorado, where he oversees the 700-plus member faculty and the annual design and instruction of more than five hundred undergraduate courses for four thousand cadets in thirty academic disciplines. He also directs the operation of five support staff agencies and faculty resources involving more than $250 million.

J. Michael Murphy, who has worked in the rocket propulsion industry for more than thirty-seven years. Murphy is vice president and chief engineer for Advanced Technology Associates Inc., which performs consulting services. He has received industry recognition for his work with the Titan missile and Space Shuttle Programs.

John H. McMasters, a program manager for the Ed Wells Initiative, a joint program between The Boeing Company and the Society of Professional Engineering Employees in Aerospace. Prior to joining Boeing in 1976, McMasters held faculty positions at Arizona State University and Purdue. He is an associate fellow of the American Institute of Aeronautics and Astronautics.

Joseph D. Mason, who retired from TRW in August 2000 after thirty-three years with the company including serving as vice president of the Systems and Integration Technology Group. His engineering career over the past forty-one years includes engineering education, control systems research and development, project management, and general management. As manager of the Tactical Systems Business Area, Mason established TRW as the leading contractor in U.S. Army command and control systems and earned recognition for leadership in missile defense systems.

And, Jerry L. Lockenour is the integrated product team leader for the Joint Strike Fighter (F-35) center fuselage for the air combat systems business area of the Integrated Systems Sector at Northrop Grumman Corp. He is responsible for all engineering and manufacturing of the $900 million project.

Dave Spencer, a 1989 aeronautics/astronautics Purdue graduate, is mission manager for 2001 *Mars Odyssey.* He was responsible for getting the spacecraft to Mars and accomplishing the objectives. He led *Odyssey's* flight team of one hundred people. The mission launched from the Kennedy Space Center on April 7, 2001, and reached Mars the following October. *Odyssey* has been orbiting Mars ever since. Its scientific work will continue through August 2004. It will provide the communications relay for the Mars exploration rovers launched in 2003.

Among current aeronautical/astronautical faculty at Purdue is Kathleen Howell, who in the fall of 2002 was named one of the fifty most prominent female scientists in the country by *Discovery* magazine. Howell has worked with NASA's Jet Propulsion Laboratory to create an "interplanetary superhighway," a method that enables spacecraft to travel through the solar system by taking advantage of the gravitational attractions of the sun and planets. The technique provides pathways that can slash the amount of fuel used by spacecraft. Howell and one of her graduate students designed such a pathway for NASA's low-fuel *Genesis* probe, launched in 2001. The probe is designed to collect samples of solar wind and return them to Earth.

In other faculty research, John Sullivan is one of the world's leaders in working with pressure-sensitive and temperature-sensitive paints. Steve Schneider is completing a Mach-6 wind tunnel that will be a unique facility in the world. James Garrison is working with global positioning satellites. C. T. Sun, Armstrong Distinguished Professor, is the world's foremost authority on composite materials. Professor Terry Weisshaar is currently leaving to run DARPA's morphing aircraft program. Professor James Doyle is the author of several structures textbooks adopted for use by other universities. Martin Jischke, a graduate of MIT in aeronautical/astronautical engineering, arrived as President of Purdue in 2000 and has led strategic planning and expansion of research efforts at the university.

Discovery Park is a new research area being constructed at Purdue. It features a $55.4 million Nanotechnology Center that will include aeronautic/aerospace faculty researchers. Other centers in Discovery Park will focus on biosciences, e-enterprises, and entrepreneurship.

At the start of the twenty-first century, NASA has located two centers in Discovery Park—one to work on small power computers, the other to work on advanced life support technologies for sustaining human colonies on Mars and elsewhere in space.

"Our department is growing in terms of faculty, research, and students," Farris says. "We're expanding our faculty to grow to about thirty in the next several years. We consistently are able to hire our first choices."

Purdue aeronautics/astronautics will be moving into a new building that will go up at the corner of Northwestern Avenue and Stadium Avenue.

"The university-owned airport is also a big boost to us," Farris says. "Under the leadership of Professor Dominick Andrisani, AAE and AvTech are now teaching a flight-test engineering course where we have our students actually fly in airplanes and in airline type simulators piloted by the aviation technology and aeronautics/astronautics students, and they collect data or aircraft performance and handling characteristics.

They get that hands-on experience, which we couldn't do if we didn't have the airport here on campus."

Students also get hands on experience through a number of internships and co-ops with industry, NASA, and the Air Force, including programs at Edwards Air Force Base in California and NASA headquarters in Houston. Through the leadership of Professor Steven Collicot, Purdue has more participation than any other university in NASA's reduced gravity flight opportunities program.

"Our plans for the next five years are to grow our faculty while keeping the undergraduate enrollment about the same," Farris says. "In the new facilities, we will have team learning modules. There will be spaces designed to help students learn to work in groups, as our industry partners would like them to do. At the same time, we'll see our research program growing, doubling the research expenditures over the next five years. We'll have more graduate students. And the graduate students also influence the experience of the undergraduate students because the undergraduates can get involved in the research. The school's world-class research laboratories will be even better with the completion of the new engineering building.

"Our goal is to be the pre-eminent program in aerospace in the country. And we are absolutely positioned to accomplish that.

"This is by far the most exciting time in my fifteen years at Purdue," Farris says. "When I talk to some of the senior faculty that have been here as long as thirty-five years, it's their most exciting time at Purdue, too.

"There's a lot of exciting work, especially associated with unmanned vehicles," he says. "There are also exciting things going on revitalizing the air-traffic management system in this country. One of our graduates, John Hayhurst, is running a new group that Boeing has started called Boeing ATM or Boeing Air Traffic Management. There are very exciting opportunities for research there."

The twentieth century has been exciting for aeronautics, space, and Purdue. And Farris sees the future offers even greater potential.

"One of our alumni, Ed Dosey, played a key role at Thiokol, came out of retirement after the *Challenger* accident, and was present for the launch of the next shuttle as the official representative of Thiokol," Farris says. "He has told me that in his lifetime, he had the experience of meeting the telegraph operator that sent the news that the Wright brothers had flown. It's just amazing that we would go from the first flight to walking on the Moon in such as short period of time.

"Try to extrapolate that and think about exciting things that are going to happen in the next century," he says. "It's really very exciting."

Tom Carney's years at Purdue span some of the most significant years of the aviation technology program. He arrived as a student in 1967 when the four-year aviation technology bachelor of science degree program was just beginning its second year. In July 2002, he was named head of the department. He is only the fourth head of the aviation technology program that is approaching its fiftieth anniversary.

All Carney ever wanted to do was fly.

"When I was in high school, the department sent out a flyer with a tear off on it if you were interested in aviation," Carney says. "It had a DC-6 pictured on it—one of the Purdue Aeronautics Corporation's airplanes. So I ripped it off, sent it in, got the materials, and applied."

He met with Jim Maris, head of the program, and once Maris understood that Carney's 3.9 grade point average was on a four-point scale and not a six-point—he was in.

"In those days, the airplanes were tied up outside," Carney says. "What we call hangar six today didn't exist. And what is now a computer lab is where we met our instructors for briefing and where we signed out the airplanes. In the spring of 1968, hangar six was enclosed. It wasn't finished, but we all moved down there. There was a big open area and lots of desks."

He graduated in the spring of 1971 and took a position teaching in the Link trainers and the DC-6 simulator. It was a one-semester appointment. When that position ran out he took a job with Reid Airways, which was a fixed-base operator at the Purdue Airport. From Reid he moved back to Purdue's aviation technology, the program he heads today.

There were fifteen to twenty students in each class of the flight program when he arrived in 1967. At the start of the twenty-first century, there are about 288 students in the aviation technology flight program.

There are three curriculum paths in the undergraduate program: first, aviation management, which is the newest of the three; second is aeronautical technology, which used to be called aviation maintenance technology; and third, professional flight, which is the pilot program.

There are a total of 613 students in all three undergraduate programs. Another twenty-one students are in the graduate program. There are twenty-eight faculty on the West Lafayette campus.

"Many people say we're the top program in the country," Carney says. "Most people who know say we're at least in the top three.

"I think we have some of the, if not the, best qualified and most experienced faculty you'll find anywhere in aviation," he says. "Our people create the excellence of this program. So the quality of the faculty is the first reason this program is considered among the best.

"The second thing that makes our program great is the quality of the students," he says. "In the case of the flight program, in particular, we have some of the best academically qualified students in the university. We vie with veterinary medicine for being the most difficult program to be accepted into. We have a number of valedictorians and salutatorians in our program—just really, really bright kids. And they are goal-oriented. They know what they want to do. They are gifted and so much fun to work with."

In 1988, 10.4 percent of applicants were accepted into the U.S. Naval Academy, 11.7 percent were accepted to the Air Force Academy, 12.2 percent were admitted to West Point. Harvard University admitted 15.2 percent and Stanford admitted 15.3. In the 1987–88 academic year, the Purdue professional pilot program accepted 7.2 percent of the external applicants to its junior-year flight program.

"Then third, there's the quality of the curriculum," Carney says. "Also the depth of the curriculum. I think it is unmatched anywhere, and I don't think anybody would seriously take us on. We're looked upon as a leader.

"And our fourth strong point is our laboratories. When you look at what we've got, in all three curricula areas—it's just excellent. In aeronautical technology and flight laboratories, we're simply unmatched. We have large-scale simulation—airline class simulators. And we've had this technology since the early 1960s. It's only recently that the other schools have gotten anything close to what we have. So we're at the cutting edge."

One of the strengths of the program is continuing opportunities for students to fly in the latest airplanes. Going back to the early 1950s and Purdue Aeronautics Corporation, students were able to fly as copilots, first on DC-3 airplanes, then on DC-6s, and finally as second officers on DC-9 jetliners, several students were checked out as DC-9 first officers (copilots). By the time Purdue Aeronautics went out of business, this copilot flight opportunity was already being expanded into aviation technology.

Before Purdue Aeronautics closed its doors, Jim Maris in aviation technology was acquiring more and more equipment, including some twin-engine airplanes. These planes increasingly were used to fly university officials to meetings. The students started flying as copilots—just as they did in the larger, Purdue Aeronautics planes.

"It was called supervised flight operations," Carney says. "As a student, my first trip as a copilot in that twin engine airplane was to take Purdue President Fred Hovde to Minneapolis. There was one full-time captain in this aviation technology program. He was on leave from Piedmont Airlines. He had cataracts and there was a new surgery to remove cataracts. Jim Maris hired him to fly and instruct in the DC-6 simulator, then became the first person to get his FAA medical certificate back after having had a double cataract operation. When he got his second class medical [for commercial pilots] he started flying the Twin Beech probably less than two hundred hours a year. It was mostly to take the president or one of the vice presidents where they needed to go."

Sometimes Carney, as a student with a commercial license, flew people on his own. "On one occasion, I had two gentlemen that I took to Bedford and then on to Connersville in March," he says. "As I flew from Bedford to Connersville, I was listening to the chatter on the radio, and I thought, gee, you know it sounds like the weather is deteriorating pretty rapidly. There was a cold front moving in. It started snowing. We got to Connersville, landed, and by the time they did their business and got back, it was snowing like crazy. I got a weather briefing and it was kind of iffy but okay, so I took off and got into a snow squall. I was only ten miles or so from the airport, so I went back and landed. I tried to rent a car to drive the two guys back, but I was too young to rent a car. I could fly these guys in an airplane, but I was too young to rent a car! They just laughed. And so in almost disgrace, I had to sit in the back of the car, and they drove back to Purdue."

The program survived on the donation of airplanes for a long time. With Maris and other qualified people on staff, they could accept these donations of airplanes, overhaul them, and make them good as new.

Carney says it was during the administration of President Steven Beering that the program became more proactive.

"Several board members were very proactive about aviation in the 1980s, including Don Powers, who was president of the board and a pilot," Carney says. "Dr. Beering was very proactive about aviation. He had been in the Air Force and worked with the astronauts. The support was just wonderful."

Beering was an Air Force flight surgeon and chief of internal medicine at what is now named Wilford Hall Medical Center at Lackland Air Force Base in Texas. It is the Air Force's largest medical facility. Early in the U.S. space program, Beering played a medical role with the astronauts who would come at intervals to the center in San Antonio for medical evaluations and tests. Beering's involvement ran from 1960 to 1969.

When Purdue's aviation technology won a special award from the federal government during Beering's presidency, he traveled with a group to Washington, D.C. Senator and former Mercury 7 Astronaut John Glenn met the group. When he saw Beering his first comment was, "You're not going to draw blood from me today, are you?"

Beering arrived at Purdue in 1983 and took an immediate interest in the aviation technology program. "I felt if we were going to be in the business of educating aviators for the twenty-first century, we had to have equipment that was compatible with what was being used in commercial aviation," Beering says. "That meant, obviously, that we had to have jets. And it also meant that we had to have simulators. Today, we've got the latest equipment and simulators. In fact, they're so sophisticated, you can get flying time on them for the airlines."

Beering said he also wanted airplanes replaced and updated in the interest of safety. "I think our program has evolved over the last several decades," Beering says. "It is probably unmatched anywhere in the world—not only in terms of size, but importantly, in quality of instruction. Tom Carney has a great deal to do with that. He deserves a huge amount of credit."

In 1989, David J. Haase, a 1964 Purdue graduate and TWA captain, received the Airline Pilot's Association Air Safety Award—the highest award for service to aviation safety.

In 1983, the university purchased its first turbine airplane, a King-Air from Beechcraft. The program grew and more airplanes were added—always with students flying as copilots.

"It became very evident, very quickly, that everybody liked the cabin-class King-Air," Carney says. "People liked the quiet. They liked the speed. We could go to Washington, D.C., in two hours and twenty minutes. That transformed what we did. Before the King-Airs, we used to get one or two trips to Washington or the east coast a year. After we got the first King-Air, we started getting a steady stream of university officials using them. And I think we've helped Purdue compete for research dollars by being able to get people to Washington and other places quickly and easily."

Next they started looking for a jet and bought one in 1987.

"It was obtained through a holding company that had been owned by a Purdue graduate," Carney says. "He called Dr. Beering and said, 'I understand you're in the market for a jet airplane.' He said he had three Diamond-1A airplanes. He would pick the best one and have it flown to us to evaluate. So, we got our first jet post–Purdue Airlines."

Purdue aviation technology instructors flew the new jet for two years before beginning a student copilot program on it. "And we've done the program ever since," Carney says.

They purchased another King-Air in 1990, and when it was time to replace the Diamond, they purchased a new Beechcraft Beechjet.

"The avionics in it are incredible," Carney says. "It's the same avionics that are in a 747-400. Our students need multi-engine time and turbine time as hiring criteria for getting a job with a corporate aircraft operator, a major carrier, or a regional carrier. This is very important to their education and career progression."

In 2003, the Purdue professional pilot program was flying two Beechcraft Super Kingairs [model B200] a Beechjet [model 400A] for the flight training of senior-level students. In addition to flight training, students in aviation technology also gain practical experience working with professional mechanics. All of the flight students have an opportunity to fly the King-Airs. They begin to become eligible for it in their junior year after receiving a commercial pilot's certificate in multi-engine aircraft and receive their instrument ratings. They get at least ten hours in the King-Airs. Some of them get upwards of forty or fifty if they work hard at it.

"They don't have to pay for that time because it's a laboratory that supports the travel needs of the university," Carney says. "So the travel needs of the university allow us to provide for the educational needs of our students."

Four to six students each year have been selected to fly the Beechjet. The number is about to move up to ten. "Not all the students are ready to fly a jet," Carney says. "But the ones who are really excel. Getting to fly that airplane and getting the experience of the avionics, the jet speeds, jet altitudes—those kinds of experiences are just incredible opportunities for them. You can see them change. When they come back from their training in the simulators for the first two trips or so—they've got a tiger by the tail.

"The instructors are really flight-training captains," he says. "That's what we do. We're faculty first. I know that when I first fly with a new student copilot, I'm essentially 'alone,' but it's okay. After about the second trip, they really hit their stride. Their rate of professional growth as an aviator, in my opinion, is almost exponential. And really as a professional training program, it's incredible. This is without peer. No one else in civilian aviation does this. You could buy flight time in a plane like this if you wanted, but that is not the same as taking an airplane, with what I call 'real people' in back—very important people—taking them on a schedule, all over the United States. You get the weather experience. Plus as a student, you're not paying for it. We put our students in front."

Carney flies with students the same way airline or corporate captains do with professional copilots. They alternate legs. "When it's my turn to fly, the students talk on the radio," Carney says. "When it's their turn, I talk on the radio." The students do landings and takeoffs as well as control the plane in flight.

In 1999, the Holleman-Niswonger Building was dedicated. The building is used for simulator training, bringing all the equipment together in one, modern facility. Scott Niswonger is a 1968 graduate of the professional pilot program. He is the CEO of Landair and Forwardair, trucking transportation companies. Niswonger donated about $1 million for the building. Charles Holleman is an aviation technology professor emeritas.

If you fly on a commercial airline, your pilot might have graduated from Purdue and experienced its training program. A majority of Purdue flight graduates move on to the airlines. "I think our graduates, from all three curriculum areas, are looked upon as leaders in the industry," Carney says. "Dr. Jischke has been very supportive of our programs and so has the provost, Dr. Sally Mason.

"Members of our faculty such as Charlie Holleman, Jill McCormick, Bill Duncan, Mike Kroes, Jim Maris, and others have had enormous impact on our programs," he says. "We also are doing a number of very interesting things in research and collaboration with aeronautical engineering and other Purdue departments and schools.

"Transportation safety and security is a very important issue for the country," he says. "We have a unique gathering of expertise and facilities here. We've got an outstanding aero-engineering program and related engineering programs. We've got an outstanding, I think, without peer, School of Technology, with a number of disciplines. And I like to think we've got the best aviation program in the country. Plus we've got a university-owned airport—the first in the nation. When you put all those things together, we're almost without peer in being able to study, research, develop, and then implement.

"You are not going to find many aviation centers like this anywhere else in the world."

David Wolf

David Wolf has spent 158 days in space. He's lived in the Russian space station, *Mir,* flown on three shuttle missions, and has performed four space walks in both Russian and U.S. space suits, logging over twenty-five hours outside the vehicle. He is currently chief of the Astronaut Office Extravehicular Activity Branch.

He is a medical doctor and among Purdue University's most distinguished graduates in electrical engineering.

What brought the Indianapolis native to Purdue? A Texas Instrument calculator played a key role.

"I was signed up for Indiana University in premed," Wolf says. "My grandmother bought me an SR-10 Texas Instruments calculator—the first one that came out. I looked at that and I thought—'I need to learn how this works.' So I took it up to Purdue during an electrical engineering orientation program the summer before my freshman year. I said, 'If I go to Purdue will I learn how this works?' They said, 'Yes.' So I signed up."

In August 1974, Wolf arrived at Purdue with a goal of joining his father as a medical doctor but using electrical engineering as his premed program. He was looking at the NASA space program as well.

"I had always followed the space program," he says. "But I realized a person needed to be something else before becoming an astronaut. So I followed my interests in engineering and medicine and flying and eventually I ended up at NASA as a biomedical engineer and eight years later became an astronaut."

It isn't the usual route. But it worked for Wolf. He received his medical degree from IU and did a medical internship at Methodist Hospital before going to NASA.

He arrived at NASA in 1983 as a bioengineer. He was in charge of building the first echocardiograph to do cardiovascular research in the space shuttle. He then became chief engineer for design of the space station medical facility. In 1986, he directed the development of the space bioreactor and associated tissue engineering and cancer research applications.

"This work led to significant advancement in tissue culture technology," Wolf says. "These bioreactors are patented and licensed for use by several companies, which make them available to all medical researchers in the areas of cancer research and tissue engineering."

Wolf has received fourteen patents. He has published more than forty technical papers. In addition to all of this, he became a private pilot and actively competes in sport aerobatic competitions.

He first applied for the astronaut program in 1983.

"I got an interview, but I didn't get the job," he says. "It took three more applications before I was finally accepted on my fourth try in 1990. I just wanted to work at NASA, but ultimately, if possible, I certainly wanted to fly, as an astronaut."

He got his first chance in 1993 on STS-58—a dedicated life-science research mission. "The crew conducted neurovestibular, cardiovascular, cardiopulmonary, metabolic, and musculoskeletal research utilizing microgravity to reveal fundamental human physiology otherwise masked by Earth gravity," NASA says.

Wolf describes the shuttle launch experience as feeling "like you're being punted into orbit."

"It's real fast, very serious," he says. "And no one ever gets tired of looking at Earth from space. It looks like another spacecraft flying in formation with you."

Wolf's next assignment was training for the Russian Space Station *Mir.*

"At first I was apprehensive about having to learn another language, moving to another country for the training," he says. "All the training was in Russian. My crewmates did not speak English. There were difficulties with logistics like what to do with your house back in America. In the end, it turned out to be one of the greatest experiences in my life. And working with another culture and working on a long duration space flight was fabulous."

He was in Russia for one and a half years of training and was stationed on *Mir* from September 1997 to January 1998.

"There was not a moment of boredom on *Mir,*" he says. "Each Mir mission had its own character, and ours was a very high workload. There was a large amount of maintenance, clean up, and repair work. (There had been a collision and fire before he arrived). I would say we worked until ten o'clock every single night of the whole mission, except Christmas, including weekends."

The most difficult part of the mission was the return to Earth.

"We had not mastered the types of exercises required," Wolf says. "We didn't have the kind of equipment required to sustain human muscles and bones. I lost 40 percent of my muscle mass and 12 percent of my bone mineral. And this really showed. In fact, for a while—for a month or so—I had doubts if I could ever readapt to living on Earth."

He had to go through rehabilitation, but the daily demands of his work with the space program cut in to his time for physical rehab.

"So it was a slow recovery over about two years," Wolf says.

He performed a space walk during the *Mir* mission and then three more during his most resent shuttle flight, STS-112 in October 2002.

"Doing a space walk is almost a religious experience," Wolf says. "Your first step out the hatch, when you clip your tether on, and step out, it's got to be one of the most exhilarating experiences that a human can feel. The view and the world you step into, is almost like *Alice in Wonderland*—dark shadows, brilliant brightness, the fabulously blue Earth, moving from plus 250 degrees to minus 250 Fahrenheit degrees with every sunset and sunrise. But you compartmentalize all that and get on with your work because space walks are serious business, and serious hard work. You have to be very careful in controlling your body because there's no resistance. The suit is heavy and hard to move in. The suit is essentially a spacecraft with all the systems of a spacecraft and you have to monitor and operate those systems. Some people report a feeling of falling when they see the earth. I did not experience that, but I practiced very carefully keeping my reference frame locked to the space station.

"When it's dark [during a space walk] all you see is the spacecraft," he says. "You have headlamps. It's just you and the light and the spacecraft floating in nothing. But when day breaks it's a brilliant fiery line that starts moving underneath you. It looks like a brilliant line of fire. And then Earth's aura lights up very suddenly, and you realize that you have this gorgeous planet down there.

"Even though my initial goal at NASA was the technology and space walks, my focus has shifted over the years in terms of what I feel is important," Wolf says. "Now I'm much more concerned that we do important work that benefits Earth—scientifically, that we continue the human spirit to explore, and that we continue to inspire the people of our planet—particularly the young people. We would definitely like to go to Mars. But for the time being, we are utilizing Earth's orbit to fully develop space faring technique, systems, and exploit the physics of weightlessness. It will be a ship, similar to our new International Space Station, in many respects, that does ultimately go to Mars. And one of those inspired young people will inspire me as they do it."

Chapter Sixteen

At Purdue University I suddenly realized that the work seemed strangely difficult, as if written in gibberish. I blinked. I didn't understand it. For someone who had always gotten good grades easily, it was a moment of reckoning, and I had to recognize that I was definitely in a new world. . . . I realized that it was time to get down to business and learn how to learn.

—Eugene Cernan, *Last Man on the Moon*

It was an incredible period, a time when great change was about to ripple through the world, impacting the way people thought and lived. But no one knew it yet.

The year 1945 brought the end of World War II. It was a place in time when people were in transition, when they were escaping the past at the same moment they were finally free to focus on their future. Events were already taking place that would lead to places no one had been before.

The pieces were starting to move into place. It had only been forty-two years since the Wright brothers flew at Kitty Hawk. Orville Wright was still alive, still living in Dayton, Ohio. The people who would take humankind beyond the bounds of Earth were positioning to meet their destiny.

Twenty-four years after the end of World War II, the first person landed on the Moon. In one incredible period of time between 1945 and 1957, five individuals who played leading roles in that triumph were at Purdue, shaping the foundation for their lives.

During many of those twelve years, three of them were on campus at any given time. While theirs would be the names that everyone would remember, they were studying and learning at Purdue alongside many others who would go on to quietly help shape aeronautical and astronautical history through their engineering and science careers.

Iven Kincheloe arrived in 1945. The media would name him the First Spaceman. Virgil Grissom enrolled in 1946. He would become the second American in space, the commander of Gemini 3 and Apollo 1. Neil Armstrong came in 1947. He would be the first man to land on the Moon. In 1952, Eugene Cernan arrived and began an amazing twenty-year journey that would culminate with the last Moon landing. In 1953, Roger Chaffee started at Purdue. He would die with Grissom fourteen years later, when a fire shot through their spacecraft during a ground test in Florida. These were five very different men from very different backgrounds who shared four common bonds: a passion for flight, a love for engineering, a thirst for exploration, and Purdue University.

Their accomplishments would open new worlds. Their accomplishments would help to seal Purdue's reputation in aeronautics and space and set the university on an irrevocable course for the future. Of the five, only two would live to tell their stories: the first and last men on the Moon.

The first Purdue graduate who would officially be titled an "astronaut" enrolled at Purdue in the fall of 1946. He arrived on a campus that was filled with young men wearing World War II military flight jackets and Army dress pants. They had an allowance of $65 a month in their pockets and up to $500 for tuition, books, and fees—all thanks to Uncle Sam and the G.I. Bill. It was a new era in education. It was a new era in America.

There were 11,462 students enrolled at Purdue the fall of 1946—49 percent more than in the fall of 1945. In 1947, enrollment hit 14,060, and in 1948 it peaked at 14,674. These students arrived at a university that would have been pushed to the limit just trying to serve the maximum number of students that had ever enrolled before—6,966.

In the fall of 1946, Purdue was as crowded as every other university in the nation with millions of young men leaving the military and anxious to get on with their lives. The G.I. Bill was the ticket to their future. And they knew it. It provided veterans with the money they needed to attend college. In the next ten years, five and a half million veterans would receive some form of higher education on the G.I. Bill, and many of them became the first in their family to receive a college degree. It changed the nation.

It was an exciting time. Eighteen-year-old farm kids who had never before been outside their home counties joined with twenty-six-year-old war veterans to form the freshman class. The veterans knew what they wanted, and they were in a hurry to get it.

This was the world Virgil Grissom entered in 1946. Grissom was a combination of everything that made up the Purdue freshman class that year. He was a veteran, although he did not have combat experience. He was from a little town in southern Indiana that was still far, far away from the hurried world.

Grissom was born April 3, 1926, in Mitchell, Indiana, two years after Frederick Martin was given command of the Around-the-World Flight and the year before Charles Lindbergh flew solo across the Atlantic Ocean. By 1926, airplanes had captured the fancy of the nation, but they were yet not a common sight in Mitchell.

Virgil was the oldest son in a family that would eventually include two brothers and a sister. He hated his name. One of his mother's sisters liked it and that's how he got it. "Can you believe anyone would let a sister name their children?" Grissom would complain to friends.[1] In order to deal with a name he didn't like, he allowed—and maybe even encouraged—people to call him by a nickname. At Mitchell High School they didn't call him "Virgil." His best friends called him "Greasy." "Greasy Grissom."

Years later at Purdue, he picked up another name. It started one evening when he was playing cards as the scorekeeper abbreviated his name "Gris" on a scorecard. A player across the table looked at the name upside down, misread it, and called Grissom "Gus" instead of "Gris." Gus stuck.[2]

In Mitchell, Grissom's dad, Dennis, worked for the B & O Railroad and the family lived simply and comfortably in town. It was a strong Christian family with loving parents.[3]

Grissom always claimed he was not a particularly good student during those early years. But in truth, he had a natural talent for math. More than anything, he just didn't apply himself, rarely taking a book home from school. He was busy working part-time jobs after school and on the weekends. He had a paper route. He worked in a grocery store. Off and on he worked at a gas station, a clothing store, and did some blacksmith work. He made model airplanes, although no more, he said, than other boys his age.[4]

Somewhere, sometime, during those early years in Mitchell the lure of flight was ignited within him. He didn't know exactly when it started. At the time, he didn't know exactly how he would use it. But it was there, and it would emerge years later to take him to the top of the U.S. space program.

Most people in a position to know say, if Grissom had lived, he would have been chosen to walk on the Moon. Some say he would have been the first.

Donald "Deke" Slayton was the man who assigned astronauts to space missions. In 1994 Slayton said, "One thing that would probably have been different if Gus had lived is that the first guy to walk on the Moon would have been Gus Grissom."[5]

Long before all of that, Grissom was a small town boy who fell in love with a small town girl and made simple plans to live happily ever after. He was a sophomore at Mitchell High School when he met Betty. She was a freshman. Grissom was fifteen years old and belonged to a Boy Scout color guard team. Betty, fourteen, was in the band and among the first high-school girl drummers in Indiana. The band and the Boy Scouts performed together at school flag ceremonies. Grissom lived in town. Betty lived just outside of Mitchell, although her father was not a farmer. Her mother was unsure about Betty dating a boy from town. Her father only wanted to know if the Grissoms were Democrats or Republicans. The answer was Republicans. The Grissom family was okay with him.[6]

Those were war years, and in 1944, Grissom signed up for the Army Air Service rather than be drafted as a foot soldier. "Flying sounded a lot more exciting than walking," he would say.[7] He was called up on August 8, 1944—two months after his graduation and D-Day. He left on Betty's seventeenth birthday.

Grissom did his basic training in Texas while Betty stayed home in Mitchell to finish her senior year of high school. She was interested in becoming an airline stewardess, but her father was against it. "Daddy wasn't convinced that airplanes were here to stay," she says.[8]

On July 6, 1945, while Grissom was home on leave, they married in the parsonage of the First Baptist Church in Mitchell. Not long after the ceremony, they began what would become an all-too-familiar ritual—separation as Grissom pursued duty and career. He returned to his Army base. She stayed home in Mitchell.[9]

Because of a backlog of men in pilot training at the end of the war, Grissom never made it to flight school. He was released from the service in 1946 and joined Betty back in Mitchell where they rented an apartment on Main Street. He worked at a company outside of town building school buses. He was restless, looking for a new job almost every chance he had. Really, he was looking for more than a job. He was looking for his future.

"One day," Betty says, "he came home and said he wanted to go to Purdue." It was that simple. And it was no surprise to her. She had already decided that a college education was her husband's best option. She was just waiting for him to catch up.[10]

Grissom decided to enroll at Purdue on the G.I. Bill to study engineering. He had an immediate problem: finding a place to live in West Lafayette. That was the rule. To enroll as a student you had to have a place to live in the community that was overflowing with ex-G.I. college students. He traveled to West Lafayette and found a room in the basement of 205 Sylvia Street.

The ritual continued. Betty moved back with her parents. "He went up to West Lafayette, and I stayed in Mitchell," Betty says. "There wasn't a place for both of us. The owner of the house where Gus lived had all the rooms rented out to students. On the main floor, there was a bedroom in the back that was rented by two guys. I don't know if they graduated or what. But when they left, I went up to West Lafayette, and we lived in that room until we got the apartment of our own on Littleton Street."[11]

Grissom attended classes all year, which was common at the time. In addition to his studies in mechanical engineering, he worked thirty hours a week frying hamburgers at a restaurant near campus. Betty found a good job as an operator for Indiana Bell.

Grissom graduated in February 1950, anxious to start his career. "What I needed was a job—and fast—because I didn't want Betty spending any more of her life at the switchboard," Grissom wrote in his book, *Gemini*. "She had made my degree possible. But I'd got the Air Force bee in my bonnet and my job hunting seemed to turn up nothing as exciting."[12]

The lure of flight was still burning within him. He considered options, including a job at a brewery. Nothing sounded as exciting as flying.

In 1950, an Air Force recruiting team visited the Purdue campus, and Grissom reenlisted to pursue his dream. He was sent once again to Texas, this time to Randolph Field for flight training. Betty, pregnant with their first child, moved to Seymour to live with her sister.

Scott Grissom was born in May 1950. While Betty visited her husband in Texas during the flight training period, Scott was six months old before he finally met his father at Williams Air Force Base in Phoenix, Arizona, where Grissom was in jet fighter training.

Grissom took to flying naturally. His five-foot, seven-inch body fit into the tight cockpit of an airplane like it had been designed with him in mind. He was doing what he loved to do.[13]

Grissom made second lieutenant in March 1951 and nine months later he was in Korea. Once again, Betty was on her own. She and Scott moved to Bedford, Indiana, ten miles from Mitchell.

In Korea, Grissom flew the F-86 Sabre Jet that had been tested and flown past the speed of sound by George Welch. Grissom named his plane *Scotty.* He received the Distinguished Flying Cross, made first lieutenant, completed his one-hundredth mission, and was shipped back home.

His next assignment was as a flight instructor in Bryan, Texas. He had already spent a great deal of his career in Texas. He was destined to spend a great deal more.

There are about fifty-seven million square miles of land on the surface of the planet Earth. For thousands of years, people living from one end of the Earth to the other have had commonalities. One of them is that they have all shared the dream of flight. Another is that they have all shared the Moon and wondered at its sight.

The first people to accomplish powered flight were brothers, Wilbur and Orville Wright. Wilbur was born in Millville, Indiana. Orville was born about sixty miles to the east in Dayton Ohio, where the brothers lived and worked. And about sixty miles north of Dayton in Auglaize County, Ohio, between the towns of Wapakoneta and St. Mary's, is the birthplace of another important person in the drama of flight: the first man to land on the Moon.

A small, rural triangle joining Wapakoneta and Dayton, Ohio, with Millville, Indiana, plays a huge role in one of the greatest stories of human accomplishment.

The first man to land on the Moon was born in 1930 in a farmhouse that belonged to his grandparents. It was a small farm. There weren't many big farms in those days in Auglaize County. Neil Armstrong's grandfather farmed about sixty acres.[14]

Armstrong's father was an auditor who worked for the state of Ohio. He audited the books at county courthouses, taking his family with him all over the state.[15]

At the start of World War II, the family settled in Auglaize County to be near relatives.[16]

In 1932, Armstrong's father took him to the airport in Cleveland to see the air races. But he was two years old and has no recollection.[17]

In 1936, his father took him flying when a man with a Ford Tri-Motor airplane was giving rides at a local airport. Armstrong was six years old. He doesn't remember that either.

"When I was nine or ten, I got interested in building model aircraft, and I did that passionately for a long number of years, throughout my youth," Armstrong says. "But at that point I hadn't really thought about piloting a real airplane. I was quite content to fly model airplanes."[18]

Armstrong arrived in the town of Wapakoneta at the end of his freshman year of high school and graduated there. He quickly found his way to Port Koneta Airport.[19]

He started flying when he was fifteen in anticipation of getting a student pilot certificate when he was legally able to at the age of sixteen.

He flew Aeronca Champ airplanes, and he remembers the excitement of flight, especially when he was able to solo. "That's a big excitement, when you're by yourself for the first time," he says. "I was very interested in it. It was very exciting, challenging, and I enjoyed it very much."[20]

It was also expensive—seven dollars an hour solo and nine dollars an hour with an instructor. "But I was making thirty cents an hour in those days," Armstrong says. "So if I was frugal, I could manage to fly occasionally."[21] He also worked around the airport doing odd jobs in exchange for flight time.

He loved to fly. But his career plans did not include working as a pilot. He wanted to design airplanes. His plan was to get an engineering degree and become part of the aeronautical industry—hopefully in aeronautical design.[22]

The next big step in accomplishing his plan was college, and he competed for a Navy scholarship. It was called the Naval Aviation College Program or NACP. The intent of the plan was to build up the reserve strength of naval aviation.

"I was fortunate to win an appointment to that program, which was a seven-year program," Armstrong says. "It included two years of college, then three years of active duty in the Navy, of which approximately two would be involved in going through flight training."[23]

At the end of the three years of active duty, participants were placed in the reserves, and they could return to college to finish their degrees.

"I actually applied for and was accepted at MIT, which had a wonderful engineering reputation," Armstrong says. "But during my junior year, I also became aware of some other engineering schools that had very good reputations, including Purdue. And you know, being an Ohio resident when, in my junior year, Purdue beat Ohio State at Ohio State, my interest grew."[24]

Ohio State was ranked number one in the nation when the Boilermakers arrived at Columbus on October 20, 1945. The Buckeyes had won twelve straight games going back to the previous season and had not been scored on that fall. The team had just been featured in *Life* magazine. The Armed Services Radio Network broadcast the game around the world.

Purdue—led by Ed Cody, Bill Canfield, and seventeen-year-old freshman quarterback Bob DeMoss—won that game thirty-five to thirteen before 73,585 stunned Buckeye fans. DeMoss threw three touchdown passes. Purdue scored twenty-two points in the first half before Ohio State made a first down.

It is considered to be among the greatest days in Purdue football history. If that game helped to bring Neil Armstrong to Purdue, it might go down as the greatest Boilermaker victory of them all.

But there was more to it than a football game. Armstrong approached his college choice the same way he appears to approach everything in life —carefully, analytically.

"My father had introduced me to a graduate of MIT who was a great booster of MIT," Armstrong says, "but he convinced me that I could get an equally good education at Purdue—particularly in the undergraduate school. He thought, perhaps, if and when I got to the graduate level, I might want to reconsider again and perhaps reintroduce the idea of going to MIT. From the sources I had available to me, I was convinced [Purdue] was as good as I could find."[25] With that, Armstrong applied to Purdue, was accepted, and arrived on campus in the fall of 1947.

Purdue's School of Aeronautics was two years old in 1947. "It did have a full aeronautical engineering curriculum and it was a four-year program," Armstrong says. "The first year was general engineering with no aeronautic courses. The second year was predominately, I would say, aligned to the mechanical engineering curriculum. But it had a couple of little introductions to aeronautical courses. The final two years had a preponderance of aeronautical engineering courses.

"I was awed by the diversity of the courses and what appeared to be the quality of the courses," he says. "From my standpoint as a young high-school graduate, it looked pretty challenging.

"There was an enormous number of G.I.s who were returning from the service. They were in all my classes—lots and lots of vets around the campus. They knew what they wanted to do. They were driven, so they made good classmates. They'd had a few years in the war to consider what they wanted to do when they got out. They were much more focused than my high-school graduate colleagues. It was a good experience being with those fellows. Many of them were married and had children. They were very good to work with."[26]

The large number of students on campus made it difficult to find a place to live. In the fall of 1947, Armstrong ran into the same problems Grissom had encountered a year earlier. "I could not get a room, anywhere in West Lafayette," Armstrong says. "I ended up living in a private home in Lafayette [about four or five blocks south of the downtown area]. A family rented me a spare room. I took the bus over to Purdue every day."[27]

By the second semester, he had found a room closer to campus in the home of a retired member of the faculty. He had no kitchen rights. He ate out, mostly at the Memorial Union.

Armstrong enjoyed working with the Purdue faculty. "Purdue had a wonderful aeronautical engineering faculty," he says. "From my perspective, they were all great. I really loved the aeronautical engineering faculty."[28]

He joined the All-American marching band led by Paul Spotts Emerick. Armstrong played the baritone horn and a little bass in the band. He also played in the Purdue orchestra. He arrived in West Lafayette with a solid musical background and a love for music. He took piano lessons when he was a boy. Even during his years as a pilot and astronaut, those who knew him say he enjoyed playing the piano.[29]

While at Purdue he did not know Iven Kincheloe or Gus Grissom, although he could come to know both very well a few years later.

Armstrong did not stay at Purdue the full two years as originally planned. The Navy called him to active duty in the middle of his sophomore year in January 1949.

He was sent to Pensacola, Florida, for flight training followed by advanced training at Corpus Christi, Texas. He received his wings in August 1950.

The Korean conflict had started two months earlier. He was sent to Korea in the fall of 1951, assigned to Fighter Squadron 51, which was subsequently placed on the the carrier USS *Essex*. He was there flying F9F2 Panthers until late spring of 1952. He loved flying off carriers.[30]

On at least one mission Armstrong ran into serious trouble. The enemy had cables strung across a canyon to harass American pilots. One of them knocked off part of his wing. Armstrong ejected in the vicinity of a U.S. Marine installation.[31]

Armstrong flew seventy-eight combat missions, and his three years of active service in the Navy program officially ended while he was in a combat zone, so he was extended until the summer of 1952.

He arrived back on campus in September 1952 and flew in a reserve squadron out of Glenview, Illinois, while finishing at Purdue.[32]

While Armstrong didn't think about it, when he returned in 1952, he was much like those World War II veterans he had met on campus in 1947. He was slightly older than traditional second-semester sophomores. And he was a war veteran.

He did not play in the band when he returned. His major nonacademic activities upon returning centered around the Phi Delta Theta Fraternity, which he joined.

"I had many friends there," Armstrong says. "I enjoyed living at the fraternity house, enjoyed the people. I thought it was good for me."[33]

Upon returning he met another young man he would know much better in the years ahead, Eugene Cernan. "He was a little younger than I was, and he was a Fiji [Phi Gamma Delta]. I don't remember how I knew Gene, but I did—although not well."[34]

Armstrong had a great experience at Purdue. "It was a wonderful experience, I enjoyed my time at Purdue immensely—before I went into the service and after I came back," he says. "I received a quality education. Purdue had a fine faculty and a wide variety of extracurricular activities to choose from, there were great intercollegiate sports. I found the only problem was that there wasn't enough time to do everything you wanted to do."[35]

Armstrong's academic career proceeded exactly according to plan. His plan was unaltered. He was going to get the aeronautical engineering degree, go into the aeronautical industry, and hopefully enter into the design world.[36]

He graduated in January 1955 and thereafter made some alterations in his plans. Ultimately, he would do some business travel that he had never anticipated while a student at Purdue.

Eugene Cernan arrived at Purdue in the fall of 1952, the same year Armstrong returned from Korea.

Cernan, born in Chicago, grew up in Bellwood, Illinois, a second generation American of Czech and Slovak descent, grew up with a love for everything mechanical. It was a trait he acquired from his father who could fix, repair, or build anything—with no formal training. Cernan was an athlete who loved sports and was even offered a football scholarship at Dartmouth. In addition to sports, Cernan had found another love as a boy in post–World War II America: flight. He grew up with dreams of flying and flying off of aircraft carriers.

The Korean War started in June 1950, and Cernan started his junior year at Proviso High School that fall. He had his sights set on a college education and if he went to Korea he was determined to go as a pilot.[37]

He applied for a Naval ROTC scholarship and planned to study engineering. "I passed [the exam] with a high score and signed up for the NROTC program at Purdue—a full-ride scholarship, plus spending money, three summer cruises, and graduation in four years as an ensign in the regular Navy," Cernan says. "The Navy, however, said the Purdue slots had already been filled and offered me the same deal at the University of Illinois. My father wouldn't hear of it because he felt Illinois wasn't a top engineering school. The Navy then offered a partial scholarship at Purdue, a program with a pittance of financial help and a commission in the Naval Reserve. I didn't want it because I knew my entire family would have to work hard to pay for me to attend Purdue as an out-of-state student. But at dad's insistence, I reluctantly agreed, knowing that not only would I get a degree, but that I could still get a commission in the Navy, albeit in the reserves, and maybe somehow could spin that into my dream of flying.[38]

"That was a big decision," he says. "My dad insisted he wouldn't have it any other way. He was right. My goal was to get a good education and get into Navy aviation—that's where I was heading."[39]

In the fall of 1952, Cernan left Bellwood for Purdue and began a journey that would take him, twenty years after he started college, to a place named Taurus-Littrow, a very long way from the Chicago area home where he grew up.

At Purdue, Cernan worked in a residence hall dining room to make cash for his expenses and won a small scholarship. His ROTC scholarship did not kick in until his junior year.

He enjoyed the social life. Cernan joined Phi Gamma Delta Fraternity and loved it. He enjoyed playing intramural sports for the Fijis. In addition to students his own age, he also became acquainted with many older men who had returned to Purdue after serving in Korea. Cernan knew Armstrong, of those returning vets, and also knew Roger Chaffee who was one year younger, but he did not know either well.

An excellent student in high school, Cernan found he smoothly completed his first semesters at Purdue. He was helped by the fact that his fraternity emphasized scholarship. "My life started on the fast track at Purdue," he says. "We had to do a lot of studying. My fraternity voted against having a TV. We thought it would be too much of a distraction. Later on, in my junior or senior year, we did get one—but we restricted its use."[40]

Eventually, even Cernan hit the wall. "I thought I had it made until I had a real wake-up call one day in a theoretical circuits course," he says in his book *The Last Man on the Moon.* "I suddenly realized that the work before me seemed strangely difficult as if written in gibberish. I blinked. I didn't understand it! My God, could I get a C in this class? Even a D? For someone who had always gotten good grades easily, it was a moment of reckoning, and I had to recognize that I was definitely in a new world. If I get a D, is it possible to fail? That certainly was not an option, not when my parents were working so hard to send me to school, not when a failure would disappoint my dad and also end my dream of flying. I realized that it was time to get down to business and learn how to learn."[41]

When he returned to Purdue from Chicago for his senior year, his father bought him a fourteen-dollar ticket to fly into West Lafayette on a DC-3 Lake Central Airlines plane. It was Cernan's first flight, and it wasn't a good one. The plane was old and outdated, and the seats were too small. Back on campus a fraternity brother took him up in a Cessna, "and as soon as the engine revved and the wheels lifted off, I knew I had made the right choice of career. Now I could look out of the small window at the passing wisps of clouds, could see the spinning propeller pull me along and hear its strong, sweet murmur as the wings flexed overhead. When my friend let me get my hands on the controls, it was as if I became part of the aircraft. Ordinary people might be pinned to that distant grass, but the skies were going to be mine."[42]

Cernan graduated from Purdue on June 6, 1956. He was commissioned an ensign in the Naval Reserves and reported to Pensacola, Florida, for flight training. Within a short time, he applied for and was accepted into the regular Navy. When he left Purdue for flight training, he was only ten years away from his first space flight. He was only sixteen years away from walking at Taurus-Littrow on the Moon.

In September 1955, Purdue freshman Martha Horn had only been on campus for two days when she and a friend, Ann Menge, agreed to a double blind date. It was decided that Menge would go with the taller of the two young men when they arrived. It was a practical matter. Horn was shorter. At five feet, nine inches, the shorter man turned out to be Roger Chaffee, a Purdue junior studying aeronautical engineering. It didn't take long for college to change Martha Horn's life. After the end of her sophomore year at the age of nineteen, she would leave Purdue to marry this young man who had such a brilliant future.

Then–U.S. Representative Gerald Ford, who would one day become president, said, "Roger Chaffee is one of the nation's great modern-day heroes . . . [who was] shooting for the moon and instead found a place in the stars."[43]

Chaffee was born on February 15, 1935. The family home was Greenville, Michigan, northeast of Grand Rapids. Roger's sister, Donna, was two years old when he arrived.

The boy's love for flight was born into him. His father loved airplanes and in 1930 had been a barnstorming pilot, flying a Waco 10 biplane at fairgrounds, carrying passengers who paid for the thrill and parachute jumpers who frightened crowds with their daring stunts.[44]

In May 1942, the family moved to Grand Rapids, where Donald Chaffee worked as chief inspector of Army ordinance at the Doehler-Jarvis plant.

In Grand Rapids, Roger Chaffee grew up in an idyllic home. He became an Eagle Scout, developed a solid work ethic running paper routes and doing odd jobs. He was an excellent student who loved making model planes. By the time he was in eighth grade, his dreams were focused on becoming an electrical engineer.

He wrote this essay in eighth grade: "For friends I like to have kids who will stick up for their own rights. I don't like girls and boys who are intolerant. I don't care for the ones that go home if they can't have their own way. I admire a person with a clean mind, one that has the ambition to make something of himself. . . . I chose electronics because I have always wanted to play with motors. . . . It is a subject in which you have the opportunity to go a long way, and that's what I like about it."[45]

By his junior year of high school, his focus had changed to nuclear physics. In an essay that year he wrote, "I think my personality and temperament are fairly well suited to this kind of job. A person in this field should have a scientific aptitude. I believe I have one. He should have an adaptability and interest in what he is doing. I am always interested in science. He should be patient. Sometimes I become a little hasty, but most of the time I can control myself. . . .

"As of right now, I don't have the financial resources necessary to attend . . . college. . . . Still, there is always a chance to win scholarships. All in all, I believe I have about a fifty-fifty chance of achieving my goal—if the Army doesn't get me first."[46]

As a high-school senior, Chaffee applied for college scholarships through three programs: The U.S. Naval Academy at Annapolis, Rhodes, and the Naval Reserve Officers Training Corps.

To enter the Naval Academy he felt he had to promise to make a career in the Navy. He might be interested, he said. But he couldn't give his word unless he was positive. "They wanted me to promise that if this is given to me, I will always remain in the Navy, and . . . I couldn't promise," he said. "I just don't know, and I don't want to lie about it."[47] His grades were good enough for the Rhodes program, but he was leaning toward engineering and Rhodes did not offer scholarships in engineering. That left the final option. Chaffee was admitted to the Navy ROTC scholarship program at the Illinois Institute of Technology beginning in the fall semester of 1953.[48]

He did very well. He joined Phi Kappa Sigma Fraternity. He made the dean's list and spent the summer in NROTC training, eight weeks of training aboard the battleship *Wisconsin*.

When he got home that summer, Chaffee examined his future more closely. And he reached a new conclusion. He wanted to be an aeronautical engineer. He wanted to attend one of the top universities in the field, and he knew which one. Shortly before the fall semester of 1954, the U.S. Navy approved Chaffee's request to transfer to Purdue.

At Purdue he lived in the Phi Kappa Sigma Fraternity house and eventually was elected president. In the spring of 1955, he and a fraternity brother, Tommy Keister, made trips to nearby Mulberry and took flight lessons from John R. "Pop" Stair. After four or five lessons he realized he would not have the money to complete the training, so he stopped.

His life started changing rapidly when he met Martha Horn on that blind date in September 1955 at the start of his junior year. She was from Oklahoma, majoring in radio and television and speech therapy.

"We had a good time on that first date, but he was an upperclassman, and I was just a freshman," Martha says. "And you know, I thought he was a little cocky. And I think he thought I was very naïve. We dated for a year before we got engaged."[49]

In the fall of her sophomore year, Martha Horn was elected Purdue homecoming queen, and Chaffee told his parents he'd found the girl he wanted to marry. In October 1956, he made it official and asked Martha. He selected a day when she was sick with laryngitis. But he was an engineer with his plan. He moved straight forward and asked. "I had lost my voice, so I really couldn't say yes or no," Martha says, "but I think he could understand by my expression that I accepted."[50]

In addition to taking courses to complete his degree in aeronautical engineering, by this time Chaffee was also teaching a lower level math course at Purdue. He did drafting work to earn some extra money. He had ROTC classes. And in the second semester of his senior year in 1957, he took up flight training again.

This time the training came as part of his NROTC program. Purdue NROTC had a contract with Purdue Aeronautics for flight training. After completing the instructions, Chaffee flew with FAA examiner David W. Kress to receive his pilot's license.

"Mr. Chaffee impressed me as being good military pilot material," Kress said in a 1967 Purdue University news release. "His ability was above average, and I recall him to be very conscientious and serious about his flying career."[51]

One of his instructors was again "Pop" Stair. Stair wrote of an early flight with Chaffee. "Landing attempts rough—tends to gain altitude."[52] Fortunately, Chaffee improved.

In 1966, about three years after Chaffee was selected for the astronaut program, Stair wrote and asked if this was the same Roger Chaffee he had instructed at Purdue. "Dear Pop," Chaffee responded in a letter dated April 4, 1966, written on NASA stationary. "Yes, I am the same Roger Chaffee you taught to fly. . . . You taught me a lot of the fundamentals of flying which I have always carried with me. I still remember how you impressed upon your students to always have an emergency landing field picked out in case of engine failure. One of the first things I do after I take off in a small aircraft is to look for a clearing or field in the event of an emergency. Of course, with the larger and faster military aircraft I am flying, this is not so important because you can only land them on a prepared surface; however, I still look around for that landing site. I will forever be grateful to the excellent instructions that you gave me in the basic aircraft and the precepts of safety that you instilled in me."[53]

Chaffee loved his years at Purdue. "He enjoyed everything about learning," Martha Horn Chaffee says. "He was an excellent student, had very high grades. He was very smart. Those two years I was at Purdue were some of the most fun years of my life. I was in Kappa Alpha Theta Sorority. I met Gene Cernan only once at Purdue. He was in charge of an ROTC program, and they were picking a queen for a ball. I was up for it, and he had to interview me. I think I was a freshman. Years later when we were reunited in the astronaut program, I reminded him of that ROTC interview. I said, 'Thanks a lot. You didn't pick me.'"[54]

After graduation in June 1957, Chaffee took a one-month job at Douglas Aircraft in Los Angeles, California. From there that summer he traveled first to Norfolk, Virginia, and then Corpus Christi, Texas, to complete his Navy training. Along the way he stopped to see Martha at her parents' home in Oklahoma City where they were busy with wedding plans.[55]

On August 22, 1957, Chaffee was commissioned an ensign. Two days later he and Martha married. He was twenty-two. She was nineteen. They spent their first few months of married life together in Norfolk, and then Chaffee was transferred to Pensacola, Florida, for flight training. His jet training began in the summer of 1958 at Kingsville, Texas. The first Chaffee child, Sheryl, was born November 17, 1958. Chaffee completed his flight training in early 1959.

Among Chaffee's first assignments was aerial photography work. He made a number of flights back and forth to Cuba. He also spent time aboard the USS *Saratoga*. On July 3, 1961, the Chaffees had another child, a son, Stephen.[56]

By July 1961, the space race was well underway. Alan Shepard had launched in May, followed by Kennedy's challenge to send a man to the Moon and back within the decade. Grissom would make his first flight on July 21.

Chaffee's vision had also expanded to space. "While we were living in Florida, he was talking about the space program," Martha says. "He mentioned several times that it really had become a goal of his to be an astronaut candidate. I was excited about it. I thought it would be fabulous. I was young, and when you're young, you never think anything is going to happen. As far as I was concerned, I knew there were going to be risks. But NASA wasn't having problems of any significance. It never entered my mind that there would be any more danger than when they were already flying every day."[57]

In 1963, Chaffee received a letter from an eight-year-old boy. The boy was the son of a man who worked in a Grand Rapids department store. As a teenager, Chaffee had worked for this man in the Boy Scout department. Chaffee wrote back,

Dear Steven,

You asked me to tell you how I became an astronaut. It is a long story that involves many people, but I will try to tell you some of it. . . .

First of all, you have to want to be an astronaut. That means you want to be a jet pilot and an engineer, and you have to want to do things that are exciting and challenging, like riding on a roller coaster or going down the biggest hill there is on a sled. . . .

But there are far more important things. You have to want to dedicate your life to a worthwhile cause, and to serve your country. You have to love your country so much that every time you see our flag, you feel warm inside. . . .

Secondly, you must always challenge your ability while you are growing up. You must be given and assume the responsibilities you can handle. . . .

The third thing you must do to become an astronaut is to study very hard. I am still studying, and I will keep on studying all the time I am an astronaut. . . .

Another thing you have to do to become an astronaut is to keep your body strong. . . . Keeping your body strong also helps you keep your mind strong. . . .

And then, Steve, if you have done a good job on all of these things and have graduated from college, you can learn to fly the big jet airplanes in the Air Force or Navy. And after you have flown them for about six years you can try for astronaut training.

It sounds like an awful lot for an eight-year-old to do and think about, doesn't it Steve? But if you always do your best and ask your mother and father and your teacher, they can tell you what to do next if you want to become an astronaut or anything else.[58]

Iven Kincheloe graduated from Purdue in 1949; Virgil Grissom in 1950; Neil Armstrong in 1955; Eugene Cernan in 1956; and Roger Chaffee in 1957. During the course of those eight years, the future of space travel—from the Bell X-2, to the X-15, to the Mercury, Gemini, and Apollo programs—all passed, in the form of five men, through one university: Purdue.

Mary Ellen Weber

Before she learned to fly, she learned to jump.

Purdue graduate Mary Ellen Weber has flown as an astronaut on two shuttle flights and logged more than 450 hours in space, but before she found a love for aviation and space, she was a skydiver.

A native of Bedford Heights, Ohio, near Cleveland, Weber was led to Purdue by the university's reputation, which Neil Armstrong, Eugene Cernan, Virgil "Gus" Grissom, and Roger Chaffee helped create.

"I became interested in Purdue because I love math and science and figuring out how things work," she says. "Purdue is the top engineering school in the country, and I wanted to learn from the best." She arrived at Purdue in the fall of 1980, months before the first space shuttle flight in April 1981.

"My first interest in flying and aviation was in skydiving and that started with the Purdue Skydiving Club, which at that time consisted of one person with a car who drove out to the drop zone," Weber says. "I just fell in love with all aspects of aviation and skydiving—which I still do today." She later became a licensed pilot with an instrument rating who ultimately flew jets with NASA.

At Purdue she majored in chemical engineering and took part in internship programs with Ohio Edison, Delco Electronics, and 3-M. "Purdue's co-ops and summer internships in engineering are among its strong points," she says. "These are invaluable experiences, and Purdue has done very well in forging relationships with industry to make these happen."

Weber graduated from Purdue in the spring of 1984. She went on to earn a Ph.D. in physical chemistry from the University of California at Berkeley in 1988 and a master's of business administration from Southern Methodist University in 2002.

"When I was in graduate school, I saw the space program as a fantastic melding of the two passions that I had—science and aviation," Weber says. "I really never dreamed it would actually come true, but I love having goals, something to strive and reach for, and that's how I viewed the astronaut program. Low and behold, it worked out."

She requested an application for the program in 1986 but waited until she had completed her Ph.D. and accomplished other things before actually sending it in 1991. Although many astronauts apply and interview several times before being selected, she was accepted on her first try. She loved the work.

"When you're in the astronaut corps you don't have a specialty, per se," Weber says. "You actually change jobs many times. On average you work in a particular area for one year or two years. Over the years, many of my assignments focused on science experiments and being the astronaut office liaison to designing the hardware for experiments and setting policies and strategies for crew training. I also became very involved in commercializing technology, looking for ways to move our space experiments to the marketplace. I found that very, very exciting."

She flew as a mission specialist on STS-70 in July 1995 and STS-101 in May 2000. Her responsibilities included checking the systems of a satellite and sending it into orbit above the equator; performing biotechnology experiments such as growing colon cancer tissues that were never before possible; flying a sixty-foot robotic arm to maneuver a space walking crewmember; and directing the transfer of over three thousand pounds of equipment.

She left NASA in December 2002 and is currently an executive at the University of Texas Southwestern Medical Center in Dallas.

Dr. Weber has accomplished more than 3,300 skydives since 1983. She is an eight-time silver/bronze medalist at the U.S. National Skydiving Championships. She participated in the world record largest completed freefall formation in 2002, with three hundred people.

"I compete every year with a sixteen-person team, and we do very well," Weber says. "In fact, we typically are only beaten by the professional skydivers. We're at the top of the 'weekend' skydivers. It's great fun competing against the best in the world. Skydiving is really all about flying your body as an aircraft, and it is incredibly challenging. That's what keeps someone like me in the sport for twenty years. It is very rewarding, and I can't imagine ever giving it up."

Chapter Seventeen

If we die, we want people to accept it. We're in a risky business, and we hope that if anything happens to us it will not delay the program. The conquest of space is worth the risk of life.

—Virgil "Gus" Grissom

January 27, 1967, Kennedy Space Center, Florida—
Virgil "Gus" Grissom, Roger Chaffee, and Ed White entered the Apollo spacecraft at 1:19 P.M. It was a routine test day in preparation for launch of Apollo 1, the first in a series of missions that would lead directly to the Moon. Many believed Grissom should and would command that first lunar landing.

The three astronauts settled into their seats wearing space suits and helmets—the same equipment they would wear at launch, scheduled for less than one month away.

Seated in their spacecraft, 220 feet high on top of the Saturn I booster at Pad 34 at the Kennedy Space Center, they connected their communication equipment and oxygen. It was Friday afternoon. It had been a long hard week and still had a long way to go.

This was what NASA termed a "plugs-out" test, meaning the umbilicals connecting the spacecraft and booster system to ground controls would be disconnected. The test would very closely resemble actual launch conditions. It would also be an opportunity to test the emergency egress system. Grissom, who was commander, had requested that. It took ninety seconds to open the hatch from the inside in an emergency. Grissom felt the crew needed to practice.

There was no fuel in the rocket. That wouldn't happen for another few weeks on February 21 when Apollo 1 was scheduled to launch. On January 27, 1967, with the launch date drawing very near, there were many problems with the command module that would carry the astronauts into space.

At 2:50 P.M. the hatch was closed, and the three astronauts lay on their seats facing straight up toward the sky. As commander, Grissom sat on the far left, with White in the middle and Chaffee on the right.

Betty Grissom had talked with her husband by telephone the night before. He told her he would be home Saturday. Her book, *Starfall,* describes the "plugs-out" test. "It was a heavy afternoon. Grissom, White, and Chaffee worked their way tediously down the preflight checklist, interrupted by a series of exasperating holds as the ground crew struggled to clear up minor, but recurrent, radio communications problems. At one point, Grissom's frustration boiled over. 'How do you expect to get us to the Moon if you people can't even hook us up with a ground station,' he demanded. 'Get with it out there.'"[1]

In fact, Grissom was very unhappy with the way Apollo 1 was progressing. He believed the spacecraft wasn't nearly ready. He believed people were rushing too fast. The last time he had been home in Houston, he had walked into his yard and picked a large lemon off a tree. He planned to place it, symbolically, on an Apollo command module—or a model of it.

At the Florida Space Center, technicians, scientists, and NASA officials were busy working in a blockhouse about one thousand feet away from the launch pad. As the day wore on, they were in a hold at T-minus ten minutes before the simulated launch, trying to correct a problem. The astronauts had been in the uncomfortable position, lying on their backs, for five hours.

A camera was focused on the spacecraft, connecting people in the blockhouse with the launch pad. At 6:31 P.M., people in the blockhouse saw a bright, white flash in the window of the spacecraft. "Fire in the spacecraft!" someone shouted. There were more shouts and static. Some people heard painful cries. A voice again shouted, "We're fighting a bad fire. Let's get out. Open her up."[2]

According to Donald "Deke" Slayton, director of flight crew operations, "Mostly it was Roger we were hearing. 'We're burning up! Get us out!' Then he screamed and that was it. We later figured it took eighteen seconds."[3]

The Grissom family, and others, would still later believe that it took much, much longer. "For awhile we were optimistic we could go in and get the crew out of there," Slayton says in his book *Deke!*. "I don't know how long it took to figure out that that was probably not too likely. Apparently it was just mass confusion up there . . . heat and toxic fumes all over the place. There was some worry the launch escape rocket mounted on the nose of the Apollo could be set off by the heat. So the pad crew just initially evacuated the area."[4]

Grissom, Chaffee, White. All three men died.

Back in Houston, the first indication that something had gone terribly wrong came when wives of NASA employees began arriving at the homes of Betty Grissom and Martha Chaffee. Husbands working at NASA had made frantic calls home with no explanation—"Just go!"

By the time the third woman arrived at Betty Grissom's home where she was preparing Friday night dinner for herself and her two sons, she understood that her life had changed. She had been the wife of an Air Force pilot for a long time. The fourth person to arrive was Dr. Charles Berry, head of medical services and chief physician to the astronauts. Berry told Betty what she already knew.

Astronaut Wally Schirra arrived later. He lived next door and had returned from the Kennedy Space Center. Betty Grissom had a question for him as soon as he walked in the door. "Did Gus get the lemon hung on that spacecraft?" she asked.[5]

It was the worst day in the history of NASA. There would ultimately be two others as equally bad. January 27, 1967, was all the more shocking because it did not occur during a flight when the unexpected can be expected. It had taken place during a test, a simulation that was supposed to conclude with people going home at the end of the day to wives and children.

As news was released to the public that Friday night, it was almost impossible to believe. But time and investigation would tell a different story. To insiders who knew what was taking place in the rush for the Moon, perhaps it was not all that hard to comprehend and understand.

Grissom's life had been racing toward this moment since he graduated from Purdue in 1950, over seventeen years before.

After Purdue and service in Korea, he continued to move forward in his career and at one point considered applying for membership in the elite Air Force precision flying group the Thunderbirds that had been formed in 1953.[6] He never did apply. He was heading in another direction, and things were moving very quickly.

In August 1955, Grissom was accepted into the Wright-Patterson Air Force Base Institute of Technology. He studied aeronautical engineering at the Institute and made a lifelong friendship with a fellow student and Air Force pilot named Gordon Cooper.

From Wright-Patterson both Grissom and Cooper advanced to Edwards Air Force Base in California for test pilot school. Grissom completed that program in 1957 and officially became a test pilot. It was a dream he had first considered during his days at Purdue. He was transferred back to Wright-Patterson for test pilot work.

"This was what I wanted all along," Grissom wrote in his book *Gemini.* "When I finished my studies and began the job of testing jet aircraft, well, there wasn't a happier pilot in the Air Force."[7]

In October 1957, the Soviet's launched *Sputnik,* and Gus and Betty Grissom, like millions of other people around the world, went out at night and tried to spot the satellite as it raced across the sky.

"Gus talked about *Sputnik,*" Betty says. "That was really a jolt. But he was busy working on an airplane they were developing. I remember one morning he said, 'Well I'm supposed to fly this plane today, but I don't know if it will even get off the ground.' He never said anything more about it, so I guess get he got off the ground.

"I don't think he ever really wanted to talk about work while he was home," Betty says. "He had enough of that during the day."[8]

In early 1958, the United States launched its own satellite. The space race was on, and no one was going to be satisfied with satellites orbiting Earth. People were going to have to fly into space.

In July 1958, the National Aeronautics and Space Administration (NASA) was created and the old National Advisory Committee for Aeronautics (NACA) was absorbed into it.

Developments continued at a rapid pace. In October 1958, Project Mercury was created to place a man into orbit and return him safely to Earth. NASA needed to develop technology to do that. It would also need to develop skilled, unflappable pilots who came to be called *astronauts.*

President Dwight Eisenhower narrowed the list for astronaut candidates. Since he saw space conquest as a military mission, he only wanted active duty military pilots. NASA added other qualifications. Candidates were to be younger than forty and no taller than five feet, eleven inches; they needed to have a college bachelor's degree or the equivalent, be in good health and physical shape, have at least 1,500 hours of flight time, and needed to be graduates of a test pilot school.[9] No women need apply, men only, although a separate application process was soon initiated for women and quickly canceled with little explanation.

The list of candidates was narrowed by the military services. In fact, out of about 200 million Americans at that time, 110 people were found to be qualified.[10] One of them was Gus Grissom.

In 1959, he was invited to apply for the space program. Grissom was at Wright-Patterson when the invitation arrived. It came in the form of a teletype message labeled "top secret." It did not explain what was taking place. Grissom recalls the day he received the message in *Gemini.* "It said that Captain Grissom would report to an address in Washington, D.C., by such and such an hour on such and such a date. What really intrigued me was the order that I should wear civilian clothing. . . . I was mystified . . . and the mystery wasn't much clarified by the instruction that I should discuss this assignment with no one. Just be there and no questions asked."[11]

A short time later Grissom was in Washington, wearing his civilian suit, wondering what was going on. He wrote, "The first person I met was a quiet-spoken sort of guy who told me he was with one of the government security agencies. He said I would shortly be in a room with a number of other people. On no account was I to say what my job was. . . . They began interviewing us privately, asking all sorts of odd-ball questions, some technical, some personal, all of them searching. . . . Finally they told me what it was all about. Nobody could order us into the space program; all of us could return to our regular assignments quietly with nobody the wiser. But it seemed I had somehow met their requirements and I was, as a result, 'invited' to join the Mercury program. 'Think it over; see how your wife feels; then let us know.'"[12]

In all, sixty-nine men had been invited to Washington, and fifty-six of them began the battery of tests and exams. By March, the number was whittled down to thirty-six who were invited to continue into the next round of examinations planned for Albuquerque, New Mexico. Thirty-two accepted.[13] Grissom remained in the running. He went home and told Betty he could still back out.

"Is it something you really want to do?" she asked.

"Yes," he said.

"Then do you even need to ask me?"[14]

After New Mexico, the next round of tests was at Wright-Patterson Air Force Base where Grissom was based. In *Starfall,* Betty says, "They took pressure suit tests, acceleration tests, heat tests, and noise tests. Each man had to prove endurance on treadmills and tilt tables, had his feet immersed in ice water, and blew up balloons until he was exhausted. . . . They had to live with two psychologists for a week and pass thirteen psychological tests for personality and motivation."[15]

The list of candidates was narrowed to eighteen with Grissom among them. NASA only wanted six, so there were more decisions to make. Unable to cut to six, they finally selected seven. The announcement was made public on April 9.

The night before Grissom, who was in Washington, called Betty to warn her about the upcoming press conference. "There might be a lot of reporters coming to the house," he said.

"I had the flu," Betty says. "I had a 102-degree temperature. So I went to the doctor, and he gave me a shot. We had a little grocery store near the house, I stopped, and while I was in the grocery these two guys came up and talked to me and said they were from *Life* magazine. They followed me back home."[16] *Life* would pay the Mercury 7 astronauts a total of $500,000 to be shared equally over four years for their personal stories and photographs.

When Betty got home, more reporters came through the door. It was a busy day. The families needed the money from *Life,* Betty says. The astronauts received standard military pay. "Thank goodness we got that money from *Life* for our personal stories," she says. "I don't think we could have made it without that. Gus had to buy a lot of civilian clothes. The astronauts did not wear uniforms. When they traveled their per diem did not cover their actual expenses, so that was more money of your pocket." As an Air Force captain, Grissom made a few hundred dollars a month.[17]

While it was clearly a risky program, Betty Grissom said she never considered expressing concern to her husband. "If you're married to a man who loves to fly, you have to let him fly," she says. "For Gus, this was just a natural progression."[18]

Perhaps not by coincidence, the Mercury 7 astronauts included three from the Air Force, three from the Navy, and one Marine. One of those Air Force pilots was Grissom's old friend Gordon Cooper.

On April 13, 1959, Grissom received his official orders. "Captain Virgil I. Grissom is relieved from assignment directorate of flight and all-weather testing, headquarters Wright Air Development Center [and is] assigned to Central Control Group, Headquarters U.S. Air Force, Washington, D.C., with permanent duty station Langley Research Center, Langley Air Force Base, Virginia, for duty with the National Aeronautics and Space Administration Space Task Group [Project Mercury]."[19] He was ordered to be at Langley on April 27.

There was a tremendous amount of work to do. The astronauts needed extensive training. There were spacecrafts to design and build along with rockets. There were tests of men and equipment. This work didn't always go well.

Deke Slayton, one of the Mercury 7, describes watching an unmanned Mercury test launch during which everything seemed to go wrong. "The countdown reaches zero . . . the Redstone [rocket] ignites for maybe two seconds, rises a couple inches, and then settles back down on the pad. Then the escape tower fires and blasts itself into the sky. Not the Mercury . . . just the tower. While we're standing there watching this fiasco, the housing on the nose of the Mercury flies off, spewing radar chaff and kicking out the parachute, just like it's supposed to do at splashdown! About ten seconds later, the escape tower comes crashing down onto the beach a few hundred yards away."[20]

Meanwhile, the Russians were also rushing into space and reports continued to filter back to the astronauts, and NASA engineers and scientists about successes on the other side of the world.

America would launch a man into space. The question was, when and who. There was considerable debate within NASA. The astronauts themselves were polled about their top choice.

According to Slayton, the astronauts were told a launch order on January 20, 1961. Alan Shepard would be first, followed by Grissom. John Glenn would be the backup for both flights.[21] Publicly, NASA only announced the names of the three finalists for the first flight and said the final decision had not yet been made and might not be made until just before the launch.[22]

In fact, the March 3, 1961, issue of *Life* magazine featured a cover that pictured Glenn, Grissom, and Shepard with this headline: "Astronaut First Team." Inside the issue was a photo of Glenn, Grissom, and Shepard with their wives and children, standing on a beach, watching a rocket launch at Cape Canaveral.

"Last week the world learned that one of these three would be chosen as the first American, and perhaps the first man, to be launched into space," Loudon S. Wainwright wrote in an accompanying article. "Sometime this spring either John Glenn or Virgil Grissom or Alan Shepard will climb into a small spacecraft on top of a Redstone rocket and wait for the most awesome journey man has ever taken. It will be the same sort of dangerous mission on which, according to persistent and believable reports, one or more of Russia's cosmonauts have already died. . . . Though all three men will be ready to do it, the one finally chosen will not be named until just before the flight. . . . The three members of the launch team have much in common. . . . But in terms of their individual approaches to life and to the mission that one of them will soon make, it would be difficult to find three more different men. All are brave and patriotic, and all are supremely willing and able to make the trip. But both by their own self-appraisals and by the appraisals of men who know them best, the similarities end right there."[23] The article almost placed the other four Mercury astronauts into an also-ran category. "The other three astronauts will still play a big part in Project Mercury," Wainwright wrote.

There were separate stories on Glenn, Grissom, and Shepard, and in this issue they were always listed and featured in that order. Grissom was pictured with his wife and children. In another shot, he was on the roof, repairing shingles of his home. He was called "a quiet little fellow who scoffs at the chance of becoming a hero."

> Virgil "Gus" Grissom, captain, USAF, is, at thirty-five, the youngest of the three man launch team. With his crew cut, short stature, and earnest face, he looks like TV's George Gobel. If any man of his experience in combat and test flying can be said to seem retiring, Grissom is that man. He is the easiest of the astronauts to overlook, a pleasant little fellow who doesn't appear to have much get-up-and-go. To the casual observer, he seems to be somewhat lost in the shadow of his larger and more outspoken colleagues. . . .
>
> But, as is true of John Glenn, Grissom's outward appearance is deceptive. . . . Grissom is simply not interested in making himself noticed and he refuses to take himself too seriously. He doesn't talk unless he has something to say and his comments are always exactly to the point. . . .
>
> Asked . . . the difference between the astronauts and other historic pioneers, he scoffed. "There's a big difference between us and Columbus and Lindbergh and the Wright brothers and all these people we're compared to. They did it themselves. We didn't think up this thing. We're just going to ride the spacecraft."
>
> "This is the best thing that ever happened to me," he says. "By the time I got into test work, it was dying out. It wasn't really flight test at all; it was mostly testing new gadgets. Here's a big new project with noth-

> ing but future. It's the first step in a great program that will go on as long as there are people. . . . Most people who know me know I'm not the hero type. Personal prestige, I couldn't care less about. Sure I want to make a success out of my military career, and this won't hurt that. But the notoriety the first man gets will only last for a little while and in a year or two the excitement of this will be forgotten in bigger things. . . . I've always been reasonably competent and whenever I've started out with something new, I've been concerned that I won't perform like the big boys. I'm always surprised to find I can do as well as anybody else. I know I'm going to be scared when I get in there, but I don't worry about my feelings and I'm not worried about being scared. I won't be scared very long. I know it's going to work."
>
> . . . The Grissoms live simply, like the country folks they are. . . . They are neither partygoers nor party-throwers. "Betty and I run our lives as we please," Grissom explains. "We don't care anything about fads or frills or the PTA. We don't give a damn about the Joneses."
>
> . . . The only astronaut ever to beat [Grissom] at [handball] is Al Shepard . . . and the other astronauts suggest that Grissom let Shepard win one game just because he wanted to so badly. That would not be like Gus Grissom. He is a stubborn competitor and Shepard is another astronaut. Each member of this unique group, in spite of any genuine camaraderie or solidarity, is interested in winning for himself. This interest applies particularly to the first flights. Asked a question about the strength of his desire for this, Grissom said, "Everything I do is influenced by it. With everything I do, I expect it. I'm here to ride the spacecraft."[24]

Scott, the Grissom's oldest son, says he believes the three finalists for the first flight amounted to a political decision. Shepard was a Navy man, Grissom was Air Force, and Glenn was a Marine. All three branches were covered. Shepard became the ultimate choice for the first American in space, he says, because the new president, John F. Kennedy, was a Navy man.[25] Others cite Shepard's capabilities, which were excellent. All three men were excellent.

Shepard launched on May 5, 1961. It was a fifteen-minute flight, and it was a complete success. There was only one setback. The Russians had launched cosmonaut Yuri Gagarin on April 12. In the view of some, America was losing the space race and the political pressure to get ahead was enormous. In fact, *Life* had forecast that the Russians would probably put a man in space first. They further speculated in that March 3, 1961 article that the U.S. space program would reach the Moon in 1972.

President Kennedy would move that timetable forward in a speech delivered in May 1961—after Shepard's flight—when he proposed landing an American on the Moon and returning him safely to earth within the decade.

Grissom was disappointed he was not the first American in space, but he knew he would have his day. And it arrived quickly.[26]

Grissom's flight was scheduled for July 18. Betty did not go to Florida. Her husband did not want her at the space center, watching, in the event that something happened. He didn't want her to see it in person. He wanted her away from reporters and TV cameras. Betty stayed home in Virginia and was joined by two other astronaut wives. They watched the launch on television.

There were weather problems. The flight was scrubbed and reset for July 21. Astronaut wives again joined Betty to watch on television. Newsmen and cameras set up in front of the house. Betty was able to talk to Gus on the telephone while he was in the spacecraft waiting for launch. "I'm fine," he told her. "In fact, if they'd stop yakking at me over that radio, I might just take a nap."[27]

Betty probably had as many problems to deal with as her husband. "When Al Shepherd's flight happened, the press kind of did some damage to his house," Betty says. "So before his flight, Gus went down, and he talked to the police department, and they sent out officers to the house. They had their dogs, and they went up and down each side of the house and kept the press out in the street. But there was another house with a driveway that had a view into our house. Well, the press got very smart, and they went around over there so they could look in."[28]

The launch went perfectly, without a problem, until some time after Grissom and his *Liberty Bell 7* spacecraft hit the ocean water. While waiting for helicopters to arrive and pick him up, the hatch blew off his spacecraft and water started pouring in.

"I just made two moves," Grissom would later say, "both of them instinctive. I tossed off my helmet and grabbed the right edge of the instrument panel and hoisted myself through the hatch. I have never moved faster in my life. The next thing I knew, I was floating high in my suit with the water up to my armpits."[29]

The spacecraft was taking water and sinking. Grissom's suit was also taking water, and he very nearly drowned before being rescued by helicopter crews. The helicopters were not able to lift *Liberty Bell 7* because it had filled with water. They left it to sink into the ocean. It was the only aircraft Grissom ever lost.

There was immediate controversy about what had happened, and it has intensified over the years. Inside the spacecraft there was an emergency plunger that, when hit, would explode the hatch open. It took a five-pound blow to do it. Some people said Grissom hit the plunger, blowing the hatch—intentionally or accidentally. Others say it was a malfunction and that everyone who hit the plunger ended up with a bruised hand. Grissom's hand was not bruised.

"I did not do anything wrong," Grissom told Betty. "That hatch just blew."[30] The spacecraft was recovered in 1999, and physical evidence supports Grissom's statement.

Grissom hated losing the spacecraft. All pilots hate to lose their vehicle. Betty says it was the media who made an issue out of the blown hatch, much more so than the people at NASA. If NASA had been unhappy with her husband, she says, he wouldn't have been so highly regarded and given more top assignments. The media, she says, would not let it drop.

Thomas Wolfe, in his book *The Right Stuff*, was particularly hard on the Grissoms unfairly, the family says. "Tom Wolfe came right here to my house and sat in the living room in his little white suit," Betty says. "He picked on us. He was going pick on somebody. He picked on us because Gus was dead. The only things that he got right in his book came from my book."[31]

Immediately after the *Liberty Bell 7* flight, Betty and the boys were flown from Virginia to Florida to be with Gus. There was a short ceremony and news conference at Patrick Air Force Base. There would be no visit to the White House—an event that had followed Shepard's launch.

According to *Starfall*, "Later Betty felt letdown. Somehow her husband had not been adequately recognized for dedicated work under pressure, which had made him almost a stranger to his family [during long absences]. After the press conference the family was driven to a guesthouse in VIP quarters at Patrick Air Force Base."[32]

The guesthouse was poorly located, Betty says. It was across a major highway from the beach where the boys wanted to swim. It was isolated. There was no one there, no TV. And Grissom informed them that he wouldn't be with them—he was due back at work the next morning. Betty didn't even have a car. She asked her husband to move them to a nearby Holiday Inn where other astronauts and their families were staying and where there was better access to the beach. He did. They had a nice stay.[33]

Betty has had disagreements with NASA over the years, which have intensified. "One thing that bothered me right at the very beginning with NASA, they wouldn't even let the families on the Cape—period," she says. "Well, Gus took us one night. We had the kids in the back seat, all covered up with a blanket or something. It was about midnight and at the guards gate they just waved him on through. He always said they knew those kids were back there because the blanket was probably wiggling. We were kind of disgusted with NASA's rules and regulations. NASA and the Air Force were very male organizations at that time. They didn't seem to deal with women very well. They didn't seem to understand women." During Grissom's Gemini flight, Betty would be asked to visit the Houston Command Center for media photos. She asked if she could bring her two sons. NASA said, "No." So Betty said she would stay home. NASA called right back and told her to bring the kids.[34]

In 1962, the astronauts and their families moved to Houston. The Grissoms liked Texas. They lived a normal life, in spite of Gus's international fame.

In January 1963, Grissom was assigned to command the first Gemini manned mission. The sixth and last Mercury mission was May 15, 1963. All the Mercury 7 astronauts flew accept for Slayton, who had been medically grounded shortly after his selection.

The Mercury flights were one-man missions. Gemini involved two astronauts, titled commander and pilot. Gemini was the next step along the way in reaching the Moon. There would be twelve Gemini flights. The objectives were to test men and equipment in flights of up to two weeks; to rendezvous and dock with another vehicle in orbit; and to perfect a system of returning on land instead of water.

The concept of returning on land was dropped in 1964. Gemini 1 and 2 were unmanned.

Grissom was commander of Gemini 3 with a new astronaut, John Young, as pilot. For this mission Grissom named his space spacecraft *Molly Brown.* A popular Broadway play and 1964 movie was "The Unsinkable Molly Brown." Everyone understood what he meant.

Launch was March 23, 1965. The flight lasted just under five hours, and the spacecraft orbited Earth three times. It did not sink in the ocean, and the mission was a total success.

The program moved rapidly. There were five more Gemini launches within a year. There were four more between June and November 1966. Twenty months after Grissom's first manned Gemini flight, the project was complete. It was time for Apollo and the Moon as NASA worked at a fast pace to keep Kennedy's timetable.

In 1966, before Gemini ended, Grissom was already at work on the Apollo program. He had been named commander of the first manned Apollo mission. The first launch was scheduled for February 1967, three months after the end of Gemini. At NASA, they called this "go-fever."

On Apollo 1, Grissom would be joined by Ed White, who had performed the first, spectacular U.S. space walk on Gemini 4, and fellow Purdue graduate Roger Chaffee. Chaffee had been on a fast track since leaving Purdue in 1957. It was about to get a lot faster. Swept up in the excitement over the Mercury launches of Shepard, Grissom, and Glenn, Chaffee had decided to give the space program a try. In 1962, when NASA announced it would begin accepting applications from a new group of astronauts, Chaffee applied. The process began in October with about 1,800 applicants.

"He started talking about it while we were stationed in Florida during 1962," Martha Chaffee, his wife, says. "He mentioned it several times that it had really been a goal of his. I think his squadron commander in Jacksonville put his name in. I was very excited about it. I was going to meet John Glenn and all those wonderful people. That's what I was excited about. I was going to meet all those people who had done such wonderful things."[35]

This would be the third class of astronauts selected. Martha Chaffee says the elimination process was tough. It was "humiliating," her husband would say. "They used to humiliate you every minute."[36]

The final astronauts selected were introduced in October 1963, a year after the process began. "We were at Wright-Patterson in Ohio," Martha says. "Roger came back from Houston after the last interview.

He knew they would let him know in a week or so. He decided to go hunting with a friend. They went bow-and-arrow hunting, and I thought, they're not going hunting. They're going camping. And that's exactly what he was doing. He just had to get away from the telephones. NASA actually did call before he got back, but they wouldn't tell me anything, which is understandable. And of course, I didn't know who had called. I just knew that the man I talked to at NASA had asked for Roger. It drove me batty. And then when he got home, he had to wait for them to call back. They finally called and told him he was in the program, but he couldn't say anything to anybody."[37]

The announcement was made October 18, 1963. There were others he knew in the group, including fellow Purdue alumnus Eugene Cernan, a fellow Navy aviator.

"It was all very exciting," Martha says. "As a matter of fact, Roger was home for Halloween, and we dressed our little son who was only about eighteen months as an astronaut."[38]

The family moved to Houston in January 1964 and soon bought a house. The Cernans lived next door and a number of other astronaut families were in the neighborhood.

In his book, *Last Man on the Moon,* Cernan says, " Roger had been a year behind me at the Naval ROTC program at Purdue and I really didn't know him during our early years as naval aviators. But when we were both among the fourteen astronauts announced in October of 1963, our lives became linked. When all else fails, line up alphabetically—Cernan then Chaffee. In the official group photo and on many other occasions, he was right beside me. . . . Roger was a workaholic, and I guess we all were. . . .We often hunted together. . . .

"At parties, Roger would challenge others to do the broom trick. He held a broom out in front of him horizontally, stepped over it, wiggled it up behind him and over his head, coming back to the starting position without ever releasing either hand. . . . We shared rental cars, hotel rooms, and often the same airplane. . . . On many a Friday night, coming home from a week-long training mission in a [two-seat] T-38, Roger and I would buzz our houses just before turning sharply left, landing at Ellington Air Force Base. From as far as San Antonio we would point the needle nose of our plane directly at the driveway separating our houses and roar over Barbuda Lane, shaking the shingles and rattling the dishes. . . . The noisy message let our wives [and neighbors] know we would be home soon. We would land, jump into our cars, and race down the two-lane Old Galveston Highway, through the single stoplight in the town of Webster, at eighty miles per hour and screech up to our houses in less than ten minutes. It was somewhat illegal but . . . we were astronauts!"[39]

"The men were very busy," Martha says. "You know, Roger would come home on Fridays and leave on Sundays. That first year was all training, survival training, everything. They went to the jungles of Panama. They'd go off and study geology. They weren't home much at all."[40]

Chaffee was focused on going to the Moon. He wanted to be on a Moon mission. "He had a map of the Moon in his office, and I would point out places and he would name them," Martha says. "He knew it very well, and he really wanted to go. He loved working with Gus and Ed. It was a really good crew. They complemented one another and they were all very dedicated. They all spent a lot of time out in California where that command module was being built."[41]

The crew was good, but there were problems with the command module. Grissom was especially vocal about his concerns. In his book, *Apollo: The Epic Journey to the Moon,* David West Reynolds writes, "[The] Apollo spacecraft was having serious technical problems. North American [the contractor] was having trouble meeting deadlines and getting everything in the spacecraft to function according to specifications. Grissom, normally the last person to say much of anything, openly criticized the spacecraft's failings. . . . In order to meet deadlines, the manufacturer was even shipping unfinished assemblies to the Cape where more work would need to be done. . . . The Apollo spacecraft was simply a much bigger beast than its predecessors. The magnitude of it was taxing everyone, even the NASA management team working with North American. Resources were not the issue, since Congress had provided a sufficient budget to accomplish the project's goal. But time and personnel could only stretch so far, and all were driven by the Russians into 'go-fever' determined to make progress no matter what."[42]

Grissom spoke very little about the space program at home. Betty was aware of his frustrations. Chaffee was also concerned. "A very good friend of mine who lived out in California was like a sister to Roger," Martha says. "He complained more to her than to me because they would meet sometimes for lunch out there. Since he was right there with the problem, he would talk about it. He didn't bring his problems home. I knew that there were a lot of problems. But he didn't go into depth. They were in a hurry. There was lots of pressure."[43]

On New Year's Day, 1967, the Purdue astronauts were at the Rose Bowl in Pasadena where the Boilermaker football team was making its first appearance. There was a Purdue float in the parade with the names of alumni—Chaffee, Grissom, Cernan, and Armstrong. Armstrong had been selected in the second astronaut group and flew as commander of a Gemini mission.

"Roger was able to take some time off, and we went and visited my parents in Oklahoma," Martha says. "We had a wonderful, wonderful Christmas. We had such a good time, and we knew that as soon as we got home from this short trip that he would be gone constantly. The launch was set for February 21, and when we got home, they started to install this little black box in our home so we could listen to the communications. Things were getting really exciting.

"The Sunday before the accident he came home, and the kids and I picked him up at Ellington Field. We went directly from church to Ellington. We picked him up and went home. He thought he was going to have to leave that night so we would just have the day together. But they called and said he didn't have to leave until the next morning. He left Monday morning. The following Saturday, Field Enterprises was going to have a big dance they had every year for the astronauts. I talked to Roger on Thursday night, and he said he didn't think he'd be home to take me to the dance. But he wanted me to go anyway—maybe with Gene and Barbara Cernan. He said they were going to do some testing. We just had a very nice visit on the telephone that Thursday night. He was killed the next day."[44]

Friday evening, the wives of astronauts and other NASA spouses started dropping by the Chaffee home. One friend stopped and said she needed to borrow some silverware. Another just stopped to talk. They didn't leave. Martha's first thought was that there couldn't be anything wrong. Roger was not flying. It was only a test. When the NASA officials finally arrived, Martha could see what had happened in their faces. It was a long night.

Gene Cernan flew in from California. "He arrived late, and I remember he hadn't eaten, so people were fixing him something to eat," Martha says. "He was still in his flight suit. He just took over from there on. He was wonderful. And Barbara Cernan was right there the whole time, too. It was so comforting to have such close friends. The astronaut program is like a fraternity, and they all come and group around you. For a long time, I was protected.

"It doesn't hit you until maybe a month later whenever things start getting back to normal, when the other husbands were coming home on Friday nights," she says. "Fridays to Sundays were the longest and the hardest to get through."[45]

Betty Grissom says what she misses most are the phone calls from Gus. That's mostly what she had once the space program began—telephone calls.[46] *Starfall* describes the scene at the launch pad during the final simulated countdown. "The two hours and twenty-five minutes scheduled before the simulated launch time stretched through the afternoon. It was past six o'clock when the ground controllers called another hold at T-minus ten minutes to resolve another pesky communications problem.

"At five seconds before 6:31 P.M. something happened—an infinitesimal change in the electrical heartbeat of the spacecraft. External displays showed a change in voltage to the instrumentation system for a fraction of a second, no more than the static on a car radio from a poor spark suppressor. Another instrument indicated loss of voltage on an alternating current bus, an interruption of power that lasted about two and a half seconds.

"Apparently at that moment, somewhere in thirty miles of wiring, one segment arced across another with a spark of fire. . . . For not quite ten seconds, the spark smoldered there in the left forward corner of the spacecraft, out of sight beneath Grissom's feet and his couch. Then, apparently, the first tongue of flame became visible. At 6:31:04, Grissom yelled 'Hey!'

"Flames spurted up the inside wall of the spacecraft and across the top of the space-suited astronauts, feeding white hot and smokeless in the pure oxygen at high pressure, feeding upon the Styrofoam padding, nylon netting, spacesuit fabric, and Velcro."[47] The pressure inside became so strong it ruptured the spacecraft on the right, base side.

The hatch was opened five minutes and twenty seconds after the fire started. Officially, NASA would say the astronauts died in seconds—but not from burns. Officially, they died from carbon monoxide gas inhalation and other noxious fumes.

The space program was put on hold during an investigation conducted by NASA. No exact cause of the fire was ever determined. According to *Starfall,* "They came close to finding it, but in the final frustration they were unable to define exactly which wire caused the fatal spark, and who or what was responsible for it. The fire had burned hottest where it started and destroyed the evidence of its own origin. For the thousands of people in NASA and North America . . . it would have been far simpler if the fire source and a personal scapegoat could have been found because the review board, in its search, uncovered a host of techniques and procedures that had been going wrong."[48]

The Grissoms do not agree with the official reports and have been at odds with NASA for a number of years. They are petitioning Congress to reopen the investigation "into possible acts of sabotage, homicide, and collusion to suppress evidence."

Scott has gone through the burned command module. He says he located a switch on the control board that had been tampered with, causing the fire. As he went through the scorched module and all its parts, he found a switch with a clearly fabricated metal plate behind it—a potentially very dangerous plate that didn't belong there.

He further believes NASA had to know about this evidence and suppressed it. The Grissoms also say their own pathology investigations indicate the astronauts lived much longer than the official reports indicate.[49]

NASA stands behind the original investigation.

Scott and Betty Grissom remain in Houston. Martha Chaffee has moved to New Mexico. Purdue offered the two Grissom and two Chaffee children scholarships. Scott and Mark Grissom took advantage of the offer and went through Purdue's aviation technology program. Scott is now a commercial pilot. Mark is an air traffic controller. Scott's daughter, Carly also attends Purdue. The university named buildings on the campus for both Roger Chaffee and Gus Grissom. Roger and Martha's daughter, Cheryl, works for NASA.

The accident remains a part of the lives of all the families. Media reporters call them on major anniversaries—five years, ten years, twenty-five years. They were called for comment after the *Challenger* and *Columbia* accidents.

"Our son Steve asked me once, he said, 'Mom, what was dad really like?'" Martha says. "He was only four and a half. He doesn't really remember. I told him, 'Your dad was a very, very kind person. He expected a lot out of people, but yet he liked to have fun.' There isn't a day that goes by that I don't think about him."[50]

Neil Armstrong remembers Grissom as, "a hard-nosed engineer, taciturn. He had strong positions on what should and should not be done. He was a contributor. He was probably Deke Slayton's number one lieutenant. If Deke wanted to get something done, he'd put Gus on the job."[51]

"Gus was good at what he did," Cernan says. "If something had to be done, he went out and did it. He knew where he was going and how he was going to get there."

"There were major improvements to that Apollo spacecraft after the fire," he says. "I have always believed if it had not been for this fire, we might never have gotten to the Moon. If it had not happened when it did, an accident could have—and most likely would have—taken place somewhere in space.

"And that might have terminated the program before we even got started."[52]

Mark Polansky

Mark Polansky grew up in the 1960s, in Edison, New Jersey, just a half hour out of New York City.

The space program was part of his life as a child. He watched the launches and was caught up in all the excitement in the days when network television covered the events live. And then there was the big event.

"I remember all the launches and watching them and just being amazed with this as a child and thinking it was really neat," Polansky says. "I remember playing spaceman as a child. You know, my parents would get a new refrigerator or washing machine, or something like that, and we'd take the old cardboard box, throw it in the cellar, and turn it into a spaceship.

"And what really excited me was when I was thirteen years old, and we landed on the Moon. I was at a baseball game in Yankee Stadium. The moment they announced it, the game just stopped. They stopped the game, announced it, and everybody cheered. The whole place sang 'God Bless America.'"

He still gets goose bumps just thinking about it.

"The whole place was just going wild," Polansky said. "And that night I was staying at my grandmother's place in Manhattan. I remember that the space walk came on kind of late, but I got to stay up and watch Neil Armstrong come down the ladder. Wow! I just couldn't believe it. It was just so exciting. It was just so exciting to think that we were actually on the Moon. I thought, gee, wouldn't it be great to do that. You know, I looked out the window and saw the Moon and thought about the fact that there were really people there. It was just such a great feeling. It was a very patriotic kind of thing, too, in those days.

"As a kid I was really interested in exploration, science," Polansky says. "I didn't know what I wanted to do, but I thought it would be kind of like a great avenue to explore. I used to read the science-fiction books, and I thought a lot about it."

He enrolled at Purdue in the fall of 1974. He picked Purdue because a friend was considering it, so he visited West Lafayette and liked it. The friend ended up at the Air Force Academy, but Polansky ended up at Purdue. And that's where, during his freshman year, he met Gene Cernan, a Purdue graduate who had just flown the last manned mission to the Moon.

"I lived in Cary Quad [residence hall], and he came through and was giving a talk in one of the lounges," Polansky says. "It was a very informal thing, just a group of students—probably about fifty to one hundred students crowding this lounge. I was five feet away from a guy who had walked on the Moon. I was just in awe of this individual. I thought, you know, somebody's got to do these things. Why not me? After that, I started looking at being an astronaut a little more seriously. I asked myself, what do the astronauts do? I looked at most of their bios, and most all of them were military test pilots. So I went backwards and said, 'Well, you have to be a military test pilot, you have to join the military and become a pilot.' So I went into the Air Force ROTC my sophomore year."

Polansky was a physics major at Purdue. "I liked physics," he says. "But it didn't like me." So at the end of the second semester of his sophomore year he transferred to aeronautical engineering—which he loved.

During his senior year he was active in the Old Masters program, which brings successful people to campus to meet with students. Polansky acted as a guide for Joe Allen during the Old Masters program. Allen had graduated from DePauw University in Greencastle, Indiana, and was an Indiana native.

There are three 1978 Purdue graduates who are astronauts—Mark Polansky, Greg Harbaugh, and David Wolf. "I knew both of them," Polansky says. "That's pretty amazing." He worked with Harbaugh on Old Masters.

Polansky received his master's degree from Purdue in December 1978. After leaving Purdue, Polansky went through pilot training and was sent to Langley Air Force Base in Virginia to fly the F-15.

"That was a great assignment, and I was just enjoying the life," Polansky says. "I really remember how enjoyable the flying on the east coast was and flying a fighter like an F-15. It was great to have the responsibility to go ahead and be a flight leader. I remember how cool it was be to be twenty-four or twenty-five years old and be in charge of a flight of four $20 million fighters coming back from a successful mission. I just thought, you know, your average twenty-four year old doesn't get to do these things. I was living life large and enjoying being an Air Force fighter pilot."

When he reached one thousand hours of flight, he put in an application to test pilot school at Edwards Air Force Base.

"And to my utter surprise, I got in the first time I applied," he says. He began to think he might actually have a shot at becoming an astronaut.

"I had a great year at Edwards, and served as a test pilot down in Florida and had an enjoyable five years there," Polansky says. "And that's when I was finally able, for the first time, to apply to the program." He applied in 1989.

"Again to my surprise, the first time I turned in the application they said, come on down for an interview. And the more I saw and the more I spoke with people, the more I said, 'You know, gosh, I really want to do this.' And then to my disappointment, I didn't get in.

"I know that is common, but you know, I had lead a very charmed life. I didn't have a problem getting good grades. I didn't have a problem getting the fighter assignments I wanted. I wasn't really used to a lot of rejection. So it was disappointing. But I thought it was a really good lesson in life, you know, about humility and how you handle yourself when things don't go your way. I had a really good job in the Air Force, so I stuck with that, and applied again for the next astronaut selection, which was 1992. I didn't even get asked to interview that year. So I almost shelved my dream. I thought, well, you know, the first year you apply, you get asked to interview. The second year you apply, you don't even get asked to interview. They're trying to tell you something—like, 'We've seen you, and thanks for coming, but you're really not our type.'"

He stayed with the Air Force, and one day received an unusual telephone call.

"It was from a good friend of mine who worked for NASA and had just been selected as an astronaut in the 1992 group," Polansky says. "He said that there was a group of pilots out there, and they were looking to add to their work force and my name had come up. Was I interested? And without even knowing a lot about it, I went, interviewed, talked with some folks, and discovered it was a good career move. So I came to NASA in 1992, just as a pilot. I got to fly with a lot of astronauts as an instructor. And it was really interesting work."

He taught the landing techniques of flying a shuttle.

"We fly shuttle training aircraft, which is a modified Gulf Stream, so it lands like a space shuttle," Polansky says. "You take it up to about twenty-eight thousand feet, and you dive into the runway, just like the space shuttle does. The astronauts fly left seat, and the instructor pilot flies right seat. I did that for a couple years, and it was very rewarding. I got to work just about every launch and landing."

Friends encouraged him to apply for the astronaut program a third time. He put them off saying last time he didn't even get an interview. "That doesn't mean anything," people told him. "Besides, all they can say is no." In 1995, he applied a third time. He was interviewed. He didn't make it.

"I said, 'Well, I think I've had enough,'" Polansky says. But his friends said no! One more time.

"I've got a lot of good friends in the astronaut office, and they were really on me to try again," Polansky says. "So I said, one more time. But this one was a little bit emotional. You know, nobody likes to be told no repeatedly. You go through a very thorough physical which is not a lot of fun. And the other thing was, there were some other avenues of life I wanted to experience. I wanted to go and get an M.B.A. I had put that off because I didn't want to start school and interrupt it in the middle and go to something else. So I applied to an M.B.A. program at the University of Houston. I got accepted to that a couple of weeks before they released the results for my astronaut class. And, you know, life's funny. When I finally said, 'Look, if I never get selected to be an astronaut, that's okay, I can live with that,' that's when I got picked." The year was 1996.

Polansky flew STS-98 in February 2001—twenty-three years after leaving Purdue with a dream to go into space.

"The most emotional moment that I had on the entire mission was the first time I got to look out the window," he says. "One of the mission specialists had told me to make sure that I didn't miss out on some of the experiences of being in space. She made sure that she put me in the overhead window and had me look at Earth for a couple of minutes. And it was the most breathtaking sight. I mean to see the curvature of the earth, to see the deep blues of the ocean, and the whites of the clouds, the browns of land masses, and then the blackness right above the thin atmosphere layer juxtaposed with this very bright, bright object of the earth, you would see total black. It was the color black like I'd never seen before. It was a very emotional thing. And then all of a sudden you just think, I'm here, I'm really, really here. You know, I've wanted to do this for so long—all your hopes and dreams and everything else, and then, you're really there. Wow!

"I felt very attached to Earth from space. You look at the earth, and you fly over troubled places on the earth. We'd fly over the Middle East, and it was just a jewel, it looked so beautiful. And you'd just sit there, and you almost want to cry, knowing the kind of stuff that happens back on the planet. You just wonder how people can be so cruel when you're up there looking at all this beauty. I'll never forget that first moment—and then it was back to work, and I never had another good chance to really look at Earth again until much later in the mission because of how busy we were."

Polansky is scheduled as pilot on STS-117 and will perform two space walks. The flight was put on hold following loss of the Shuttle *Columbia* and its crew.

Chapter Eighteen

Once you walk on the Moon you can never 'unwalk.' No one can ever take that step away from you. It's a unique opportunity, but it carries a responsibility as well. You're one of twelve human beings who have lived and called another planet in this universe home—and I refer to the Moon as a planet because that's what it felt like for me after three days. You have a responsibility to make sure that other people know what it was like. What did it look like? What did it feel like? Were we scared? Did we feel closer to God? People want to know. I tell them it's really not so much what we saw as what we felt—the almost spiritual experience of standing on the Moon.

—Eugene Cernan

It was after 3:00 P.M. Houston time on Sunday, July 20, 1969. Neil Armstrong and Edwin "Buzz" Aldrin were standing in their lunar module, *Eagle.* They were flying—uniquely down—toward the Moon. The *Eagle* had first separated from the command module, *Columbia,* in an upside-down position, and as it descended it pitched from side to side, but in the weightlessness of space, it didn't matter to the astronauts.

Everything had been tested and retested in the Apollo program. The lunar module had flown before. But it had never landed on the Moon, and it had never launched from the Moon. Over the next day, these possibilities would be attempted for the first time in actual lunar conditions.

It had been eight years and two months since President John F. Kennedy proposed landing a man on the Moon and returning him safely to Earth within the decade. The decade was drawing to a close. The "go-fever" rush of NASA had reached this moment. At mission control in Houston, everyone fell silent. People were barely breathing.

There had been alarms on the lunar module—several of them. Computers were overloading. Steve Bales at mission control was the guidance officer. The decision to go or abort was his. Some top people at NASA thought it was all over, but Bales made his decision instantly. "Go. . ." It would by okay. He was twenty-six years old, about the average age of the people manning monitors in the control room that day.[1]

As the astronauts skimmed over the surface of the Moon, reading instruments and looking out large triangular windows, Armstrong realized the computer guidance system was taking them down in an area filled with large boulders. He took over manual control as had been planned. He looked for a place to land, and as he searched, Aldrin rattled out numbers providing information about their descent. Houston radioed information concerning remaining fuel:

> Charlie Duke [Houston Control]: Sixty seconds of fuel.
> Aldrin: Okay. Seventy-five feet. And it's looking good. Down a half, six forward. . . .
> Aldrin: Sixty feet, down two and a half. [Pause] Two forward. Two forward. That's good. . . .
> Aldrin: Forty feet, down two and a half. Picking up some dust.
> Aldrin: Thirty feet, two and a half down. [Garbled] Shadow . . .
> Aldrin: Four forward, four forward. Drifting to the right a little. Twenty feet, down a half . . .
> Duke: Thirty seconds . . .
> Aldrin: Drifting forward just a little bit; that's good. . . .[2]

Standing in the lunar module, working the controls, Armstrong's heart rate hit 150 beats per minute.

The landing radar on the lunar module had been made by Ryan Aeronautical whose chairman was T. Claude Ryan. Forty-two years earlier his Ryan Airlines had built the *Spirit of St. Louis* for Charles Lindbergh. Ryan believed Armstrong and Lindbergh had a lot in common, including "great self-confidence."[3]

People in Houston Control watching computer monitors and people around the world watching television knew two things: time was running out and the lunar module hadn't landed. There was hushed silence listening to the voices calling from another world. As Charlie Duke would later say, everyone was about turning blue.

Armstrong was at peak performance. No one at Houston could see what he was doing, but he knew exactly what to do and how he would accomplish it. He had trained hard for this moment. He was not about to come this close to the Moon and fail. In a sense, Neil Armstrong had prepared for this moment his entire life, going back to Purdue University and even before.

As he approached his January 1955 graduation from Purdue, Armstrong's vision was still set on a career in aeronautical engineering design, but his military experience had given him a lot of opportunities to fly. He was rethinking. He was becoming interested in flight testing, which combined his aeronautical engineering and aviator experience.

He had learned about the fascinating work being done by the National Advisory Committee for Aeronautics (NACA) in their research airplane program at Edwards, California.

He applied to the NACA installation at Edwards for a piloting job. They didn't have any openings. He was looking for other alternatives and interviewing with people from various aeronautical organizations when he received a call from the NACA laboratory in Cleveland. They asked if they could talk to him about a possible position there. NACA Edwards had forwarded his application to the other laboratories. He interviewed with NACA on the campus and accepted an offer at Cleveland.[4] He went right to work and loved it, learning a great deal in the process.

After about six months, an opening appeared at NACA Edwards. They contacted him to see if he would be interested in that position. He accepted the transfer to Edwards in the summer of 1955.[5]

At Edwards he met fellow Purdue graduate Kincheloe.[6] In late 1955, NACA and the Air Force tentatively let the contract for building of the X-15 aircraft. At that time, NACA announced three pilots, the Air Force two and the Navy one, to be the initial X-15 pilot team. Armstrong was the junior member of the NACA team. Kincheloe was the senior member of the Air Force team.[7]

Armstrong's career advanced very quickly. The X-15 in the late 1950s was simply the hottest airplane in the sky. Some people were talking about it as more than airplane. "There was a lot of conversation in the popular press about the X-15 being the first spacecraft," Armstrong says. "It wasn't in today's sense of what space is. But at that time when airplanes had only flown to a little over Mach 2 [two times the speed of sound], an airplane that could go outside the atmosphere, and fly three times as fast as anything that had flown before, was certainly space flight in the imagination of most people. And indeed, in a technical sense, it had all the same characteristics as a spacecraft. It was, I think, properly categorized as a spacecraft."[8]

In a foreward to the book *At the Edge of Space,* by fellow X-15 pilot Milton Thompson, Armstrong wrote, "The X-15 was to be capable of a speed of 6,600 feet per second and an altitude of 250,000 feet. It was to carry a pilot and a payload of 800 pounds of research instruments and recorders. At the time is seemed audacious. It had taken half a century for aircraft to reach Mach 2 and 80,000 feet. Now, one new design would attempt to triple those achievements. The X-15 would accomplish all its goals and more. In 199 flights over nearly a decade, it would become the most successful research airplane in history."[9]

The X-15 was taken up under the wing of a huge B-52 bomber. It was released in flight, its engine fired, and when it had expended all its fuel it glided to the dry lakebeds at Edwards Air Force Base. Thompson says, "One very unusual thing about the visibility of the X-15 windows was that the pilot could not see any part of the airplane. He could not see the nose, he could not see the wings—nothing."[10]

Armstrong flew the X-15 for twenty months from November 30, 1960, to July 26, 1962, taking seven flights. In the X-15, he hit Mach 5.74 or 3,989 miles per hour. He reached a maximum altitude of 207,500 feet. He was the seventh pilot to fly the plane and the third to leave the program.[11]

Armstrong wasn't the only Purdue person flying the X-15. Only twelve pilots flew the plane and two of them were connected to Purdue. The second Boilermaker was William "Pete" Knight.

Knight is a year older than Armstrong and was born in 1929 in Noblesville, Indiana, just north of Indianapolis. The family moved to Ohio when he was young, but he continued spending summers on his parents' Indiana farm. In 1947, he graduated from high school in Mansfield, Ohio. As a boy he wanted to be a horse trainer or a pilot. Upon graduation, he set his sights on being a patent attorney.

Knight enrolled at Butler University in Indianapolis, but transferred to an extension of Purdue in Indianapolis in 1950. He was switching his career to engineering. "I figured if I was going to get into engineering, Purdue would be the place to go," he says.[12]

Knight spent one year as a Purdue student before being drafted for the Korean conflict in December 1950, six months after the action started. He had an option to join the Air Force so he did. He went into a cadet program and received flight training. He graduated as a second lieutenant in March 1953.

Knight ended up flying in the air defense command. In 1954, he won a national air show race in Dayton, Ohio. Following that success, he enrolled in the Air Force Institute of Technology and moved on to test pilot school, graduating in 1959.

In 1960, he was assigned to a project titled Dynasoar. The pilots assigned to it went through the same selection process as the original Mercury 7 pilots. Dynasoar was the first U.S. manned space project that resulted in aircraft hardware development.

Dynasoar emerged in the late 1950s as a joint Air Force/NACA project with the military taking the lead. It resulted in development of the X-20 airplane that was to be placed on top of a rocket, such as a Titan, and launched into space. It looked and sounded much like the shuttle program that eventually emerged in the 1980s.

Armstrong also was involved in Dynasoar. When the program was canceled, in addition to Knight, another Purdue graduate, Hank Gordon, a 1950 alumnus born in Valparasio, Indiana, was among five pilots still with the program.

Knight went into the X-15 program in 1965, remaining until September 1, 1968. He flew sixteen X-15 flights with a maximum speed of Mach 6.7 or 4,520 miles per hour. His maximum altitude was 280,500 feet.[13]

Knight knew Armstrong from their early days at Edwards. "He was a nice guy," Knight says, "But he couldn't play gin rummy too well. I liked Neil, and I still stay in contact with him."[14]

Knight's speed of 4,520 miles per hour accomplished on October 3, 1967, was a record when he did it. It still stands. "And that's unfortunate," Knight says. "That's a travesty. That indicates we haven't advanced that kind of technology for more than thirty years. That's not consistent with this nation."[15]

After the X-15 program, Knight was sent to Vietnam. He later went to Wright-Patterson and worked on the F-15. He also served as vice commander at Edwards and retired from the Air Force in 1982. In later years, he worked in industry and became involved in politics, serving as a councilman and mayor and finally a member of the California State Senate.

By the time the X-15 rolled out, the Russians and Americans had both placed satellites in orbit, and the space race was on. However, Armstrong was not focusing on a space career. "I was trying to really understand the elements of flight mechanics and the flight testing world," he says. "I was learning. I was young, fairly inexperienced. The X-15 was a pretty good airplane. It had some areas where its controllability was substantially degraded. But it had a long life, a very productive research existence. It will be well remembered in aeronautical history. All the work we were doing was exciting."[16]

Armstrong was not up for consideration when NASA selected the original Mercury 7 astronauts. Only military pilots were considered, and he was a civilian at this time.

The future was unknown. There were several programs with space potential up and running, and no one knew what the future held, who would be the "one."

"We didn't even know at that point in time whether Mercury would ever become a real project or whether it would die," Armstrong says. "I was on Dynasoar. It was equally or more exciting than Mercury, but it never happened. But that wasn't surprising to us. In that world, projects come and go. Some of them become real, and some never become real. And you can't tell at the time what will happen."[17]

In addition to flying the X-15 and being in Dynasoar, Armstrong was involved in a number of other projects, but he did have his eyes on what was happening on the east coast and the Mercury launches at Cape Canaveral. "I was interested in the sense that a lot of people who were running that program came from Edwards," Armstrong says. "People left Edwards to become top executives of the Mercury program, like Kenny Kleinknecht, a Purdue fellow. Kenny became the Project Mercury manager."[18]

In the 1970 book *First on the Moon*, Armstrong is quoted as saying, "We [at Edwards] even worked on the Mercury project's drogue parachute, which in the early days tended to be unstable at sonic speeds. . . . At the time we were doing this, the Mercury project looked like a dark horse to us. We thought we were far more involved in space flight research than the Mercury people. I judged them wrongly."[19]

The second class of NASA astronauts was announced in 1962. This time they accepted a civilian—Neil Armstrong. NASA asked him to apply, and he decided that the excitement in the program was sufficiently strong enough to give it a try.[20]

When he arrived in Houston, the Space Center had not yet been built. NASA was just moving from Langley. It was operating in Houston out of rented offices in the suburbs.

Armstrong didn't have to wait long for an assignment. He was named to the backup crew for Gemini 5, which launched August 21, 1965. As soon as Gemini 5 cleared the launch tower at liftoff, he was cleared for another assignment. He was placed in command of Gemini 8 and went into intense training.

Even as crews were being selected for Gemini, NASA was thinking ahead. As early as 1964, Donald "Deke" Slayton, the Mercury 7 astronaut who was medically disqualified to fly and was put in charge of matching crews and flights, was thinking all the way to the Moon landing.

Early in 1964, two years after Armstrong arrived, Slayton estimated he would need ten Gemini crews and eight Apollo crews before the moon landing. The Gemini manned flights started in 1965 and ended in 1966. Gemini did use ten crews, but there were only four Apollo crews before the moon landing.

In his book *Deke!* he writes, "My mission was to create a pool of guys who had the necessary experience in rendezvous and docking (Extra Vehicular Activity or space walking) and long duration before I had to select which three would attempt the first lunar landing." He made a list of guidelines:

"Everybody was considered to be qualified and acceptable for any mission when brought to NASA. That is, if we hired the guy and kept him around, he was eligible to fly.

"But some are more qualified than others for specific seats on specific missions. That is, guys with command or management or test pilot experience were more likely to be handed the more challenging assignments.

"I would try to match people in a crew based on individual talents and, when possible, personal compatibility.

"I always kept future requirements and training in mind. When I wanted to assign somebody for an assignment in Gemini, I had to think how that would affect Apollo. So I had a long-term plan that was updated regularly.

"I assumed a 10 percent attrition rate."[21]

Armstrong's Gemini 8 launched on March 16, 1966, after a one-day delay. The main objective was to rendezvous with a target vehicle named an Agena. A space walk was also planned.

Gemini 8 did not go according to plan. The problems began after docking—a key step NASA was practicing in preparation for the moon landing effort. After docking, "the Gemini-Agena combination had yawed out of alignment by thirty degrees," Slayton says. "They were literally bending in two. . . . Over the next few minutes the Gemini-Agena yawed and rolled a bit. Then it settled down. Neil and [fellow astronaut] Dave [Scott] kept trying to turn off the Agena control system figuring that it was . . . causing the problems. Eight minutes after Dave first noticed the big problem, the whole thing started rolling pretty seriously, literally beginning to spin. The vehicles were also yawing—moving from side to side. Neil and Dave were worried that the docking adaptor was going to break.

"They managed to get things to slow down enough so they could undock. The moment they backed away from the Agena, however, Gemini started rolling and tumbling. . . . Nothing Neil could do with the hand controller seemed to make any difference. Pretty soon they were doing a 360 every second. Their vision was getting blurred and they were worried that pieces of Gemini were going to start flying off."[22] Armstrong was able to bring it under control and his cool command during the pressure of the situation earned him a great deal of respect.

The next flight, Gemini 9, also featured a Purdue graduate. Eugene Cernan had arrived at the space program. He had graduated with an engineering degree from Purdue in the spring of 1956, and he immediately began fulfilling his longtime dream to be a Navy aviator.[23]

His first job was learning how to fly, and his training began in earnest in January 1957. "Once it began, flying was very easy for me," Cernan says. "My dad had taught me about engines, Purdue had taught me how to learn, sports had taught me how to compete, and preflight taught me about the aircraft."[24]

He received his Navy wings on November 22, 1957. It was a significant time in flight. Nineteen days earlier the Soviet Union had added to its already alarming success with the *Sputnik* satellite by launching a dog, Laika, into orbit.

The U.S. Mercury astronauts were introduced on April 9, 1959, and if Armstrong was unsure where this program was going, it definitely caught the attention of Cernan. "I was fascinated by their assignment," he says. "How did one get to be an astronaut?[25]

An applicant had to be in the military, which qualified Cernan. He was the right age and held the right degree. But that was it, and he believed by the time he built his credentials to qualify, the space race might be over.

"I thought it would be great to do that someday," Cernan says. "But I thought by the time I qualified, all the pioneering would be over and there wouldn't be anything left to do."[26]

May 1961 was a huge month for Cernan and the U.S. space program. On May 5, Alan Shepard launched into space. On May 6, Cernan married.

"While trying to keep my mind on the thousand things that needed to be done before the wedding, I had stayed glued to the television set, mentally putting myself inside that little Mercury capsule and imagining the wild, thundering ride of Alan Shepard," Cernan says. "If someone had tapped me on the shoulder at that moment and told me that, the next time Alan flew in space, his backup would be a veteran astronaut named Gene Cernan who had two flights under his own belt and had gone to the Moon, I would have laughed out loud."[27]

Cernan's career reached a turning point. His committment in the Navy was coming to an end, and he considered other opportunities. Then he got a great offer. The Navy offered him the opportunity to earn a master's degree while continuing to fly jets in return for another six-year commitment. He accepted, and Cernan and his wife, Barbara, moved to the Monterey Peninsula of California.

But he still kept one eye on the space program. The second group of nine astronauts was announced in September 1962. Since the first group was called the Mercury 7, it was logical that the new group be named the Next Nine.

Cernan saw familiar names on the list—including fellow Purdue graduate Armstrong. He also noticed changes in the selection criteria. The top age had been lowered to thirty-five. In addition to engineering degrees, NASA started accepting people with degrees in physical and biological sciences. NASA continued to look for applicants who had test pilot experience, who had graduated from a military test pilot school, or had equivalent credentials. Cernan was not a test pilot, and he wondered if he would ever meet all the requirements to take part in the program.[28]

"I never really did decide I wanted to get into the space program until I received a call from the Navy saying they had been reviewing personnel and wanted to recommend me to NASA for further evaluation," Cernan says.[29] That call came in June 1963.

The nomination was just the first step. Cernan was next interviewed. His background was reviewed. There were physical examinations at Brooks Air Force Base in San Antonio, near where Charles McAllister and Charles Lindbergh had collided and parachuted to safety just thirty-eight years before. Cernan cleared every obstacle and kept moving closer and closer to a possibility he still found hard to believe.

In the fall of 1963, he was told he had a telephone call from NASA headquarters. When he picked up the receiver, "Deke" Slayton, head of the astronaut office, was on the line. In his book *The Last Man on the Moon*, Cernan recounts the conversation: "'Geno,' Slayton said. 'If you're still interested in coming down here, we've got a job for you.' Somehow I must have replied in the affirmative," Cernan says. "But I was so elated that I don't even remember hanging up."[30]

He was seven years out of Purdue and eight and a half years away from walking on the Moon.

Among the thirteen others selected for the program was fellow Purdue graduate Roger Chaffee. Also in the group were two men who would fly on Apollo 11 with Armstrong—Edwin "Buzz" Aldrin and Michael Collins. If time moved quickly before Cernan was selected for the space program, it moved even faster once he had moved to Houston with his wife and their daughter, Tracy.

In November 1965, he was assigned as backup pilot for the Gemini 9 mission.

All the astronauts played a guessing game about what being assigned to a certain backup position would mean to their future flights, Cernan says. He believed that as part of the backup crew for Gemini 9, he would probably be pilot on Gemini 12, the last in that series. Gemini 9 was scheduled for May 1966. The primary commander for Gemini 9 was Elliot See. The pilot was Charlie Basset. Joining Cernan on the two-man backup crew was Tom Stafford.[31]

On February 28, 1966, the Gemini 9 primary and backup crews flew separate NASA, dual-seat, T-38 jets to St. Louis. The weather was rainy and snowy. The plane carrying Basset and See crashed, killing both men.

Cernan was now the primary pilot for the May Gemini mission with Stafford in command. Launch day was Tuesday, May 17. Mission plans included a space walk by Cernan. As they dressed for the flight, Slayton called Stafford aside for a private talk. It would be years before Cernan learned what it was all about. Stafford was told that if anything went wrong during the space walk, Cernan might be left with no way to get back inside the capsule. If that happened, Stafford's only choice would be to cut his partner lose and return to Earth without him.[32]

Like Armstrong's mission, Gemini 9 included a rendezvous with an Agena. One of Cernan's jobs was to make calculations for the Gemini rendezvous using pencil, paper, and a slide rule, a tool he had learned to use at Purdue.

On May 17, the Agena they were to dock with launched and plunged into the ocean 130 seconds after liftoff. For Cernan and Stafford, the wait to reach space would last a little longer.

On June 1, they came within two minutes of launch before computer problems caused another delay. On June 3, they tried again. At 8:49 A.M. EDT, they launched. Minutes later, Cernan was in space. Only days before *Surveyor 1* lunar probe had sent back 144 photographs of possible landing sites for the coming Apollo program. Cernan was only six and a half years away from his walk on the Moon.

It didn't take long for troubles to emerge on Gemini 9. When the two astronauts finally got close enough to see the space vehicle with which they were scheduled to rendezvous, nicknamed the "Blob," serious problems were spotted. The Blob was spinning and turning very slowly but obviously out of control. The nose cone, which was supposed to have fallen off, was still attached and in two pieces. It looked like a huge, open jaw. The Blob, in fact, looked like a giant alligator, rolling and floating in space, waiting to strike.

Later, when Cernan did his space walk, there were more problems. Attached to the spacecraft by a long umbilical cord, he found it difficult to control what he was doing in space. Cernan was only the third person to do this. The other two were an American, Ed White, who had died in Apollo 1, and a Russian.

"My only connection with the real world was through the umbilical cord, which we called the 'snake,' and it set out to teach me a lesson in Newton's law of motion," Cernan says. "My slightest move would affect my entire body, ripple through the umbilical, and jostle the spacecraft. . . . Since I had nothing to stabilize my movements, I went out of control, tumbling every which way, and when I reached the end of the umbilical, I rebounded like a bungee jumper and the snake reeled me in as it tried to resume its original shape."[33]

Cernan set a new record for time spent outside a spacecraft and he decided the snake was "the most malicious serpent since the one Eve met in the Garden of Eden."[34]

The beauty of the universe overwhelmed him as he floated in space with nothing to impede his view. Here is his description of what he saw as he floated high above the earth:

"The naked sun, an intense ball of gleaming white fire, stared at me, a tiny interloper in its realm. The view of Earth was incredible from my tree house in the galaxy as my home planet swooshed beneath my boots. The blue horizon had vanished at sunrise and now was merely a tissue-thin, curbed band of cerulean color terminating in black space. From up where there was no weather, I looked down on the tops of thunderstorms and the giant cottony fingers of hurricane Alma. In the open seas I could make out the V-shape wakes of ships and, on land, the dark grids of major cities. Mountain ranges spawned graceful rivers that slid toward the oceans, and I could see the Mississippi wiggling down to New Orleans. A rainbow-wide palette of colors presented emerald rainforests and bronze deserts, sapphire water, ivory clouds, and above it all—total blackness. Try to imagine a place with no boundaries, a room with no walls, an empty well as deep and limitless as your imagination, for that is where I was. And it was . . . my home for [several] hours."[35]

As he went about his work, Cernan became the first human to orbit the entire Earth during a space walk. The walk attracted a great deal of media attention on Earth, and Roger Chaffee went to the Cernan home to explain to Barbara everything that was happening.

There was a lot to explain. Problems continued on Gemini 9. Cernan's facemask fogged up. He had trouble turning valves. As he turned a valve in one direction, his entire body would spin the opposite way. The fogging became so serious that he could barely see. In fact, there were serious concerns that he would not be able to complete the job of getting back into the space capsule because he would not be able to see at all. He barely did make it, after having spent two hours and nine minutes in space. His walk had been 36,000 miles.

Re-entry was spectacular as the astronauts watched the ball of fire created by friction against the spacecraft. "A streak of orange flashed past, a skinny lightening bolt that instantly vanished into space," Cernan says. "From the other side, a dark green streak zipped by, then, all around us, brilliant stripes of blue, red, and purple came faster and faster as the blunt end of Gemini 9 collided with the thick atmosphere. [A] slight corkscrewing movement made the long tongues of flame trailing along behind us like sleek wings, swirl and curve over each other, brightly fluorescent in the darkness. Shades of oranges and yellows and glowing reds, shining blues, and greens intermingled, coiling in a colorful spiral. . . . Then the fire completely enveloped us, the blaze coating the spacecraft and spread from the burning heat shield all the way back beyond the nose, merging at some unseen point far behind."[36]

Cernan worried that he might be blamed for problems with the space walk. But when similar—and even worse—problems were encountered on Gemini 10 and 11 space walks, changes were made in equipment and procedures.

His confidence was energized on December 22, 1966, when it was announced he would be on the backup crew for the second manned Apollo mission. Cernan was convinced that being named backup on the original Apollo 2 mission meant he would be on the prime crew for Apollo 5. And he believed there was a chance that might be the big one—the first lunar landing.[37] But that possibility changed when Apollo 2 was scrubbed, and Cernan, along with Tom Stafford, became a backup crew for Apollo 1 instead.

In January 1967, Virgil "Gus" Grissom, Chaffee, and Ed White were lost in the Apollo 1 command module fire. The rush to reach the Moon was put on hold.

During the lengthy investigation, new planning, and building for the space program, Cernan and some of the other astronauts grew restless. Cernan had always felt it was wrong for him to receive the hero treatment for his mission on Gemini 9. The real heroes in his mind were the men fighting in Vietnam. When the space program slowed after Apollo 1, he and several other astronauts asked if they could leave NASA for a while and join other fighter pilots in Southeast Asia.

Slayton told them the decision to leave the space program was always up to them, but he would not promise them a job when they returned. Top military officials at the Pentagon eventually ruled the astronauts would not be put into combat.[38]

Cernan says all the astronauts wanted to be first on the Moon. They all wanted whatever flight was being assigned and as many flights as they could get, he says. It was a very competitive atmosphere—and a positive one.

"It was extremely competitive," Cernan says. "But once somebody got assigned to a flight, everybody was behind him. We were all pulling the wagon in the same direction. When someone got assigned to a flight, everyone was helping them."[39]

Cernan says no one had a circle around his name as the chosen astronaut for the moon landing. "Neil wasn't picked to be first," he says, "but it worked out to be the best choice because I don't think anyone could have handled being the first man on the Moon with any more dignity than he has. It's a lot on your shoulders to be the first human being to walk on the Moon."[40]

Cernan says in April 1967, just three months after the fire, Slayton called eighteen of the astronauts into a room for a meeting. He told them the Apollo missions would be assigned from the group of men in that room. The first manned mission to go would be designated Apollo 7 with crew Wally Schirra, Donn Eisele, and Walt Cunningham. Cernan was named backup lunar module pilot for Apollo 7.[41]

As time passed quickly, Cernan says other astronauts were assigned to flights: Jim McDivitt, Dave Scott, and Rusty Schweickart on Apollo 8; Frank Borman, Mike Collins, and Bill Anders on Apollo 9; Cernan, Tom Stafford, and John Young on Apollo 10.[42]

There were changes in assignments. The basic plan was to have each flight test various aspects of the mission necessary to ultimately land on the Moon—each taking progress another step forward. NASA would only land when it was determined the program was ready.

Cernan believed there was a chance for his Apollo 10 to be first. "If all of those tests [on Apollo 7, 8, and 9] went well, there was a good chance that Apollo 10 would fly all the way to the Moon," he says.[43] It might also come with Apollo 11, or 12, or 13. It all depended on how fast developments progressed. "It could have been any number of people who would have been first," Cernan says. "Crews were switched, people got hurt, backup crews were changed. All that happened."[44]

Twenty-one months after the Apollo 1 fire, Apollo 7 launched. The date was October 11, 1968. It was a complete success.

Apollo 7 had gone so well that plans were changed for the next mission. Instead of orbiting Earth, Apollo 8 would circle the Moon. Apollo 8 did circle the Moon in December, and on Christmas Eve the astronauts read from the Bible, the book of Genesis.

There was still a great deal of speculation about which Apollo flight would provide the first opportunity for a moon landing. "My operating rule was to have a pool of guys trained so that anyone could handle anything," Slayton says in his book *Deke!* "With the success of Apollo 8, it was time to name the Apollo 11 crew. On the planning charts, this might very well turn out to be the first manned lunar landing. No one knew for sure. The lunar module was still a couple months away from a test flight. There was the Apollo 10 lunar orbit mission, too. Some people were thinking if 9 went well, we should . . . have the 10 crew make the landing. So it wasn't a cut-and-dried decision as to who should make the first steps on the Moon. . . . With Gus [Grissom] dead, the most likely candidates were Frank Borman and Jim McDivitt. I had full confidence in Tom Stafford [commander on Apollo 10], Neil Armstrong [commander on 11], and Peter Conrad [commander on 12]. The system had put them in the right place at the right time. Any one of them might very well make the first landing."[45]

Slayton wrote, "Later on, people would talk about the process as if it was some kind of science, or as if politics had controlled it—the fact that Neil was a civilian. All I can say is that a lot of factors, most of them beyond anybody's control, put these guys in the right place at the right time. I called Neil, Mike [Collins], and Buzz [Aldrin] into my office on Monday, January 6 [1969] and told them, 'You're it.'"[46]

That January it was announced that the Apollo 9 mission would go as planned—a deep space orbit to test equipment including the lunar lander. Apollo 10 would go to the Moon and do everything but land. Apollo 11 could not be committed to attempting a lunar landing until Apollo 10 results could be analyzed.

Cernan kept a close eye on the preparation of the equipment that would take him to lunar orbit. He saw one interesting development. Technicians had to remove oxygen tanks from the service module in order to do some repair. New tanks were put in. The original tanks were refurbished and eventually placed in Apollo 13 "where they would contribute to a disaster in space. One never knows," Cernan says.[47]

Apollo 10 launched on May 18, 1969. The night before, Cernan was given special permission to visit his wife and daughter, with the threat that consequences would result if anyone saw and recognized him. On his way back to the Kennedy Space Center, driving back roads, Cernan was speeding in his rental car. He was stopped by a police officer. He recounts the incident in his book.

"Where y'all going in such a hurry?" the officer asked.

"Officer, if I told you, you wouldn't believe me," Cernan said.

There were many questions. Cernan had a California driver's license, but he admitted he lived in Houston. He was driving a rental car without any rental papers or registration. The officer kept asking questions. Cernan kept declining to answer, hoping he'd just get a ticket, would be sent on his way, and no one would be the wiser.

Finally, the officer decided to take Cernan to the police station and asked him to step out of the car. Cernan visualized the morning headlines. "Astronaut Arrest Scrubs Moon Mission." At the last second before the handcuffs would have gone on, Guenther Wendt of NASA, happened by and saw Cernan. He took the officer aside and explained.

"I've heard a lot of cock-and-bull stories in my life, and if you think I'm going believe that one, you're crazy," the officer said. "Thousands of people around here and I'm supposed to believe I caught me an astronaut on the way to the Moon? But it's such a good story—get out of here. And go to your Moon!"[48]

It was customary for astronauts to name their space vehicles and the names chosen for Apollo 10 were popular with the media and the public. The command module was *Charlie Brown* and the lunar lander was *Snoopy,* from the *Peanuts* cartoon strip.

They lifted off right on schedule, but soon after launch the astronauts heard groaning from their ship and there were severe vibrations. Questions emerged about whether the vehicle would hold together. At Houston, all the data said everything was fine, and they went with the data, although Mission Commander Stafford kept his hand on the abort handle. All he had to do was twist it. Finally, they broke away from their Earth orbit and started the flight to the Moon.

Color television was still fairly new to most American homes. Apollo 10 took color TV all the way to the Moon. It was the first American space mission to carry color television cameras. The results were so good that they won an Emmy.

The view of Earth from this great distance was different from what Cernan had seen during his Earth orbit on the Gemini flight. "In Gemini, we had flown across coastlines, lakes, and cities as we traversed around the world, but now as we rapidly moved away from Earth we could see entire oceans and continents in a glance," Cernan says. "In orbit, the horizon curved like a giant rainbow, but now it closed in upon itself and the earth evolved before our eyes. . . . Our cloud-wrapped blue globe was surrounded by a blackness of such great depth that for the first time I realized that I was truly on a space voyage."[49]

At the halfway point, NASA played Frank Sinatra singing "Fly Me to the Moon."

Cernan found time to be philosophical, to ponder some great questions. "Looking back at Earth, I saw only a distant blue and white star," he says. "There were oceans down there, deep and wide, but I could see completely across them now and they seemed so small. . . . Out where I was dashing through space, I was wrapped in infinity. Even the word *infinity* lost its meaning because I couldn't measure it, and without sunsets and sunrises, time meant nothing more than performing some checklist function at a specific point in the mission. . . . Stars and eternal blackness everywhere. There is no end. . . . When I looked around, I saw beauty, not emptiness. No one in their right mind can see such a sight and deny the spirituality of the experience, nor the existence of a Supreme Being. . . . Someone, some being, some power placed our little world, our sun and our Moon where they are in the dark void, and the scheme defies any attempt at logic. It is just too perfect and beautiful to have happened by accident."[50]

When they got their first sight of the Moon up close, they were like "three monkeys in a cage, scrambling to get to get to the windows," Cernan says.[51]

On the dark side of the Moon, out of sight and communication with Earth, Cernan and Stafford crawled into the lunar lander. The third astronaut on the mission, John Young, stayed behind and at the precise moment, pulled the command module away. Hearts stopped everywhere on Earth as people waited to learn what had happened. The Madrid, Spain, tracking station reported first. They were picking up signals coming from behind the Moon. And it wasn't one spacecraft they were seeing. It was two, flying about fifty feet apart. "The guys at mission control wore smiles so big, they would have eaten bananas sideways," Cernan says.[52]

The next job for *Snoopy*, the lunar lander, was to head down and take an even closer look at the Moon. Cernan and Stafford went into an orbit that took them within 47,000 feet of the surface. Among their tasks was to take pictures of a place known as the Sea of Tranquility. That was where the lunar lander from Apollo 11 would land. Even as they worked, Apollo 11 was being taken out to the launch pad.

Their work complete, they prepared to fire rockets that would send them back up toward the command module. In a second, everything broke loose. "*Snoopy* went nuts," Cernan says. "We were suddenly bouncing, diving, and spinning all over the place as we blazed along at 3,000 miles per hour, less than 47,000 feet above the rocks and craters—much closer if you consider those mountains to be grinning around us like gigantic decayed teeth. . . . The computers were confused and useless. The spacecraft radar that was supposed to be locking onto *Charlie Brown* had found a much larger target—the Moon—and was trying to fly in that direction. . . . Things went topsy-turvy, and I saw the surface corkscrew through my window, then the knife edge of a horizon, then blackness, then the Moon again, only this time coming from a different direction. We were totally out of control. . . . Tom overrode the computers and grabbed manual control of the spacecraft. Then, as swiftly as it had started, the horrifying little episode ended, a fifteen-second lifetime during which we made about eight cartwheels above the Moon. . . . After analyzing the data, experts later surmised that had we continued spinning for only two more seconds, Tom and I would have crashed."[53]

Stafford and Cernan spent twelve hours standing in the lunar module.

Once back in the command module, there was one more critical step that had been accomplished only once before by Apollo 8 the previous Christmas. It was called a trans Earth injection, or in NASA-speak, a "TEI." Rockets had to fire to take the command module out of lunar orbit and send it back to the earth early. If it failed, there would be no going home.[54] It worked.

During the next three hours, the astronauts shaved and brushed their teeth—more breakthroughs for a space mission, and they played a tape of Dean Martin singing "Going Back to Houston."[55]

As lunar module pilot, Cernan had no re-entry duties and was able to watch out the window. "The fireball formed, and I wondered if it would be as spectacular as the greens and blues and reds I had seen on Gemini," he says. "I could not have guessed what was about to unfold before my eyes. The different shape of the capsule and our enormous speed drastically altered the formula, and a ball of white and violet flame slipped around us like a glove. It grew in intensity and flew out behind us like the train of a bride's gown, stretching a hundred yards, then a thousand, then for miles, and the whole time we were being savagely slammed around inside the spacecraft. White shimmering flames chewed at the outside of *Charlie Brown.* Then another little round burning ball, a tiny golden sun, formed inside the fire train and stayed perfectly balanced in the furious river that glowed behind our cooking spacecraft, which rode inside a purple shield of pure heat. Everywhere in the South Pacific, we were seen as a brilliant shooting star flashing across the sky."[56]

When they landed in the Pacific Ocean, about four hundred miles from Pago Pago, the first helicopter to arrive from a nearby aircraft carrier had "Hello, there, Charlie Brown," written on its bottom. The flight had been eight days, three minutes, and twenty-three seconds.

One of Cernan's most frequent questions upon return centered on whether or not he was disappointed he didn't have the opportunity to land on the Moon. "Would I like to have had a shot at it? You bet I would," Cernan says. "However, we all believed in the importance of our mission because we knew Apollo 11 was going to need every scrap of information we could gather if it was to have a successful flight of its own."[57]

Everyone had a role to play. Besides, Cernan planned on making a landing himself as a commander, not a lunar module pilot.

When it became clear that Apollo 11 stood a strong chance of becoming the first mission to land on the Moon, Aldrin began to ask who would be first to walk on the Moon. He felt he should be first since his title was lunar module pilot and the designated pilot had always done the space walks during Gemini.

According to Cernan, "Buzz had worked himself into a frenzy with his campaign to be the first man to walk on the Moon. He came flapping into my office at the Manned Spacecraft Center one day like an angry stork, laden with charts and graphs and statistics arguing what he considered to be obvious: that he, the lunar module pilot, and not Neil Armstrong, the mission commander, should be the first one down the ladder on Apollo 11. Since I shared an office with Neil, who was away training that day, I found Aldrin's arguments both offensive and ridiculous."[58]

Slayton says the issue finally reached his desk. According to Slayton, Aldrin's father, a man with a long history in flight, was also involved. Says Slayton, "He wanted to know why his son was getting the shaft about being the first guy to walk on the Moon. I guess he got it in his head that Neil was chosen because he was a civilian. Buzz raised the question with Neil who was noncommittal. [Nothing had been written in stone yet.] . . . [The decision] bounced . . . to me, and I told Buzz I thought it should be Neil on seniority. Neil had come into the program a year ahead of Buzz, so he had first choice."[59]

Slayton also says from a technical standpoint, the way the hatch in the lunar module had been designed, it was easier for the person standing on the left to exit first. That was Armstrong. The issue was settled by April.[60]

At 9:32 A.M. on Wednesday, July 16, 1969, Apollo 11 launched. It was an international event attracting attention and live television coverage across the globe. The Apollo 11 mission to the Moon would bring the world together for eight days, first in anticipation, next in amazement as people watched the first walk on the Moon, and finally in celebration as the astronauts returned and landed.

The flight to the Moon went smoothly and according to plan. The lunar lander, *Eagle*, with Armstrong and Aldrin on board, separated from the command module, *Columbia*, on July 20. The world collectively held its breath.

Armstrong says the plan had always been for him to take control from the computer and land the module himself. "The computer didn't have any way of knowing where it was going," he says. "It knew a set of numbers, but it didn't know what was there when we got there. The craft, theoretically, had the ability to land automatically. But nobody would ever do that. Not with people on board. It was going into a bad area, so I had to go find a good area. And I did that."[61]

In the book *First on the Moon*, Armstrong is quoted as saying the computer alarms had occupied their attention before the landing. "Supposedly in this time period, the crew member is supposed to look out and see the landing area and if any small changes where the automatic system is taking him are required, he initiates those himself manually. . . . We got tied up with computer alarms and were obliged to keep our heads inside the cockpit to assure ourselves that we could continue flying safely. So all those good pictures Tom Stafford took for me on Apollo 10, in order to pick out where I was going and to know precisely where I was, were to no avail. I just didn't get a chance to look out the window. In fact, when the problems were less important and I did get a chance to look out at about 3,000 feet, we had already passed most of the landmarks I had memorized. . . .

"As we dropped below a thousand feet, it was quite obvious that the system was attempting to land in an undesirable area in a boulder field surrounding [a] crater. I was surprised by the size of the boulders; some of them were as big as small motorcars . . .

"I was tempted to land, but my better judgment took over. We pitched over to a level altitude, which would allow us to maintain our horizontal velocity and just skim along over the top of the boulder field. That is, we pitched over to standing straight up. Then the automatic throttle was still giving us a descent rate that was too high, and it was going to get us down to an altitude where we would be unable to look out ahead far enough. That was when I took command of the throttle to fly the LM [lunar module] manually the rest of the way. I was being absolutely adamant about my right [not] to be wishy-washy about where I was going to land, and the only way I could buy time was to slow down the descent rate.

"There are three kinds of throttle control on the LM, I chose the semiautomatic version in which I controlled the altitude and the horizontal velocity and let my commands, in conjunction with computer commands, operate the throttle. I changed my mind a couple of times again, looking for a parking place. Something would look good and then as we got closer it really wasn't good. Finally, we found an area ringed on one side by fairly good size craters and on the other side by a boulder field. It was not a particularly big area, only a couple of hundred square feet, about the size of a big house lot. It looked satisfactory. I was quite concerned about the fuel level, although we apparently had a little bit more than our gauge had indicated. It's always nice to have a gallon left when you read empty. But we had to get on the surface very soon or fire the ascent engine and abort."[62] Estimates are there were about fifteen seconds of fuel left when they landed.

In Houston, they began to hear radio traffic from the *Eagle* using terms they well understood.

"Aldrin: Contact Light.

Armstrong: Shutdown.

Aldrin: Okay. Engine Stop.

Aldrin: ACA out of Detent.

Armstrong: Out of Detent. Auto.

Aldrin: Mode Control, both Auto. Descent Engine Command Override, off. Engine Arm, off. Four-thirteen is in.

Charlie Duke [Houston Control]: We copy you down, *Eagle.*

Armstrong: Engine arm is off. [Pause] Houston, Tranquility Base here. The *Eagle* has landed."[63]

Armstrong and Aldrin shook hands. Mission Control in Houston erupted. "The whole [place] was pandemonium," Slayton says. It took fifteen seconds to regain order and seconds were vital. The *Eagle* was only cleared to stay on the Moon for one minute while they checked to make certain everything was okay. Then they cleared it for another minute. And another. After twelve minutes they were okay to stay.[64]

There was plenty of work to do aboard *Eagle* and Armstrong and Aldrin went about it. They were scheduled to have a rest before walking on the Moon, but they requested to walk first. It had been assumed they would make that request, and the walk was on.

About six hours after landing, Armstrong stepped carefully down the ladder to the Moon. He had been thinking about what he might say when he first placed his boot on the surface. He made a final choice of words sometime after landing and had them in his head as he descended the ladder.

When he reached the bottom he said, "That's one small step for [a] man, one giant leap for mankind." It was 9:56 P.M. in Houston. More than a half billion people watched on television around the world, incredulous at what they were seeing. Live from the Moon. Unbelievable!

Armstrong says he had plenty of time to decide what to say after the landing. And to him, the landing itself was far more significant than the first step on the Moon. Years later, he would be widely quoted as saying, "Pilots like to fly, not walk."

There is a fascination with walking on the Moon. However, landing on the lunar surface was the severe engineering challenge, very difficult and risky. Walking was much less so. The important accomplishment in Armstrong's mind was the landing.

To Armstrong the most important words he spoke on July 20, 1969, were not "that's one small step . . ." They were "The *Eagle* has landed."[65] That meant Apollo 11 had accomplished half its mission. The other half was getting home.

But first, before attempting to lift off from the Moon, rejoin *Columbia*, and return to Earth, there was that walk on the lunar surface to accomplish.

Armstrong says walking on the Moon is quite a bit different from walking on Earth. The backpack causes you to learn forward. Since there is less friction, you start slower. And stopping is a whole other issue in the one-sixth gravity of the Moon. "Turning from a standing position is slightly slower than on Earth due to the lower frictional force available at the sole of the foot," he explained in a 1971 speech. "But adequate turning rates can be readily accomplished. Acceleration from a standing position to forward motion is noticeably slower than on Earth as a result of the low frictional force available at the sole of the boot. Two methods of acceleration are available: (1) a series of three or four steps adding a small increment of velocity with each step; (2) leaning very far forward and pushing off vigorously, gaining the desired velocity in the first step."[66]

Armstrong says you move forward on the Moon by walking, hopping, or loping. Loping results when you try to walk fast. "At higher speeds, the force at the foot necessary to maintain the speed will provide sufficient upward force to lift the person off the ground before the other foot comes down," he says, "This mode of locomotion . . . is the preferred method of traveling over substantial distances. The loping pace is like running in that both feet are off the ground at the same time, but unlike running in that the legs are moving rather slowly. It gives one, in fact, the feeling of running in slow motion. Running, as we know it here on Earth, cannot be performed on the Moon. Hopping with both feet leaving and hitting the surface simultaneously was found to be a satisfactory method of movement, but was not a preferred method by any of the crewmen.

"Stopping from a walk can be achieved in one or two steps, but stopping from the loping mode requires three or four. In general, movement on the lunar surface requires somewhat more planning and attention than movement here on Earth.

"Of course, the low gravitational force invites astounding jumping antics. Free jumps could be controlled up to about a meter. Jumps above that provided an unstabilized period of time that made the guarantee of a stable landing difficult."[67]

He says the maximum jump was two meters while balancing with the handrails on the ladder.[68]

Armstrong says astronauts did fall on the Moon, but the falls were "of little consequence. The falling rate is so slow that no damage is expected. Usually the fall can be prevented once an unbalance is noticed, simply by turning in the direction of the fall and taking a step in that direction. Having fallen, a recovery to a standing position can be performed unassisted fairly easily for a face down position and with somewhat more difficulty from a face-up position."[69]

Apollo 11 changed the world. But the Apollo program was not finished. Flights to the Moon went on. There would be six more missions to the lunar surface. All but one succeeded. Apollo 13 was forced to return early.

Among the men who deeply wanted an opportunity to land and walk on the Moon was Cernan, who had come so close on Apollo 10. He was offered his chance. Slayton assigned him to the backup crew for Apollo 13. He would be backup lunar module pilot, the same position Aldrin had on Apollo 11. According to the rotation they were following, Cernan believed the odds were then good that he would then be assigned lunar pilot on Apollo 16.

He turned it down. He wanted to walk on the Moon, but not as lunar module pilot. He wanted to be commander of the mission.

Slayton warned him that budget cuts were coming and Apollo 16 very likely could be the last Moon mission. "If you don't go, I don't know if you'll ever fly again," Slayton said. Again Cernan said no. In fact, the odds were even worse than Cernan realized.[70]

But within months after the success of Apollo 11, Cernan learned he was being named backup commander for Apollo 14. He believed that meant he would get the command position on the Apollo 17 moon landing—if there was an Apollo 17.

Shepard commanded Apollo 14 to a successful mission and took the first golf shots on the Moon.

Apollo 15 took off with a lunar rover so astronauts could drive long distances from their landing site. With Apollo 16 up next, the decision was finally made on the crew for number 17. Cernan officially was named the commander. Apollo 17 would be the last mission of the series. In addition to the title he always wanted, commander, Cernan would get a title he never wanted: Last Man on the Moon.

John Young commanded Apollo 16. Another success. Now, there was only one mission left to go.

A crowd of 700,000 people showed up in Florida to witness the historic last launch. Cernan's invited guests included friends like John Wayne, Connie Stevens, Bob Hope, Don Rickles, Dinah Shore, Johnny Carson, Henry Mancini, and Eva Gabor.

At 12:33 A.M. on December 7, 1972, Cernan and his crew were on their way. It is incredible experiencing a launch on top of the huge Saturn V used in Apollo, Cernan says. He is one of three astronauts who have launched on top of the Saturn V twice, and the only one who has launched both in daylight and darkness. "It is unique," he says. "The experience begins even before you go up that elevator and get in the spacecraft. You sort of grow with that thing as soon as it reaches the pad because it's your baby, it's your booster, its what is going to get you there.

"It really comes alive. On Apollo 10, they started fueling the night before. We went out there, and the spotlights were on and that thing was literally alive—it was almost breathing; the cryogenics, the hydrogenised oxygen, is sort of boiling and venting overboard, and it has a life of its own."[71]

With Apollo 17, he had even more personal feelings because at launch he had the control near his hand to shut it down. "I sat on that hand because that was one thing I didn't want to do by mistake," he says "There was another switch, and if I didn't like what the guidance looked like, I could have flipped that switch and taken over and flown 7.6 million pounds of thrust with a joy stick in my right hand. I had done that so many times in a simulator, I'm convinced I could have done it in a real launch."[72]

The launch experience changed as it went through stages. "It lifts off very, very slowly, until after you get airborne," Cernan says. "It takes fifteen seconds to clear the tower. It shakes a lot and rumbles, the thrust-to-weight ratio is so marginal it literally barely gets off the ground. If you lose an engine in that first fifteen seconds, you're coming back down. After fifteen seconds, four [of five] engines can sustain flight because you've burned off enough fuel, enough weight. It's just a heck of a ride. The first stage when you pick up four to four and a half Gs and then suddenly go to nothing is what John Young called 'The Great Train Wreck.' And I guess that's what a great train wreck might be like because you get bounced back and forth. Then all of a sudden, it's quiet and you're pulling less than a G, and you smooth out. The second staging is not nearly as violent as the first."[73]

You don't sleep well the night before launch, Cernan says. You doze. At the end of the first day of the Apollo missions, Cernan was tired. "But now you're on your way to the Moon," he says. "That interferes with your sleep. We didn't really sleep well until we were on our way home."[74]

Apollo 17 landed on the Moon on December 11 with Cernan at the controls and lunar module pilot Jack Schmidt at his side.

"That lunar lander is a major challenge," Cernan says. "It is probably twelve to fourteen of the most dynamic minutes of your life. You start down from about 50,000 feet, you've flown over the site one revolution earlier, and now you're lying on your back and you're starting on down and your firing that engine and it's vibrating and shaking and there's noise. The ground [Houston] is talking to you. You're taking vector updates, your copilot is reading numbers, and you are slowly pitching to where you can see the horizon of the Moon through the windows. At 7,000 feet, you make a major pitch over and the vibration, the noise, the talking, everything is going on at once, and you head down to 200 feet where you bite the bullet because if you have an engine failure at 200 feet, you can't stage quick enough to get out of there before you hit the surface. You have to descend fast enough that you don't run out of fuel, and you have to come down slow enough to land, not crash. It's not like landing an airplane on Earth. Once you start a movement you have to take it out. At eighty feet you hit all that dust. The ground [Houston] is telling you how much fuel you have left, your copilot is giving you numbers. I finally said, 'Jack, no more numbers. I've got it.' By that time, you pick out your landing site and go down fairly slow. You have to shut the engine down about nine feet above the surface because if you land with the engine running, you could blow the vehicle apart."[75]

The quick drop the last nine feet made their stomachs jump. "The next moment was the most impressive to me," Cernan says. "The ground is not talking, they don't have anything to say. Your copilot is overwhelmed. No noise there. There are no vibrations. The engine is shut down. The dust is gone and the only thing you can hear is the purr of the environmental control system. It becomes the most quiet, still, untarnished moment a human being can ever experience. You look out the window and see what human eyes have never seen before. This valley we landed in, surrounded by mountains on three sides, higher than the Grand Canyon, is deep. You are now where no one has been before. That experience may have lasted for two or three seconds, or five seconds, or five minutes—it didn't last for five minutes but it seemed like it lasted a long time and it was just one of those moments you remember. It was complete absence of noise, of dust, of anything on this far away planet. And then you get your breath, and you tell them back home 'Houston, tell America the *Challenger* has landed.'"[76]

Moondust and rocks on the lunar surface are shades of gray, Cernan says. It gets into everything from your spacesuit to your fingernails when you take your space suit off back in the lunar module. "There's a film of lunar dust all over, almost like beach sand but with the fineness of graphite," Cernan says. "It could be three inches deep. It could be three or four meters deep. You look around, and you're standing in sunlight and the blackest black you can conceive in your mind surrounds you. Not darkness—blackness.

"And one of the first things you see when you're out of the spacecraft is the earth and all its beauty and splendor: the blues of the ocean and the whites of the snow and the clouds. It is three-dimensional out there in that blackness. All the way down on our descent, not only was I looking at where we were going to land and the radar and listening, I wanted to look at the Earth. You just wanted to freeze the lander and stand there and look at it, but you didn't have time.

"I didn't feel closer to God on the Moon. You can feel close to God anyplace," Cernan says, "but I certainly was witness to a small part of his creation. There's no question in my mind about that at all. I was at a place in time and space where science met its match. There were things I saw in terms of the purpose and logicality of the earth as it moved through space—it didn't tumble, its overpowering beauty, the fact that I could literally look alongside the edge and there was this blackness in which the earth was three-dimensional! You could put your hand around the earth and almost focus on the endlessness of time, the endlessness of infinity. Can I show it to you? No. Can I draw you a picture of it? No. But I can tell you it exists because I saw it with my own eyes."[77]

Earth is small from the Moon. An astronaut can hold out his gloved thumb and block it from view. "The earth is your identity with reality, and suddenly, you can block it out with your thumb and that's overwhelming because that's existence, that's life, that's family, that's love, that's past, that's future, and all of a sudden you can block it out of your sight," Cernan says. "And yet you have a couple billion people who can watch every move you make."[78]

On Wednesday, December 13, day three of mankind's last visit to the Moon, the Cernans' nine-year-old daughter appeared on the NBC TV *Today Show.* Dressed in a long skirt that featured her father's Apollo 17 patch, a light top, and a ribbon in her yellow hair, she sat on a high stool and watched a television monitor as the astronauts worked on the Moon.

Cernan described what was said in his book. "It looks like they're having a ball up there," Tracy said as she watched her dad jumping on the lunar surface. *Today* host Jim Hartz asked if they might find water on the Moon. "If they find water," Tracy said, "they're in the wrong place."

Hartz asked Tracy if her dad was bringing her a souvenir from his business trip to the Moon. "I can't tell you," she said. It was a secret. Hartz kept gently nudging. Finally Tracy gave in. She said, "He's going to send me back a Moonbeam."[79]

Cernan was the last of the two astronauts to go back into the lunar lander at the end of the last day. As he stepped off the lunar surface and onto the ladder, he made a statement that summed up his feelings. It was spontaneous. "As we leave the Moon," he said, "we leave as we came, and God willing, as we shall return, with peace and hope for all mankind. As I take these last steps from the surface for some time to come, I'd just like to record that America's challenge of today has forged man's destiny of tomorrow. Godspeed the crew of Apollo 17."

Cernan was thirty-eight years old when he left the Moon. Armstrong was also thirty-eight when he left the moon.

People often point to the Moon today and ask Armstrong and Cernan if they still think about it. How can they not? "Sometimes I look up and see a place where I've been," Armstrong said on the tenth anniversary.

Cernan's grandchildren call it "Popie's Moon."

"That period of my life passed so fast, sometimes I wonder—did I miss it?" Cernan says. "Did I really do all that? I grew up in a blue-collar family in Chicago and had a chance to go to the Moon twice, to live there, and command a mission there. And I do not take all that for granted. I'd love to go back and take a look at that place where I lived for three days some thirty years ago. That won't happen, but no one can ever take away the memories.

"What was accomplished? Mankind has left the planet," he says. "We have called another body in this universe our home. That's a significant step, a significant accomplishment. But I've always felt that it's going to take fifty or one hundred years before we ever fully appreciate the significance of what this means. Neil's one small step was one giant leap for mankind, but I'm not sure we know yet what that giant leap was or what it means. It will take several generations for it to evolve. How long did it take before people understood the meaning of the voyage of Columbus?

"I'm a little disappointed it's taking us so long, but there is no question in my mind, none whatsoever, that we will go to Mars," he says. "When I talk to third and fourth graders I look them right in the eye and say, 'You are the ones who are going to make it happen.' As long as we give them the tools, as long as we give them the education and the inspiration, there is no question in my mind that they will take us to Mars. Where it's going to lead, who knows? But I can tell you this with absolute certainty—it is going to happen. Apollo 17 was not the end. It's just the beginning."[80]

Andrew Feustel

Andrew Feustel was born in 1965 when the Mercury space program was long completed and Gemini was nearing its end. He was four years old when Neil Armstrong walked on the Moon.

Today Feustel, a space shuttle astronaut, is carrying on the tradition of Neil Armstrong, Eugene Cernan, Virgil "Gus" Grissom, and Roger Chaffee. He is also carrying on the tradition of Cliff Turpin, Jimmie Johnson, George Welch, Malcolm Ross, Iven Kincheloe, and many, many others—flying faster, higher, and farther into new horizons that hold the promise of the future.

A NASA mission specialist since 2000, Feustel is Purdue University's newest astronaut.

A native of Lake Orion, Michigan, near Pontiac, Feustel grew up with space travel as a fact of life. The Space Shuttle Program had been under way for two years by the time he graduated high school in 1983.

"In high school, a few of my buddies and I used to talk about how we were going to become astronauts," Feustel says. "We were going to become Air Force fighter pilots, and then go on to be astronauts."

After three years at Oakland Community College, in Michigan, Feustel received an associate science degree with minors in geology and industrial design. He enrolled at Purdue in the fall of 1986. "I have to admit, when I went to Purdue, I always had it in my mind that, hey—a lot of astronauts graduated there. It's the right place for me to go."

But it wasn't the lure of space that attracted him to Purdue so much as tradition. His great uncle graduated from Purdue in 1905—in engineering. His uncle and father graduated from Purdue in 1963 and 1965—in engineering.

"I kind of thought of it as a family obligation to go attend Purdue," Feustel says. But not in engineering. He received a B.S. in solid earth sciences in 1989 and a master's degree from Purdue in geophysics two years later. He went on to earn a Ph.D. in geological sciences specializing in seismology at Queen's University, Kingston, Ontario, Canada, in 1995.

Feustel is more than the first nonengineer in his family. He is the first nonengineer Purdue astronaut—although pre-astronaut Malcolm Ross majored in radio and communications.

"I always had the thought that I was going to grow up to do this," Feustel says. "It wasn't as much a matter of wanting to do it, as it was this is what I thought I was going to end up doing. I always had it in my mind, with the path that I took, that somehow my planetary sciences and geophysics would all get tied in to being an explorer, an astronaut."

While at Purdue, Feustel served for three years as Grand Prix chairman and team go-cart driver for Sigma Phi Epsilon Fraternity.

Working and studying in Kingston, Ontario, he maintained a friendship with a fellow Purdue graduate who was working in Ottawa, Ontario, at the same time and who later took a job with Exxon in Houston, Texas. For three years Feustel was a geophysicist for the Engineering Seismology Group in Kingston, installing and operating microseismic monitoring equipment in underground mines throughout Eastern Canada and the United States.

In 1996, the friend with Exxon called with information about job opportunities. Feustel moved to Exxon Mobil Exploration Company in Houston in January 1997 as an exploration geophysicist designing and providing operational oversight of land, marine, and borehole seismic programs worldwide.

In the summer of 1999, he applied for the astronaut program and was accepted in the eighteenth class July 20, 2000—the thirty-first anniversary of Neil Armstrong's lunar landing.

Feustel can expect a several year wait after being selected before taking his first flight. Sometimes the wait is even longer. He's excited about the possibilities for the Space Shuttle Program, the International Space Station, and beyond.

"But I'd like to see us actually talking about manned missions to Mars and maybe going back to the Moon in preparation for that," he says. "I think we've fully established ourselves in low-Earth orbit. It's time for us to have a vision for the future—not only to explore, because that's what we do as humans, but also to pursue the longevity of our existence here on the planet. I don't think we'll last here on this planet forever unless we start trying to figure out ways to get out and explore the solar system and beyond and make some inroads into space."

He loves his work, even as he waits for his first opportunity to launch into space.

"For me personally, this job is great, even without space flight," Feustel says. "The job is very exciting and challenging, aside from the space flight. So that really just becomes the icing on the cake. A very significant part of what we do here as astronauts is groundwork in support of missions. It's a great place to work."

The story of flight has been brief, accomplishing a great deal in one hundred years, Feustel says.

"I wish in the last twenty or thirty years we could have had an even steeper growth curve," he says. "I was just a young kid when we first started flying in space—a baby. We have certainly come a long way, just in my lifetime. And I'm willing to believe that, maybe not in my career, but I'm almost certain in my lifetime, we'll see manned missions to Mars, if not farther.

"That's what I'd like to do. I'd like to be going to Mars. I'd like to do some surface reconnaissance, seismic experiments, and geophysical observations there and all the things that geoscientists do when they go out in the field.

"Somebody's has to do it," he says. "You know, a great thought that has been wandering around in my mind lately is that with opportunity comes obligation. For those of us who have been lucky enough to get this opportunity, we're obligated to work and carry through to the best of our abilities, applying our skills. That's how I face this job and the opportunities that I have. It's a unique experience.

"And maybe today we're at the turning point."

Notes

Chapter One

1. *Lafayette(Indiana) Daily Courier,* 10 June 1908, evening edition.
2. Ibid.
3. Tom Crouch, *The Bishop's Boys* (New York: W. W. Norton and Company, 1989), 268.
4. Bill Gunston, *Aviation Year by Year* (New York: DK Publishing, Inc., 1992), 13.
5. Ibid.
6. Ibid.
7. W. H. Brands, *The First American* (New York: Knopf Publshing Group, 2002).
8. Gunston, *Aviation Year by Year,* 17.

9 Roger Bilstein, *Flight in America: From the Wrights to the Astronauts* (Baltimore: John Hopkins University Press, 2001), 5.

10. Ibid.
11. Ibid., 6.
12. *Lafayette (Indiana) Daily Courier* , 17 August 1859.
13. Ibid.
14. Ibid.
15. Ibid.
16. Ibid.
17. Ibid.
18. Ibid.
19. Ibid.
20. *Lafayette (Indiana) Daily Courier,* 18 August 1859.
21. Ibid.
22. Ibid.
23. Ibid.
24. *Lafayette (Indiana) Daily Courier,* 17 August 1859.
25. *Lafayette (Indiana) Daily Courier,* 18 August 1859.
26. Bilstein, *Flight in America,* 5.

27. Purdue School of Mechanical Engineering, *One Hundred Years of Progress* (West Lafayette: Purdue University, 1963), 14.

28. H. B. Knoll, *The Story of Purdue Engineering* (West Lafayette: Purdue University, 1963).

29. Purdue Mechanical Engineering, *One Hundred Years of Progress.*

30. Knoll, *Story of Purdue Engineering,* 15.

31. Purdue Mechanical Engineering, *One Hundred Years of Progress.*

32. Ibid.

33. Ibid.

34. Knoll, *The Story of Purdue Engineering,* 207.

35. Purdue Mechanical Engineering, *One Hundred Years of Progress.*

36. Crouch, *The Bishop's Boys,* 23–66.

37. Ibid., 170.

38. Ibid., 164.

39. Wilbur Wright to the Smithsonian Institution, letter, 30 May 1899, Wright Collection, Smithsonian Institution.

40. Brief and Digest of the Evidence for Complain on Final Hearing *The Wright Company* v. *Herring-Curtiss Company and Glenn H. Curtiss,* Wright State University Archives; Crouch, *The Bishop's Boys,* 161.

41. Fred C. Kelly, *The Wright Brothers: A Biography* (Mineola: Dover Publications, 1943), 225.

42. Ibid.

43. John Gillespie Magee Jr., "High Flight"

44. *The Lafayette (Indiana) Daily Courier,* 10 June 1908.

Chapter Two

1. Turpin family, interviewed by author, January 2002.

2. Early Birds biography James Clifford Turpin, Smithsonian Institution Air and Space Museum Archives, Early Birds of Aviation, Inc. Collection

3. Tom Crouch, *The Bishop's Boys* (New York: W.W. Norton and Company, 1989) 281–282.

4. Ibid., 392.

5. Early Birds biography of Turpin, Smithsonian Institution Air and Space Museum Archives.

6. *Purdue University Alumnus* (1954).

7. Early Birds biography of Turpin, Smithsonian Institution Air and Space Museum Archives.

8. Crouch, *The Bishop's Boys*, 426.

9. Fred C. Kelly, *The Wright Brothers: A Biography* (Mineola: Dover Publications, 1943), 274–275.

10. Dayton, Ohio, newspaper article, 1910, James French and Richard French, Cliff Turpin Scrapbook Collection.

11. H. H. Arnold, *Global Mission* (New York: Harper & Brothers, 1949), 16.

12. Ibid., 17.

13. Ibid.

14. Ibid., 18–19.

15. Ibid., 20.

16. Ibid.

17. Ibid., 21.

18. Crouch, *The Bishop's Boys*, 429.

19. Ibid., 431.

20. Ibid.

21. Sedalia, Missouri, newspaper article, 1 October 1910, James French and Richard French, Cliff Turpin Scrapbook Collection.

22. Ibid.

23. Aero Club of America.

24. Ibid.

25. *Phi Delta Theta Magazine*, November 1910, James French and Richard French, Cliff Turpin Scrapbook Collection.

26. Newspaper article, November 1910, James French and Richard French, Cliff Turpin Scrapbook Collection.

27. Fred Fisher(musical score) and Alfred Bryan (words), "Come Josephine In My Flying Machine"

28. Frank R. Robertson, newspaper article 1910, James French and Richard French, Cliff Turpin Scrapbook Collection.

29. James French and Richard French, Cliff Turpin Scrapbook Collection.

30. A. F. Grandt Jr., W. A. Gustafson, and L. T. Cargnino, *One Small Step: The History of Aerospace Engineering at Purdue University* (West Lafayette: Purdue School of Aeronautics and Astronautics, 1995), page XVIII, pamphlet.

31. Ibid.

32. *Lafayette (Indiana) Morning Journal*, 14 June 1911.

33. Ibid.

34. Ibid.

35. Ibid.

36. Ibid.

37. Ibid.

38. Ibid.

39. Ibid.

40. Ibid.

41. Ibid.

42. Grandt, Gustafson, and Cargnino, *One Small Step*, XVIII–XIX.

43. *Sunday Standard Times* (New Bedford, Mass.), 1911, James French and Richard French, Cliff Turpin Scrapbook Collection.

44. *Chicago Tribune*, 11 August 1911.

45. Ibid.

46. *Chicago Tribune*, 13 August 1911.

47. John McCutcheon, *Drawn From Memory* (Indianapolis: Bobbs-Merrill Co., 1950), 239.

48. John McCutcheon, *Chicago Tribune*, 13 August 1911.

49. Ibid.

50. Ibid.

51. Ibid.

52. *Chicago Tribune*, 17 August 1911.

53. Ibid.

54. Ibid.

55. Ibid.

56. McCutcheon, *Drawn From Memory*, 239.

57. *Colorado Springs Gazette* article, James French and Richard French, Cliff Turpin Scrapbook Collection.

58. Ibid.

59. Ibid.

60. Ibid.

61. Ibid.

62. Ibid.

63. Ibid.

64. Ibid.

65. Grand Rapids, Michigan, newspaper article, 13 Sept 1911, James French and Richard French, Cliff Turpin Scrapbook Collection.

66. Springfield, Illinois, newspaper, James French and Richard French, Cliff Turpin Scrapbook Collection.

67. Peoria, Illinois, newspaper, James French and Richard French, Cliff Turpin Scrapbook Collection.

68. *Sunday Standard Times* (New Bedford, Mass.) article, James French and Richard French, Cliff Turpin Scrapbook Collection.

69. *Louisville (Kentucky) Courier Journal* article, James French and Richard French, Cliff Turpin Scrapbook Collection.

70 Crouch, *The Bishop's Boys*, 435.

71 St. Louis newspaper article, James French and Richard French, Cliff Turpin Scrapbook Collection.

72 James French and Richard French, Cliff Turpin Scrapbook Collection.

73 *Sunday Standard Times* (New Bedford, Mass.) article, James French and Richard French, Cliff Turpin Scrapbook Collection.

74 *New York Times*, 16 January 1912.

75 James French and Richard French, Cliff Turpin Scrapbook Collection.

76 Ibid.

77 Dayton, Ohio, newspaper article, James French and Richard French, Cliff Turpin Scrapbook Collection.

78. Ibid.

79. *Sunday Standard Times* (New Bedford, Mass.) article, James French and Richard French, Cliff Turpin Scrapbook Collection.

80. Cliff Turpin to Orville Wright, letter, 13 February 1912, Wright Collection, Library of Congress.

81. *New York Times*, January 1912.

82. *Los Angeles Tribune*, 29 January 1912.

83. Ibid.

84. Ibid.

85. Cliff Turpin to Orville Wright, 13 February 1912, Wright Collection, Library of Congress.

86. Ibid.

87. Ibid.

88. Ibid.

89. Ibid.

90. Ibid.

91. Frank H. Ellis, *Canada's Flying Heritage* (Toronto: University of Toronto Press, 1980).

92. Ibid.

93. Ibid.

94. *Los Angeles Times*, 31 May 1912.

95. Ibid.

96. Ibid.

97. Ibid., 2 June 1912.

98. Ibid.

99. Crouch, *The Bishop's Boys*, 434–435

100. Early Birds biography of Phil Parmalee, Smithsonian Institution Air and Space Museum Archives, Early Birds of America, Inc. Collection.

101. *The Purdue Engineering Review* (1916).

102. Letters between Cliff Turpin and H. H. Arnold, James French and Richard French, Cliff Turpin Scrapbook Collection.

103. *Cap Cod Standard Times*, 25 December 1964.

104. Ibid.

Chapter Three

1. Edith Doff Culver, *Tailspins: A Story of Early Aviation Days* (Santa Fe: Sunstone Press, 2001).

2. Germantown, Ohio, newspaper article, Johnson Family Collection.

3. National Aviation Hall of Fame biography of William Mitchell, <http://www.nationalaviation.org/museum.asp?eraid=2§ion=museum>

4. Ibid.

5. Early Birds of Aviation on-line collection, Walter Lees story.

6. Johnson family interviewed by author, August, 2001.

7. *Dayton Daily News*, 13 June 1956, Smithsonian Institution Air And Space Museum Archives.

8. Wright Patterson on-line history< http://www.ascho.wpafb.af.mil>

9. Ibid.

10. Ibid.

11. Ibid.

12. Ibid.

13. Smithsonian Institution Air and Space Museum Archives, Jimmie Johnson File.

14. Germantown, Ohio, newspaper article, Johnson Family Collection.

15. Ibid.

16. Trudy Johnson interviewed by author, August 2001

17. Trudy Johnson Speech, Johnson Family Collection.

18. Ibid.

19. Ibid.

20. Ibid.

21. Ibid.

22. Ibid.

23. Ibid.

24. Ibid.

25. Ibid.

26. Ibid.

27. Ibid.

28. Ibid.

29. Ibid.

30. Ibid.

31. Ibid.

32. Ibid.

33. Ibid.

Chapter Four

1. H. B. Knoll, *The Story of Purdue Engineering* (West Lafayette: Purdue University 1963), 341.

2. *Exponent*, 18 May 1910.

3. Knoll, *Story of Purdue Engineering*, 341.

4. Ibid., 344.

5. Ibid., 341.

6. Tippecanoe County Millennium Committee, specifically Bob Kriebel, Fern Honeywell Martin, Ernest Wilkinson, and Paula Alexander Woods, *Tippecanoe County at 2000: A Hoosier County Recalls its Past* (2000) 94.

7. George Haskins Jr. interviewed by author, 15 March 2003.

8. Ibid.

9. News article in Haskins Family Collection.

10. *Exponent*, 8 June 1919.

11. *Lafayette (Indiana) Morning Journal*, 9 June 1919.

12. Ibid.

13. Idid.

14. Idid.

15. Idid, 11 June 1919.

16. Idid.

17. Knoll, *Story of Purdue Engineering*, 344.

18. Ibid.

19. Idid.

20. *Lafayette (Indiana) Journal*, 9 June 1919.

21. Knoll, *Story of Purdue Engineering*, 344.

22. Ibid.

23. Ibid., 344–345.

24. Ibid., *Story of Purdue Engineering*, 345.

25. Ibid., 346.

26. *Purdue Engineering Review* (May 1920), 9–14.

27. Ibid., 24–37.

Chapter Five

1. *Purdue Alumnus,* 11 (April 1924), 5.

2. *Air Force Magazine,* 82, No. 9 (September 1999).

3. *Purdue Debris* 1908.

4. Carroll V. Glines and Stan Cohen, *The First Flight Around the World* (Missoula: Pictorial Histories Publishing Company, Inc.), 1.

5. Ibid.

6. *Air Force Magazine,* 82, No. 9 (September 1999).

7. Ibid.

8. Ibid.

9. Glines and Cohen, *First Flight Around The World,* 156.

10. Ibid., 159.

11. "The Great Race of 1924", The American Experience, Public Broadcasting System, 1990.

12. Ibid.

13. Ibid.

14. Glines and Cohen, *First Flight Around The World,* 43.

15. "The Great Race of 1924"

16. Glines and Cohen, *First Flight Around The World,* 43.

17. Ibid., 44.

18. Ibid., 50.

19. Ibid.

20. "The Great Race of 1924"

21. Glines and Cohen, *First Flight Around the World,* 52.

22. Ibid., 53.

23. Ibid., 54.

24. *New York Times,* 2 May 1924.

25. Idid., 3 May 1924.

26. Ibid., 3 May 1924.

27. Glines and Cohen, *First Flight Around The World,* 64.

28. Ibid., 61.

29. *New York Times* 12 May 1924.

30.Glines and Cohen, *First Flight Around The World,* 61.

31. *New York Times,* 13 May 1924.

32. Ibid.

33. Ibid.

34. Ibid.

35. *New York Times*, 26 May 1924.

36. Ibid.

37. Ibid.

38. Carroll V. Glines, *Around The World in 175 Days: The First Round-the-World Flight* (Washington, D.C.: Smithsonian Institution Press, 2001), 60.

39. Ibid.

40. "The Great Air Race of 1924"

41. Glines, *Around The World in 175 Days*, 60.

42. Ibid., 60–61.

43. "The Great Air Race of 1924"

44. Glines, *Around The World in 175 Days*, 60, 62.

45. *New York Times*, 26 May 1924.

46. "The Great Air Race of 1924"

47. Glines, *Around The World in 175 Days*, 61.

48. *New York Times*, 26 May 1924.

49. Ibid.

50. Ibid.

51. Ibid.

52. *New York Times*, 4 June year 1924.

53. Glines and Cohen, *First Flight Around The World*, 133.

54. *Seattle Post Intelligencer*, 29 September 1924.

55. Glines, *Around The World in 175 Days*, 64.

56. *New York Times*, 25 May 1924.

Chapter Six

1. *Orange County (California) Register* article, McAllister Family Collection.

2. Jean Elrod (daughter of McAllister) interviewed by author, March 2003.

3. Irvin Aerospace history, <www.airbornesystems-na.com/history.html>, March 2003.

4. Ibid.

5. Scott Berg, *Lindbergh* (New York: Berkley Publishing Group, 1999), 65.

6. Ibid., 66.

7. Ibid., 79.

8. Ibid.

9. Ibid.

10. Maxwell Air Field History, <http://www.maxwell.af.mil/42abw/hq/history/index.html>.

11. Ibid.

12. Ibid.

13. *Orange County (California) Register* 1995.

14. *The Wartime Journals of Charles A. Lindbergh*, Charles Lindbergh (New York, Harcourt, 1970).

15. Jean Elrod, interviewed by author, March 2003.

16. Berg, *Lindbergh*, 114.

Chapter Seven

1. U.S. Centennial of Flight Commission, "Air Transport—Commercial Aviation: An Overview," by T. A. Heppenheimer, <http://www.centennialofflight.gov/essay/Commercial_Aviation/Tran-OV.htm>

2. Ibid.

3. U.S. Centennial of Flight Commission, "The Pioneering Years: Commercial Aviation 1920–1930," <http://www.centennialofflight.gov/essay_cat/8.htm>.

4. Ralph Johnson, interviewed with author, May 2003.

5. Ibid.

6. Ibid.

7. Ibid.

8. Ibid.

9. Ibid.

10. Ibid.

11. Ibid.

12. U.S. Centennial of Flight Commission, "Airmail Pilots: Firsts and Legends," by Roger Mola, <http://www.centennialofflight.gov/essay_cat/7.htm>

13. U.S. Centennial of Flight Commission, "Airmail 1918 to 1924: The Post Office Flies the Mail," <http://www.centennialofflight.gov/essay_cat/7.htm>.

14. Ibid.

15. Ibid.

16. Ibid.

17. Ibid.

18. "Airmail Pilots: Firsts and Legends," <http://www.centennialofflight.gov/essay_cat/7.htm>.

19. U.S. Centennial of Flight Commission, "Airmail: The Airmail Act of 1925 through 1929," <http://www.centennialofflight.gov/essay_cat/7.htm>.

20. Ibid.

21. U.S. Centennial of Flight Commission, "Airmail and The Growth of The Airlines," <http://www.centennialofflight.gov/essay_cat/7.htm>.

22. Ralph Johnson, interviewed by author, May 2003.

23. "Air Transport—Commercial Aviation: An Overview," <http://www.centennialofflight.gov/essay_cat/7.htm>.

24. Ralph Johnson, interviewed by author, May 2003.

25. "Airmail and The Growth of The Airlines," <http://www.centennialofflight.gov/essay_cat/7.htm>.

26. Ibid.

27. Ralph Johnson, interviewed with author, May 2003.

28. Ibid.

29. Ibid.

30. Ibid.

31. *RUPA News (Journal of the Retired United Pilots Association),* November 2002.

32. U.S. Centennial of Flight Commission, "Commercial Flight in the 1930s," <http://www.centennialofflight.gov/essay_cat/8.htm>.

33. Ralph Johnson, interviewed by author, May 2003.

34. Ibid.

35. Ibid.

36. Ibid.

37. *RUPA News (Journal of the Retired United Pilots Association),* November 2002.

38. Ralph Johnson, interviewed by author, May 2003.

Chapter Eight

1. *Purdue University Alumni Record and Campus Encyclopedia,* June 1929 (West Lafayette: Purdue University, 1929), 574.

2. H. B. Knoll, *The Story of Purdue Engineering* (West Lafayette: Purdue University, 1963) 346.

3. Tippecanoe County Millennium Committee, specifically Bob Kriebel, Fern Honeywell Martin, Ernest Wilkinson, and Paula Alexander Woods; *Tippecanoe County at 2000: A Hoosier County Recalls Its Past* (2000) 94.

4. Knoll, *The Story of Purdue Engineering,* 346.

5. Ibid.

6. Ibid., 347.

7. Ibid.

8. Tippecanoe County Millennium Committee, *Tippecanoe County at 2000,* 94.

9. Knoll, *The Story of Purdue Engineering,* 347.

10. Ibid.

11. Wright-Patterson Air Force Base on-line history, <http://www.wpafb.af.mil/museum/history/wwii/ce43.ht>.

12. Stephen Ambrose, *D-Day* (New York: Simon & Schuster, 1994) 220.

13. Knoll, *The Story of Purdue Engineering,* 347.

14 Lawrence "Cap" Aretz's daughter interviewed by author, March 2003.

15. Tippecanoe County Millenium Committee, *Tippecanoe County at 2000,* 96.

16. Knoll, *The Story of Purdue Engineering,* 78.

17. Ibid.

18. Ibid.

19. Ibid., 348.

20. Ibid.

21. Tippecanoe County Millenium Committee, *Tippecanoe County at 2000*, 95.

22. Knoll, *The Story of Purdue Engineering*, 348, 349.

23. Ibid., 349.

24. Ibid.

25. Ibid., 348.

26. Ibid., 353.

27. Ibid., 348.

28. Smithsonian Institution Air and Space Museum online, <www.nasm.edu/nasm/aero/aircraft/lockheed_5c.htm>.

29. *New York Times*, 10 April 1935, 23.

30. Ibid.

31. Knoll, *The Story of Purdue Engineering*, 350, 351.

32. *Lafayette (Indiana) Journal and Courier*, 15 April 1935, page 1.

33. Ibid.

34. Ibid.

35. Ibid.

36. Ibid.

37. *New York Times*, 15 April 1935, page 1

38. *Lafayette (Indiana) Journal and Courier*, 16 April 1935, page 1.

39. Ibid.

40. Ibid., 17 April 1935.

41. Ibid.

Chapter Ten

1. Grove Webster, "The Civilian Pilot Training Program," *Aerospace Historian Magazine* (March 1979), 34–39.

2. Ibid.

3. Ibid.

5. Ibid.

6.U.S. Centennial of Flight Commission, "Civilian Pilot Training Program," by Roger Guillemette, < http://www.centennialofflight.gov/essay/GENERAL_AVIATION/civilian_pilot_training/GA20.htm>.

7. "The Civilian PilotTraining Program," <http://www.centennialofflight.gov/essay/GENERAL_AVIATION/civilian_pilot_training/GA20.htm>.

8. Grove Webster, taped interview with Thomas Boyle.

9. *A Record of the University in the War Years*, ed. H. B. Knoll, (West Lafayette: Purdue University Archives, 1947).

10. U.S. Centennial of Flight Commission on-line, <http://www.centennialofflight.gov>.

11. "The Civilian Pilot Training Program," <http://www.centennialofflight.gov/essay/GENERAL_AVIATION/civilian_pilot_training/GA20.htm>.

12. Ibid.

13. Ibid.

14. U.S. Centennial of Flight Commission on-line, <http://www.centennialofflight.gov>.

15. Tippecanoe County Millennium Committee, specifically Bob Kriebel, Fern Honeywell Martin, Ernest Wilkinson, and Paula Alexander Woods; *Tippecanoe County at 2000: A Hoosier County Recalls Its Past* (2000), 96.

16. U.S. Centennial of Flight Commission on-line, <http://www.centennialofflight.gov>.

17. Tippecanoe County Millenium Committee, *Tippecanoe County at 2000.*

18. H. B. Knoll, *The Story of Purdue Engineering* (West Lafayette: Purdue University, 1963) 354.

19. Frank K. Burrin, *Edward Charles Elliott: Educator* (West Lafayette: Purdue Research Foundation, 1970).

20. Knoll, *War Years*, 53.

21. Ibid., 54.

22. E. F. Bruhn, *A History of Aeronautical Engineering and Research at Purdue for Period 1937 to 1950,* Purdue University, pamphlet, 15

23. Ibid., 27.

24. Ibid.

25. Ibid.

26. A. F. Grandt Jr., W. A. Gustafson, L. T. Cargnino, *One Small Step: The History of Aerospace Engineering At Purdue University* (West Lafayette, Purdue University School of Aeronautics and Astronautics, 1995), 39.

27. "A History of Aeronautical Engineering and Research at Purdue for period 1937 to 1950," Purdue University, 44.

Chapter Eleven

1. Distinguished Service Citation
2. Layton Allen, *A Few Recollections of George Welch.*
3. George J. Frebert, *Delaware Aviation History* (George J. Frebert, 1998).
4. Al Blackburn, *Aces Wild: The Race for Mach 1* (Wilmington: Scholarly Resources, 1999) 91.
5. Allen, *A Few Recollections of George Welch.*
6. Blackburn, *Aces Wild*, 91.
7. Allen, *A Few Recollections of George Welch.*
8. Ibid.
9. Ibid.
10. Blackburn, *Aces Wild*, 91.
11. Ibid., 92.
12. Ibid.
13. Lyle F. Padilla and Raymond J. Castagnaro, "History, Legend and Myth: Hollywood and the Medal of Honor (1998), <http://www.users.voicenet.com/~lpadilla/mohintro.html>.
14. Corey C. Jordan, "The Amazing George Welch: The Tiger of Pearl Harbor"(Jordan Publishing, 1998).
15. Blackburn, *Aces Wild*, 94.
16. Ibid.
17. Ibid., 95.
18. Ken Taylor, interviewed by author, 15 May 2003.
19. George Prange, *December 7th, 1941: The Day The Japanese Attacked Pearl Harbor* (New York: McGraw-Hill Book Company, 1988), 200.
20. Ibid.
21. Ibid.
22. Ken Taylor, interviewed by author, 15 May 2003.
23. Ibid.
24. Ibid.

25. Ibid.

26. Prange, *December 7th 1941*, 200.

27. Ibid.

28. Ken Taylor, interviewed by author, 15 May 2003.

29. Blackburn, *Aces Wild*, 82.

30. Prange, *December 7th, 1941*, 287.

31. Distinguished Service Medal Citation

32. Blackburn, *Aces Wild*, 83.

33. Ibid.

34. Prange, *December 7th, 1941*, 289.

35. Distinguished Service Medal Citation

36. Ibid.

37. George Prange, *At Dawn We Slept* (New York: McGraw-Hill, 1981), 534.

38. Blackburn, *Aces Wild*, 97.

39. New York World-Telegram, December 16, 1941, Smithsonian Institution Air and Space Museum Archives.

40. Prange, *At Dawn We Slept*, 89.

41. Ibid.

42. Ibid.

43. Ibid., 89, 91.

44. Ibid., 91.

45. *Martin-Bellinger Report.*

46. Ibid.

47. Ibid.

48. Prange, *December 7th, 1941*, 194.

49. Pearl Harbor Congressional Investigation Committee, *Attack Reportof the Joint Committee on the Investigation of the Pearl Harbor Attack*, United States Congress.

50. Prange, *December 7th, 1941*, 189.

51. Ibid., 190.

52. Ibid., 347.

53. Pearl Harbor Congressional Investigation Committee, *Pearl Harbor Attack Report.*

54. *Herald Tribune*, 26 May 1942, Smithsonian Institution Air and Space Museum Archives.

55. Blackburn, *Aces Wild*, 97.

56. Ibid., 98.

57. Ibid., 99.

58, Ibid., 100.

59. Ibid., 102.

60. Ibid., 103.

61. Ibid.

62. Ibid., 104.

63. Ibid., 136.

64. Ibid., 141.

65. Ibid., 142.

66. Ibid., 144.

67. Ibid., 146.

68. Ibid., 147.

69. Ibid., 149.

70. Ibid., 154.

71. Ibid., 159.

72. Ibid., 165–168.

73. Ibid., 170.

74. Ibid., 170.

75. Al Blackburn, interviewed by author, 15 May 2003.

76. Ken Taylor, interviewed by author, 15 May, 2003.

77. Letter by Robert Reiland, *Air and Space Magazine* (April/May 1991) 7.

78. Ken Taylor, interviewed by author, June 2003.

79. Blackburn, *Aces Wild*, 244.

Chapter Twelve

1. Jerry Goldman, interviewed by author, winter 2001, spring 2003.

2. Ibid.

3. Ibid.

4. A. F. Grandt, Jr., W. A. Gustafson, and L. T. Cargnino, *One Small Step: The History of Aerospace Engineering at Purdue University* (West Lafayette: Purdue School of Aeronautics and Astronautics, 1995), page XVIII, pamphlet.

5. Purdue Aeronautics Corporation minutes, 12 May 1942, Purdue Research Foundation.

6. Ibid., 7 July 1942.

7. Ibid., 19 January 1943.

8. Ibid., 30 June 1943.

9. Grandt Jr., Gustafson, and Cargnino, *One Small Step*, 47.

10. Ibid., 47, 48.

11. Ibid., 48.

12. Ibid., 49.

13. Ibid.

14. Ibid., 54, 55.

15. Ibid., 50.

16. Ibid., 50.

17. Purdue Aeronautics Corporation minutes, 18 May 1945.

18. Idid.

19. Jerry Goldman, interviewed by author.

20. Purdue Aeronautics Board minutes, 19 January 1954.

21. Purdue Research Foundation minutes, 14 May 1952.

22. Purdue Research Foundation Investment Committee minutes, 19 December 1951.

23. Ibid., 20 February 1952; 10 April 1952.

24. Jerry Goldman, interviewed by author.

25. Purdue Research Foundation Investment Committee minutes, 25 September 1952.

26. Purdue Research Foundation minutes, 14 May 1952.

27. Jerry Goldman, interviewed by author.

28. Purdue Aeronautics Corporation Board minutes, 28 December 1954.

29. Ibid.

30. Jerry Goldman, interviewed by author.

31. James Maris, interviewed by author, May 2003.

32. Ibid.

33. Ibid.

34. Ibid.

35. Ibid.

36. Ibid.

37. Ibid.

38. *Indianapolis Star*, 16 October 1959.

39. Jerry Goldman, interviewed by author.

40. National Public Broadcasting Archives at the University of Maryland Libraries.

41. *FAA Aviation News* (February 1966) 8.

42. Ibid., 9.

43. Jerry Goldman, interviewed by author.

44. Purdue Aeronautics Corporation minutes, 3 June 1967.

45. *Lafayette (Indiana) Journal and Courier*, 23 March 1971, 1

46. Jerry Goldman, interviewed by author.

47. *Lafayette (Indiana) Journal and Courier*, 19 April 1962.

48. Civil Aeronautics Board Accident Report, 17 November 1964.

49. Jerry Goldman, interviewed by author.

Chapter Thirteen

1. *New York Times*, 5 October 1957, 1.

2. Ibid.

3. Ibid.

4. Ibid.

5. *New York Times*, 7 October 1957.

6. *New York Times*, 5 November 1957.

7. Tony Reichardt, *Air & Space Magazine/Smithsonian* (August/September 2000).

8. Ibid.

9. Ibid.

10. Richard P. Hallion, *Test Pilots: The Frontiersmen of Space* (Washington, D.C.: Smithsonian Institution Press, 1981) 215.

11. Reichardt, *Air & Space Magazine* (August/September 2000).

12. James Haggerty Jr., *The First Spaceman* (Duell, Sloan, and Pearce, 1960) 9.

13. Ibid., 10.

14. Ibid., 11.

15. Ibid., 12.

16. Ibid., 14.
17. Ibid.
18. Ibid., 18.
19. Ibid., 21.
20. Ibid., 21.
21. Ibid., 21.
22. Ibid., 25.
23. Ibid., 27.
24. Ibid., 33.
25. Ibid., 58.
26. Ibid., 60.
27. Ibid., 61.
28. Ibid., 61.
29. Ibid., 69.
30. Ibid., 69.
31. Ibid., 70.
32. Ibid., 72.
33. Ibid., 92.
34. Ibid., 92, 101.
35. Ibid., 83.
36. Ibid., 87.
37. Ibid., 87, 117.
38. Ibid., 99–100.
39. Ibid., 101.
40. Ibid., 102.
41. Ibid.
42. Ibid., 104.
43. Ibid., 117.
44. Ibid., 119.
45. Ibid., 121.
46. Ibid., 136.
47. Ibid., 137.
48. Ibid., 138.
49. *U.S News and World Report*, 17 January 1958.

50. Haggerty Jr., *The First Spaceman*, 144, 145.
51. Ibid., 147.
52. Ibid., 7.
53. Neil Armstrong, interviewed by author, June 2003.

Chapter Fourteen

1. *National Geographic*, Vol. 120, No. 5 (November 1961) 674.
2.Ibid., 672.
3. Ibid., 672.
4. Ibid., 672, 674.
5. Ibid., 672.
6. Craig Ryan, *The Pre-Astronauts: Manned Ballooning on the Threshold of Space* (Annapolis: Naval Institute Press, 1995), 212.
7. Ibid., 218.
8. Malcolm Ross short autobiography, Smithsonian Institution Air and Space Museum Archives.
9. Ibid.
10. Shirley Thomas, *Men of Space*, Vol. 4 (Philadelphia: Chilton Company, 1962) 142.
11. Charles B. Moore, interviewed by author, June 2003.
12. Benson Saler, Charles A. Ziegler, and Charles B. Moore, *UFO Crash at Roswell: The Genesis of a Modern Myth* (Washington, D.C.: Smithsonian Press, 1997), 67–68.
13. Ibid.
14. Ibid.
15. Ibid.
16. Ryan, *The Pre-Astronauts*, 106.
17. Charles B. Moore, interviewed by author, June 2003.
18. Ibid.
19. Official U.S. Navy Biography, Smithsonian Institution Air and Space Museum Archives.
20. Charles B. Moore, interviewed by author, June 2003.
21. *National Geographic* (February 1957) 269.
22. Ibid., 273.
23. Ryan, *The Pre-Astronauts*, 228.

24. *National Geographic* (February 1957) 278.
25. Ibid., 278.
26. Ibid., 279.
27. Ibid., 279.
28. Ibid 282.
29. Ryan, *The Pre-Astronauts*, 230.
30. *National Geographic* (February 1957) 282.
31. Ibid.
32. Ryan, *The Pre-Astronauts*, 230.
33. Smithsonian Institution Air and Space Museum Archives.
34. *New York Herald Tribune*, 4 February 1958, 7.
35. Ibid.
36. Thomas, *Men of Space*, 161.
37. Ibid., 153.
38. Ryan, *The Pre-Astronauts*, 232.
39. Ibid.
40. Thomas, *Men of Space*, 160.
41. *The Washington Daily News*, 1 December 1959, Smithsonian Institution Air and Space Museum Archives.
42. Ibid.
43. *The Evening Star* (Washington, D.C.), 30 November 1959, 6, Smithsonian Institution Air and Space Museum Archives.
44. Ibid.
45. Ryan, *The Pre-Astronauts*, 236.
46. *National Geographic* (February 1957), 675.
47. Ibid., 675.
48. Ibid., 676, 677.
49. Ibid., 676.
50. Ibid., 677.
51. Ibid., 679.
52. Ibid.
53. Ibid., 683.
54. Ibid.
55. *New York Times*, 5 May 1956.

56. *National Geographic* (November 1961) 684.
57. Thomas, *Men of Space,* 137.
58. *Lafayette (Indiana) Journal and Courier,* 18 October 1962.
59. Thomas, *Men of Space,* 136.
60. Neil Armstrong, interviewed by author, June 2003.
61. Ibid.

Chapter Sixteen

1. Betty Grissom, interviewed by author, March 2003.
2. Ibid.
3. Virgil Grissom, *Gemini,* (London: The Macmillian Company, 1968), 17.
4. Betty Grissom, interviewed by author, March 2003.
5. Donald Slayton and Michael Cassutt, *Deke!: U.S. Manned Space: From Mercury to the Shuttle* (New York: Tom Doherty Associates, 1994), 191.
6. Betty Grissom, interviewed by author, March 2003.
7. Grissom, *Gemini,* 18.
8. Betty Grissom and Henry Still, *Starfall* (New York: Thomas Y. Crowell Company, 1974), 17.
9. Ibid., 18.
10. Betty Grissom, interviewed by author, March 2003.
11. Ibid.
12. Grissom, *Gemini,* 19.
13. Grissom, *Starfall,* 31; Betty Grissom, interviewed by author, March 2003.
14. Neil Armstrong interview with author, June 2003.
15. Gene Farmer and Dora Jane Hamblin, *First Men On The Moon: A Voyage With Neil Armstrong, Michael Collins, Edwin Aldrin, Jr.* (Boston: Little Brown and Company, 1970), 112.
16. Neil Armstrong, interviewed by author, June 2003.
17. Ibid.
18. Ibid.
19. Ibid.
20. Ibid.

21. Ibid.
22. Ibid.
23. Ibid.
24. Ibid.
25. Ibid.
26. Ibid.
27. Ibid.
28. Ibid.
29. Ibid.
30. Ibid.
31. Ibid.
32. Ibid.
33. Ibid.
34. Ibid.
35. Ibid.
36. Ibid.
37. Eugene Cernan and Don Davis, *Last Man On The Moon*, (New York: St. Martin's Press, 1999), 23–24.
38. Ibid., 24.
39. Eugene Cernan, interviewed by author, June 2003.
40. Ibid.
41. Cernan and Davis, *Last Man On The Moon*, 26.
42. Ibid., 29.
43. C. Donald Chrysler and Donald L. Chaffee, *On Course To The Stars*, (Grand Rapids: Kregel Publications: 1968), ix, x.
44.Ibid., 16.
45. Ibid., 44.
46. Ibid., 49, 50.
47. Ibid., 51.
48. Ibid.
49. Martha Chaffee, interviewed by author, March 2003.
50. Ibid.
51. Chrysler and Chaffee, *On Course To The Stars*, 64.
52. Ibid., 65.

53. Roger Chaffee to John "Pop" Stair, letter, Clinton Prairie Canaltrek on-line history project, <http://www.dagwood.wvec.k12.in.us/cpes/stair.html>.

54. Martha Chaffee, interviewed by author, March 2003.

55. Ibid.

56. Chrysler and Chaffee, *On Course To The Stars*, 75.

57. Martha Chaffee, interviewed by author, March 2003.

58. Chrysler and Chaffee, *On Course To The Stars*, 47, 48.

Chapter Seventeen

1. Betty Grissom and Henry Still, *Starfall* (New York: Thomas Y. Crowell Company, 1974), 185.

2. Ibid., 186.

3. Donald Slayton and Michael Cassutt, *Deke!: U.S. Manned Space: From Mercury To The Shuttle* (New York: Tom Doherty Associates, Inc., 1994), 189.

4. Ibid.

5. Grissom and Still, *Starfall*, 189.

6. Betty Grissom, interviewed by author, March 2003.

7. Virgil Grissom, *Gemini, A Personal Account of Man's Venture Into Space* (Toronto:The Macmillian Company, 1968), 19–21.

8. Betty Grissom, interviewed by author, March 2003.

9. Grissom and Still, *Starfall*, page 54.

10. Ibid.

11. Grissom, *Gemini*, 21.

12. Ibid., 22.

13. Grissom and Still, *Starfall*, 54.

14. Ibid., 55.

15. Ibid., 57.

16. Betty Grissom, interviewed by author, March 2003.

17. Ibid.

18. Ibid.

19. Grissom and Still, *Starfall*, 57.

20. Slayton and Cassutt, *Deke!*, 90.

21. Ibid., 93.

22. Ibid., 94.
23. *Life* 50, no. 9, (3 March 1961), 24-25.
24. Ibid., 28–29.
25. Scott Grissom, interviewed by author, March 2003.
26. Betty Grissom, interviewed by author, March 2003.
27. Grissom and Still, *Starfall*, 96.
28. Betty Grissom, interviewed by author, March 2003.
29. Ibid., 101.
30. Ibid., 104.
31. Betty Grissom, interviewed by author, March 2003.
32. Grissom and Still, *Starfall*, 107.
33. Betty Grissom, interviewed by author, March 2003.
34. Ibid.
35. Martha Chaffee, interviewed by author, March 2003.
36. Ibid.
37. Ibid.
38. Ibid.
39. Eugene Cernan and Don Davis, *Last Man On The Moon*, (New York: St. Martin's Press, 1999), 8–9.
40. Martha Chaffee, interviewed by author, March 2003.
41. Ibid.
42. David West Reynolds, *Apollo: The Epic Journey To The Moon*, (New York: Harcourt, Inc., 2002), 67.
43. Martha Chaffee, interviewed by author, March 2003.
44. Ibid.
45. Ibid.
46. Betty Grissom, interviewed by author, March 2003.
47. Grissom and Still, *Starfall*, 186.
48. Ibid., 194.
49. Betty and Scott Grissom, interviewed by author, March 2003.
50. Martha Chaffee, interviewed by author, March 2003.
51. Neil Armstrong, interviewed by author, June 2003.
52. Eugene Cernan, interviewed by author, June 2003.

Chapter Eighteen

1. Gene Farmer and Dora Jane Hamblin, *First On the Moon, A Voyage with Neil Armstrong, Michael Collins, Edwin E. Aldrin, Jr.,* (Boston: Little Brown and Company, 1970), 240.

2. Apollo 11 Transcript, "Lunar Landing," NASA.

3. Farmer and Hamblin, *First On the Moon,* 238–240.

4. Neil Armstrong interview with author, June 2003

5. Ibid.

6. Ibid.

7. Ibid.

8. Ibid.

9. Milton O. Thompson and Neil Armstrong, *At the Edge of Space, The X-15 Flight Program* (Washington, D.C.: Smithsonian Institution Press, 1992), xii.

10. Ibid., 38.

11. Ibid., 362.

12. Pete Knight, interviewed by author, 2001.

13. Thompson and Armstrong, *Edge of Space,* 363.

14. Pete Knight, interviewed by author, 2001.

15. Ibid.

16. Neil Armstrong, interviewed by author, June 2003.

17. Ibid.

18. Neil Armstrong, interviewed by author, June 2003.

19. Farmer and Hamblin, *First On the Moon,* 119.

20. Ibid.

21. Donald Slayton and Micheal Cassutt, *Deke! U.S. Manned Space: From Mercury to the Shuttle* (New York: Tom Doherty Associates, 1994), 136.

22. Ibid.

23. Ibid.

24. Eugene Cernan and Don Davis, *Last Man on the Moon,* (New York: St. Martin's Press, 1999), 29.

25. Ibid., 30.

26. Ibid., 42.

27. Eugene Cernan, interviewed by author, June 2003.

28. Cernan and Davis, *Last Man*, 48.
29. Ibid., 51.
30. Ibid.
31. Ibid., 59.
32. Ibid., 87.
33. Ibid.,105.
34. Ibid., 132.
35. Ibid., 133.
36. Ibid., 134.
37. Ibid., 148.
38. Ibid., 161.
39. Ibid., 163.
40. Eugene Cernan, interviewed by author, June 2003.
41. Ibid.
42. Cernan and Davis, *Last Man*, 165.
43. Ibid., 171.
44. Ibid., 180.
45. Slayton and Cassutt, *Deke!*, 223.
46. Ibid.
47. Eugene Cernan, interviewed by author, June 2003.
48. Cernan and Davis, *Last Man*, 187.
49. Ibid., 194.
50. Ibid., 205, 206.
51. Ibid., 209.
52. Ibid., 210.
53.Ibid., 213.
54. Ibid., 218.
55. Ibid., 219.
56. Ibid., 220.
57. Ibid., 221.
58. Ibid., 221, 222.
59. Slayton and Cassutt, *Deke!*, 234.
60. Ibid.
61. Neil Armstrong, interviewed by author, June 2003.

62. Farmer and Hamblin, *First On The Moon*, prologue.
63. Apollo 11 transcript, "Lunar Landing," NASA.
64. Slayton and Cassutt, *Deke!*, 244.
65. Neil Armstrong, interviewed by author, June 2003.
66. Ibid.
67. Neil Armstrong, "Lunar Surface Exploration," delivered at COSPAR, Leningrad, Russia, 1971.
68. Ibid.
69. Ibid.
70. Cernan and Davis, *Last Man*, 228.
71. Ibid.
72. Eugene Cernan, interviewed by author, June 2003.
73. Ibid.
74. Ibid.
75. Ibid.
76. Ibid.
77. Ibid.
78. Ibid.
79. Ibid.
80. Ibid.

Index